Information Assurance for the Enterprise: A Roadmap to Information Security

Corey Schou
Idaho State University

Dan Shoemaker
University of Detroit Mercy

McGraw-Hill
Irwin

Boston   Burr Ridge, IL   Dubuque, IA   Madison, WI   New York   San Francisco   St. Louis
Bangkok   Bogotá   Caracas   Kuala Lumpur   Lisbon   London   Madrid   Mexico City
Milan   Montreal   New Delhi   Santiago   Seoul   Singapore   Sydney   Taipei   Toronto

**McGraw-Hill
Irwin**

INFORMATION ASSURANCE FOR THE ENTERPRISE: A ROADMAP TO INFORMATION SECURITY

Published by McGraw-Hill/Irwin, a business unit of The McGraw-Hill Companies, Inc., 1221 Avenue of the Americas, New York, NY, 10020. Copyright © 2007 by The McGraw-Hill Companies, Inc. All rights reserved. No part of this publication may be reproduced or distributed in any form or by any means, or stored in a database or retrieval system, without the prior written consent of The McGraw-Hill Companies, Inc., including, but not limited to, in any network or other electronic storage or transmission, or broadcast for distance learning.

Some ancillaries, including electronic and print components, may not be available to customers outside the United States.

This book is printed on acid-free paper.

1 2 3 4 5 6 7 8 9 0 DOC/DOC 0 9 8 7 6

ISBN: 978-0-07-225524-9
MHID: 0-07-225524-2

Editorial director: *Brent Gordon*
Executive editor: *Paul Ducham*
Editorial coordinator: *Alaina Grayson*
Marketing manager: *Rhonda Seelinger*
Project manager: *Jim Labeots*
Production supervisor: *Gina Hangos*
Senior designer: *Artemio Ortiz Jr.*
Lead media project manager: *Cathy L. Tepper*
Cover design: *Artemio Ortiz Jr.*
Typeface: *10/12 Giovanni*
Compositor: *International Typesetting and Composition*
Printer: *R. R. Donnelley*

Library of Congress Cataloging-in-Publication Data

Schou, Corey.
    Information assurance for the enterprise: a roadmap to information security / Corey Schou, Dan Shoemaker.
        p. cm.
    ISBN-13: 978-0-07-225524-9 (alk. paper)
    ISBN-10: 0-07-225524-2 (alk. paper)
    1. Computer security. 2. Data protection. I. Shoemaker, Dan. II. Title.
    QA76.9.A25S3523 2007
    005.8–dc22

                        2006048178

www.mhhe.com

ABOUT THE AUTHORS

Corey D. Schou, Ph.D., is first and foremost a teacher. He is a professor of Computer Information Systems, an Associate Dean in the College of Business, the University Professor of Informatics, and director of the Informatics Research Institute at Idaho State University. In his nearly 40-year career, he has taught collegiate courses in areas as diverse as comparative anatomy and biology to international law and compilers. He currently heads the congressionally funded National Information Assurance Training and Education Center (NIATEC) to support solving Critical Information Infrastructure problems in the United States.

Dr. Schou is an internationally recognized expert in information assurance, and travels the globe consulting and speaking to industry, government, and academic leaders. He has more than 30 years experience in computer science, information systems, and information assurance yielding over 400 publications, books, and articles. As part of his research stream, he has developed systems for integrated group decision support, training management systems, and instructional design.

Twenty years ago, he developed the eDACUM process that has been used to develop the major information assurance standards used by both industry and the United States government, including NIST, CNSS, and NSA. Throughout his career, he has been an active consultant to major organizations such as the United States Senate, Federal Express, Apple, General Motors, United Airlines, Microsoft, Boeing, Department of Energy, and the Department of State.

He is a founder of The Colloquium for Information Systems Security Education (CISSE), the first non-government recipient of the Federal Information Systems Security Educators Award, and the recipient of the highly prestigious Tipton Award in Computer Security. Professor Schou has also received several awards from his university recognizing not only his research, but his service to the profession.

A dedicated inventor and systems developer who is constantly manipulating ideas—as well as flint—he is currently working with colleagues on an artificial intelligence project to classify Native American arrowheads.

He is an active member of many professional organizations and is an avid traveler. Most importantly, he is dedicated to his family who has remained patient throughout his professional journey.

Dan Shoemaker, Ph.D., is the Director of the Centre for Assurance Studies, a National Security Agency (NSA) Center of Academic Excellence in Information Assurance Education at the University of Detroit Mercy, where he is a professor and the Chair of the Computer and Information Systems Program since 1985. His Ph.D. is from the University of Michigan in Ann Arbor, and he has held various professional IS roles at that institution, as well as at Michigan State University. His two books, *Engineering a Better Software Organization* and *GOT-ITFine Tuning Your Software Organization* sold extensively to the U.S. military as well as overseas.

Serving as an expert panelist on three national working groups within the Department of Homeland Security's Cybersecunty Division, Dr. Shoemaker is an author and one of three domain editors for the Software Assurance Common Body of Knowledge. He also serves on the Assurance Business Case Working Group and the Workforce Education and Training Working Group.

Lectures on cybersecunty, information assurance, and software engineering related topics have taken Dr. Shoemaker throughout the United States and Canada. He founded the International Cybersecurity Education Coalition (ICSEC), connecting higher education institutions located in Michigan, Ohio, and Indiana. ICSEC's mission is to extend and support the teaching of standard information assurance curricula within the Midwest.

Dr. Shoemaker has been a formal U.S. partner of the British Standards Institution (BSI) since 1994 and he has worked with the recently released ISO/IEC 27000 International Standard Series for Information Security since its inception in 1995. In addition, Dr. Shoemaker is a member of the advisory panel for Automation Alley, a designated academic advocate for the Information Systems Audit and Control Association (ISACA), and he teaches a COBIT based Sarbanes-Oxley audit to managers up and down the Big Three's automotive supply chain in Detroit.

Dr. Shoemaker loves to travel with his wife, his little white dog, and any of his four grown children who might be willing to come along. He has a particular fondness for England, where he attended school in his youth and he always spends some of his summers in London.

CONTENTS AT A GLANCE

CONTENTS

PREFACE

This text is based on two assumptions. First, written, spoken, and electronic information is valuable—it is an asset; the information assurance function should be able to protect any information asset the organization owns. Second, information assurance has to be complete and continuous. All safeguards must be in place and operating correctly at all times.

Most organizations do not even know what information they have much less what threatens it. They cannot even evaluate risks they are accepting because they do not know the

- **Scope**—companies just cannot get their arms around their own assets
- **Value**—shifting understanding of the value of information that a company DOES hold
- **Risks**—knowing all of the ways that information can be threatened
- **Assigned Accountability**—putting the right people in charge of the process

To ensure the right level of security the organization has to create a complete, clearly understandable, and economically feasible protection system. The system must ensure the security of all information of value; it must account for all likely risks and address them with appropriate countermeasures.

This text describes the elements and procedures involved in protecting information. It explains how the elements inter-relate and how they can be used to build an information assurance strategy that is continuously effective and reliable over time. That strategy details how to design, implement, and maintain a comprehensive and coordinated information assurance solution. That solution must address a broad spectrum of security requirements, not just those that are convenient. It must be systematic and maintainable as a long-term operational process and it must directly support the business case requirements.

The information assurance solution merges all required procedures and controls into a single coordinated process. The reliability of that process must be objectively measurable. The process must evolve continuously to meet the changing environment. The process must provide a trustworthy long-term assurance capability, which addresses all probable threats and responds to all incidents appropriately. Consequently, the information assurance process should be holistic. That is, a proper information assurance solution must incorporate all of the factors necessary to satisfy all the security needs for a given situation. That condition is termed "total protection."

The book covers the essential material for the DHS Centers of Academic Excellence in Computer Security Education as well as (ISC)2 Common Body of Knowledge and the Draft ACM Computing Curriculum (2005). It also addresses the principles of ISO-17799.

Background of the Field: From COMSEC to IA

The concept of total protection has evolved through several stages mirroring the evolution of computer technology itself. There continue to be a many ways in which information security is understood and approached because of those evolutionary steps.

The idea of computer security surfaced with the widespread use of computers in the 1960s, therefore, security solutions for the first 20 years were almost exclusively technology-focused. Although technological solutions are still fundamental to the field, a strictly technology-centric approach is the narrowest possible way to approach security.

Typical technological approaches involving the essential practices for assuring hardware and software functionality (COMPUSEC) and network operation (COMSEC). These are machine-oriented disciplines and they are relevant to an entire range of concerns associated with the electronic processing, storage, and transmission of data. Their limitation lies in the fact that they cannot ensure that the information being processed is trustworthy or that the physical space is secure.

For instance, classic COMPUSEC and COMSEC employ documented procedures to ensure trusted access to the computer and network equipment (authentication and authorization), as well as to insuring the secure transmission of digital information (integrity checking and encryption). However, they do not incorporate safeguards to ensure that equipment itself is not damaged or stolen. Nor do they guarantee that the system will not be misused. Since these approaches ensure secure processing and transmission of electronic data, that omission is appropriate. However, it is also a potential source of serious vulnerability, if the aim is to ensure the protection of all information stored on the computer.

Information security (INFOSEC) provides functions to improve control over the external elements. It provides that assurance by using procedures similar to those employed to secure financial or physical assets. INFOSEC relies heavily on monitoring and audit functions to enforce its practices.

Since INFOSEC uses one or both of the technological disciplines (that is, COMSEC, or COMPUSEC), it is capable of securing a broader and less tangible range of assets. For instance, INFOSEC does not simply ensure that the system is password protected. It ensures that accesses under a given password are logged for the purpose of regularly monitoring use as well as identifying misuse for corrective action.

The classic INFOSEC model does not account for conventional environmental threats such as physical infrastructure and routine operational failures. This failure is a source of vulnerability, because threats like terrorist acts, power failures, or even violations of the law can be disastrous.

Security of operations protects the organization against environmental threats by ensuring that the actual operation of the system is reliable, consistent, and complies with contractual and regulatory requirements. It is a procedural rather than a technical discipline and it does not imply the supplementary use of COMSEC or COMPUSEC.

Security of operations involves equipment and standard operating procedures to assure the safety of the physical elements of the system. An effective security-of-operations function is important, because it focuses on maintaining the system's continuous availability.

The weakness of the security-of-operations concept lies in the fact that it does not specifically include measures for securing electronic transmissions and storage. Furthermore, because of its orientation toward physical protection, it is often administered separately from the information assurance function.

Consolidating Approaches: IA

COMPUSEC, COMSEC, INFOSEC, and security of operations are all valuable aspects of overall security. However, the problem with each of them individually is that they address part, but not all, of the problem creating the potential for exploitation of unsecured areas. This has led to the recognition that every avenue of attack must be safeguarded in order for the assurance to be correct.

The means for accomplishing that is characterized by a relatively new term, "information assurance," or IA. IA takes a comprehensive view of the assurance responsibility. Essentially, it involves the creation of a persistent, organization-wide assurance system, which contains the policies, procedures, and technical and managerial functions needed to guarantee security in every area of threat throughout the information life cycle. It is necessary to establish information assurance through a strategic planning process because of its all-inclusive process focus.

Information assurance is the broadest and most intuitively attractive of the assurance disciplines because it incorporates the strengths of the other methods into a holistic approach focused on ensuring total security. Nonetheless, beyond establishing a top-level architecture, the IA concept does little more than integrate the conventional assurance activities of COMSEC, NETSEC, INFOSEC, and security of operations into a single system.

The Information Assurance Life Cycle: The Organization of the Text

Properly functioning systems produce consistent outcomes. To achieve consistency, systems incorporate a common set of elements into a logical process. With systems, the term for that process is a life cycle. System life cycles always have a defined beginning, follow repeatable steps, and produce predictable outcomes. Every component within the life cycle has a specific purpose and contributes differently to the overall outcome.

In this text, you will learn about the standard elements and interrelationships of the information assurance life cycle. Each chapter presents one of the elements of that process and focuses on describing the qualities that each component adds to the overall assurance picture. In addition it tracks how that element subsequently interacts with the other elements in the process to establish trustworthy and sustainable security.

The book is organized along the lines of the information assurance life cycle and is divided into four sections, as follows.

Section One: Understanding the Risks

The first section, composed of two chapters, outlines the two primary principles that are the starting place for the information assurance process. These are necessary because information is intangible. Therefore, there has to be an initial stage to identify and label the information that the organization owns and recognize what threatens it.

The first chapter presents a process to ensure that all items of value to the organization are identified and accounted for. Without this process, the organization would not know what to secure. Once each information asset is identified and catalogued, a risk assessment is carried out to define the specific things that might harm each item. Specific knowledge of the risks is a precondition to establishing a correct response. Chapters in this section are

- Chapter 1: Understanding the Form of the Asset
- Chapter 2: Assessing Risks

Section Two: Sustaining a Relevant Response

To ensure trust, the information assurance process has to be sustainable. Sustainability requires a concrete and repeatable infrastructure of processes that are continuously appropriate and persistent. Section Two discusses the principles that the organization must address to ensure a systematic response. Chapters in this section are

- Chapter 3: Establishing an Overall Process
- Chapter 4: Building and Documenting an Information Assurance Framework
- Chapter 5: Maintaining Security of Operations
- Chapter 6: Controlling Access

Section Three: Deploying the Countermeasures

The countermeasures are the traditional areas of security. This section is composed of eight chapters, organized into management and technical countermeasures. All these areas are broad and deep and each contains more material than could possibly be presented in a single textbook because they represent substantive actions. Consequently, we concentrate on discussing their general application and their interrelationship with each other. The individual reader may choose to do greater in-depth research into specific areas of interest using the chapter as a starting point. Chapters in this section are

- Management Countermeasures
  - Chapter 7: Personnel Security
  - Chapter 8: Physical Security
  - Chapter 9: Assuring Against Software Vulnerabilities
  - Chapter 10: Continuity Planning and Implementation
  - Chapter 11: Laws, Regulations, and Computer Crime

- Technical Countermeasures
  - Chapter 12: Network Security
  - Chapter 13: Cryptology
  - Chapter 14: Ensuring the Secure Use of Software

Section Four: Sustaining a Security Culture

Finally, two aspects of the assurance process do not fit directly within a life-cycle model. Those are ethics and human factors. These are higher-level principles, which support the "security behavior" of the organization. Although they appear to be peripheral to establishing a security system, they are critical to its long-term success. We provide a discussion of each as well as suggest how they contribute to the establishment and operation of the information assurance system.

- Chapter 15: Human Factors: Ensuring Secure Performance
- Chapter 16: Ensuring an Ethical Organization

Intended Audience

Our assumption in writing this book is that information assurance is not limited to securing information assets in electronic form. It must secure all information of any value, in whatever form. Thus, electronic protection approaches by themselves are insufficient. In addition, genuine assurance implies that all elements necessary to ensure reliable protection have been established. Consequently, in addition to technical controls, the security solution must also incorporate all relevant organizational and human factors into a total system of protection.

This book provides a comprehensive, in-depth survey of the field of information assurance. The audience includes everybody from students interested in understanding what information assurance is, to instructors who want to teach information assurance from a holistic perspective.

In many cases, we have taken liberties with the technical details to ensure that the principle is clear to a broader audience. Because of its breadth and application focus, the audience for this book extends from business and technical managers who want to learn how to ensure security within their particular areas to top-level executives who want to provide leadership for an effort in this field.

Knowing What to Secure

In this chapter, you will learn:
- Why "knowing what to secure" is the first step in the security process
- Why information has to be controlled like any other organizational asset
- Why change has to be rigorously planned for and managed

Information is like no other asset: it is intangible; therefore, it cannot be accounted for like car parts or soapboxes. It is valuable; yet it is hard to establish a precise dollar value for knowledge. These two characteristics, lack of tangibility and ambiguous worth, pose a fundamental dilemma for the assurance process because it creates a situation where you are unsure of what to protect.

Therefore, the first step in the assurance process is to identify and label every useful bit of information that the organization owns. This is a simple inventory process. Every item of information is catalogued and a value is assigned. The recording process is called **baselining** and the catalogue that it produces is called a **baseline**. The baseline is the starting point for the security response.

A baseline is the precise specification of the content and interrelationship of all of the organization's information items. By definition, the baseline contains only items that the organization considers valuable. The baseline documents the *information resource base* of the organization.

Because the actual contents of the baseline are intangible, this documentation is the proxy for the asset itself. Since the baseline constitutes the only tangible record of the asset base, that documentation has to be maintained as a living entity throughout the information assurance process. The protection scheme is geared to protecting the contents of the baseline. Therefore, the goal of the baselining process is to assure a continuously accurate picture of the components and status of the information base.

The information base is dynamic because the information contained is constantly changing. Most information of value is directly related to the business case. Therefore, asset bases evolve with the business case over time.

It is important to maintain alignment between the baseline and the business case, because the baseline contains the information that supports the organization's mission and purpose. As such, a formally documented and highly disciplined process should be employed to evaluate and control any changes to the baseline.

A disciplined process is necessary because information is hard to keep track of and the business case is complex. Strict discipline assures that all items of value to the organization are accounted for.

For example, a change to the organizational business case, such as a new product line, will produce new information. The new information may be extremely valuable to the overall success of the product and the organization. Therefore, there has to be certainty that any new information added will be identified properly and assured adequately. Without a formal process to make certain that changes are reflected accurately, it is likely that the organization's understanding of the contents of the asset base will be lost. This creates the potential for valuable new items to be unprotected, or even for the organization to lose track of its assets entirely.

Ensuring Continuous Knowledge

The process that assures that the contents of the information base are always known and documented adequately is called **asset management**. Asset management establishes and maintains a precise description of the information asset base, its constituent elements, and their interrelationship. It assures a permanent, accurate accounting and enables the status of the asset base to be known at all times.

Asset management assures that the documentation is accurate and that all security policies are correctly implemented. Asset management is a complex organizational process composed of six interdependent activities. These are

1. Process implementation
2. Asset identification
3. Control of change
4. Status accounting
5. Asset evaluation
6. Version management

Process Implementation

It takes a plan to establish a persistent organizational process. In the case of asset management, this is called the **asset management plan**. That plan enumerates the activities that make up the entire asset management process. This includes all of the necessary procedures as well as all the points in the process where those functions will be performed. The plan defines and assigns organizational roles, responsibilities, and personal interrelationships while specifying the interactions between each activity.

The product is a complete, correct, and fully documented life-cycle strategy. That strategy lays out the overall approach to accounting for and maintaining the status of all information of value to the enterprise. The resulting plan should precisely specify the process that will be used to identify and label information and maintain a correct representation. Because the plan sets the strategic direction and dictates the procedures for meeting organizational objectives, it must also be sensitive to changes in organizational context. Therefore, the organization must make a commitment to continuous planning and updating throughout the life cycle.

The plan must make certain that the status of the information asset is known and kept up-to-date. It must assure that valid baselines and versions exist. In conjunction with the requirement to maintain baseline integrity, rules must be laid down to assure that the repositories that contain the formally constituted baselines are properly maintained and archived. Finally, the plan should specify an up-to-date list of the **decision makers** who are authorized to approve alterations to the form of the asset base. That list should itemize the authority, scope, and responsibility of each decision maker.

One of the most important benefits of a well-managed asset baseline is that it underwrites the way that risk is managed and **disaster recovery** is assured. The **risk management** function is an essential feature of the information assurance process because it maintains the organization's planned response to all identified threats. The risk management plan is based on an assessment of the threat to the information base that each risk represents. Risk management is aided by well-defined baselines because a clear picture of the form of the asset assures that only relevant threats will be dealt with.

Effective disaster recovery is another outcome of good baseline management. Disaster recovery plans assure the ability to recover assets after a disaster. This is an important element in ensuring organizational continuity. The contribution of the asset management plan to the disaster recovery process is the assurance of precise knowledge about the contents of the asset base (this precise knowledge enables the timely restoration of normal functions) to a specified recovery point.

Periodically it is necessary to archive a well-defined baseline. Periodic archiving assures that an up-to-date picture of the asset is available for recovery. The rules and procedures for archiving each baseline have to be defined and documented in order to do archiving properly. Thus, the asset management plan has to describe both the **timing** and the execution steps required to back up and preserve each baseline. That includes fundamental considerations such as establishing the priority for what is to be protected, as well as itemizing the requirements for sequencing and scheduling the recovery steps in the case of a disaster. At a minimum, the following concerns should be addressed:

- Is all the necessary information and associated equipment needed to re-create the baseline available in the archive?
- Are all necessary media protected from disaster?
- Is there a need to maintain copies of the controls that have been set to assure each item of information?
- Is there a requirement to maintain copyright records for a specific set of assets?
- What is the mode of retention, including the media and format, as well as the location of stored baselines and the tools for maintenance?
- What length of time will baselines be kept? The goal is to preserve the baseline for only as long as is necessary to support disaster recovery.

This section has provided an overview of the implementation process. Before we move on to the next section, which focuses on the details of how the process is executed, we would like you to answer some questions about overall concepts.

Cross Check

1. Why is the specific identification of items to be secured a precondition for the security process?
2. Why is the asset identification process best done in a hierarchical fashion?
3. What is asset accounting and why is it important?
4. Why should there be a plan to implement asset accounting?
5. How is disaster recovery related to asset accounting?
6. Why is asset accounting an essential support for the disaster recovery process?

Asset Identification

The goal of the **asset identification** function is to establish an accurate record of the precise form of the items in the information asset base. To assure proper representation, all items that comprise the information asset base have to be identified and labeled unambiguously. Once this is done, the documentation is continuously updated.

Asset identification is based on a formal identification scheme. The identification scheme assures that everything worth protecting is identified and labeled properly. As a result, the asset identification scheme is the cornerstone of good asset management. Identification and labeling of the asset is an essential requirement because the information base is a theoretical construct, which might have many forms. Practical security requirements demand that a complete and correct picture of the form of the information asset is maintained at all times. This implies a process to assure that the relevant characteristics of each item of information are known and properly recorded.

An asset identification scheme establishes the "day one" form of the asset and it is kept current throughout the life cycle. With new organizational systems, this process is carried out during the design phase. If the function is already part of an existing system, then a retrospective analysis of existing systems is required.

Such after-the-fact analysis can be costly and difficult for a manager to justify because it may require documenting the functions of hundreds of thousands of lines of code that could be decades old. However, it is essential to the overall responsibility to provide assurance, because legacy systems are usually insecure. That is, it would not be sound practice for the organization to be able to say with certainty that 10 percent of its systems—those that represent new code—were secure, but that the status of the other 90 percent was unknown.

Because of the necessity to secure only those items of value, the identification scheme is always guided by the business case. There are two separate steps involved in documenting the identification scheme. First, the decision criteria to be used to identify and characterize the individual asset items must be explicitly agreed to. For instance, criteria like … *"The information item must be directly traceable to and support a business process"* can be used to decide whether or not an asset is worth protecting. Then, once the right decision criteria are established, it is important to assure that the people responsible for conducting the actual identification and labeling process will correctly use them.

Each item of information that will go into the asset base is identified and appropriately labeled. As we said earlier, this is a documentation process. The description of the item, its area of application, and its general use is recorded and a label is created. This documentation and labeling process actually requires two passes.

The first pass describes the components of the baseline at a high level of functioning. The aim is to describe the large components of a particular real-world operation, for instance, invoices and accounts. This high-level characterization should be all-encompassing, rather than detailed. It should focus on communicating the general form of the asset base to managers and users. This is done to obtain feedback. The aim is to assure a clear relationship between the documentation of the asset base and the associated elements of the business process.

The actual **asset base** typically contains multiple representations. These are called versions. For example, data from tax forms for different years would constitute different versions of the same basic item, which is "tax form information." Once that high-level understanding is achieved, a second pass is required to detail each of the large components. The outcome of this second pass is a detailed description of each of the information items that were identified in the first pass. Figure 1-1 illustrates this two-pass approach to identifying and representing the information asset.

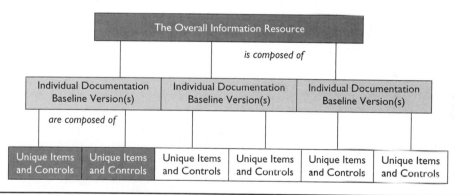

Figure 1-1   Hierarchy of documentation baselines

The labeling employed to characterize the relationship of each individual component to all other components is based on and reflects the hierarchical structure. In actual application, the labels will employ mnemonics unique to each item. That facilitates automated management, in a database for instance. However, the labeling must always correlate to the element's location in the hierarchy of the identification scheme.

Items defined at each level are given specific labels associated with the structure itself. These labels must be unique and should designate and describe the position of the item in the overall **family tree** of the asset base. A label should provide a unique name of the item, the name of the baseline, and the version designation. Furthermore, the overall labeling scheme must be expressed in such a way that the relationship between all components can be understood. It is a good idea to use naming standards to guide the labeling process in an organization of any size.

During the identification process, all information items that make up the information base are described and labeled. They are arrayed in a logical framework based on their interrelationships and interdependencies. This structure represents the form (configuration) of the asset.

As we have said, an aggregate set of related information items is termed a baseline. The individual components constituting this baseline are identified and labeled. That structure is then maintained as a coherent array of the information items that compose it. Moreover, once the baseline is established, it is maintained through the life cycle of the system that it describes.

The most common model for representing the components of a baseline is hierarchical. However, as we said earlier, the business case evolves over time; therefore, the form of the asset base also evolves. Consequently, the labels that characterize information are subject to alterations in their relative position within that hierarchy, as well as in the relationship to other items at the same level. The identification scheme must accommodate such changes.

The organization then establishes the practical countermeasures that will be used to assure each component at a desired level of security. Depending on the degree of assurance required, information can be described at one or all of these levels (as shown in Figure 1-2):

- The baseline (for example, an entity's complete set of assets)
- Baseline components (for example, a single asset—a document, for instance)
- The unit (for example, an individual item—a field on a document)

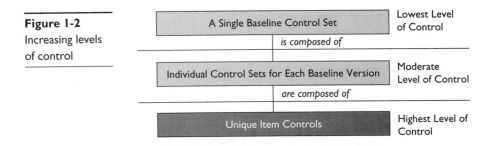

Figure 1-2
Increasing levels of control

A Single Baseline Control Set — Lowest Level of Control

is composed of

Individual Control Sets for Each Baseline Version — Moderate Level of Control

are composed of

Unique Item Controls — Highest Level of Control

The asset base can be assured this way because the classification and tagging of the elements provides a tangible representation of the items to be secured.

The structure is maintained top-down, ranging from a view of the information asset as a single entity all the way down to a designation of the explicit items that constitute it. The baseline representation that emerges at the lowest level in this decomposition process is a detailed and concrete architecture. That **concrete architecture** represents the only tangible depiction of the asset.

The general approach to this design process is outlined in Figure 1-3. Please remember, this is provided as an illustration only. The approach is the same in all cases, but the form of each particular implementation will vary with the individual business model of the organization.

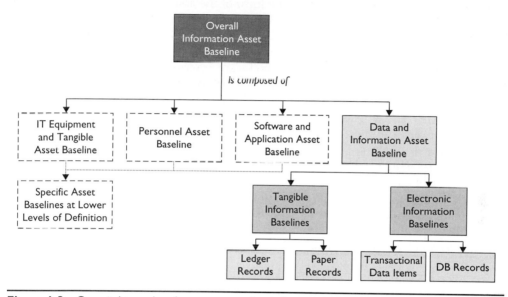

Figure 1-3   Generic hierarchy of components of an information base

Figure 1-3 is a general representation of the mechanism that identifies and arrays the distinct items of information that comprise the asset base. The decomposition process illustrated demonstrates how the goal of establishing successive levels of understanding is achieved. At the lowest level of decomposition, the baseline scheme that emerges represents the detailed architecture of the asset base of the organization.

Because the array of items and their position in the hierarchy is subjective, that decision should be based on consensus. It should be made using the input of many stakeholders, ranging from the technical staff to the business case owners of a given item of information. However, independent of who makes the decision, once it is established, the formal asset baseline is kept in some sort of formally designated repository, which is maintained accurately throughout the life cycle.

Control of Change

Change control is a continuous process. It assures that the documentation of the items that exist within the baseline is accurate and that their precise status is known at all times. Its aim is to manage the natural evolution of an entity in such a way that it preserves its overall integrity. An effective process for the control of change offers two advantages. First, it assures the integrity and correctness of a baseline. Second, it allows for the maintenance of continuous knowledge about status.

Change control is a sensing, analysis, and authorizing function. It is necessary because information evolves. Items are continuously added to baselines and the form and content of individual baselines changes as the business model evolves. Moreover, the countermeasures required to assure each item are always changing in accordance with alterations in policy, as well as to the form of the asset itself. Thus, there has to be a process to manage the natural evolution. Otherwise, the understanding needed to assure the asset base would degrade quickly. For that reason alone, effective information assurance depends on rigorous change control.

The functional parts of asset management are interrelated, in that the capability to conduct effective **change management** depends on the prior process (asset identification). The information assets of the organization are intangible. If change were not controlled, the rest of the assurance process would become pointless. That is because the organization would not know what it was protecting. Therefore, change management is a critical requirement.

Any change to the baseline can have serious implications because any modification to the form of the information asset may change the protection requirements. Consequently, the appropriate manager must authorize all proposed changes. That decision-making process must be supported by an analysis of the implications of the change.

That analysis should consider such things as how the changed item will be reintegrated into and interface with the other items in the assurance scheme. As a requirement, there should be an estimate of the affects and resource commitments required to modify the form of the protection. Change control is such an important process that its detailed implementation will be discussed in detail in the next section.

Status Accounting

Identification and change control establish and maintain a correct and continuously evolving image of the content of the information base. This image is documented by the status accounting function. **Status accounting** maintains running documentation of all asset baselines and performs the routine reporting activities necessary to transmit that knowledge to the appropriate managers.

This record is typically maintained in an electronic repository or *"ledger."* This ledger is the concrete documentation of the asset base. The ledger is referenced by change control to perform the impact analysis, prior to the authorization of a change. It is updated in a timely fashion once a change has been approved and implemented. In many organizations, the person responsible for doing the status accounting is the information resource manager. Because this manager essentially maintains the baselines, this individual is sometimes referred to as a *baseline manager*.

Asset Evaluation

The point of asset evaluation is to assure the operational integrity of the asset base itself. That assessment is an important continuous review process. It involves a formal inspection of a designated baseline. Inspection targets will normally depend on the requirements of the situation. Evaluations are done on a routine, scheduled basis.

The schedule is typically developed as part of the initial planning. It is important to maintain a disciplined inspection process, because the basic principle of *integrity* is involved.

The evaluation assesses the degree of correctness of the baseline. It tests the accuracy of the description, the placement of the item in the hierarchy, and labeling of each information resources within the baseline. In conjunction with these steps, it also evaluates the appropriateness and effectiveness of the specific safeguards that have been established for each element.

The result of each evaluation is communicated to appropriate designated executives. By rule, any findings of nonoccurrence or identified anomalies must be resolved through action by the manager responsible for the affected item. Immediate executive action is required because these anomalies are, by definition, latent vulnerabilities. The reporting process itself, as well as the explicit criteria for judging whether the problem has been resolved, is outlined in the asset management plan.

Version Management

Version management is necessary because there are usually simultaneous representations of the same asset baseline and is really a library administration function. It keeps each authorized version of the asset baselines secure, each in its own repository. Since those representations are maintained electronically, the repositories are usually just another organizationally sanctioned database. These databases are individually maintained, and are labeled uniquely.

In addition to maintaining a record of all current versions, all superseded versions are archived separately. This archive is similar to the repositories that hold the current versions, in the sense that it is a secure electronic storage location. The archives of old versions are useful to security because they provide a rollback capability in the case of disaster, as well as serve as a source of time-series data for root cause analysis. Many useful things can be learned about the long-term behavior and evolution of the resource by studying these data.

Maintaining Integrity

In this part of the chapter, you will learn about the components that are necessary for maintaining integrity in the organization.

Establishing the Checkpoint

The integrity of information must be supported by management function because it is a critical quality for assurance. One of the most commonly accepted ways of performing that function is outlined in Figure 1-4.

The location for receiving and processing requests must be established at a single identified point in the organization because the information resource is both intangible and dynamic. As such, any changes to its representation have to be carefully coordinated. This is the checkpoint where changes are analyzed and authorized. Its purpose is to make certain that a responsible party approves any changes to a secured baseline.

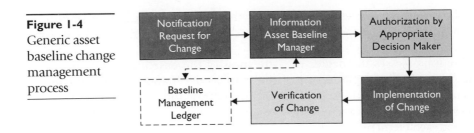

Figure 1-4
Generic asset
baseline change
management
process

The generic term for this process is *"change management."* Change management assures continuous integrity by controlling *all* changes to *all* formally established baselines.

Change management analyzes requests for changes to the form of the asset base. The aim is to determine all of the potential implications and impacts on the affected baseline. Once these are all understood, the next step is to obtain the authorizations.

Documenting the Decision

The method for requesting changes must be both understood clearly and applied consistently throughout the organization. To assure consistency, the format of the documentation should be standardized. No single format is applicable to all assurance situations. The following is the minimum information that needs to be supplied in order for a decision to be made:

- Organizational requirements that necessitate the change
- The operational timeframe and proposed schedule
- Information items impacted
- Controls impacted
- Costs and resource commitments
- Staff capabilities required
- Any software or tool requirements
- Any anticipated changes in procedure caused by the change
- Any anticipated change in the way the baseline is kept (for example, libraries)
- Any audit considerations
- Any disaster recovery considerations
- If they exist, the impacts on the various versions

Assigning Authority

Decisions about the form of the asset base have to be made by a responsible party. This assures accountability. Therefore, as part of the process the person who should appropriately make the decision has to be identified and decision-making authority has to be assigned formally.

The first step is to identify and designate the proper decision maker. The authority for authorizing change is typically assigned based on operational responsibilities. That is, the person who should be held accountable for approving changes to an information asset should also be the one responsible for managing its generation and use.

The process of identifying and designating that decision-making authority requires that the organization understands the operational implications for the information itself. Policies should be made about questions such as whether low-level technical activities, for instance routine maintenance changes, should be approved by any person higher in the organization than technical workers.

Structural change to a baseline takes place when new items are created or added. The decision to change a baseline can be approved only by the **authorized decision maker**. From the standpoint of maintaining a disciplined approach, the decision maker empowered to approve changes must also be the one with the authority to enforce the decisions that they make. That is, the decision maker should be in a position to allocate the resources and oversee the activities to assure the integrity of the change.

Implementing the Change

Any change to the form or substance of a baseline element is initiated through a formal process. A request for change is submitted to the person responsible for maintaining the accuracy of the baseline. This responsibility is established as part of the planning for the assurance function. The subsequent responsibility of that individual is to assure that the change is appropriately authorized, and will not affect the integrity of either the item or the asset baseline as a whole.

All changes have to be approved. At one end of the spectrum, if the change represents a high risk or is resource-intensive, the approval might come from an executive decision based on a thorough analysis of impacts. If the change is determined to be low risk or have minor impact, this approval might be nothing more than a simple sign-off from a technical manager.

The change is made once authorization is received and the person responsible for making modifications to the **controlled repository** where the baseline is kept and implemented. For example, they could change the labeling, add elements, or alter the form of the element itself.

Once this is done, the person responsible for maintaining the overall integrity of the asset base must inspect and verify the change. The purpose of the inspection and verification is to assure that the change was implemented correctly. If the change is important enough, the entire baseline should be audited afterward to verify that integrity has been maintained. Once the up-to-date status of the baseline is confirmed, the labeling is modified to reflect the form of the new baseline.

When the integrity of the baseline can be confirmed, its new status is recorded. Affected parties are notified and, in the case of electronic items, affected systems are inspected to assure they comply with the new status. Most operational baselines are complex. They may have thousands of components and interrelationships that must be maintained to keep an accurate picture of the asset. Ensuring that their representation is up to date is a resource-intensive exercise; however, it is an absolute condition for security. If the representation of the asset is not assured deliberately and rigorously, the painfully constructed understanding of the information asset base will eventually be lost.

Changes at any level in the representation are always maintained at each relevant level, and they must reflect correctly and accurately the changed status of the actual asset base. For instance, even adding an extra field to a financial record requires that data administration reformat the database to capture the new information. At the same time, from an assurance standpoint, if the form of the record is changed, there is now something additional to secure (for example, the new item), so it is necessary to update the baselines that contain that information item to reflect its new status, along with changes to the controls.

Accounting for Information

It is necessary to create a formal organizational accounting function to assure that the contents of the asset base are always accurate and known. In that respect, each baseline is treated as if it were a separate account in a ledger. Individual transactions affecting the form of those baselines, or the overall structure of the asset base itself, are entered as they occur. The aim is to document and record all transactions for that baseline. This function is not responsible for actually ensuring that the process of making the change is carried out. Its purpose is to assure that up-to-date answers about the status of a given baseline are available. The following data has to be gathered to assure that this function operates as intended:

- The label and description of the information item
- How formally the item is controlled
- A description of the controls
- Measures appropriate to support the monitoring of the integrity of the item

Other Considerations

Escalation policies must always be considered because changes to the business case can modify the security requirements of a particular information item. For instance, an information item generated by a software system under development will always have different sensitivity requirements than the information that flows through the same application when it begins supporting the core operation. Once that system and its data are moved up to operational status, it takes a different level of authority to approve changes to the representation of the information it processes. This approval requires some sort of procedure to assure that it actually happens. To assure that the asset baselines integrity is maintained as they evolve, it is a good idea to keep track of the individuals who requested the change. This allows security managers to validate sensitivity and use for example.

Finally, in complex and outsourced situations typical of modern information system work, it is an absolute requirement that asset baselines evolve through a single integrated and coordinated function. An organization's information resources frequently include contributions from external participants—customers and subcontractors, for instance.

There should be a formal mechanism that assures that contributions do not inadvertently (or intentionally) damage the integrity of the organization's understanding of its own assets. Otherwise, if third parties had the capability to change baselines without authority, there would be the extreme danger that the integrity of the entire asset could be destroyed without anyone in the organization knowing it.

There is no greater threat to the integrity of information than uncontrolled change. If the evolution of the baselines that represent the information asset is not controlled properly, critical information may be threatened because the necessary countermeasures were not in place. This is not a trivial hazard and so it is essential that unauthorized changes to the form of the asset base will not occur. Nevertheless, before we proceed to the next section, which focuses on the actual steps to be taken to implement a reliable process for controlling change, here are some questions to test your understanding of the process.

Cross Check

1. What is an information asset baseline and why is it critical to create one before embarking on an information assurance process?

2. Why are asset baselines formulated hierarchically? What is the advantage of approaching information identification that way?

3. Why are information asset baselines constantly changing? Is this a particular problem in IT organizations?

4. Why is it important to control carefully changes that take place in the information asset baseline?

Establishing the Assurance Function

In this part of the chapter, you will learn the details of establishing the assurance function.

Basing the Response on the Risks

Information assurance maintains the integrity of the information asset base. That is, once a baseline is established, explicit countermeasures can be put in place to assure the protection of every organizational information asset. The assurance function cannot be deployed, however, until the risks are understood fully. So, once the baselines are established, it is necessary to do a rigorous threat assessment to identify the measures that must be taken to resolve each threat.

A control that has been deliberately set to counter an identified threat is a **countermeasure**. To identify the appropriate countermeasures, the organization must move item by item through the baseline and decide what threats apply. Most of the rest of this text discusses the types of specific countermeasures that may be used in various areas of assurance. That is not our purpose here, because we are examining the process by which all the vulnerabilities for every baseline are identified and recorded and the threats that could exploit them are evaluated. The outcome of the process is an explicit inventory of risks and the associated countermeasures.

The rigor of the process is always based on the degree of risk. The risk assessment can be either formal or informal, but the idea is to identify all logical vulnerabilities. The details of how to conduct a risk assessment are provided in the next chapter. Here we are discussing the reasons for doing one and the general conditions that apply.

The risk assessment produces an initial characterization of the type and origin of all reasonable threats to a particular information item. The next step in the process is to determine the feasibility of each of the potential countermeasures that could put in place to address every identified threat. That requires an accurate understanding of the precise threat-countermeasure relationship, which involves characterizing four related factors:

1. Timing requirements
2. Corrective action requirements
3. Financial factors
4. Likelihood

Timing Requirements

Deciding the timing of the countermeasure is applied is important because the value of the **corrective action** depends on the ability to deliver it in sufficient time. The old axiom about "closing the barn door after the horse has escaped" is an example of how timing is a security issue.

Nonetheless, every threat has different timing requirements. Therefore, the feasibility of the countermeasure should be evaluated based on the question of whether it can react quickly enough to overcome the threat. For instance, an electronic penetration must be detected and responded to almost instantly or it will never be countered. That is because the appearance of the threat is moving at the speed of the computer itself. By comparison, an attempt by a thief to break into the computer room allows a little more time to respond. Thus, timing has to be factored into any consideration of feasibility.

Corrective Action Requirements

The same is true with corrective actions. A corrective action is the specific response that an organization deploys for a given situation. There is a range of possible corrective actions that could apply to a given threat. However, the most effective ones may not be feasible because of technical, physical, or resource limitations. For example, if a software countermeasure is identified as the best defense against a particular threat, it is prudent to assure that it is compatible with the requirements of the current system. Otherwise, it would be useless at best, and in the worst case it could constitute a threat.

The same considerations apply to physical countermeasures. For instance, it would be hard to convince the Board of Directors to build another information systems building because the first is situated in a flood plain. That would be the case, even though that might be the most effective countermeasure to the threat of floods. The salient point is that corrective actions are always assigned on a sliding scale, which factors feasibility and cost into the equation. The outcome is typically the selection of a countermeasure that is the most practical, rather than the one that is the best in all cases.

Financial Factors

The most important element and the one that is most easily understood and accepted by the people in the organization, is **financial factors**. Financial factors typically describe the return on investment (ROI) for a given countermeasure. If the cost of implementing a countermeasure is greater than the conceivable loss, it is pointless to consider it. This may seem unlikely, but in the case of low-value assets, there is always the possibility that the expense of maintaining a given level of security outweighs the financial loss resulting from compromise. Therefore, a decision might be justified to let the item sit unprotected.

Likelihood

Likelihood is composed of two factors. The first is the frequency of occurrence (of the threat) and the second is the extent of the harm that might result. The extent of harm should never be confused with frequency of occurrence. For instance, fires might happen infrequently. Yet if they do, the likelihood is very high that significant harm will occur. Therefore, a countermeasure to protect your house against fires would be highly justified, even if they were unlikely to happen. Conversely, if there is little harm from one incident of a threat but a high rate of occurrence, then some sort of countermeasure might be justified because the aggregate impact of the resulting harm over time may be significant. Frequency and probability have to be balanced in that respect to establish a countermeasure set.

Hoping for the Best and Planning for the Worst

Of course, it is important to base the threat assessment on an uncertainty factor. The term **uncertainty** describes the priority of the threat. It is expressed as a percentage, in the same way weather forecasters predict rain. It is important to communicate the threat in layman's terms because threat assessment is never an exact science and yet people, especially decision makers, have to understand the situation in sufficient depth in to build an appropriate response. This problem is a particular concern with an entity as complex and abstract as information.

Uncertainty is expressed as a level of confidence—from zero to 100 percent. What this confidence level communicates is the threat's immediacy and impact. For instance, a statement that a threat should be considered to be 100 percent likely to occur and cause harm, in essence, states that the countermeasures are absolutely required.

Documenting the Countermeasures

Once the analysis of the risks is complete, the organization will know two different and highly related things. First, it will know precisely what information assets it holds. This has already been recorded in the set of baselines. Second, the organization will know the type and priority of each of the threats to every one of the items in the baseline as well as the countermeasures established to mitigate them. Figure 1-5 describes that relationship.

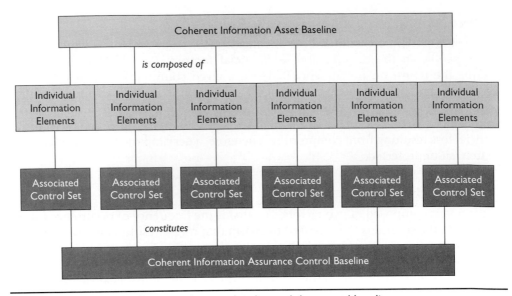

Figure 1-5   Relationship between the asset baseline and the control baseline

Therefore, the countermeasures that have been selected for each item in the asset baseline must be recorded as well. The final version of the representation of the asset base has both the information item and the associated countermeasures tightly bound to each other. Changes to either type of baseline component are maintained in that way—in essence, the information and the associated countermeasures have to correspond. It is unacceptable to have controls that do not specifically reference an information item or information items that do not have an associated control in any asset baseline.

Documenting the Assurance Solution

Preparing and documenting a specific set of **work practices** establishes a concrete link between each specific item of information and the countermeasures that are set to protect it. Detailed work practices assure that the operational steps necessary to maintain a correct relationship between the information and its countermeasures are documented, understood, and practiced across the organization. In order to make certain that these work practices are designed and documented correctly, the following factors have to be considered:

- Sequence and timing of countermeasures
- Specific monitoring practices

- Accountabilities
- Documentation and reporting
- Problem resolution responsibilities

Sequence and Timing

Countermeasures are generally not applied at the same time. Instead, they must be sequenced properly. For example, these might be the countermeasures specified for the personnel function:

1. Background checks will be performed for all new hires.
2. An initial employee orientation will be held to obtain confidentiality agreements.
3. Employees will receive regularly scheduled security training.
4. Employee violations of policy and procedure will be disciplined.
5. Employees will be given periodic random background checks.
6. Employees will report all security incidents they see.
7. Employee-reported security incidents will be recorded and quantified.
8. Employees leaving the organization will be processed using secure personnel practice.
9. Unfriendly terminations will be processed as security incidents.

There is a logical sequence for how these are deployed. For instance, it is impossible to quantify an incident before it has been reported, and some of these items might take place at the same time or interchangeably. However, it is not good practice to assume that everybody knows the sequence. As a case in point, it is a matter of organizational choice whether employees sign a confidentiality agreement before or after their credentials are verified. While there are potential security risks associated with not verifying a person's credentials, there is little threat to confidentiality since the employee has not been hired. As such, it is important that the personnel manager understand what task to do first, and that knowledge cannot be assumed. This is a minor item, but it serves to illustrate the point that sequence needs to be considered in the design process for countermeasures.

Monitoring

Monitoring has two purposes: First, it assures that the relationship between the information and its countermeasures will be supervised; second, it allows the organization to evolve continuously the countermeasures as threats arise. A focused monitoring process assures both of these functions. This function is established by developing work practices that specify the participants, schedule, and responsibilities for each monitoring activity, as well as the reporting requirements.

Accountabilities

Explicit accountability for oversight and problem resolution should be assigned as part of the description of the countermeasures. Otherwise, their application will not be supervised properly. This requires that individual supervisory roles and responsibilities be defined for each countermeasure, including the change management authority discussed earlier in this chapter. Then, performance of these duties needs to be overseen using the monitoring process just discussed. To assure evenhanded administration of discipline, the consequences of a failure to meet assigned obligations must be spelled out.

Documentation and Reporting

The documentation and reporting function is established and maintained through a statement of the specific steps required to assure proper recording and reporting of incidents. That statement defines what information will be captured and specifically how it will be recorded and reported. Customary reporting lines have to be specified to assure this. The statement must also identify all management reports to be produced down to their specific layout.

Problem Resolution

Finally, a statement has to be made about how problems will be resolved. This set of work practices is usually called a problem resolution process. The process defines how typical problems with operations will be handled as they are identified, who is responsible for their resolution, and the criteria that will be used to determine if the problem has been resolved properly. This function closes the loop in ensuring consistent application of the process, because it guarantees that problems that arise during operation will be dealt with systematically.

Keeping the System Aligned

As the final point, remember the importance of keeping the baseline properly aligned with the evolution of the operating infrastructure of the organization. This is an iterative process in the sense that it is inappropriate given the complex demands of even the simplest organizational situation to develop a static representation and to fail to maintain it. Therefore, effectiveness implies a commitment to continuous monitoring, adjustment, and updating of the baseline.

This process should entail solicitation of continual and regular feedback from the operational environment. The feedback is important because, in addition to providing guidance, a well-executed feedback system generates a high degree of organizational buy-in. This final benefit—universal acceptance—justifies fully the work required to obtain that feedback because it assures disciplined performance of the security work. We are now going to move on to the specific elements of information assurance, but before we do so, we would like you to review a final set of key questions to check your understanding of the ideas in this chapter.

Cross Check

1. In terms of focus, what is the difference between the selection of the controls for information assurance and the deployment of the actual response? Why should these be considered different aspects?

2. What is the role of the change control process and why might it be the single most important success factor?

3. Why is it necessary to conduct operational risk assessment on an ongoing basis? How are the outcomes of this process used?

4. What are the organizational and business case issues and constraints involved in control selection? Why are these critical determinants of the ongoing effectiveness of the information assurance system and how can they be affected by change?

5. Why is it necessary to maintain a classic change management process for the information asset baseline? What is the role of the information baseline accounting ledger in this process and why is it important?

6. Why is it necessary to value controls to implement information assurance? What does the organization lose by *not* doing this (for example, what would be the situation if this were not done)?

7. What is the role of threat assessment in the overall control formulation process? Why is threat assessment a primary success factor for operational implementation?

8. Why is it necessary to follow the steps in the process? What is the likely consequence of jumping ahead a few steps to conclude things?

Chapter 1 Review

Chapter Summary

- The asset management process is composed of six interdependent organizational activities. These are process implementation, asset identification, change control, status accounting, asset evaluation, and version management.

- The baseline identification is important because the deployment of assurance controls is directly referenced to the structure and content of the asset being managed.

- Change control is necessary because information assets are constantly evolving and there should be an organizational process to manage that natural evolution.

- Without change control, the ability to account for the information base with certainty would quickly disappear.

- Status accounting maintains a running account of all asset baselines and performs the routine reporting activities required to convey that information to the appropriate people when needed.

- Asset evaluation constitutes a formal inspection of the target baseline. It should be performed on a scheduled basis.

- The asset management process is formally defined and specifically implemented by means of an asset management plan.

- One of the primary benefits of well-managed asset baselines is that they fully underwrite the risk management and disaster recovery process.

- The identification and baselining process is the essential element in the establishment of an effective asset management program and, as a result, the cornerstone of asset management is the asset identification scheme.

- In practice, that aggregated set of related information assets is termed a "baseline."

- Items defined at each level are provided with unique and appropriate labels. Generally, these labels are associated with the structure itself.

- At the lowest level of decomposition, the baseline scheme that emerges will represent the concrete architecture of the target information asset.

- A change management process is necessary to establish and maintain explicit control over the information asset baselines and associated controls.

- Change management starts with having a defined mechanism for processing change requests. This is a documentation activity.

- Changes at each level in the structure of the information asset baseline are maintained at all relevant levels in that ledger. They must reflect correctly and accurately the changed status of the actual information item.

- Operationally, a control set is assigned once the target asset is unambiguously understood.

- The actual process of designing the control set necessitates a step-by-step analysis of the precise protection requirements of each individual element comprising the information resource.

- The purpose of assessment is to assure the effectiveness as well as confirm the coverage of the assurance scheme.

- The assessment operation is carried out much like other conventional testing activity. The practical outcome of this process is a formal analysis of effectiveness.

- The final form of the system is composed of two independently formulated, but interrelated, baselines.

- These are the information asset baseline, which describes the form of the resource, and the control baseline, which provides the actual assurance.

- The application of the required controls for each information item must be spelled out in the form of itemized work practices.

- Effectiveness implies a commitment to continuous monitoring and adjustment.

- This process should be centered on constantly seeking feedback from the operational environment.

Key Terms

asset base (5)
asset identification (4)
asset management (2)
asset management plan (2)
authorized decision makers (11)
baseline (1)
baselining (1)
change control (7)
change management (8)
concrete architecture (6)
controlled repository (11)
corrective action (14)
countermeasure (13)
decision maker (3)
disaster recovery (3)
family tree (5)
financial factors (15)
risk management (3)
status accounting (8)
timing (3)
uncertainty (15)
version management (9)
work practices (16)

Key Term Quiz

Use the preceding vocabulary terms to complete the following sentences. Not all terms
will be used.

1. Testing to refine the control set in its operational environment is called _____.

2. Each information item is identified by a unique and appropriate _____.

3. Essentially, _____ types of baselines are involved in asset management.

4. The baseline that provides the specific assurance function is called the _____.

5. The goal of authorization is to assure that the designated _____ authorizes all
   changes to information and control _____.

6. Implementing work practices involves consideration of their _____.

7. Threats to information are identified by means of a _____.

8. _____ is necessary because an organization's information can legitimately be
   in more than one form, tax records for instance.

9. Measures to resolve problems are called _____.

10. _____ maintains an up-to-date record of the form of the asset.

Multiple Choice Quiz

1. Information asset management:
   A. is irrelevant to information assurance
   B. implements policy
   C. involves AT&E
   D. is unnecessary

2. Baselines:
   A. are abstract
   B. are intangible
   C. are hierarchical
   D. must be programmed

3. The process of formulating the control set should be based on:
   A. best guess
   B. confidence
   C. iteration
   D. a sense of humor

4. To do its work properly, the status accounting function relies on the use of:
   A. code reviews
   B. repositories
   C. controls
   D. verifications

5. Information asset management is always based on:
   A. a plan
   B. an analysis
   C. best guess
   D. best practice

6. Version management is necessary because:
   A. there are often multiple examples of the same information
   B. software comes in multiple versions
   C. there might be two organizations involved
   D. versions are difficult to identify

7. A disciplined change process is necessary because:

    A. discipline is important

    B. the protection scheme must be continuously aligned to the business case

    C. items that are left out of the protection scheme will still be protected

    D. change never happens

8. Documented baselines serve as:

    A. a warning against threats

    B. the model for good security practice

    C. the basis for access control

    D. a proxy for the information asset itself

Essay Quiz

In your own words, briefly answer the following:

1. Why is it important to control changes to asset baselines?

2. Why is the labeling process approached hierarchically?

3. Differentiate asset baselines from control baselines.

4. How do the asset management procedures relate to overall information assurance policy?

5. What is the role of risk assessment when it comes to baseline formulation?

6. Why is organizational buy-in so important to good asset management?

7. What is the purpose of version management, why is it necessary, what are the outcomes if it is not practiced?

8. Why is it logical to begin the information assurance process with an information identification step?

9. Why must labels be unique, what purpose does unique labeling serve in the real world?

10. Why is assignment of accountability important? What would be the consequence of not having it?

Case Exercise

Complete the following case exercise as directed by your instructor:

Refer to the Heavy Metal Technology Case in Appendix A. You have been assigned the baseline management responsibility for the project to upgrade the target acquisition and display (TADS) for the AH64-D Apache Longbow attack helicopter. To start the process, you know you must first identify and array a complete and coherent baseline of high-level documentation items. Using the project materials outlined in the case (and others you want to add because you feel they are appropriate), perform the following tasks:

- Identify all distinct types of documentation.
- Relate these documentation items to each other. If there are implied relationships, what are they?
- Provide unique labels for each item that reflects their relationship to each other and through which another reader could easily see that relationship.
- Formulate these items into a coherent baseline.
- Define a change control system to assure that the integrity of each of these items will be preserved over time
- Justify the effectiveness of that control scheme.

Assessing Risks

In this chapter, you will learn:

- The elements of risk assessment
- The role and purpose of risk assessment in information assurance
- The fundamentals of how to perform a risk assessment
- How the audit process serves to identify and track risks

The information assurance process is founded on the ability to anticipate and manage risks. A **risk** is the possibility that a **threat** is capable of exploiting a known **weakness** or **vulnerability**. The operational process by which risks are identified and characterized is called **risk assessment**.

Within the context of the information assurance life cycle, the term "risk assessment" describes an explicit, repeatable process, which is well understood and followed continuously by all responsible parties. In this chapter, we will discuss the various ways to ensure that this process is both repeatable and continuous.

Risks—An Overview

Risk assessments are important because they help decision makers understand the things that could go wrong, how likely they are to occur, and the consequences if that were to happen. Obviously having that knowledge is an essential precondition to planning an effective security response.

Knowing Where You Stand

In this subsection, you will learn the terminology, definitions, and methods of risk assessment so you will understand how to do proper risk assessments.

Understanding Threats: Where Risk Assessment Fits

Like the information identification principle discussed in Chapter 1, risk assessment is a prerequisite rather than a discrete countermeasure area. Once all the information of value to the organization has been identified, the next logical step is to itemize the risks to it. Therefore, the other necessity for effective deployment of countermeasures is an understanding of the nature of the risks involved. That rule applies in every substantive area of security, from barrier fences to electronic encryption.

Identifying Risks versus Managing Them: A Distinction

The term "risk assessment" is sometimes used interchangeably with "risk management" because knowing where the risks lie is a fundamental precondition for managing risks. That is not correct, since these are not the same processes.

Risk assessment focuses on understanding the nature of all feasible risks. It identifies and evaluates each relevant threat, determines its potential impact, and itemizes the safeguards that will be needed to control it. Risk assessments delineate both the strategy to reduce the likelihood of a risk *occurring* **(preventative measures)**, *as well as the measures to respond effectively if a risk becomes a direct threat* **(reactive measures)**.

Risk management on the other hand, maintains the effectiveness of those measures once they have been put in place. Thus risk management ensures effective and up-to-date alignment between identified threats and the countermeasures deployed to mitigate them. This is typically part of the day-to-day operation. Therefore that process is normally termed "Operational Security." The risk management process will be discussed in Chapter 5, "Security of Operations."

Providing Useful Answers: Certainty versus Impact

Risk assessments should always answer two distinct but highly related questions. The first is: "What is the *certainty* of the risk?" This is typically expressed as **likelihood**. The second is: "What is the anticipated *impact*?" That is normally conveyed as an estimate of the loss, harm, failure, or danger if the event does happen.

Ideally, both questions can be answered in easily understood and believable terms. Understandability and credibility are key factors, because the results of the risk assessment guide operational decision makers in the deployment and management of the security process.

Shaping the Response: Risk versus Consequences

There are risks in every endeavor. In the case of information assurance, the risk applies specifically to threats that might cause harm to *information* assets. All risk assessments provide two specific pieces of information, the **probability of occurrence** and the **estimate of the consequences**. As we said in the preceding section, these independent, highly related factors determine the security features required.

Nevertheless, there is an implicit order to how these two issues should be approached. The first consideration has to be *likelihood* since, in a world where time is money; a highly unlikely event might not be worth the cost of further consideration. However, it is the estimate of the consequences shapes the form of the response. That is because there is never enough money to secure against every conceivable risk and so the potential harm that each risk represents has to be balanced against the likelihood of its occurrence.

For instance, an event that might cause catastrophic loss will sometimes justify consideration, even if it is improbable. For example, the unfortunate consequences of the Earth running into an asteroid justifies spending considerable money to track the movement of those things, even though the odds of an asteroid striking the earth are negligible.

Priorities: Matching Resources against Potential Harm

The primary goal of the risk assessment process is to maximize operational deployment and resource use. It accomplishes that purpose by identifying risks with the greatest probability of occurrence *and* which will cause the greatest degree of harm. The options these represent for the organization are arrayed in descending order of priority and addressed based on resource availability.

Since all of the decisions about the tangible form of the security system will depend on getting these priorities correct, it should be simple to see why a rigorous and accurate risk assessment process is critical to the overall success of any information assurance system.

Methodology: Ensuring Confidence in the Assessment

It is easy to have confidence in an estimate that is based on tangible things, an engineering problem for instance. However, that confidence will diminish quickly if the estimate is based on an entity as complex and hard to visualize as "information."

Consequently, information assurance risk assessments are built around tangible **evidence**. That evidence is obtained by conducting **interviews** and documenting observations of both organizational and human behavior. In addition, auditing system logs and examining other relevant technical or managerial record provides insight.

The collection process has to be systematic and coordinated because the sources of data are diverse. Every risk assessment should reflect a commonly accepted and repeatable methodology, which will produce independently verifiable concrete evidence.

Scope: Making the Overall Assessment Process Efficient

The gathering, compilation, analysis, and verification of risk data can be time consuming and resource intensive. To ensure the effectiveness and accuracy of any particular risk assessment, the scope of the inquiry has to be defined precisely and be limited to a particular problem.

Operationally it is acceptable to approach the understanding of risk in a highly focused and compartmented fashion, as long as the organization understands that the results of any risk assessment characterize only a part of the problem. In fact, the need to paint a detailed and accurate picture of all threats usually implies a series of specifically-targeted, highly integrated risk assessments that take place over a defined period.

Risk assessments target various areas of threat—electronic, human, and physical. The insight gained from each assessment is aggregated into a comprehensive understanding of the total **threat picture**, which serves as the basis for deciding how each will be addressed.

Ensuring Continuity: Tracking Evolving Threats

Risk assessments identify specific vulnerabilities and the threats that could exploit them. That understanding is called a **threat profile or picture**. However, because threats are constantly appearing, that profile has to be updated continuously. Consequently, the risk assessment is ongoing. That process maintains continuous knowledge of three critical factors:

1. The existence and interrelationships among all of the organization's information assets

2. The specific threats to each asset

3. The precise business, financial and technological issues associated with each threat

These are separate considerations, in that conditions for any one of them can change independently. However, they are also interdependent in that changes to one factor will most likely change the situation for the other two.

Making Threats Visible: Risk Classification

The risk assessment process itself has two components. The first is risk *classification* and the second is *risk response*. Since the form of the response depends on the type of risks involved, we are going to discuss that activity first. The latter activity—which is divided across two sections, *strategy formulation* and *deployment*—will be discussed in the subsequent sections.

Risk classification involves two procedures, **risk identification** and **risk estimation**. Because these activities both entail assessment of risks to an entity as abstract as information, they tend to be more qualitative than quantitative. They both result in plausible evidence to support decision making about the response. Figure 2-1 outlines their relationship.

Figure 2-1
Stages of risk
assessment

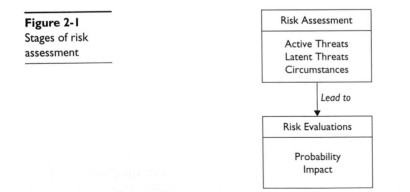

Gap Analysis: A Standard Approach to Identifying Risk

In professional settings, the initial itemization of risks is usually based on the identification of **gaps** between *ideal* practice and the current operation. Thus, risks in operations are identified by comparing the current operation to the requirements of ideal best practice. These requirements are normally expressed in a reference model.

The product of that analysis identifies the gaps between the best practices specified by the model and the current operations. These gaps are assumed to represent vulnerabilities that must be addressed by the security system. Figure 2-2 illustrates this.

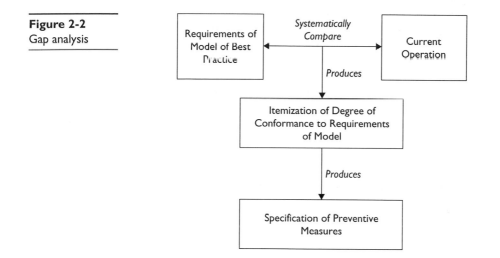

Figure 2-2
Gap analysis

In the first stage of the process, recommendations for best practice are compared to current practices within the organization. An alignment between the two is determined. A vulnerability is assumed to exist where a gap exists; that is . . . where the ideal state does not match the actual performance.

The goal of this analysis is to understand the kind of vulnerability that each gap represents. The results of that analysis drives the decisions about the actions that must be taken to alleviate that specific area of weakness.

There are at least four major universal **standards** used to perform a gap analysis. Each defines a useful set of control objectives, which can be tailored to both assess the current state of best practice, as well as provide recommendations for countermeasures. In that respect, each has the potential to serve as the basis for a complete solution. These are the ISO 27000 series, which includes a standard for risk assessment; NIST 800-18 (NIST SP 800-37); as well as the GASSP and COBIT models.

Risk Identification

Risk identification is range-finding activity. It is the simplest form of risk classification. It identifies potentially harmful risks. Consequently, a gap analysis is an ideal way to do risk identification. A particular threat may not have much impact within a given situation. So, variations from ideal practice that are identified through the gap analysis all have to be evaluated to differentiate only those gaps that would create vulnerabilities.

Risk identification documents the characteristics of every vulnerability, including itemizing a list of all of the threats that would be able to exploit it.

Risk identifications should characterize unambiguously and communicate the precise area of threat, as well as identify the information assets affected. Accurate risk identifications normally require exhaustive detective work including extensive interviews with participants, detailed analysis of technical processes and documentation. In some cases, strategic business process analysis is included.

The same careful investigative process needs to be followed to track known vulnerabilities after they have been identified. That is because of the potential for a **latent threat** to become active. A latent threat might not have immediate consequences because the conditions that make it harmful are not yet present. Latent threats are normally ignored in the process of developing the security strategy. This is understandable, since resources ought to be concentrated on the threats that are known to cause harm. However, a latent threat can become an active one if those conditions change. Therefore, all latent threats that could exploit a known vulnerability have to be tracked.

For example, insider theft might not be an immediate threat if the organization is small and every employee is known and trusted. However, if the organization has to bring in many subcontractors to meet a new project deadline, the potential threat of insider theft would become a very active one indeed, and as a result explicit countermeasures would be immediately required. Consequently, it is very important that the circumstances that turn a latent threat into an active one are specified within the risk identification phase and the recommended actions highlighted.

Risk Estimation

Unlike risk identification, which is a simple classification activity, risk estimation is a data-driven process. Risk estimations measure and quantitatively describe each potential risk. As such, risk estimation is the mechanism that provides the substantive data that will serve as the basis for the **risk analysis**. Therefore, it is important that information arising from the risk estimation is reported in as unambiguous and timely a fashion as possible to the appropriate decision makers.

Risk estimation determines the probability and impact of all threats that have been identified through risk identification. It provides the data for the analysis and decision making about the form of the response. That is, any number of countermeasures might be appropriate to a given vulnerability. However, in the operational world it is always necessary to pick just one. That decision is guided by the information that is developed through the risk estimation process.

Quantitative factors that might be included in the risk estimation includes assets affected, the potential duration of the threat, and the severity of adverse impact. Severity is typically expressed in common quantitative terms such as money or time lost. Because likelihood is an important factor, risk estimations must state the both the *probability of occurrence* and known *cause-and-effect linkages* to each information resource.

Strategy Formulation: Deciding About the Response

At this stage, the assumption is that the right group of decision makers will plan the countermeasure deployment. That decision-making process is based on factors such as return on investment (ROI), the likelihood that harm will ensue, and the probability that the event will occur. This should all be supported by the analyses done during the risk estimation phase.

ROI: Making the Business Case

Since the adverse impacts of threats inevitably cost money, it is important to factor applicable return on investment (ROI) issues into the eventual security response. One obvious reason for that is to ensure that the countermeasure does not cost more than the harm that the threat could cause.

Trade-Offs: Balancing Likelihood, Frequency, and Cost

Cost benefit and likelihood of occurrence have to be balanced when formulating a security response. The question is whether the threat will involve substantial cost within a given period of time. In essence, what has to be determined is the dollar value of the damage from a given threat within the specified planning period. This is balanced against the cost of deploying and maintaining a countermeasure over the same period.

Since the frequency of occurrence within a specified period of time, as well as the unit cost for each occurrence determines the actual dollar value of the damage, those considerations have to be traded off against each other.

Decide what the expected frequency and likelihood and the resultant cost will be. If the historical rate of occurrence were high, then even though the harm might be minor, a countermeasure might make good business sense. Remember the cost from the harm of each occurrence would add up quickly. The opposite is also true. A catastrophic threat is not necessarily dangerous if it only happens every 10,000 years. Therefore a valid risk mitigation decision might be to ignore it completely.

Making a Practical Decision: Annualized Exposure Loss

The decision-making that supports these trade-offs is based on annualized loss exposure (ALE). That is, the estimated expense of maintaining a countermeasure over one year is evaluated against the costs that would be incurred if the threat were to happen. If the expense is greater than any possible harm, then the countermeasure is not included in the security response. The formula for determining annualized loss exposure (ALE) is:

$$ALE = \text{Annual Cost of Deployment} - (\text{Annual Rate of Occurrence} \times \text{Cost per Occurrence})$$

Certainty Factors: Assuring Credibility

It has to be recognized that there is always uncertainty in the decision-making process. In practice, the risk analysis will probably identify threats where the likelihood and extent of damage are not clear. Those cases will outnumber the ones where the harm is evident and the probability certain. Quantitatively, the degree of certainty of the estimate should be expressed as a level of confidence from zero to 100 percent. This establishes the credibility of the associated estimate.

Knowing the probability of events is useful because it will tell the organization where immediate investment in security is required. Decision makers have to have confidence in the data they are using for their actions. Expressing the likelihood of an event as a probability estimate will communicate the importance of a timely response to decision makers. On the other hand, a failure to integrate an estimate of certainty into the analysis will reduce the overall level of stakeholder confidence in the results.

Documenting Outcomes: The Risk Mitigation Report

The outcome of the strategy formulation phase is a report which is distributed to the people charged with the responsibility for implementing the risk mitigation strategy. The mechanism for communicating information about risk is the **risk mitigation report**. This document specifies the steps selected for each risk and itemizes the countermeasures that will be implemented as well as the parties in the organization who will be responsible for accomplishing each task.

The risk mitigation report sets the security process in motion. The risk mitigation report dictates the form of the operational response by identifying threats that must be managed. It communicates the harm that ensues from each threat and suggests the various alternatives for response. The risk mitigation report is arguably the single most influential element in aligning the security solution with the requirements of the situation since it communicates the response blueprint.

The Security Solution: Deploying Countermeasures

A response to known threats is deployed in this stage of the process. The functional elements that make up that response are called **countermeasures**. Countermeasures are the steps that will be taken to mitigate a given risk.

Response deployment is another two-stage process. It starts with a more in-depth analysis, called **operational security analysis**, which leads to the deployment of a concrete security solution. The operational security analysis is a different type of analysis than the risk estimation because its purpose is much more applied. It ensures that the previously defined strategy and countermeasures are valid and fit the overall security aims of the organization. The implementation stage actually puts the response in place. Figure 2-3 illustrates this.

Risk Analysis: Understanding the Deployment Situation

The task of the **operational security analysis** is to understand precisely the implications of the threat picture developed in the risk identification and estimation stage. The goal is to refine further the general understanding of the risks to a point that can be acted on by decision makers.

For operational decision making, it is important to specify a minimum degree of protection. Minimum levels of protection must be specified because the management

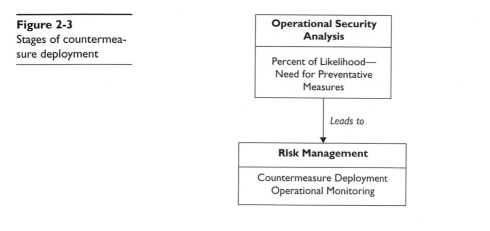

Figure 2-3
Stages of countermeasure deployment

role is deciding about what level of risk the organization can reasonably afford in its day-to-day operation. The decision is called a *risk-tolerance* decision. An intelligent risk-tolerance decision has to be supported by a focused investigation.

Assigning Priorities: Understanding Operational Costs and Benefits

An **operational security analysis** provides the information needed to assign operational priorities. To achieve that goal, the analysis should describe the value of an information asset. It expresses the value in terms such as how significantly the loss of that information would affect the organization.

Operational security analyses are performed to obtain a reliable, databased understanding of the **cost/benefit** situation for all identified vulnerabilities. Accordingly, the typical analysis always includes an assessment of the level of **acceptability** of the risk in dollars and cents terms.

This leads to a decision about how the risk will be handled, which is termed a **risk-mitigation** decision. Risk-mitigation decisions are the choices made about how to reduce the severity or affect of a known risk. All risks must have a documented risk-mitigation decision associated with them. As such, it is acceptable for a risk-mitigation decision to range from: "Spend whatever it takes to ensure that this risk does not occur," all the way to: "The harm the risk would cause does not justify the cost of addressing it."

In addition to recommending specific actions to prevent the risk, risk-mitigation decisions also specify ways to recover from the risk. The most common way of ensuring recovery is through a **risk transfer**. This specifies how any foreseen impact can be reallocated, or spread, so that the loss is not permanent or catastrophic. Much of disaster planning (discussed in Chapter 10) is supported by these kinds of decisions.

Asset Valuation: Involving the Business Case

The product of the operational security analysis is a security strategy. Therefore, the risk analysis must contain the needs, issues, and concerns of the various organizational stakeholders. Risk evaluations are painstaking processes. They use a systematic method to establish a substantive, resource-based, link between each risk and the benefits of countering it successfully. Operational factors that enter into the analysis of risk include such issues as: "What is the level of criticality of each particular information asset and what is the specific degree of resource involvement?" As such, at a minimum, risk evaluations have to answer one key question: "What is the value to the organization of a specific asset?"

It should be clear that, since information assets are abstract, it is imperative to use a uniform and consistent methodology to obtain an organizational value for each asset. Consequently, the critical success factors for a risk valuation lie with the business case, rather than the technical one. There are numerous ways of obtaining an organizational value for an asset. Popular examples include the following methods.

- **Applied Information Economics**—this approach assigns a standard unit of measure (usually financial) to variables, such as customer satisfaction, and uses statistics to calculate the value of the information to each variable.

- **The Balanced Scorecard**—this is the traditional "valuation" method employed by most organizations. It associates organizational performance with information value using four different global factors. These will be discussed further in the next section.

- **Economic Value Added**—this is the conventional cost analysis approach. It assigns value by subtracting costs from any value returned. The IT function charges each unit for information it uses. Thus, revenue as well as costs can be tracked.

- **Economic Value Sourced**—this assigns value four ways: increased revenue, improved productivity, decreased cycle time, or decreased risk. By using risk, it places security functions directly into information asset valuation equation.

- **Portfolio Management**—works like a stock portfolio. A responsible party, like the CIO, manages the portfolio of information items. With this approach, considerations such as size, age, performance, and risk determine the value of each item.

- **Real Option Valuation**—this is option based. It constantly considers the value of each information item over time in order to determine what the asset contributes.

A Sample Approach: The Balanced Scorecard

Although these approaches all have a reasonable number of adherents, we will use the Balanced Scorecard to illustrate the risk valuation process because it is arguably one of the easiest approaches to use. Originally conceived by Robert S. Kaplan and David P. Norton, the Balanced Scorecard allows companies to assess performance against four general criteria.

The Balanced Scorecard requires that every information item should be traceable to a specific organizational goal. In application, the organization's "scorecard" is tailored by means of a planning process whose purpose is to develop measures to portray accurately the non-financial as well as the financial condition of the organization. Since this is situational, the Balanced Scorecard does not recommend a specific set of measures. Instead it assesses value from four "perspectives." These perspectives and potential measurement factors are shown in Figure 2-4.

Figure 2-4
Categories of measures for four perspectives of the Balanced Scorecard

Financial Perspective Measures
Net Income
Operating Margin
Economic Value Added
Revenue Growth

Operational Perspective Measures
Safety
Process Enhancement
Operational Efficiency
Productivity

Customer Perspective Measures
Customer Satisfaction, External
Customer Satisfaction, Internal
Customer Loyalty

Learn/Grow Perspective Measures
Employee Personal Development
Employee Satisfaction
Organizational Enhancement

The data developed by the Balanced Scorecard allows an organization to value *all* assets appropriately. The valuation is essential if the overall aim of the risk assessment process is to prioritize and assign security protection to the complete range of assets. The organization institutes the process either by collecting new data or by analyzing existing data.

Ensuring Confidence: The Value of a Standard Method

The organization can then assign a quantitative, or at least objective, value to each information asset that it wishes to protect. It can confidently allocate a security priority from that value, which is based on all or some of these relevant categories.

The benefit of a standard methodology such as the Balanced Scorecard is that the organization will have data to support decisions about which item to secure and in what order. The best part of any standard method such as this is that, as data is collected and refined over time, the organization will be able to increase its predictive accuracy and thus sharpen its security control.

Operational Risk Assessment

Operational risk assessment is a continuing obligation of the process. Continuing periodic assessments of risks are necessary because the security situation is invariably changing. Thus, it is important to assure the validity of the strategy and countermeasures on a periodic basis. As we said earlier, operational risk assessments are conducted as part of the risk management process, which is in the domain of the security-of-operations principle (Chapter 5).

However, we will discuss the actual process of operational risk assessment in this chapter because the activities involved are planned and implemented in the same way as the other risk assessments. That is, operational risk assessments employ risk identification and estimation as the primary data-gathering mechanism and they use the **risk evaluation** function to decide about the nature of emerging threats.

Rather than producing a strategy, operational risk assessments are used to fine-tune the security response over time. Their aim is to maintain the desired level of assurance. The goal of the operational risk assessment is to say with certainty that the currently deployed set of countermeasures address the right threats and that these continue to be effective given the aims of the organization. If that is not the case, then the operational risk assessment provides the information necessary to help decision makers make the necessary changes to achieve the desired state.

The primary difference between traditional risk assessments and operational risk assessment is that the risk report is passed to the people responsible for maintaining the operational security and assurance system rather than the people who formulated the response.

This is a different set of individuals, with different needs. The people responsible for maintaining the security system tend to be lower in the organization, with a routine procedural/technical focus rather than a strategic one. As such, the operational risk assessment has to be designed to communicate to the people in that role. In particular, operational risk assessments should provide explicit implementation advice about changes that must be made to countermeasures.

Establishment: Planning for Operational Risk Assessment

The overall purpose of information assurance is to maintain an appropriate set of countermeasures at all times. Operational risk assessments are a critical part of that purpose because countermeasures have to be evaluated periodically to ensure that the protection is relevant and maintains its effectiveness. The process must be continuous. To make certain that the operational risk assessment process functions as intended, it has to be planned carefully. Consequently, it is necessary to tailor an effective, routine risk assessment process as part of the planning for the overall risk assessment function.

Planning for operational risk assessments involves establishing a standard schedule for the performance of each assessment as well as a defined process for problem reporting and **corrective action**. As such, the organization has to treat operational risk assessment exactly as it would any other continuous process. It must be resourced and staffed to ensure it functions as a part of everyday organizational operation.

Judging Performance: The Importance of Standard Criteria

Operational risk assessment does not typically involve the strategic gap analysis that supports the creation of the security strategy. Instead it makes use of a defined set of performance criteria, which are typically laid down during the formulation of the initial risk mitigation strategy.

Therefore, each countermeasure must have a set of observable criteria built into its specification. These criteria should be both measurable and capable of being recorded and reported meaningfully. In addition, the assumptions about cost and occurrence that were part of the original decision to deploy each control also must be stated.

Standard performance criteria allow decision makers to judge with certainty, at any time, for any countermeasure, whether that control is performing as desired and continues to achieve its purpose. The organization will use the data produced by the operational assessment process to monitor and ensure the effectiveness of its information assurance scheme. Accordingly, that data has to be unambiguous and easy for decision makers to use.

Implementing the Operational Risk Assessment Process

As we said in the prior section, operational risk assessments are established by plan. That planning process is no different from the one that establishes any other element of the assurance function. The actual planning is based on organizational goals and policies and the outcome of the process must be a relevant infrastructure of procedures.

To meet the demands of a changing security environment, risk assessments have to be exceptionally flexible. Therefore, the plan should specify specific roles and responsibilities, rather than dictate actions to be taken. The plan ensures that a responsible party will always be in place to address any contingency. The subsequent accountabilities should fit all of the requirements of the security situation.

It is necessary to plan the operational assessment process because it ensures that adequate resources are available to support the assessment activities. Furthermore, because it is sometimes hard to tell whether the goal has been reached, the operational risk assessment plan should specify the means or criteria that will be used to determine whether the goals of the process are met.

Standard Measurement: Ensuring Consistent Interpretation

Plans for risk assessment should ensure that each assessment produces consistent data. Consistency is important because third parties, primarily strategic decision makers, use that data to interpret the degree of risk exposure, as well as the types of countermeasures that have to be deployed. As such, all measurement data produced by the quantitative and qualitative measures of risk discussed earlier must be defined in the plan. Those definitions can be used to ensure that the information obtained in the assessment process is consistent across all areas of the organization.

Consistency is critical because stakeholders have to be on the same page when it comes to understanding the precise nature of the threats to the organization and the required response. If the people responsible for identifying and managing threats interpret the information differently, there is a potential for uncoordinated and ineffective responses.

Also, credibility is always an issue when it comes to operational information. If there is no clear definition of the basis for the information in front of them, it is hard for decision makers to rely on it. Therefore it is important to make certain that there is consistent understanding of what a given piece of information means.

This can be assured only through clear and consistent knowledge of the origins and meaning of the underlying data. Proper understanding has to be ensured across all of the stakeholders in the organization and that understanding can be reached only if there are common and consistent definitions. If the basis is consistently understood, standard information collected over time can also provide a valuable source of historical data for trend analysis.

Audit

Although audit is used for purposes other than risk assessment, it is the only process for in-depth monitoring and so it should be discussed in a chapter dedicated to understanding the nature of threats. Effective overall assurance requires a specifically designated organization-wide watchdog to monitor the ongoing performance of the security function, as well as ensure the continuing integrity of the security solution. Audit provides the deliberate and disciplined means to that end.

Audit assures the integrity of the security solution from the pervasive influence of **process entropy**. Process entropy is the natural tendency for any organized system to degrade over time due to the changing conditions. Audit verifies that the necessary knowledge and accountability are in place to guarantee continuous performance. It confirms that the implemented security procedures are working as intended within the normal business setting. It identifies nonconformances with accepted practice and identifies new risks. If new risks or nonconformances are detected, audit notifies the parties responsible for restoring conformity. Figure 2-5 outlines this.

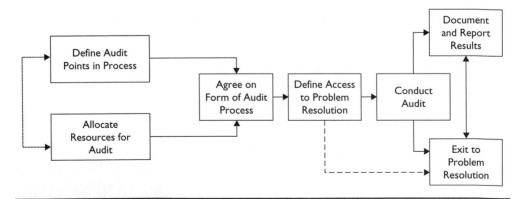

Figure 2-5 The audit process

There are many reasons why an organization might conduct an audit. A client might initiate an audit because a contract demands it or a regulatory agency requires it.

A **follow-up** audit might be undertaken if a previous audit indicated that a follow-up was necessary to confirm compliance. There are even situations where the people who requested the audit are the ones being audited. That is the case with **internal audit**.

In most instances, audits are mandated by contract through the **client organization** to verify **compliance** with requirements or procedures. In the case of information assurance, the primary reason for an audit is verification of conformity with a particular strategy, plan, standard, regulation, or guideline. Although they are less common, security audits may be requested by third parties to verify compliance with a specified requirement.

Audits are done to determine something about the four "Cs": contract, capability, compliance, or certification. Audits are frequently aimed at determining whether a specific situation, or deliverable, meets a customer's contractual requirements. Contractual audits are not within the scope of a security audit unless what is being assessed is the potential for breaches or the robustness of security features.

In the case of subcontractor and outsourced work these audits are almost the only method for assessing operational risks in the outsourced work and controlling and ensuring the integrity of the final product. In the case of outsourced work, rigorous audits must be performed to determine the extent to which the audited organization has followed proper procedure in carrying out the work. An external party should always perform the audits that extend down the supply chain from prime contractor, through sub- and sub-sub-contractors. The aim of these types of audits should be to confirm that requirements adhere to contractual specifications for proper security procedure at all levels in the supply chain.

Ensuring Continuity: Information Assurance Audits

Information assurance audits assess the execution of a defined set of security processes. The audit verifies the performance of those processes continuously. Audits are applicable in two operational areas—compliance and certification. In both cases the audit is performed to determine whether the assessed organization's processes are in the desired state of conformance with specified requirements. Three aspects of effective performance are normally audited:

1. The completeness and correctness of the policies that guide the process

2. The execution of the procedures to carry out the process

3. The capability of the management

Aims of an Audit: Compliance or Certification

The client for an audit is usually a specific customer, a regulatory body, or the government. The auditors can be either external or internal to the organization. If external auditors are performing the audit, it is typically termed an "audit." If internal auditors are performing it, it is called an "internal audit." In both cases auditors are looking for **noncompliances**, sometimes termed **nonconformances**, with particular, specified **audit criteria**. The customer establishes these criteria in advance of the audit.

In the case of certification, the basis for the audit is a general standard, or model that is typically specified by a third party. The standard or model is used to accredit the audited organization to some specific, required level of performance, or achievement. What is audited is the relationship between the organization's current operating performance and the requirements of the standard, contract, or regulation. In all of these cases the audit underwrites authoritative certification that the proper set of policies is in place and that the correspondingly acceptable set of procedures is being followed.

The point of both types of audits, either a general audit or certification audit, is to determine whether the **auditee** has achieved its stated objectives.

Ensuring Continuity: The Audit Framework

Audit involves a number of related processes, but they all serve the same aim, which is to establish and enforce ongoing organizational compliance with a specific criterion, or standard model. It ensures that compliance within an explicit audit framework. In the specific case of information assurance the items that are addressed within that framework include such things as

- Software integrity and controls
- Hardware integrity and controls
- Database integrity and controls
- Compliance with **contracts** and procedures
- Event and incident logs

Audit and Accountability

The audit process maintains accountability for performance. Therefore, it has to examine relevant aspects of the execution of each target function. It does that by observing objectively and documenting the behavior of the elements that compose that function. Each element is termed a **control objective**. Control objectives are focused behaviors with observable outcomes. Validating the functioning of control objectives provides an indicator of the security system's current level of compliance with a required level of performance. That continuous assurance of compliance is the best way of ensuring that the security system remains valid and effective.

Audits are necessary adjuncts to the risk assessment. Risk assessments are often snapshots, to identify what risks currently exist. In the case of such an approach, this often captures only a single point in time. It is rarely sufficient for proper management. An audit accounts for the execution of a required set of procedures over time. Audits therefore maintain the status of all designated security procedures on an ongoing basis. Regular audits combined with a good risk management process should help ensure that the integrity of the security response is maintained on a continuous basis.

Committing: Establishing the Audit Process

Audits tend to be costly so the requirement to perform regular audits is normally established by contract or regulation. That sort of legal obligation is necessary, because audits are so resource intensive. Audits are scheduled by plan to be held at predetermined milestones as part of the execution of that contract. Audits are always carried out based on a specific set of audit criteria because they often involve legal considerations. Parties have to agree in advance on what these are.

Auditing personnel have to be given specific responsibility for performing the audit. This assignment is necessary because people and organizations normally do not enjoy being audited. As a result the mandate to perform the audit process has to be formally established.

The resources needed to conduct the audits should be specified and cross-referenced to the audit objectives by contract. To ensure this, the parties involved in the audit have to specifically agree on how the audit will be conducted—the scope, procedures, and entry and exit criteria for the process. In addition the process to be followed to resolve noncompliances must be specified. Upon completion, the audit results must always be documented and provided to the audited party.

It is the responsibility of the party who requests the audit to define its overall purpose. That party must:

- Define the steps that the audited party should take
- Inform the audited party about the audit procedure they should follow
- Indicate the standards that will be used to evaluate compliance
- Select the elements, activities, and locations that should be audited

Managing the Audit Process

An audit manager is appointed to ensure the audit process is managed separately and is independent of the organization being audited. The role of this manager is to supervise, monitor, and evaluate the activities of the audit team. In that capacity, the audit manager plans and schedules audit activities, assumes responsibility for the **audit reporting** process, and controls the follow-up procedures. Figure 2-6 outlines this.

Audit Planning

Planning for an audit requires the organization to confirm that the necessary resources are in place. Once this confirmation is received, the organization schedules the process, selects the auditors, and assigns the audit roles and responsibilities. As we said earlier, at this stage formal steps must be taken to guarantee the integrity of the process by ensuring the organizational independence of the auditors. Once this can be confirmed the audit process is ready to be executed. Traditionally, there are four types of participants in an audit process:

- **Auditee**—The organization being audited
- **Lead Auditor**—The chief auditor
- **Auditor**—The audit team
- **Client**—The organization that engaged the auditors

Figure 2-6
Managing the
audit process

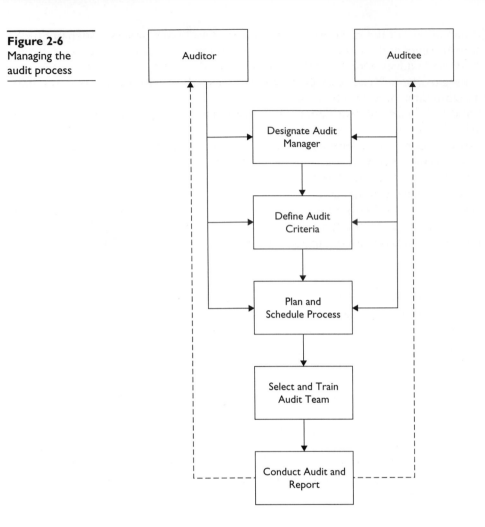

Audits are performed using concrete criteria. Thus the people who have requested the audit have to identify all relevant standards and specify those criteria. The audit is initiated by an opening meeting with the audited party's senior managers. The auditors are then responsible for ensuring that an appropriately qualified and capable team of auditors is selected.

A specifically designated **lead auditor** always manages the team. The lead auditor should always have sole authority for the process. Because lead auditors are responsible for the success of the audit, they are always considered to be third parties—even when the audit itself is internal. The responsibilities of the lead auditor are to manage the audit, assign audit tasks, help select auditors, orient the audit team, prepare the audit plan, and define auditor qualifications. Lead auditors are responsible for clarifying audit requirements and communicating them to all participants.

The auditors themselves must have the technical and professional expertise required to perform a proper audit. They must understand the system being audited and the standards that will be applied and be familiar with the auditee's operation. They must have a working knowledge of the **laws and regulations** that govern the activities of the audited organization.

The overall goal of the audit team is to guarantee consistent interpretation. It must be ensured that all auditors will make the same observations and draw the same conclusions when faced with the same evidence. In addition, audit managers should adopt and enforce a code of ethics to govern the overall audit. The prime directive of that code should be to protect the confidentiality of audit information.

The audit process starts with the detailed planning of the event and the approval of that audit plan between the audit team and the initiator of the audit. The audit performs the audit setup requirements by reviewing documents that describe the current system. An audit plan is then prepared by the lead auditor and approved by the client before the audit begins.

Details of Execution: Performing the Audit

The audit process involves a number of related steps, many of which are documentation intensive. In practical terms this means that the audit activity at each stage revolves around either preparing or reviewing **audit documentation**.

The auditors prepare working documents from each audit. These working documents are tailored to the situation. They include the checklists that auditors will use to evaluate the various compliance elements and the forms that will be used to document observations and evidence.

The preparation, validation, and distribution of the audit forms and checklists is one of the most important activities in the audit process because they drive the rest of the process. Forms and checklists are critical documentation items because they guide the performance of the process. That is the case because, if a procedure or other audit target is not on the checklist, it will not be reviewed.

Establishing a good **checklist** is one of the most important success factors in information assurance (IA) audits, because many of the important information assurance and security controls are embedded in software. Usually this is the operating system, but it could include the network support utilities, such as the firewall. The records generated are kept in **event logs**, which are automatically maintained by the system and essentially invisible to users unless specifically designated and called out by the documentation. Auditing these is an essential element of the information assurance function. However, they are not traditionally thought of as audit material, so they have to be identified and accounted for at the beginning of the process.

It is important in structuring the overall process to keep two things in mind. First, electronic records have to be audited using the same methodology and level of rigor that is applied to the more traditional body of audit evidence. Second, the outcomes and conclusions of the review of electronic records have to be fully integrated and appropriately supported in the body of audit findings in the exact same fashion as the traditional audit evidence.

These are two important factors unique to auditing information assurance work. Obviously all parties in the audit need to know what problems were discovered and that can only result from an examination of the complete body of evidence. Consequently, a successful audit process requires a systematic and exhaustive effort to identify, catalogue, and examine all relevant documentation, including both paper records and electronic ones.

The worst possible situation would be to examine only one type of record, leaving whole procedures in another form unexamined. The auditors collect the evidence using the following tools. Audit evidence is typically collected by:

- Interviewing personnel
- Reading documents
- Reviewing operational manuals
- Studying operational records
- Analyzing operating data
- Observing routine activities
- Examining routine environmental conditions

Authenticating Audit Evidence

After the collection phase, evidence obtained through interviews must be authenticated. For the sake of consistent interpretation, interview evidence should be confirmed by a more objective means. From the accumulated evidence, clues that point to possible nonconformities should be investigated thoroughly.

The audit process gathers sufficient reliable, pertinent, practical evidence to demonstrate that the requirements of specified procedure have been satisfied. Therefore, at the point where the audit is deemed complete, all objective data and conclusions must be authenticated by means of a suitable analysis. This must also be further justified through a careful consideration of the meaning of that evidence. This general process is outlined in Figure 2-7.

The responsibility of the auditor is to draw conclusions about the target designated by the client. That duty is supported by the audit tasks agreed to in the audit plan. The aim of the auditor is to maintain the team's effectiveness with respect to those requirements. However, in the execution of an audit there are a couple of critical success factors that must be considered.

The first of these is the importance of **confidentiality** in the audit process and specifically with respect to audit findings. This quality is important because it will determine the level of cooperation of the audited party and the ability of the auditors to do their job properly. It is difficult enough to get the right evidence to draw a proper conclusion without having to wrestle the people in the organization for their documentation, which is exactly what will happen if they believe the information will be leaked. Ensuring confidentiality is so important that an audit should be terminated if confidentiality is breached.

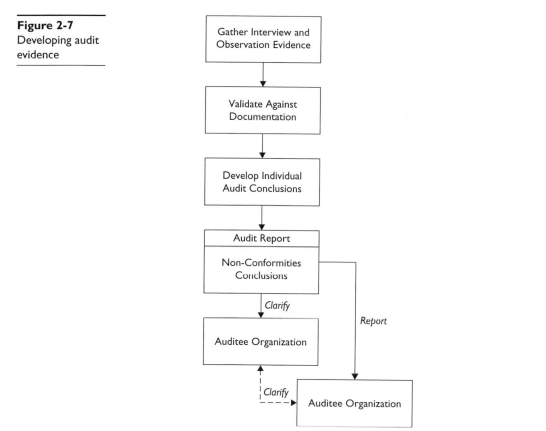

Figure 2-7
Developing audit evidence

The second success factor is **impartiality**. Even though a conclusion will inevitably have to be drawn, it is important that all findings are supported by unambiguous evidence. This evidence should be either directly observable or expressed in terms that can be verified objectively. All assumptions must be stated in every case. The classic example of the way this should be done is the case of the old auditor who, when asked what color the whiteboard in the conference room was, responded that he could only draw a conclusion about the color of the front, because he couldn't see the back. That is exactly the degree of evidence-based inference required to underwrite the impartiality of an auditor's findings. This is an extremely important element of the process because if those findings are seen as biased, they will not be relied on.

The auditors document a list of the key nonconformities based on that evidence. The auditors can also draw general conclusions about how well the system is doing in achieving its objectives. A high degree of competence is necessary in audits where the conclusions might be controversial or demonstrate something other than simple noncompliance. That is essential in the case of situations where the audited party is attempting to hide something. There is no such thing as double jeopardy in an audit. The most commonly invalidated audit findings are those where the audited organization initially passed the audit, only to have subsequent facts uncovered indicating that the auditor was unable to fully assess the situation correctly.

This may seem like a side issue, but the fact is that audit evidence is often conflicting, so the auditor has to weigh and balance the overall findings in order to reach a conclusion. Success rests on the ability of the auditor to get the evidence on the table so it can be examined. Electronic information can be more difficult to gather than paper records, but it is also harder to tamper with. Accordingly, one of the primary questions that an IT auditor has to answer is: "Does the electronic record substantiate the paper one?"

Finally, the audit team discusses their findings, observations, conclusions, and non-conformities with the auditee's senior managers. It is traditional to do this before they prepare a final audit report.

Preparing the Audit Report

Normally there is a meeting with the audited party during the preparation phase; the goal of this meeting is to clarify concerns and discuss action items. After the meeting, the auditors report their preliminary conclusions, including problems encountered.

Follow-ups to audits are normally carried out to document that problems identified in the original audit have been addressed and corrective actions taken. This is followed by a formal set of recommendations. The final report will contain statements outlining:

- The purpose and scope of the audit
- The audited organization
- Audit targets
- Applicable control structures and standards
- Evaluation criteria
- Observation list classified by major and minor findings
- The timing of follow-up activities

The Importance of Validation

The actual reporting is a multistage activity built around an iterative communication process between the auditor and the auditee's management and staff. Most audits support conclusions about capability and certification; the audit process must accurately reflect the status of the organization. Accordingly, it is important for the members of that organization to assist in the validation of the findings.

Since much of audit is a matter of expert opinion, auditors must make every effort to ensure their perspective is correct. This can be accomplished only by testing their inferences with the people who do the work. That is not to say that auditors should seek feedback in order to shape their conclusions. It is to suggest that it is important to validate perspectives by discussing them with participants, and time devoted to this end should be built into the audit schedule.

C&A: The Federal Government's Use of Audit

Finally, audit within the federal government takes on a special form called Certification and Accreditation (C&A). This is a special application of the audit process to support the special needs of very large organizations, ones where trust in products and services must be established in advance. It deserves examination because it is an excellent example of the use of audit to pre-designate levels of trust through the universal analysis and certification of the level of risk for subsequent customers.

The federal government's C&A process generates a document that management can use to identify and accept the residual risk in any system. It is a product-oriented approach. However, the same process can be used to certify services and even organizations. The C&A process is a comprehensive evaluation of the technical and non-technical security features of the entity being tested. It assesses safeguards, to establish the extent that a particular entity meets a set of specified information assurance requirements.

The outcome of a C&A process is a recommendation to the senior systems manager (SSM), the chief information officer (CIO), or the designated approving authority (DAA) that the system should be accredited as secure, provisionally accredited, or not accredited. Certification of a system is the outcome of an information assurance analysis in the following areas:

- Physical
- Personnel
- Administrative
- Information
- Information Systems
- Communications

Once a system has gone through certification it is ready to be accredited. Accreditation is the formal declaration by the senior systems manager (SSM) that an information system is approved to operate in a particular security mode using a prescribed set of safeguards at an acceptable level of risk. This declaration establishes the risk tolerance levels of the system and allows the system administrator to prescribe the appropriate set of access controls.

An advantage of using this type of process is that it relies on defined steps that bring responsible participants together to implement uniform C&A practice. That practice then is applicable throughout the life cycle of the system, which is why this type of continuous process is a popular part of acquisition and development project strategies.

Example of a C&A Process: The Federal Government's DITSCAP

The DoD Information Technology Security Certification and Accreditation Process (DITSCAP) is the primary means to obtain audited certification of the adequacy of the information assurance and security features of any system that might be used by the federal government. In a bureaucracy as large as the federal government, the DITSCAP process is particularly important to ensure that prospective customers know what all of the risks associated with a given system are.

This process applies specifically to the software in systems; however, it can also be used to certify the risk status of other aspects of the system that interface with the software, such as the business process the software supports. There are four phases to a DITSCAP evaluation:

- Definition
- Verification
- Validation
- Post Accreditation

Each phase contributes to the process of ensuring acceptable qualification of the system for federal use. It would be very difficult to characterize the sensitivity of the data—and thereby designate the access control scheme—without complete performance of each of these steps. As a result, security models like Bell-LaPadula and Biba, which are discussed in the chapter on access control (Chapter 6), depend on the system first going through a DITSCAP evaluation.

Phase 1: Definition   In the first phase, key players agree on the intended system's mission, attendant security requirements, the scope of the C&A boundary, the audit schedule, the level of effort, and resource commitment. The agreement is documented in the System Security Authorization Agreement (SSAA) that describes the system. During the definition phase, the certifier will

- Define the system functions, requirements, and interfaces
- Define information category and classification
- Prepare the system architecture description
- Identify principal C&A roles and responsibilities
- Define Certification and Authentication level of effort
- Draft System Security Authorization Agreement (SSAA)
- Agree on the method for implementing security requirements (documented in SSAA)

Phase 2: Verification   During this phase individuals called certifiers determine the system's compliance with SSAA requirements. They seek to identify the integrated system for certification testing and accreditation. Main tasks during this phase are

- System architecture analysis
- Software design analysis
- Network connection rule compliance
- Integrity analysis of integrated products

- Life-cycle management analysis
- Security requirements
- Validation procedures
- Vulnerability evaluation

Phase 3: Validation   Validation of the system is a hands-on process, the aim of which is to validate compliance with the SSAA requirements. The goal is to obtain full approval to operate system (accreditation). Primary tasks during validation include

- Security test and evaluation (ST&E)—Determination that the Confidentiality, Integrity, Availability, and Accountability (CIAA) elements are implemented as documented in SSAA and perform properly
- Penetration Testing—this includes exploitation by both insiders and outsiders
- Communication security compliance evaluation
- System Management Analysis (Maintain Management/Configuration Management/Architecture)
- Contingency Plan Evaluation—this would include backup, continuity of operations, recovery, and so on
- Site Accréditation Survey (SSAA compliance, environment)
- Risk Management Review (acceptable risks to CIAA)

This effort results in the development of a Certification Report and Recommendation for Accreditation in which the certifier recommends whether the system should be accredited. Another alternative might be that the system will be given an interim accreditation, or be unaccredited. The end of this phase is marked by the accreditation decision from the senior systems manager (SSM/DAA/CIO).

Phase 4: Post Accreditation   This phase starts after site accreditation has been accomplished and its objective is to maintain an acceptable level of residual risk. Responsibilities for keeping the system running shift from the certifiers to site normal operations groups, and this responsibility remains with them until the system is terminated.

The main tasks during this phase include a review configuration and security management. The certifier documents that the organization follows the change management scheme documented in SSAA and determines that system security management continues to support mission and architecture. The certifier will usually conduct a risk management review to confirm that risk to CIAA is acceptable. The certifier will ensure mechanisms are in place to enable continued compliance with SSAA requirements, current threat assessment, and concept of operations

In addition, post accreditation requires that the SSAA is recognized as a living document, which continues to represent agreement among the senior systems manager, the certifying authority, the user representative, and the program manager. This document is developed in Phase 1 and updated in each phase as the system development progresses and new information becomes available. At minimum, the SSAA should contain the information in Table 2-1.

Steps	Examples
Mission Description and System Identification	This section describes the system being accredited in terms of its role, mission and criticality
Environment Description	This section describes the overall operational environment of the system
System Architectural Description	The system design and structure
System Security Requirements	
Organizations and Resources	What is the hosting organization and what resources it has
Tailor Plan	Example
	Programmatic considerations
	Security environment
	IT system characteristics
	Reuse of previously approved solutions
	Tailoring summary
Tasks and Milestones	What needs to be done and when
Schedule Summary	Bringing the schedule together
Level of Effort	How much work
Roles and Responsibilities	Who does what

Table 2-1 Minimum Content of an SSAA

Chapter 2 Review

Chapter Summary

- The systematic process by which risks are identified and countered is termed risk assessment.
- The aim of a risk assessment is to identify, evaluate, and manage information security risks.
- In order to do that, the **scope of the assessment** has to embody the entire set of organizational and technical issues.
- The risks that may exist for a given information asset are itemized in terms of the threats and vulnerabilities that they represent for each specific asset.

- It is important to first specify the precise body of information assets that will fall within the scope of the assessment process.

- In practical terms the risk assessment poses the common-sense questions: "What could go wrong? How likely is it to occur? What are the consequences if it does? And what are the steps that I can take to mitigate that circumstance?"

- Risk assessment processes operate under the assumption that as threats are identified the appropriate countermeasures can be developed and put in place to prevent them from happening or contain them if they do.

- Risk assessment entails an ongoing process, which is performed to ensure the long-term survival of the information asset base.

- The first stage is usually made up of two practical steps, risk identification and risk estimation.

- Risk identifications can only be done after extensive investigative activity within the organization itself.

- Risks have to be tracked and monitored using these same processes.

- Risk estimation is a quantitative endeavor that involves the actual evaluation of the circumstances of the potential risks.

- Quantitative factors that may be included in a risk estimation could include such things as an inventory of the assets affected, the potential length of occurrence, and the degree of adverse impact measured in such common terms as money or time.

- The stage of the process where the actual steps are taken to mitigate or control the identified threats involves both risk analysis and substantive risk management.

- Risk analysis seeks to define the preventative measures that may be employed to reduce the likelihood of a risk ever occurring as well as the countermeasures that will be needed to respond effectively if it does.

- Risk management deploys the countermeasures and monitors their effectiveness.

- The **risk analysis report** shapes the operational response by identifying those threats that have to be managed.

- Essential security controls are deployed based on the identified threats and the priority assigned to all vulnerabilities identified in the risk assessment.

- Specifically, all quantitative and qualitative measures of risk and impacts must be unambiguously defined in a plan.

- The risk management plan should provide a specific mechanism to control the risks that are associated with **third-party work**.

- Audit ensures the monitoring and enforcement of the control procedures that have been specifically designed and installed to provide the appropriate level of assurance for a given setting.

- Audit establishes and enforces ongoing organizational accountability within some sort of control framework.

- Because audits often involve contractual considerations, they should always be performed based on audit criteria.

- The auditors make a list of key nonconformities based on the evidence obtained.

- Then the auditors draw conclusions about how well the system is applying its policies and achieving its objectives.

- Once an **audit conclusion** has been reached, it is packaged into a report, which is normally reviewed with the auditee's upper management prior to release.

- The responsibility of the auditor is to evaluate the audit target that is defined and designated by the client.

- The sole aim of the auditor is to comply with those requirements.

- Audit evidence is the tangible documentation that the auditors have obtained, which provides sufficient **proof of compliance**.

- This documentation is used to support the **analysis and interpretation of the evidence** as well as underwrite the findings of the audit report.

- It is the record of the audit work performed as well as the evidence that supports the auditor's findings and conclusions.

Key Terms

acceptability (33)
analysis and interpretation of the evidence (52)
audit (38)
audit conclusion (52)
audit criteria (39)
audit documentation (43)
audit reporting (41)
auditee (40)
checklist (43)
client organization (39)
compliance (39)
confidentiality (44)
contracts (40)
control objective (40)
corrective action (36)
cost/benefit (33)
countermeasures (32)
estimate of the consequences (26)
evidence (27)
event logs (43)
follow-up (39)
gaps (28)
impartiality (45)

internal audit (39)
interviews (27)
latent threat (30)
laws and regulations (43)
lead auditor (42)
likelihood (26)
noncompliances (39)
nonconformances (39)
operational security analysis (32)
(preventative measures) (26)
process entropy (38)
probability of occurrence (26)
proof of compliance (52)
Quantitative (30)
(reactive measures) (26)
risk (25)
risk analysis (30)
risk analysis report (51)
risk assessment (25)
risk estimation (28)
risk evaluation (36)
risk identification (28)
risk management (26)
risk mitigation (33)
risk mitigation report (32)
risk-tolerance (33)
risk transfer (33)
scope of the assessment (50)
standards (29)
third-party work (51)
threat (25)
threat picture (27)
threat profile or picture (28)
vulnerability (25)
weakness (25)

Key Term Quiz

Complete each statement by writing one of the terms from this list in each blank.

1. _____ provides probabilities that a risk will occur as well as the cost/benefit impacts if it does.

2. The least quantitative type of risk assessment is called a risk _____.

3. Decisions about the deployment of the security response are based on _____.

4. One mechanism for assessing whether to deploy countermeasures is the Balanced _____.

5. The only way to ensure accountability is through _____ of risk performance.

6. Measurement requires established _____.

7. The process that ensures that control objectives are being met is called _____.

8. There are essentially two types of risk assessments: _____ and _____.

9. The document that ensures that nonconformities are brought to management's attention is called a _____.

10. Audit conclusions are only based on _____.

Multiple Choice Quiz

1. A control framework ensures that:
    A. defects are prevented
    B. vulnerabilities don't happen
    C. procedures are followed
    D. no risk is ignored

2. Confidentiality is important in all types of assessments because:
    A. it ensures cooperation
    B. it prevents leaks
    C. it identifies threats
    D. it reduces cost

3. Continuous risk management is underwritten by:
    A. plans
    B. project management
    C. risk assessment
    D. procedures

4. Most risk assessments are conducted against:
    A. reference models of best practice
    B. gaps
    C. specified criteria
    D. the technology

5. Besides the effectiveness of security controls, audit can assure:
    A. security technologies
    B. security processes

C. safety

D. security work

6. A gap analysis looks at:

   A. the best practices

   B. the difference between current and ideal practice

   C. the presence of non-conformities

   D. the audit evidence

7. A likelihood estimate is important because:

   A. people like estimates

   B. knowledge of probability of occurrence supports decision making

   C. investment in security is easy to make

   D. likelihood drives cost

8. A risk estimation is different from an operational security analysis in that:

   A. risk estimations are quantitative and security analyses are not

   B. risk estimations deal with probability

   C. the aim of the security analysis is to determine whether the strategy is correct

   D. the aim of the security analysis is to determine ROI

9. Scope is essential to risk assessment because:

   A. it defines the range of things that will be examined

   B. it sets the security perimeter

   C. it establishes the types of analyses that will be needed

   D. it is a component of the risk mitigation strategy

10. Risk assessments are:

   A. basic countermeasures

   B. unnecessary because threats are always evolving

   C. features that are found in the security of operations function

   D. an essential precondition to planning the response

Essay Quiz

1. It is important to validate audit interviews by other means. Why is that the case and what can happen if this is not done?

2. Risk assessments always embody some form of probability estimate. Why is that necessary and what does it prevent?

3. What is the role of Annualized Exposure Loss in security system formulation? What may happen if the ALE is ignored?

4. Forms and checklists are important in all types of assessments. Why is that the case and what do they essentially provide for the process?

5. Security audits are different from risk assessments in that they are regular and ongoing. What is the primary benefit of a continuous process?

6. Gap analyses are most easily accomplished if they are based on standards. Explain why?

7. Certification is a very useful aspect of the risk process. Explain how certification can assure against risks.

8. One of the most important aspects of the practical security process is the risk mitigation report. Explain what purpose it serves and why it is a key element of security.

9. How does risk assessment relate to the information identification process?

10. What is the role of risk identification in the overall process? Why is risk identification a necessary step?

Case Exercise

Complete the following case exercise as directed by your instructor:

Heavy Metal Technologies (HMT) is a defense contractor headquartered in Huntsville, Alabama. HMT was recently contracted by the Army to upgrade the fire control system for the MH64-D Apache Longbow attack helicopter. Because the contracted enhancement is so important to the continuing success of the main ground attack helicopter program and thus because of its importance to national defense, the Army wants a total commitment from HMT that the integrity, confidentiality, and availability of project information will be assured. Therefore the Army would like HMT to address the following five organizational control concerns. Please provide a written solution for each of these.

- The Army requires a procedure that all security concerns will be identified and addressed.

- The Army requires a procedure to assure that performance of the security process will be continuous.

- The Army requires a procedure to assure that the control processes will be cost efficient.

- The Army requires a procedure to assure that the comp will be able to satisfy its contractual and legal obligations.

- The Army requires a procedure to assure that all third-party work will meet security criteria.

Security Policy

In this chapter, you will learn how to:

- Define the terms information assets, risks, and countermeasures
- Structure a synergistic information assurance solution
- Identify the role of policy in the information assurance process
- Design a functional information assurance and security management system

Protection of information is crucial in a society where cybercrime and cyberterrorism are household words. Nevertheless, it is becoming increasingly difficult to ensure that protection when the threats to information continue to grow in number and sophistication. Between 1988 and 2003, a total of 319,992 security incidents were reported to the Community Emergency Response Team Coordinating Center (CERT/CC) at Carnegie Mellon University. These focused on one of four attack types: unauthorized access, malicious code, denial of service, or inappropriate usage. It is important to note that 219,623 of these events occurred during 2002 and 2003 alone. Or, to put that statistic into context 69 percent of all attacks on information in the entire fifteen-year period from 1988 through 2003 happened in the last two years!

Product vulnerabilities follow the same pattern. Vulnerabilities are flaws that allow an attacker to usurp privileges, regulate operation, or compromise data. Over the past 16 years, 12,946 product vulnerabilities were reported to the CERT/CC. Of these, 7,913 or approximately two-thirds, surfaced since September 11, 2001 and the trend is expected to increase!

Many factors contribute to these statistics; however the implication is clear. It is essential to establish and maintain an effective, continuously evolving defense. Yet, there are still significant problems with ensuring that defense. The major findings of a recent Government Accountability Office (GAO) study of the national infrastructure revealed the following weaknesses:

- Risk-based information assurance plans were not developed for major systems.
- Information assurance policies were not documented.
- Programs for evaluating the effectiveness of **controls** were not implemented.
- Controls for application development and change control were not implemented.

- Implementation and use of software products had inadequate control.
- There are too few people who know how to select, implement, and maintain information assurance controls.

Significantly, the reported weak points are in the areas of **policy** and **process**, rather than technology. Breakdowns in security are most likely to occur because of a failure to understand the problem, set proper goals, and follow **correct** procedure. This chapter discusses the various ways to ensure that policies and procedures areas are truly **responsive** to information assurance requirements.

Definitions: Assets, Risks, and Countermeasures

Data are observations of the environment, including raw facts and figures. Information is a collection of those data assembled into a relevant and useful picture. Information is used to support decision making. If the information is integral to good decisions, it is an asset. An asset is anything a person or organization owns that is valuable, including tangible and intangible things.

In the case of information processing operations, the value of the tangible assets lies in their ability to support the storage, processing, and delivery of necessary information. The value of intangible assets is harder to express, however it is done frequently in terms of the replacement costs or the value of the information to a specific organizational function.

The information assurance process protects information of value from all predicted threats by deploying a set of actions to prevent or slow an impending attack. These actions are the countermeasures discussed in Chapter 2.

Any circumstance or event that might cause injury to information assets or information processing systems through unauthorized access, destruction, disclosure, modification of data, and/or denial of service is a **threat**. Threats are any event that can have an undesirable affect on the condition of an asset. Threats are categorized by the degree of risk that they represent. A risk is the likelihood that a particular threat will produce a harmful effect. Risks are assessed in terms of their impact and probability of occurrence.

Risks increase or decrease based on the number of vulnerabilities present. **Vulnerabilities** are flaws or weak points in a protection scheme. When a threat can exploit a vulnerability, the vulnerability becomes a **weakness**.

For instance, unlocked doors are a vulnerability and a burglar is a threat. If no burglars are in the neighborhood, then an unlocked door is not going to be exploited. If burglars are in the neighborhood and the door is locked, there would also be no vulnerability. Only if a burglar is in the neighborhood and the door is unlocked would there be the probability that harm would ensue.

The unlocked door constitutes a weakness. The correct response to an identified weakness is a countermeasure. Countermeasures reduce the probability of harm by either eliminating the vulnerability or lessening the impact of the threat, thereby reducing the risk. Thus the response to the weakness cited in our example would be to eliminate the vulnerability by "always locking the door" or eliminate the threat by ensuring that burglar are not in the neighborhood.

It is a daunting task to identify the right set of countermeasures because security situations are complex. Simply looking at the problem will not solve it. As a result, it is necessary to adopt and follow a systematic process to ensure that everything that needs to be considered will be addressed properly. This "thinking through and responding correctly" is the "information assurance process." The goal is to be certain that there are no exploitable gaps in a security response.

The Common Characteristics of an Information Assurance Process

The assurance process supports three common characteristics to ensure the value of information: availability, integrity, and confidentiality. The first characteristic, **availability**, is the quality that ensures that the information is provided to the authorized users when it is required. The best way to understand the value of availability is to ask, "What would happen if an asset disappeared entirely?" For example, what would happen if the organization's payroll data were erased on payday? Imagine the chaos in a big organization like General Motors if they were unable to pay their employees at the usual time.

The second characteristic is **integrity**. Integrity of data or processes centers on the qualities of authenticity, accuracy, and completeness. It is easy to appreciate the value of integrity in information assurance. For example; if a bank could not depend on its account balances, it would be out of business.

The third characteristic, **confidentiality**, describes an organization's need to restrict access to information or data. From a system point of view, confidentiality is the assurance that access controls are enforced. If the organization's data and information could be made public without harm, there would not be a need for this attribute, but this is rarely the case. One way to visualize the value of confidentiality is to imagine how much competitors might pay to have access to data and information, or the cost of litigation if a legal requirement to observe privacy were violated.

Establishing the Information Assurance Process

The information assurance process is established by organizing an appropriate set of countermeasures into a seamless and effective response profile. The outcome of this process must be synergistic, which means that the effect of the combined countermeasures should be greater than the sum of the individual parts of the solution. Consequently, each element of the assurance scheme has to be selected carefully to achieve the desired effect. This is a design activity, which is no less involved than the design of any complex system. It requires integrating a range of elements into a working solution.

Ensuring Coordination: Integrating Functions

Comprehensive information assurance solutions encompass measures from a diverse range of disciplines, including business, computer science, ethics, law, mathematics, and military science. Each discipline contributes elements that will be part of the eventual response; any one of these could be a key component of a correct solution.

Each discipline adds a new set of considerations. The expansion in scope creates a problem because it increases the coordination demands. For instance, good policies and procedure are essential for a proper security response. Yet the responsibility for defining that policy rests with upper management, while the responsibility for assuring information is usually vested with operations and IT. The people who set the policies are rarely the ones who implement and maintain them. Since the policy-making and technical functions are normally at different strata in the organization, they rarely communicate with each other. Consequently, that relationship has to be coordinated for the information security process to be effective.

In business planning, auditing, information systems, and human resources all share responsibility for information assurance. Yet these units almost never coordinate among themselves. That lack of coordination causes gaps in the protection scheme, even if each function is effectively performing their assurance tasks for their area of responsibility.

For instance, business planning sets assurance priorities, but it is the information systems function that implements them. The human resources function does the background checks and provides the security staff, yet it is the auditing function that actually monitors the work that is being done. Consequently, of that typical division of labor, work has to be done to ensure that these functions are intelligently integrated into a single seamless operation. If not, they will not properly coordinate with each other and that lack of coordination will inevitably cause gaps in the protection scheme.

Creating the Assurance Process: The Role of Design

Coordination is complex. A formal and comprehensive design process is the first step in overcoming that complexity. The goal of this design process is to implement three governing principles:

- Effective information assurance programs demand integrated business and technological processes.
- Effective information assurance programs must be designed deliberately and deployed through a strategic planning activity.
- Information assurance solutions must be composed of an integrated set of responses, embedded in day-to-day operation in such a way that they are invisible to end users.

The goal of the design is to incorporate these three principles into a tangible, comprehensive, and dynamically evolving information assurance system. Systems are a set of components assembled by plan to meet a specified purpose. However, the question remains: "What is the role of policy in designing that system?"

Security Infrastructure: Making the Process Systematic

An information assurance system ensures trustworthy protection of all assets within its scope. Identifying the scope and components is not accidental. Explicit guidance is necessary to assure that the system is implemented and managed to fit organizational and operational requirements. Policy ensures that guidance. Policies are guiding principles. Sound policies are the prerequisite for organized work.

Policies regulate the functions of the entire organization. Therefore, only senior management defines security policies. To ensure that policies are implemented properly , senior managers should delegate the operational roles and responsibilities to the right people in their organization. Finally, senior managers should be responsible for defining the measures necessary to demonstrate achievement of organizational security goals and should enforce accountability for performance based of those measures.

The combined set of policies, roles and responsibilities and accountabilities for a given organization is called a **security infrastructure**. A security infrastructure is unique to the organization.

Planning: Formalizing the Assurance Process

A security infrastructure takes exhaustive planning, constant study, and a commitment to continuous improvement to formalize and maintain the assurance process. Strategic planning is the first step in any assurance process. **Planning** is a critical part of assurance because that activity turns abstract policies into concrete actions.

The next section discusses the fundamental principles that underpin the planning process. It presents a method for differentiating organizational needs and formalizing the organization's intentions. Finally, the section explains how the organization can integrate its policies into a working solution. That integration is the first step in creating an effective information assurance response.

Policy and Information Assurance

Assurance requires strategic thinking. That is because the *complete set* of things that threaten the organization have to be identified and addressed by a response, not just *some* of the things. The goal of the strategic planning process is to spell out the role and relationship of every security element that involved in the overall solution.

The strategic planning process ensures that all critical elements necessary to assure information are identified, aligned, and established seamlessly as routine organization practice. As such planning is a strategic organizational function, rather than a narrow technical one. Planning is approached at the strategy level because a correct solution requires the integration of diverse components across the entire organization. That process is guided by the organization's information assurance policies.

To ensure seamlessness, policies must be uniform across the organization. Policies are valuable because they build a shared understanding the process to be followed. Polices coordinate work across the organization and establish the critical path to assurance for the organization.

The policies an organization defines are based on a standard. Standards express the commonly accepted best practices in a given field. Since they communicate expert advice, they serve as the "ideal" conceptual model for practice. As we said earlier, there is a small range of publicly accepted standards available and an wide variety of proprietary ones.

The standard could be generic or proprietary, but whatever the source, the purpose of the standard is to provide a common basis to guide the approach. Policies that fit the specific requirements of the standard are tailored from its recommendations. The policy should explicitly state the "what," but not the "how," of assurance. In information assurance, policies support five common aims:

- **Prevention**—denotes those organizational, operational, and physical methods deemed necessary to keep an assured system secure from both internal and external penetration, and prevent the occurrence of undesirable activity.

- **Detection**—seeks to find and help people react to the nature, existence, presence, or fact of an assured system penetration.

- **Containment**—focuses on keeping sensitive data within the assured system.

- **Deterrence**—describes those policies, procedures, and actions that are designed to discourage penetration of an assured system.

- **Recovery**—details the actions necessary to restore a system's processing capability and data files after a failure or penetration. It includes the restoration of an asset or assets to a specified prior state (assured system).

To make the process effective, policies and procedures should be understood and supported organization-wide. Everyone from executive decision makers to the operational levels must be aware of what the policies mean. Three different types of policies are associated with specific types of decision making. Figure 3-1 describes the policy focus at each level.

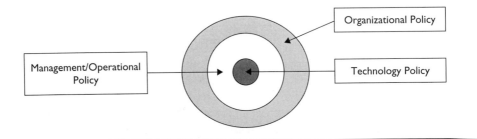

Figure 3-1   Levels of application and support of policies

As can be seen, information assurance solutions are multilayered and multifaceted. All components must be present to establish a response. The approach must be coordinated because the environment contains individuals (black hats) who seek constantly to exploit the vulnerabilities in a defense. Experience has shown that if a flaw is found it will be exploited eventually.

Of course, black hats do not cause every problem. Frequently, well-intentioned individuals make mistakes that inadvertently create exploitable flaws. Therefore, all necessary policies, procedures, and physical safeguards must be maintained to assure the **confidentiality, integrity,** and **availability** of information.

These are called security **controls**. The term control has a slightly different meaning and it is slightly broader in its application than the term *countermeasure*. Controls are routine behaviors. They might be part of the security countermeasure set but they can just as easily be in place to ensure performance in some other area, such as financial accounting. In most security systems the countermeasures constitute a large part of the control set. However, the specific policies, procedures, and work instructions adopted by the organization are also a form of control.

The *security infrastructure* is the control set that the organization has planned for itself. These controls are established and embedded seamlessly into day-to-day operation and ensure the desired level of protection. Seamlessness is a necessary requirement for control sets because if controls are too intrusive they will be circumvented. Worse, the workers themselves will sabotage controls that interfere with day-to-day work.

All security controls are designed around competing considerations. The aim is to tailor the most effective solution for each situation without being too intrusive. An illustration of this balancing act is the password. Passwords control access to almost everything; they are critical. However, it is hard for people to remember complex passwords, so individuals use ones that are easy to remember and easy to guess. That makes the system susceptible to threats like brute force or dictionary attacks. However, if the password is hard to remember, users will inevitably write them down and that creates a different type of vulnerability.

There is no common set of controls because each problem set is unique. Therefore, the control set has to be actively tailored to fit the specific needs of the environment. The goal is to address the threats that occur in that environment in an organized way. Standards and policies dictate the structure, while the countermeasures that are evolved within that policy framework make up the response.

In most organizations, the development of an effective policy structure is a very complex activity because it is necessary to understand all the problems involved. As such the development process must include all potential stakeholders. Open **communication** among all the participants is an essential first condition and can be a single point of failure.

Using our prior example, the Chief Executive Officer (CEO) and the Chief Security Officer (CSO) are all responsible for information assurance policies. However, the technical people within the IT function implement and oversee the policies. In most cases the CEO and the IT worker have little shared background. They do not speak the same language nor do they have the same organizational values. However, it is imperative that they share a common vision of the problem and the steps that have to be taken for the security response to be comprehensive and correct. That top-to-bottom understanding is difficult to maintain and is not created by accident. It requires a continuous organized effort to ensure the flow of communication among all parties.

Information assurance is an intangible condition, not a concrete object. So agreeing on the approach will probably involve resolving conflicting points of view and political undercurrents. The conflict is the reason why a formal process is needed to develop a common understanding. That process has to allow all participants to bring up, examine, and discuss every aspect of the problem.

The outcome of this discussion is a planned assurance system. The plan develops from a formal design process. The design communicates the organization's understanding of how it will implement information assurance. The design must provide an **unambiguous** statement of the basic policies and assumptions that it implements. In addition the design must ensure the acceptance of these policies. Furthermore, it should help managers understand how to implement the operational relationships needed to turn those policies into day-to-day practices. The design must allow people at all levels to understand their personal responsibility with respect to assurance.

The required level of understanding is established by building organization-wide awareness. Awareness is necessary to support proper and consistent practice. At a minimum, that definition process should include the following steps:

- Definition of information as an organizational asset

- Identification and evaluation of the sensitivity of organizational systems and data

- Creation of plans to ensure security and control of each identified system

- Development and implementation of training programs to enable and enforce the understanding and the use of proper information assurance measures

The Relationship between Policy and the Assurance Process

Organizations have an ethical and fiduciary obligation to keep sensitive data confidential. This obligation includes securing such routine things as personnel records, client, and payroll data as well as corporate strategic plans and intellectual property. In addition, the competitive position of an organization depends on its trustworthiness. A comprehensive and effective plan is essential to ensure trustworthiness. As such a formal information assurance planning exercise is essential to the development of a tailored, organization-wide assurance scheme. This is shown in Figure 3-2.

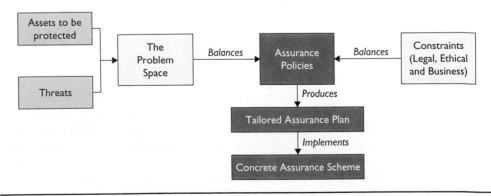

Figure 3-2   Planning and assurance

A well-executed planning process specifies the steps needed to address all assurance requirements of the organization. The plan ensures that the necessary resources are available to implement properly assurance policies within the organization's operational environment. The planning process ensures that policies are internally consistent and that the resources provided are focused on the most important goals of the organization. The plan brings all organizational security activities into a single, coherent, continuously evolving scheme.

Every organization has strategic aims. Organizational policies for information assurance should flow from these aims. Ideally, the board of directors and senior management set the direction that the information assurance function will take. The duty of the management team is to develop and communicate policies that will best achieve the goals. Examples of the right policies vary from organization to organization. However, they will form a complete specification of the general steps necessary to ensure an integrated and organization-wide security solution and information assurance process.

General Requirements for the Information Assurance Process

Because every organization is unique and each implements assurance differently, the steps to assure these three requirements differ. However, all information assurance solutions have the same conditions. These criteria are as follows:

- Information integrity, confidentiality, availability, authentication, and nonrepudiation must be assured.

- All relevant information assurance needs must be represented in the solution.

- The responsibility for performing the various information assurance functions must be assigned and understood explicitly.

- A system of accountability and enforcement must exist.

- Regular and systematic assessments must be performed.

- All participants must understand the importance of information assurance.

- Continuity of operation must be ensured even if the IT function fails.

- Information assurance functions must conform to legal requirements.

- Expense must be kept proportionate to impact and likelihood of risk.

- The organization must ensure that information is used ethically.

Organizations follow a standard process to implement these requirements. The process must have a strategic focus since it involves long-range considerations. It incorporates all the elements of the organization in its scope and it reaches to the boundaries of the organization.

Figure 3-3 outlines the functional elements of the comprehensive long-range information assurance planning process.

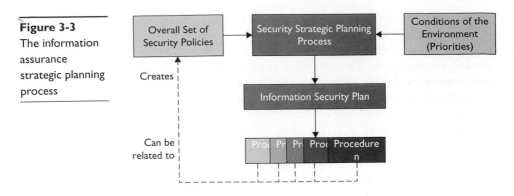

Figure 3-3
The information assurance strategic planning process

The outcome of this process is an organization-wide information security plan that balances the aims of security policy with real-world conditions and environmental constraints. The atomic-level components of the plan are a set of procedures that ensure the required level of security. These procedures should be directly traceable back to the policies that defined them. This is a closed-loop process in that the ongoing alignment of procedures to policies fine-tunes the actual security response and ensures its effectiveness in functional settings.

Cross Check

Complete these statements by filling in the blanks:

1. Planning defines all of the actions necessary to achieve policy _____.
2. The practical outcome of the information assurance planning process is a _____.
3. Information assurance is an important organization consideration because it underwrites _____.

Developing an Assurance Plan

If policy provides the aims, planning supplies the outcomes. That relationship is captured in a tailored assurance plan. Operationally, this plan is the formal representation of how the organization intends to address its policy requirements. As such, strategic planning and strategic plans should include all of the following common characteristics:

- **Complete**—the plan addresses clearly the entire set of issues.
- **Correct**—elements logically required to do this are present.
- **Understandable**—the elements can be understood.
- **Unambiguous**—the elements cannot be misunderstood.
- **Traceable**— items are traceable to each other and to the baseline requirements.

The strategic plan defines an approach to security in an assurable system. Each plan should be tailored to the situation. Because it has to be managed, the strategic plan should also provide a description of the way that the system should be evaluated.

That evaluation insures that the operation of the system meets the goals defined by the plan. It contains a set of quantitative measures that can be used to judge performance against those goals. To be effective, information assurance solutions have to be "baked" into the current organization and technology environment, rather than strapped on after the fact. The plan must offer clear, unmistakable recommendations for how a baked-in solution will be assured. This is itemized in the form of explicit and unambiguous procedures.

The plan may be anything from a simple document to a large-scale project that produces a formal specification of necessary activities. This is typically the case when the strategic situation is either extensive or complex. The plan itemizes the specific steps to be taken to implement security, as well as to maintain the operational solution. The aim is to keep the plan aligned with technological and organization goals as the organization evolves.

A detailed plan ensures a completely integrated solution. Completeness implies that all necessary components and relationships are present in the response. The principle of completeness is important with assured systems because those solutions will be deployed in an environment where some practices already exist. A comprehensive strategic planning process reduces the problem of component integration. It ensures the steps needed to achieve a desired state of assurance and combines existing activities with any new elements to satisfy the overall purpose. The plan might require modifying or elimination current activities. The only goal of the plan is to achieve an optimum solution that meets all assurance needs.

The planning process is essential because an incomplete or uncoordinated response leads to unintended consequences. For example, a highly secure network without personnel policies can be **breached** no matter how sophisticated the technology because the human element is uncontrolled. Therefore every assurance plan has to contain every necessary countermeasure to be considered correct.

Cross Check

Complete these statements by filling in the blanks:

1. A strategic plan is a formal expression of how an organization will address specified _____.

2. Operationally strategic plans tailor a response to fit the given _____.

3. The problem is that information assurance solutions are deployed into a _____ environment where _____.

Designing a Functional Information Security Management System

The customary outcome of the planning process is a formal Information Security Management System (ISMS). "**ISMS**" is an industry term that describes a comprehensive set of discrete management controls arrayed into an operational solution. The ISMS ensures optimum assurance of the data and information assets it is set to manage. An ISMS contains specifically tailored technical and organization procedures. These make up an effective system, as Figure 3-4 outlines.

Figure 3-4
The Information
Security
Management
System

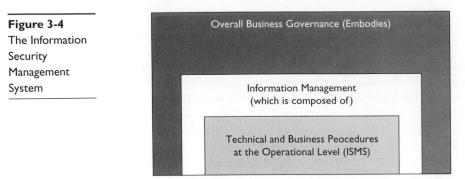

An ISMS substantiates each assurance policy by installing an identifiable control. A well-developed ISMS ensures a uniform control structure is in place and that it reaches to all levels of the organization because information is an organizational asset and resource. The development of an ISMS must originate with the senior management because information affects every part of the organization, not just information technology. All aspects of the organization management hierarchy should be involved, as Figure 3-5 outlines.

Figure 3-5
The flow of
responsibility
for information
assurance

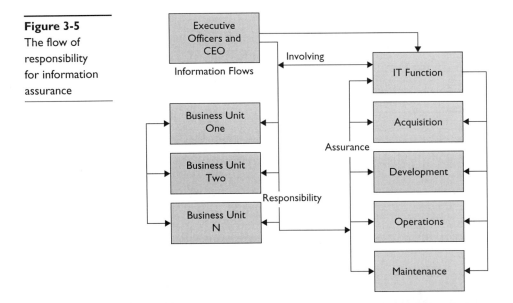

Properly implemented information assurance systems are always under the sponsorship of executive management. Senior sponsorship is critical because those managers have the authority to ensure that the design will meet every requirement and that everyone in the organization will adopt it. Unfortunately, ISMS are often shuffled off to the information systems department. This transfer is dysfunctional because the management of an information systems operation rarely has anything to do with defining overall organization strategy and it has no authority to enforce policies outside its domain. That inappropriate location of accountability for the overall information assurance function is the root cause of the problems reflected in the GAO study cited earlier in this chapter.

An ISMS should be implemented to fit requirements as a life-cycle process. The life-cycle model used for design and deployment of an ISMS is similar to the system's development life-cycle model. It moves from specification through design, implementation, and testing prior to deployment as a working system. The first step in the life-cycle process is to define the scope of the ISMS by establishing what will fall within the boundaries of the assurance scheme and what is not.

Defining the Information Assurance Boundaries

It is not hard to build an adequate defense if the problem boundaries are well established and unchanging. However, that is rarely the case with information. It is an abstract entity and the threats continually evolve. The problem is aggravated by the fact that it is difficult to detect a theft of information. Information is the only asset that can be stolen, while the organization retains possession of it. It is hard to set proper boundaries with any certainty.

Information assurance boundary setting is based on the concept of perimeters. An **information assurance perimeter** is the outer boundary of the space to be secured. The first step in establishing a boundary is to establish the perimeter of the ISMS. That requires defining what the system protects. Defining a perimeter is complicated by the feasibility factor. **Feasibility** is the likelihood that a task or purpose can be accomplished. In information assurance, feasibility is based on whether the perimeter selected assures all priority assets and fits within the available resources and capabilities of the organization.

No matter how elegant the solution, it is useless if it is not feasible. For example, sophisticated biometric technologies can be used for access control. However, biometric solutions do not fit within the budget of the average computer lab. Thus, a biometric solution for a minor application is questionable because it does not fit within the financial constraints. That would be the case even if the biometric control itself worked properly and fulfilled its purpose in all respects. A circumstance that might change this would be if the information contained in the system were highly sensitive. That might justify the added cost and trouble of employing biometrics. However, if there were no obvious threats to the equipment or information, the cost would probably not justify the effort.

A central part of the planning and deployment of the information assurance system is to assess and trade off the effects of threats against the financial and staff resources. Factors that enter into this thinking include answers to questions such as the following:

- What is the level of criticality for each of the information assets that falls within the scope of the system?

- What is the degree of assurance required for each?

- What are the effects of identifiable threats?
- How accessible is the data?
- How complex and critical is the system?

Figure 3-6 summarizes the decision process that underlies setting the boundaries for the ISMS based on the value of the asset. The figure demonstrates how a nonessential or low-value resource might be left outside of the defensive perimeter. Nevertheless, if the decision to leave an asset out of the protection scheme is made, that choice is based on precise knowledge of its value; this is informed risk. A decision maker uses this prioritization process to maximize resource use, and to optimize information assurance and security protection.

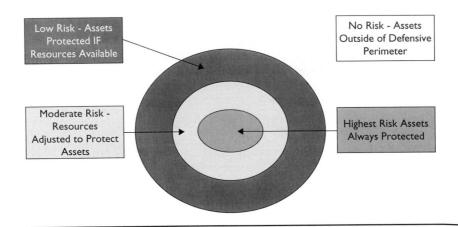

Figure 3-6   Prioritized value and risk acceptance

Ownership of information rests with the people who create or use it. These are called **stakeholders** because they are the ones who will be harmed if their information is damaged or compromised. Therefore, they are the ones to be consulted when the protection strategy is formed. As such, it is critical to include representatives from the organization, as well as concerned third parties, in the boundary definition process.

Involvement is important in formulating a working information assurance system, because real-world information assurance boundaries are dynamic. With information assets, the borders of the system are subject to ongoing refinement as threats and resources evolve. Therefore, the level of significance has to be assigned by people who understand the consequences. This rarely includes the people in the IT function itself. IT should be viewed as the information custodian, with responsibility for overseeing and implementing the necessary safeguards to protect the information assets.

The working principle of the boundary-setting process is that the organizational units are the owners of the asset. The owners should provide the assessment of its worth. This applies to formally defined information assets, as well as other controlled legal, contractual, and/or organization assets. The goal of ownership involvement is to ensure that critical functions are protected adequately within the resources available. Protection requires an ongoing appraisal of the effectiveness of the system. Over time, the organization fine-tunes the deployment of information assurance controls. Approved modifications to the controls can be accomplished based on feedback from the operational units.

Cross Check

Complete these statements by filling in the blanks:

1. An effective ISMS is realized through a tailored set of _____ and _____ procedures.
2. The eventual working solution has to fit within the available _____ and _____ of the organization.
3. Because the organization owns the information, it is critical that stakeholders from the _____ are involved in system definition.

Building the Information Assurance System

Every information assurance system specifies rules for the behaviors needed to counteract threats to the organization's information assets. Because every organization has different information assurance needs, the system has to be built like any other tangible entity. It starts with a framework that is refined down to a tailored set of controls.

Chapter 2 details the types of controls used and the methods for arranging them. However, the controls evolve from policies and are established by planning. The process is universal and generic. That is, although the situation will vary, the elements of the process should always the same. All information assurance processes embody five fundamental activities that should be recognizable to anybody familiar with systems work:

1. Top-down understanding and refinement
2. Progressive (or iterative) enhancement
3. Optimization based on feasibility
4. Continuous control
5. Measurement and assessment

Threats to data and information occur at various levels in the organization and appear in many forms. These threats range from sophisticated penetrations of the network to ordinary thefts perpetrated by people who knowingly, or unknowingly, take something of value from the organization's information asset base. The first step in forming an information assurance response is the identification of realistic threats. Those are the threats within the organization's technical or operating environment that might lead to the loss of any information, of any value. Figure 3-7 outlines the elements of this process.

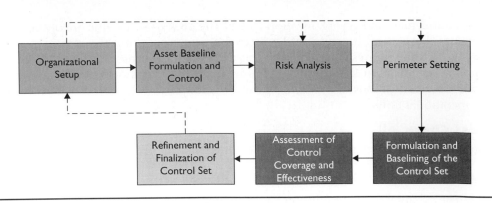

Figure 3-7 Steps in formulating a control set

As can be seen, the overall outcome of this process is an optimum set of controls. Seven steps are involved in developing these:

1. **Organizational Setup**
2. **Asset Identification** and Baselining
3. Risk Analysis
4. **Asset Valuation**
5. Selection of the Control Set
6. Operational Testing
7. Finalization of the Baseline Control Set

Step 1: Organizational Setup

The first step is to launch the process. This establishes the need for information assurance and the characteristics of the response. It is an awareness exercise. The outcome should be publicized organization-wide and acknowledged by all stakeholders.

An awareness activity is essential because major ISMS projects are costly and disruptive. The process requires the total up-front commitment of the entire organization to be successful. The commitment might be expressed in something as simple as a project charter written under the auspices of an executive sponsor. Or it may involve a detailed specification derived from requirements and a contract, which supports the education and buy-in of all of the people involved in the design and implementation of the system. The rule is that once this agreement is obtained, the direction provided must be followed. The formulation of that agreement must not be taken lightly because it determines the form of the rest of the process.

Step 2: Asset Identification and Baselining

Information assets exist in three different forms: electronic, paper, or human knowledge. Information can be recorded electronically, on paper, or in both media—all at the same time. Or, it can reside only in somebody's head and never actually be recorded anywhere.

However, if it is important to safeguard that piece of information it might be necessary to take specific actions to secure it in all three states.

Therefore, before a protection scheme can be developed the form of the asset must be known and categorized. The identification process entails a meticulous classification and labeling of each item placed under the information assurance scheme. Identification is not a trivial exercise. It is prerequisite for subsequent risk assessment because it establishes the "day one" state of the organization's entire inventory of information assets. This is discussed in detail in Chapter 1; because it is essential to establishing the overall information assurance process, it will be outlined here.

The aggregate set of secured assets is termed a **baseline**. All the individual components that constitute that baseline are identified and labeled as part of the process. The baseline is the sum of the information assets that are protected by the information assurance system. A precisely defined information-asset baseline is a prerequisite for conducting the rest of the process.

The baseline is a concrete structure. To formulate it, the organization must classify and tag asset elements based on their logical interrelationships. The resulting classification is maintained as a top-down hierarchy of elements that range from a view of information as a single entity down to the items that constitute the resource.

The decisions that establish the baseline are made using the input of many participants. These participants range from the technical staff to executive owners of a given piece of information. The decision may be political, so the process should be conducted in such a way that the outcome can be validated.

Each item placed in the hierarchy is given a unique and appropriate label, associated with the overall structure of the information asset base itself. The label should designate and relate the position of any item to the overall family tree of items in the baseline. Once established, the formal baseline is kept in an electronic ledger, which is fully accounted for and maintained as an asset throughout the life cycle of the information assurance scheme.

Because information and technology evolve, procedures should be defined to manage change systematically. For example, simply adding an extra data element to a record requires that the organization update the baselines that contain that data element to reflect its new status. If the baseline is not updated in a systematic and **disciplined** fashion, knowledge of the form of the information asset will move out of the organization's grasp, leaving the organization to secure information items that do not exist and not securing things that do.

Step 3: Risk Analysis

Once the asset baseline is established, the organization must identify and evaluate the risks to its contents. The risk assessment is a critical part of the process because it documents the potential threats to the asset. In addition, it evaluates the damage that might occur and analyzes and categorizes the acceptable options. This is normally accomplished through a gap analysis, performed against an expert model of best practice.

Because they are based on best practices, expert models are employed typically as the means of implementing the functioning security system. The expert model serves as a benchmark of correct practice that the organization should adopt in order to be considered secure.

Benchmarks used to judge performance are commonly accepted and repeatable points of reference. The "ideal" practices specified in the expert model provide the point of comparison. The current operation is compared to the benchmark to determine how close the organization comes to satisfying the requirements of those ideal practices.

The general body of knowledge (BOK) for information assurance is full of expert models. These models all define the practices that should exist in a properly functioning security system. Any of these can be adopted to serve as a benchmark. That includes models from International Standards Organization (ISO), National Institute of Science and Technology (NIST), Information Systems Audit and Control Association (ISACA), Committee on National Security Systems (CNSS), and the International Information Systems Security Certification Consortium (ISC²). If none of these expert models are acceptable, then the organization might even develop a unique set of benchmark practices to assess its current operation.

Any model of best practice can serve as the point of reference. The only rule is that the model must be established before the gap analysis starts. Then, any gap between the current practice and best practice (as defined by the benchmark) can be considered to be a potential security vulnerability, by definition. Once the vulnerabilities have all been identified, decisions can be made about how to safeguard the organization.

Step 4: Asset Valuation

Asset valuation is important to information assurance because there is a direct relationship between the resources required to establish a given level of assurance and the size of the system it is possible to secure. Operational factors that enter into that consideration include answers to the following questions:

- What is the level of criticality of each particular information asset in the asset baseline?
- What is the specific degree of resource commitment required to assure it?

The valuation step is needed because there are never sufficient resources to secure all elements in the asset baseline and because the baseline is dominated by abstract entities, so the value of the asset base is not known. It is essential for every organization to systematically value and prioritize the information assets to develop a targeted protection scheme.

There are many ways to value assets. Most of these are standard economic analysis techniques, such as Economic Value Added and Economic, Economic Value Sourced, Real Option Valuation, or the Balanced Scorecard. Because these are economic models, the critical success factors are always rooted in the organization operation. Independent of the technique selected, however, the benefit of a valuation approach is that it helps the organization identify the sequence for securing the most valuable assets. Criteria used to make that decision are based on the assurance policies that have been established for the information asset.

As data are collected and refined over time, the organization improves its valuation effectiveness and sharpens its control over the asset base. The eventual outcome of this process is an empirical understanding of the value of the major items in the information baseline. This knowledge sets the boundaries of the system, implementation priorities, and the degree of protection required.

Step 5: Selection of a Control Set

Information assurance controls are defined once the information asset baseline has been determined and the threat picture established. The information assurance controls specify the countermeasures or information assurance responses to be deployed and maintained for each information item. Selecting a control requires an item-by-item evaluation of each element to characterize the actions that will be required to secure it. That assessment evaluates every possible countermeasure and then deploys a set of practical controls for every baselined item.

The majority of the work involved in setting up a formal ISMS involves the specification, design, scheduling, and installation of a working **control set**. The outcome of this activity, is the security infrastructure of the organization. We have devoted an entire chapter to describing how an infrastructure model is formulated because it is such an important element of assurance. Keep in mind during the formulation process that the control set establishes the assurance function details and it must be maintained under strict organizational control.

To ensure this control, each defined countermeasure has to be engineered for optimum performance. The control is then related to all other countermeasures and placed into a formal baseline called the control baseline. A control baseline must be maintained in alignment with the information asset baseline for every ISMS.

The control baseline is the valid control set for the designated information asset. It is kept under strict control using exactly the same process used to ensure the information baseline formulated at the beginning of the process. The two baselines, **information** and associated **controls**, must be directly **traceable** to each other. Every information item must be referenced to the control set that is maintained for it. That is the only way to be certain that the ISMS addresses the security requirements of that particular information resource. Therefore the maintenance of the integrity of these two baselines is an important overall responsibility of the assurance process.

Step 6: Operational Testing

Once the control set has been implemented, it must be validated to ensure that the proposed ISMS satisfies the requirements of the plan or contract. The validation of this relationship that takes place after the deployment of the system in its working environment is called **operational testing** because the system is now embedded in the environment it is meant to secure. From a validation standpoint, this requires ongoing analysis of actual outcomes against the performance criteria established in the planning phase. Security within an assured system is a critical requirement.

That assessment is planned, implemented, and administered just like any other testing activity. It employs assumptions developed in the **risk analysis** as the basis for assessment; however, operational issues identified after implementation may also be added. The aim is to say with certainty that the aggregate set of controls is effective given the assurance goals of the organization.

This assurance requires the conduct of validating and verifying activities over a specified duration, as well as a formal reporting and decision-making process to ensure that problems that are identified are resolved. Each control must have a set of assigned criteria that can be used to assess its ongoing performance because the goal of this stage of the process is to produce a final product. This ensures a thorough evaluation of each component. As such, each control must have a behaviorally observable result associated with it. This is outlined in Figure 3-8.

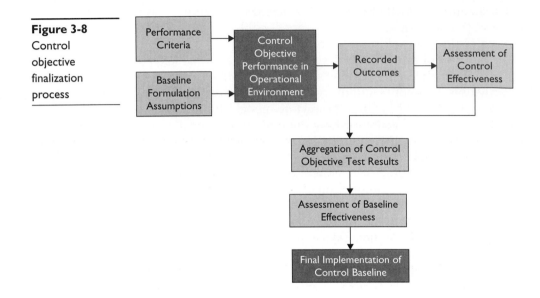

Figure 3-8
Control objective finalization process

Step 7: Finalization of the Baseline

The organization uses the outcome of the operational testing phase to assess the effectiveness of the control set. The assessment is based on the observable performance of each control against established criteria, as well as any assumptions about cost that were part of the baseline process. Once the testing is **complete**, the aggregate controls are finalized into the released version of the security system.

Since these controls are the operational form of the information assurance system. The baseline that represents them is maintained under strict configuration management. The system can be considered to be mature at this point. Therefore the operational model that emerges at this stage is the organization's specific assurance infrastructure. The only rule with this system is that the organization must maintain it as a stable resource.

Maintaining Information Assurance over Time

Information assurance operates in the background of the day-to-day operation. It identifies, analyzes, and controls harmful or undesirable events as they occur during normal operations. The aim of the **maintenance process** is to ensure that the information assurance system continues to be appropriate to the environment. Because that environment is constantly evolving, the form of the response and its scope will have to change accordingly. Therefore, a disciplined and systematic process is used to guarantee that the protection will be maintained as required.

Maintenance is a continuous process. Maintenance is based on continuous feedback from operations. The discipline that is necessary to ensure effective information assurance has to be continuous and reliable, even when it is tempting to cut corners or leave out a step. This means that information assurance functions must be monitored and enforced. This can be both intrusive and difficult to sustain unless the day-to-day functions of the information assurance system meshes with the operating philosophy of the organization.

Handling Exceptions

Information assurance operates under the dark star of **process entropy**. That term describes the wicked brew of competitive pressure and mind-numbing advances in technology, which cause well-defined processes to eventually fall apart. Change is inevitable in the case of information assurance. That is because unforeseen and escalating threats are always just over the horizon. A proper information assurance system has to include a mechanism for dealing with unanticipated threats in a disciplined fashion.

The response to unanticipated threats is a systematic problem-solving approach. These are "**exception processes**" that serve as the rapid response agents who respond when a new or unexpected incident is reported. In practice, this is formalized as the organization's incident-handling process. **Incident handling** is invoked only when the organization encounters a problem within its information assurance function that it has not seen before.

Such a process is important in today's environment because of the increasing sophistication of attacks. Because attacks are becoming more complex, the countermeasures have to be agile and adaptive to provide defense in depth. To be effective, they must embody the following attributes:

- **Timely**—response times ensure effective remediation.
- **Responsive**—the response is evolved directly from the threat.
- **Disciplined**—the process is structured and followed systematically.
- **Usable**—the process involves all types of users in the solution.

Timeliness is essential because the majority of information assurance problems are unanticipated. Consequently, organizations need to create robust exception-handling processes that allow them to react rapidly to unanticipated threats. Responsiveness is important because it ensures that the defense reacts to the threat in the optimally.

Usability is important because the effectiveness of the defense is typically proportional to the number of people who are involved. If incidents can only be recognized and responded to by a few people, it is likely that something new or unique will slip past them. If, however, each member of the user community is knowledgeable, aware, and involved, it will be more likely that unplanned or unanticipated events will be identified immediately.

The Essential Role of Accountability in Maintaining Assurance

Accountability is the glue that holds the information assurance process together. It enforces management discipline by linking individual responsibility to the requirements of the controls. **Accountability** is the mechanism that enables the internal control function. It ensures that the human component of the assured system is aligned with the information assurance plans of the organization.

Accountability is not a technical function; it is an organizational concern and may be political. Accountability must be enforced through the assignment of suitable duties to every individual in the organization and then consistent **monitoring** of performance. The organization should execute the following generic tasks to establish accountability:

- Establish a direct link between identified risks and accountable parties
- Ensure that accountable parties understand their duties
- Ensure that the accountable parties have accepted their responsibilities
- Ensure that accountable parties are capable of responding to incidents

Enforcement should be tailored to the information assurance policies adopted by the organization. Therefore a comprehensive understanding of the business case is necessary to maintain consistent enforcement. In addition to understanding the organization requirements, it is important that the individual capabilities of the individuals responsible for security are maintained. That requires hiring and personnel evaluation practices to ensure an adequate level of individual performance among the security staff.

Communicating Organizational and Technical Direction

The essential leadership quality for any successful operation is common understanding of requirements. Therefore, the success of the information assurance process rests on effective communication. All participants must understand the rules of behavior. There is no way the organization can hold an individual accountable if he or she was not given adequate information about how to behave.

Unfortunately, information assurance schemes are complex and subject to change so this behavior must be attuned to the situation. For example, individuals should protect their passwords. This is essential to the overall integrity of the system and is critical to the proper functioning of the access control system. However, the impact of failure to protect a password depends on the circumstance. Sharing a password for a home computer might not be particularly significant. Sharing a password for a highly critical national defense system containing classified information is a federal crime. Therefore the behaviors in both cases have to be understood and applied appropriately.

Ensuring Organizational Awareness

All applicable policy and procedure goals, as well as the nuances of operation, must be communicated to all constituents and stakeholders in the organization. The communication process should be structured formally and managed carefully to ensure the proper level of individual awareness. It is important that everyone who has anything to do with the information assurance system understand the reasons for adequate protection.

This understanding is ensured by an awareness or "buy-in" program prior to establishing the system. It is well established that the long-term success of any organizational function depends directly on the level of support it has. Therefore, the buy-in process is important, from senior management on down.

Enforcing Discipline

Consistent performance is essential to the success of any organizational system. Therefore, the operational information assurance management system must continuously assure day-to-day work. This is where most information assurance operations fail, because necessary activities are not performed on a disciplined basis and in a repeatable way. Effective control relies on the ability to supervise and enforce individual and group behavior. Employee assessment is a required component of that process.

Monitoring of employee performance is needed to enable and enforce organizational information assurance discipline. The practice of effective information assurance is a discipline no less rigorous than training for a sporting event. It requires the willingness and ability of individuals to follow procedure continuously on a daily basis.

The level of discipline required to ensure continuous security behavior is difficult to instill in most organizations because it requires that people change their routine. Those changes might apply to individual work, daily practices, job responsibilities, and the daily functions of the operational unit. Whatever the change, there is a tendency to resist because old habits are comfortable. Without enforcement, workers revert to their old practices.

The Review Process

It is necessary to review systematically individual and group performance to assign accountability and enforce policy. That enforcement is ensured through a formal and continuous review process. Reviews are necessary because information assurance involves behavior, which requires human judgment to assess. Two types of reviews are normally done as part of information assurance monitoring and enforcement. These are

- Management reviews
- Technical reviews

The most common inspection activity is the management review, which evaluates the performance of individuals as well as the execution of the process. Management reviews are carried out to support decisions about boundary settings, corrective actions, and allocation of resources. The review team ensures this by evaluating information assurance plans against their substantive outcomes. The review team identifies and reports variations from that plan and/or the defined procedures.

Management reviews are performed to inform supervisory personnel and staff—who have direct responsibility for information assurance—about a failure to perform properly. These reviews always involve the participation of the individual who has been assigned accountability for the process; however, a review leader facilitates the actual activity. Review teams are composed of management and technical staff. If any external stakeholders are involved in the process, for instance a federal contractor, they can also participate as appropriate.

The outcome of these reviews and the eventual resolutions are always documented because they are part of the organizational record. Management reviews target failures to meet defined performance criteria. Likely targets are variations from policies and goals, deviations from the plan, or breakdowns in procedure. These assessments prepare status reports. They also present any evidence that addresses a specific concern. Rules for the conduct of these reviews are stipulated in the overall implementation of the system. Review intervals are tied to milestones or terminal events, such as migrations to new technologies.

Management reviews are initiated by establishing ground rules for the conduct of the inspection including the definition of how the findings will be reported and to whom. Reviewers meet and assess the issues that have been raised. They document and classify the problems they find. The documentation might entail interviews with individuals involved with the problem. Once the facts have been clarified, the review team provides an itemized list of action items and specification of how these might be resolved. Review teams are problem identifiers, not problem solvers. The resolution of issues identified as the result of a functional management review is left to the individuals who manage and operate the system.

The difference between a management review and a technical review is the depth and focus of the inspection. The depth of technical coverage is important. Therefore, many companies have dedicated positions called Information Security Officers who perform these types of inspections.

Technical reviews focus on items related to the performance of the technology against requirements. Therefore, the evaluation focuses on the performance aspects of a technical component or process, such as hardware, software, and documentation. This entails questions such as whether the technology has been implemented properly and/or whether its performance conforms to specifications. In addition to the common questions of whether the technology has achieved its purpose, reviews might go as deeply into the issue as an examination of the installation procedures and other performance data.

Technical reviews support the technical and management personnel who have direct responsibility for the system. These reviews discover and report vulnerabilities that affect the performance of the system. Their goal is to evaluate the effects of vulnerabilities, or software defects, on the immediate information assurance aims of the organization.

Technically adept people have to perform these reviews. That group might include such people as system managers, system engineers, security software administrators, network information assurance specialists, and even Software Quality Assurance (SQA) specialists. Because these reviews give insight into the performance of enabling components of any information assurance system, routine technical reviews ought to be defined and scheduled early in the initial planning phase of the information assurance system implementation process.

Formal Versus Informal Reviews

Management and technical reviews might be conducted as either inspections or walk-throughs. The primary difference between these two reviews is the level and degree of rigor. With inspections, there is considerable analysis prior to the generation of findings.

In walkthroughs, findings are reported as minutes with the action items coming as general recommendations. Trust is ensured through audit.

Audits are a different process; they are conducted for the same reason, which is to provide feedback on performance. These were discussed in Chapter 2 (Risk Assessment) since audits are the best means of identifying emerging problems, as well as certifying performance.

Because of the certification aspect, third parties are frequently involved in/audits. The third party might be an outside agency or it could be an inside agent, such as internal audit designated as an independent authority by the organization. Independence is the key to status as an auditor. The auditors do their work as disinterested third parties whose only aim is to generate evidence-based conclusions. Thus audits offer independent certification of conformance to a standard or contract. Audits should generate trust due to their impartiality. Audits are often conducted for information assurance purposes because of the trust element. Given their certification aims, audits usually require a common model, or standard, as the reference point.

Audits also require sound documentary evidence of processes, procedures, and other deliverables to support findings. A lead auditor facilitates the process. An external body, such as ISACA, or the U.S. Department of Defense, usually accredits them. The lead auditor directs an audit team that is composed of subject matter experts trained specifically in auditing techniques.

Audits are required by customer organizations to verify compliance with a defined set of information assurance requirements. They may verify compliance with designated plans, regulations, and standards within their scope. Statistical techniques are employed to analyze data and communicate findings. The outcome of an audit is always a listing of the applicable standards and criteria, as well as the evidence that supports audit conclusions. These conclusions are aimed at certifying compliance with a given standard. This field may become one of the largest and fastest-growing professions in the next ten years because of new laws involving information assurance and control.

Measuring Performance

The ability to base management decisions on data is an important aspect of an ongoing information assurance maintenance process. Information technology work involves the management and control of virtual assets. To be managed properly, these assets have to be understood. Therefore, information assurance systems that entail quantitative measures of performance have an advantage over ones that are not measured. This capability lets the organization evaluate ongoing performance, as well as assign accountability in a systematic way.

Measurement programs allow managers to make decisions based on evidence, not assumption. Properly established and maintained, the measurement program allows the organization to assess the performance of the information assurance function and bring deviations to the right person's attention. This is ensured by regularized reviews of each operational element, at preplanned, mutually agreed-on times.

An effective assessment program provides consistent monitoring of the information assurance operation. An operational assessment program ensures that confidence in the information assurance solution is assured by data on an ongoing basis. It confirms that the appropriate controls are in place and functioning. An effective assessment program should exhibit these attributes:

- **Factual**—Values are directly observable versus inferred.
- **Adaptable**—Measures are used that appropriately fit the circumstance.
- **Meaningful**—Outcomes are **understandable** to all stakeholders.

There are no universally recognized **metrics** for assessing information assurance performance. Because information assurance operations are oriented toward the recognition and **prevention** of security breaches, there is at least a need for a uniform organization-wide definition of these events. Security breaches are any incident that involves a violation or compromise of any one of the five information assurance principles: confidentiality, integrity, availability, authentication, or nonrepudiation of origin.

All breaches have tangible consequences. Therefore, it should be possible for the organization to delineate the measurable characteristics of any act that might constitute a breach. The rule for this is: whatever measures are selected must be applied consistently and uniformly.

Chapter 3 Review

Chapter Summary

- Every sector of the global economy depends on assured information.
- Information assurance is a complex topic embodying diverse fields, such as business, computer science, ethics, military science, law, and mathematics.
- Effective information assurance programs demand an integrated set of business and technological processes.
- Effective information assurance programs must be deliberately designed and deployed through a strategic planning activity.
- Information assurance responses must embody an appropriate set of interacting components that function as an integral part of the day-to-day operation.
- Every organization must maintain a comprehensive, robust, and continuously evolving information assurance response to deal with hazards as they arise.
- Assurance starts with the concept of policy. Policies are the necessary precondition for any kind of organized work because they set the direction.
- Policies are valuable because they underwrite group understanding and commitment, as well as coordinate work across the entire organization.

- Policy supports five common aims: prevention, **detection, containment, deterrence**, and **recovery**.

- Strategy is the traditional means to implement policy.

- Implementation constitutes the first step in building an effective information assurance response.

- There are three common characteristics of assurance: availability, integrity, and secrecy/confidentiality.

- The outcome of the planning process is an organizational information assurance plan that balances the aims of policy against the inevitable real-world conditions and constraints.

- In practice, this relationship is expressed through a tailored strategic plan.

- Operationally, the strategic plan tailors a response to fit a given situation.

- Planning produces an Information Assurance Management System (IAMS).

- The right set of controls has to be identified and put in place to support the purposes of the organization.

- The aim of the maintenance process is to sustain an information assurance response that is appropriate to the changing requirements of the situation.

- All information assurance system planning has to include a process for dealing with unexpected events in a disciplined fashion.

- This process is particularly important in today's climate because the growing sophistication of attacks and attackers means that protection has to be in-depth and adaptive.

- Accountability enforces management discipline by linking individual responsibility to the requirements of the controls.

- Consequently, accountability is the mechanism that underwrites the internal control function.

- The first essential requirement for successful information assurance system operation is understanding. This attribute is underwritten by effective communication.

- With any deliberately designed system, precise and consistent control are the essential ingredients of success. And an effective control process relies on the ability to monitor individual and group performance.

- A measurement process is a requisite component in a formally planned and systematically deployed information assurance system. That process is required to enable and enforce organizational information assurance discipline.

- Properly established and maintained, the measurement program will allow managers to monitor the actions of the information assurance function and bring any deviations to their attention.

Key Terms

accountability (78)
asset identification (72)
asset valuation (72)
availability (59)
baseline (73)
breached (67)
communication (63)
complete (76)
confidentiality (59)
containment (83)
control set (75)
controls (57)
correct (58)
detection (83)
deterrence (83)
disciplined (73)
exception processes (77)
feasibility (69)
incident handling (77)
information assurance perimeter (69)
integrity (59)
information (75)
Information Assurance Management System (ISMS) (67)
maintenance process (76)
metrics (82)
monitoring (78)
operational testing (75)
organizational setup (72)
planning (61)
policy (58)
prevention (82)
process entropy (77)
process (58)
recovery (83)
responsive (58)
risk analysis (75)
security infrastructure (61)
stakeholders (70)
threat (58)
traceable (75)
unambiguous (64)

understandable (82)
usability (77)
vulnerabilities (58)
weakness (58)

Key Term Quiz

Use terms from the Key Terms list to complete the following sentences. Not all terms will be used.

1. Information assurance comes from effective _____, as well as good _____.

2. _____ from internal sources are the most frequent cause of loss to businesses. This is addressed by proper _____.

3. The attributes of information assurance are _____ , _____, and _____.

4. The five common aims of information assurance are _____, _____, _____, _____, and _____.

5. All information assurance system planning has to include a _____ for dealing with unexpected events in a _____ way.

6. Most information assurance systems fail because the required processes are not performed on a _____ basis and in a _____ way.

7. Handling and control of virtual assets has to be made _____ and _____ to be managed properly.

8. _____ is the glue that holds the information assurance framework together because it enforces _____.

9. All information assurance systems embody a deliberate set of _____ aimed at managing every plausible _____ to an organization's information assets.

10. Before a practical protection scheme can be built, the _____ has to be known and categorized.

11. The outcome of information assurance system development is a complete set of practical _____ for every necessary _____.

Multiple Choice Quiz

1. Policies underwrite ____.

    A. mutual understanding

    B. organizational commitment

    C. cost analysis

    D. practices

2. ISMS implementation should be sponsored by _____.

    A. the designers

    B. the highest level in the organization

    C. the workers

    D. information assurance gurus

3. It is necessary to define the form of the information asset because _____.

    A. information is intangible

    B. information is useful

    C. information changes

    D. information is hard to manage

4. Accountability can be enforced only by _____.

    A. definition of the rules

    B. monitoring

    C. laws

    D. hard work

5. Quantitative measurement ensures _____.

    A. rational decision making

    B. scientific understanding

    C. information assurance

    D. good decisions

6. Strategic thinking is required because:

    A. the security solution must be complete

    B. the security solution must be short-term

    C. the security solution must be in-depth

    D. the security solution must fit the need

7. A security control is:

    A. a software feature

    B. something that has an observable outcome

    C. a button on the dashboard

    D. an objective

8. Design is important because:

    A. ISMS must be designed

    B. security systems are abstract and hard to understand

    C. security systems are abstract and must be formalized

    D. security systems have to evolve

9. With security, the competitive position of an organization depends on its:

    A. responsiveness

    B. trustworthiness

    C. reliability

    D. due diligence

10. Models are essential ways to benchmark:

    A. gaps

    B. security defects

    C. security performance

    D. security best practice

Essay Quiz

In your own words, briefly answer the following questions.

1. Why does effective planning require understanding the precise circumstance?

2. Why is executive sponsorship important to maintain the response?

3. What is the purpose/function of management reviews?

4. Why is discipline an important element of information assurance?

5. Why is feasibility an important element of formulating the information assurance boundary?

6. What is the role of measurement?

7. What is the role of chance in maintaining security systems

8. What is the role of asset valuation in developing security systems? Why is it important?

9. Why are gaps vulnerabilities?

10. What is the role of communication in security system formulation?

Case Exercise

Complete the following exercise as directed by your instructor.

Heavy Metal Technology Case in Appendix A

You have been assigned the task of answering the security consultant's concerns for Heavy Metal Technology's Sunnyside West facility. Prepare a complete and coherent set of policy recommendations. These recommendations should address the issues listed in the following list:

- Entrance from the parking structure is controlled by swipe card access
- Entrance from the loading dock is not secured
- None of the support employees has a security clearance
- Access to the server farm is available from the hallway
- Access to the network is controlled through a single firewall
- Access to the employee facilities is not monitored
- Engineers can come and go through their own entrance
- No fire suppression equipment is in the machine room
- There are no disaster contingency plans for this facility

Now, trade work with another member of the class and perform a management review of their response. Is this a complete and coherent solution? Can you see any areas that might require additional policies to cover them?

Building and Documenting an Information Assurance Framework

In this chapter, you will learn:

- The difference between policies and procedures
- What an information assurance infrastructure is
- How to tailor an information assurance infrastructure
- How to document and information assurance infrastructure

In the last chapter we learned that a comprehensive system of carefully planned and designed controls was the way to assure ALL the information that lies within an ENTIRE organization. We learned that to build that system all of the necessary technology, people, and process had to be harnessed to a functional, fully integrated, organization-wide set of information assurance controls. We learned that controls were the observable behaviors used to assure a process and that as a set, these controls must ensure an effective response is available to counter all relevant threats.

In this chapter you will learn that the control process is implemented through a framework of coherent, rational, and understandable standard procedures tailored for efficiency and effectiveness within the organizational environment. In addition we will learn about the accepted ways of creating those procedures and ensuring their continuing effectiveness.

What is a Procedure?

A **procedure** is a specification of the sequence and timing of the steps of a response and describes the action to be taken to achieve a given goal. The **documentation** of a set of information assurance and security procedures is the first step in creating an assurance process because the procedures describe the actions required to ensure the day-to-day performance of information assurance and security duties.

The difference between policy, discussed in the last chapter, and procedure, discussed here, is the level of focus. The focus of policies is long-term and strategic, the focus of procedures is short-term and day-to-day. Procedures define the actions performed as part of routine operation. In the case of information, they specify the set of assurance activities that must be executed to ensure security.

Procedures define all information assurance and security actions. This definition must be in sufficient detail so the performance of these actions can be overseen and controlled. The term *procedure* implies the method, rather than the outcome. However, procedures can also serve as a tangible mechanism for evaluating whether the information assurance and security system has met its intended goals. That evaluation is based on whether all required procedures have been properly and consistently executed.

The purpose of this chapter is to teach you about the issues and concerns that are involved in developing a comprehensive set of regular and consistent operating procedures. It also discusses the common approaches that can be taken to define those steps.

We will demonstrate how an organization establishes a concrete and sustainable assurance process through a framework of specially designed procedures. In organizational terms that framework is referred to as an **infrastructure**, or more accurately an **information assurance infrastructure**.

Infrastructure and the Five Pillars of Assurance

An information assurance infrastructure is an essential part of security because the process for assuring **information** has to be tangible for it to be understood and executed properly. Although information has the same characteristics of cost, utility, and worth as material assets, the resource itself is abstract. That simple lack of substance is what makes information hard to secure.

An information assurance and security infrastructure plan specifies the steps the organization will take to ensure security. This specification makes the process, if not the resource itself, tangible. It describes how all information assurance and security practices will be established and enforced.

That description ensures that the information within the infrastructure is overseen and managed. Therefore, to be complete, the procedures embedded in the information assurance infrastructure must enforce the five common pillars of security:

- Confidentiality
- Integrity
- Availability
- Authorization and Authentication
- Non-Repudiation of Origin

Confidentiality ensures that information is not disclosed to unauthorized persons, processes, or devices. This factor requires discrete functions such as information labeling and the establishment of need-to-know rules. Confidentiality is related to privacy. Privacy is usually considered to be associated with protection of personal information.

Integrity reflects the logical correctness of such essential components as the operating system. It denotes the reliability of the hardware and software entities that implement the protection and the consistency of data structures and occurrences of stored data. In information assurance, integrity frequently implies specific protection against unauthorized modification or destruction of data in its transmission, storage, and processing. Thus integrity is the condition that ensures data will arrive at its destination in exactly the same form as it was sent. In that respect, integrity assures trust.

To guarantee the desired level of trust, the integrity function must continuously ensure the accuracy, relevancy, and completeness of the data. In addition, to assure integrity the system must be robust. Cryptography and error-detection techniques play a role in making certain that sufficient integrity is maintained throughout the process of transmitting, storing and processing information.

Availability provides authorized users with timely, reliable access to data and information services. Availability is characterized by best practices in information system management, such as provision of backup power, spare data channels, off-site capabilities, and continuous signal. By providing an assured level of function in day-to-day operations, availability ensures the system's purpose, which is to provide necessary information as required.

Availability ensures the flow of information within the operation and it is the quality most closely associated with the business case. Because it is driven by the business case, the degree of availability is dictated by factors that fall outside the pure system assurance considerations. For instance availability factors are often traded off against purely security-related services, such as need-to-know. For example, a situation might occur in which the availability of a piece of information is more important than maintaining its confidentiality. The decision to sacrifice other information assurance services for the sake of enhanced availability requires a cost-benefit trade-off analysis and a risk mitigation decision.

Authentication is the security service that establishes the validity of a transmission, message, or originator. It is the means by which an **authorization** to acquire specific items of information is confirmed. Authentication is employed by the organization to ensure that instances of unauthorized access are reduced.

Individuals, organizations, or computers must be able to establish their identities to be secure. For the computer, this implies that clients can be authenticated to servers and that servers can authenticate to clients. Authentication requires an authorization procedure that manages how the system will regulate access to resources. Access is based on the identity of the particular entity.

Non-repudiation of origin provides the data sender with proof of delivery and it ensures the sender's identity to the recipient. Neither party can later deny that the data was legitimately sent and received. Non-repudiation has implications for a broad spectrum of applications—from purchases on eBay to modern battlefield orders.

Instituting a Sustainable Security Operation

Two conditions have to be satisfied to assure all of these basic services are embedded and sustained within the day-to-day operation. First, a concrete reference point has to be adopted and documented to guide the process. The second condition is that the organization has to follow all specified security practices rigorously.

The Role of Policy in Creating an Infrastructure

Policies are the organization's statement about the approach that will be followed to ensure authentication, non-repudiation, integrity, confidentiality, and availability of information. Policies should be both comprehensive and coherent, because they constitute the framework that dictates the scope and application of the subsequent **information assurance process**.

Procedures define the steps to be taken to enable and enforce each policy. As such, every policy must be composed the right set of procedures to enact it. The requirement for completeness is satisfied through a multi-level hierarchy of control statements. At the top, this hierarchy is composed of statements about intent, which are successively broken down into clear performance and practice statements.

To achieve sufficient detail, the process is iterative. Meaning the procedures that substantiate each policy are progressively refined into increasingly explicit control statements, until the desired level of control is established. The eventual product of this logical decomposition process is the finalized information assurance infrastructure.

An information assurance infrastructure is an array of control behaviors, designed to ensure security at all organizational levels. In effect, there are control statements within that infrastructure that are applicable at each level of organizational functioning; *policy, management* and *operations*. As part of the design of the information assurance process, these must be articulated logically within the hierarchy.

For instance, an access control policy is usually required at the policy level. This policy might state that all users must be authenticated. Then at the management level a number of associated control procedures would have to be designed and put in place to assure that the authentication is done correctly, ranging from assignment of identity, all the way down to password control procedures. Finally, at the operations level, there would typically be a number of concrete activities, called **work practices**, which would be specified to embed each procedure into the day-to-day operation. As an example, password control necessitates the creation of functions to authenticate each identity, assign rights, and monitor use.

To complicate things further, all organizations are different. Therefore, the quantity and rigor of the controls embedded within a given infrastructure will differ between organizations. That means that feasible policies, procedures, and work practices must be designed within the context of that specific operation. For instance, password control policies, procedures, and work practices at a secure installation will be more extensive and rigorous than they would be for a video rental store.

All information assurance infrastructures have to be fitted to their context. This process is called **tailoring**. We discussed the process for tailoring a control structure in Chapter 3. In that chapter we saw that, because the task of tailoring information assurance controls into an infrastructure is complex, it requires some form of guidance. Most control structures are tailored from the best practices specified by a model.

Two common models for security are ISO 27000 and CoBIT. Both specify detailed control statements that can easily be turned into procedures. For example, ISO 27000 specifies 132 security control statements at the level of procedural detail represented by these two items.

> 4.7.5.3 User identification and authentication. All users shall have a unique identifier (user ID) for their personal and sole use so that activities can be traced to the responsible individual.

> 4.7.5.4 Password management system. A password management system shall be in place to provide an effective, interactive facility which ensures quality passwords.

All standard approaches have similar characteristics. First, they are concrete and can be tailored into a specification of the tasks to be performed in each instance. Second, because these control statements are concrete, their outcomes can be used to judge whether the information assurance process is operating properly. Finally, the outcomes of these tasks can be assessed because specific responsibility can be assigned. That establishes tangible **accountability** for information assurance and security performance for all responsible parties.

Ensuring a Disciplined Process: Establishing the Culture

The second critical success factor involves human factors. We have said earlier in this text that **information assurance procedures** must be followed systematically. But the problem with procedure is that it is usually seen as intrusive and unnecessary. The only way to assure security is by demanding disciplined performance of assigned duties.

The goal of continuous sustainable assurance requires a high degree of disciplined practice by the people responsible for carrying out information assurance tasks. Therefore, care must be taken to ensure the right level of information assurance and security practice among the managers and workers involved with the assurance process. Recent statistics indicate that over two-thirds of the information assurance breakdowns in corporate America have managerial or behavioral origins (CSI, 2004). Therefore, it goes without saying that an effective information assurance process has to ensure that the people within the system are operating in secure manner. As shown in Figure 4-1, this makes information assurance a people-and-processes problem, as much as it is a technical one.

Figure 4-1
The informa-
tion assurance
pyramid

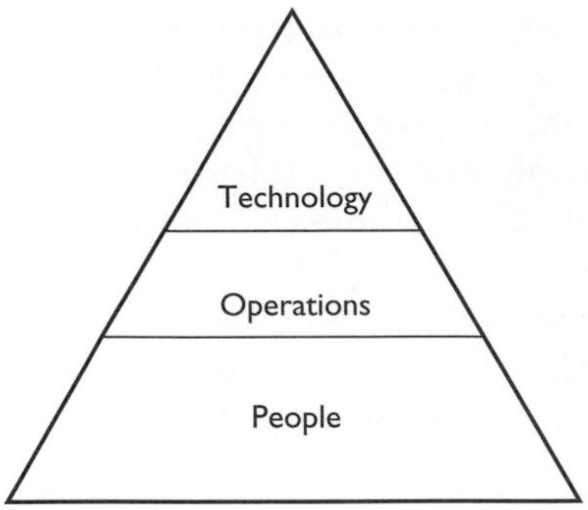

Technology

Operations

People

Information assurance safeguards are aimed at identifying suspicious or undesirable behavior. That behavior can be both technical and people based. Therefore, it is critically important to build a baseline of acceptable, or normal, practices to judge performance against.

The need to ensure routine information assurance and security performance within a baseline of acceptable practice is a different issue than the need to evaluate the performance of controls against a baseline of established criteria, (discussed in Chapter 3). To tell whether the system is operating properly workers must distinguish appropriate, from inappropriate behavior. Therefore, the first steps in building a formal information assurance and security system should be aimed at embedding a comprehensive understanding of information assurance policies, procedures and work practices within the organization. That understanding has to be complete and include both technical and behavioral level issues at all levels of performance.

This requirement is an important issue with information assurance because the organization's own people are likely to be the first ones to encounter a new or unique form of attack. As such, everybody within the organization has to be fully aware of what constitutes correct behavior, to identify incorrect behavior. Therefore, a mechanism has to be provided to ensure that all workers understand correct practice, so that they will be able to detect and report suspicious events.

Developing An Information Assurance Infrastructure

The information assurance infrastructure operates in the same way as any other organizational control system. Examples are the accounting, finance, and physical inventory systems in most organizations. Consequently a sound information assurance infrastructure demonstrates nine essential qualities of a correctly functioning system:

- **Suitability**—all necessary system attributes are present and appropriate to specified tasks.
- **Accuracy**—the system ensures that all information is correct, or that agreed-on results or desired effects are present.
- **Interoperability**—the system will correctly and efficiently interact with other specified systems.

- **Compliance**—it can be confirmed that the system adheres to specified criteria, standards, conventions, or regulations and laws.

- **Integrity**—the system can be confirmed to prevent unauthorized access, whether accidental or deliberate, to programs and data.

- **Maturity**—It can be reliably confirmed that faults are not present that might cause the system to fail frequently.

- **Fault tolerance**—if faults are present or if the system fails, attributes are present that allow it to maintain or regain a specified level of performance with a specified time.

- **Recoverability**—the system is capable of re-establishing a requisite level of performance, as well as recovering the data directly affected in the case of a failure.

- **Replaceability**—the system purposes can be achieved by another specified system in the case of extended or catastrophic failure.

The infrastructure should always provide a correct and explicit response to all threats. Because all environments are different, this implies that all infrastructures must be fitted to their precise situation. This involves blending technology with operational factors in such a way that the continuing control coverage effectiveness is assured. This is called **tailoring**.

As we saw in Chapter 3, the approach to defining that infrastructure goes through eight focusing steps to ensure a systematic development process and that everything that needs to be considered in that process is addressed.

The infrastructure development process drills down from a high-level view of the problem. That high-level perspective ensures that the infrastructure will be both comprehensive and complete. However, since the outcome of the development process is a set of controls, it implies a set of successively more focused statements that ensure the necessary procedures and work practices are specified in detail. The final product of the refinement process is a set of concrete policies, procedures, and work practices, which precisely fit the specific requirements of the information assurance environment. That process is illustrated in Figure 4-2.

Ensuring Common Understanding: Metrics and Security

Tailoring specifies a set of information assurance requirements. These are derived from the policies itemized in the information assurance and security plan and expressed as a formal specification. The requirements must be complete. All stakeholder perspectives—such as those of users and line managers within the organization—must be captured and represented within requirements. The outcome should be a substantive set of documented practices, which characterize the information assurance functions for the organization.

Those requirements must be communicated in unambiguous terms. This is a very important consideration because ambiguity is a potential point of failure. For instance, a term like "threats" may have a different meaning for a manager versus a technician.

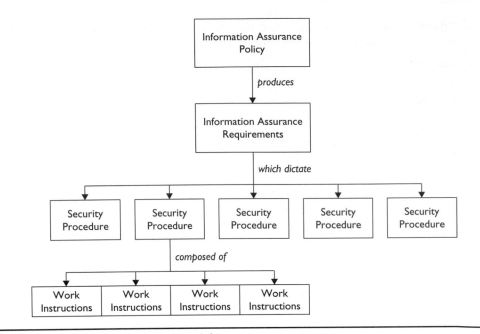

Figure 4-2 The information assurance definition process

A network security specialist might characterize a threat as malicious code, intrusions, network interruptions, and denial of service, and would measure it by the things that affect them; such as occurrences, or downtime. Managers on the other hand are more likely to understand and characterize threats in terms that are meaningful to them such as lost production, cost, and operational interruption time—expressed in dollar value or cost. That can be a source of confusion in the eventual day-to-day operation of the system.

Therefore, if the aim is to ensure consistent performance of security duties across all levels of the organization all terms and measures used should be integrated into a single document. That implies the need for a deliberate program to develop an appropriate set of common metrics.

The organizational environment determines the metrics to be used, because the nature, rigor, and application of the measures will vary based on the demands of the security situation. For instance, a highly secure government facility is likely to require extensive and rigorous metrics based around the complete set of technology and process requirements, while an organization might be more interested in just those measures that are related to productivity and performance.

The basis for any decision about metrics is the level of control that will be required to establish an assurable system. Broad measures, such as number of incidents, are acceptable where the required level of control is not particularly high. However, where a great degree of security is essential it is necessary to employ a detailed set of measures to define the requisite control.

The level of detail is achieved by continuing to break down each measure into sub-factors. The creation of sub-factors continues until the required level of understanding is reached. By rule, the attributes of each sub-factor must be directly traceable to the higher-level measures they were derived from. For example, network intrusions expressed as "number of occurrences" at the highest level should be translated into a specific set of categories of attack at the operational level. Sub-factors should also be traceable through the hierarchy of measures up to the top-level system requirements. This is a dynamic process. The sub-factors and their associated measures constantly change. Therefore, the measurement set must be refined continuously and continuously updated.

Accommodating Human Factors in the Infrastructure

Human factors are important considerations in the operation of any organizational infrastructure because disciplined performance determines how correctly each procedure will be followed. The alignment of incentives and the assurance of human factors is a critical aspect of the information assurance process, and Chapter 15 is devoted entirely to the discussion of this important topic.

The behavior of the humans within the infrastructure is ensured by the monitoring and enforcement of compliance of documented procedures. Any information assurance and security requirements associated with the technology are easy to monitor because the behavior of technology is predictable. On the other hand, human performance is harder to assure since it is governed by perceptions and emotions rather than logical rules. It is important to ensure that all human behavior rules are clearly defined, properly understood, and are accompanied by a set of enforcement criteria.

Motivating people to follow procedure is a challenge that has been compared to "herding cats" and it requires continuous oversight and strict enforcement. The only feasible response to human factors is a coherent and explicit definition of acceptable behavior.

Any procedure associated with ensuring human behavior has to assign explicit responsibility for performance to every individual. This is necessary to judge whether an information assurance or security procedure has been followed correctly and to enforce accountability. Once the rules have been established, the monitoring and control function can be concentrated on ensuring that each employee complies properly.

Documentation: Conveying the Form of the Infrastructure

To be effective, every information assurance infrastructure has to be documented completely. This documentation should communicate the three vital elements of the process—policies, procedures, and work instructions. The mechanism that is employed to document an organization's policies, procedures, and work practices is the **Information Assurance Manual**.

The Information Assurance Manual

The organization's information assurance policies are documented and communicated through an *information assurance manual.* That manual communicates the organization's specific approach to information assurance and security. The manual serves as a reference point for developing *standard operating procedures.* It integrates all required procedures and work practices for each policy into a statement of purpose.

Although it takes a lot of work to develop one, a well written information assurance manual has many advantages. It is critical to implementing and ensuring the continuous performance of the information assurance management process. It is a valuable tool for communicating the information assurance policy, goals, and objectives to stakeholders. If the information assurance manual is maintained properly, it advertises new information assurance initiatives and accomplishments to employees and customers.

The information assurance manual itemizes every procedure the organization will follow to comply with each stated policy. In addition, it specifies the work practices to be followed for each procedure. The one rule in creating an information assurance manual is that each procedure and its associated set of work practices must be traceable upward to the policy that it implements. That traceability facilitates the day-to-day assignment of specific employee responsibility for the execution of work practices. To ensure proper monitoring, the information assurance manual also specifies that metrics be employed to assess the performance of each work practice.

Finally, the information assurance manual is a key mechanism for demonstrating due diligence in performance of information assurance. Due diligence is important to ensure proof that legal, regulatory, and contractual considerations have been satisfied and to protect the organization from litigation. A detailed and comprehensive manual helps avoid liability problems by stating clearly the approach chosen and then fairly and honestly documenting the reasons for the choice. The manual has to be thorough, convincing, and provide sufficient information to enable people who are not part of the assurance process to understand what was done and why.

Ensuring Sustainability: The Documentation Set

To make policies real and sustainable it is necessary to document all procedures and work practices. To ensure enforcement these procedures and work practices have to be expressed in terms that everyone understands and follows. The procedures and work practices, together with the information assurance manual itself, form the complete **documentation set** for the information assurance process.

Once the manual has been prepared and approved, a complete set of operating procedures is written to implement each policy. Each **operating procedure** defines what will be done on a day-to-day basis. In addition to the specification of procedures, there is an accompanying designation of the individuals responsible for performing of every task.

Work practices are developed for each procedure. These **work practices** itemize the behaviors that the organization designates to accomplish each procedure. For example, if there were frequent instances where employees kept their passwords after leaving the organization, the documentation at this level would itemize the steps to be taken to ensure that passwords were deactivated when an employee termination took place. The documentation might specify a different set of work practices for situations of friendly versus unfriendly termination. The operating principle behind the development of statements of procedure and practice at this level is that the more explicit the specification, the more likely it is that the problem will not occur.

Implementation: Achieving the Right Level of Detail

The point has been made several times in this chapter that care and effort has to be taken to ensure that procedures and work practices are documented at the right level of detail. Documentation should always include specification of the responsibilities and qualifications of the individuals who execute these tasks. At a minimum, every documented procedure states the

- Steps to be taken, their measurement, and evaluation criteria
- Expected output, the measurement, and evaluation criteria
- Interrelationship with other procedures
- Qualifications and skills of the people performing the procedure
- Tools, rules, practices, methodologies, and conventions employed

At least ten areas of information assurance should be itemized using this policy/procedure/work instruction model. These are

- Physical security practices—discussed further in Chapter 9
- Personnel security practices—discussed further in Chapter 8
- Operational security practices—discussed further in Chapter 5
- Network security practices—discussed further in Chapter 12
- Software security practices—discussed further in Chapter 14
- Development process security practices—discussed further in Chapter 9
- Transmission security/encryption practices—discussed further in Chapter 13
- Business continuity practices—discussed further in Chapter 10
- Legal and regulatory compliance practices—discussed further in Chapter 11
- Ethical practices—discussed further in Chapter 16

Walking the Talk—the Role of Detailed Work Practices

The complete set of work practices for the organization is the detailed description of how information assurance and security will be implemented and enforced. Work practices clearly explain how each procedure will be executed. The key to success is consistent execution. Each work instruction has to have a set of metrics and measurement methods associated with it. These measures help managers judge whether the work has been satisfactory performed.

Because specification at this level of detail requires a good deal of description, work practices are typically long documents. They can be unwieldy unless they are broken into three types of specifications. These specifications are not mutually exclusive, instead, each specification reinforces the other. The specifications communicate the steps chosen to ensure an end-to-end information assurance process. These are as follows:

- Specification of Management Practices
- Specification of Operations Practices
- Specification of Assurance and Accountability Practices

The **management specification** lays out the details of the management oversight and control function. Adequate performance of the practices specified in the management specification ensures that the information assurance process will meet its stated goals. In other words, this specification defines the details of the management framework for the information assurance process. A management specification assigns roles and responsibilities and defines the detailed accountability mechanisms. It also specifies in depth how performance of each assurance work practice will be monitored, measured, and assessed.

The **operations specification** is the roadmap for the execution and maintenance of the specific process. It itemizes the practices that constitute the day-to-day performance of information assurance and security duties. Operations specifications describe the execution of each practice. Managers frequently refer to these documents when advice is required about performance of the process. Such issues might include when to use or assess a specific procedure and what exceptions might apply.

The **assurance specification** documents how the organization verifies and validates the execution of the assurance function. (In this context, "verify" ensures that the process establishes the relevant policies and "validate" ensures that the process is working correctly.) These specifications are intended to ensure consistent and reliable performance of the process. Therefore, the person who will be responsible for assessing that performance must be specified, as well as the specific measures that will be used to evaluate the performance of each practice.

Tailoring a Concrete Information Assurance System

Effective information assurance and security depends on establishing the right set of policies, procedures, and work practices, tailored into a concrete infrastructure. To ensure that this infrastructure is correct it is necessary to satisfy at least five generic requirements. The policies, procedures and work practices must consistently:

1. *Understand the resource*—the nature and characteristics of the information resource must be fully understood including its potential for use and the limitations associated with it.

2. *Maintain the resource*—the information resource must be acquired, maintained, and operated in a way that ensures that it consistently meets the requirements of the organization.

3. *Develop the resource*—the information resource must be developed deliberately to maintain close alignment with the goals and purposes of the organization.

4. *Use the resource*—the information resource must be used efficiently and effectively in support of the day-to-day operations of the organization.

5. *Manage the resource*—the use of the information resource must be substantively and effectively managed. The aim of this management activity must be to achieve a desired result in an optimum fashion, given resources available.

Every information assurance process should be tailored uniquely to its environment. In that respect, the tailoring process ensures that the process is correctly aligned with the environmental, sensitivity, and information assurance requirements of the situation. The generic tailoring process involves the preparation of a relevant response to six areas:

1. Context
2. Scope
3. System Operation
4. General Purpose
5. Environment
6. Sensitivity

Context

The first aspect to understand is the **context** in which the system operates. That is because context determines the assurance approach. For instance, there will be a different set of procedures where the context demands very rigorous approaches versus a situation where information assurance and security are not as important. Consequently the context in which the assurance system operates has to be clearly defined to move forward with scope definition. That is an initial condition of the tailoring process.

Scope

Once the context is understood, the scope of the assurance system must be defined. That definition should be the product of a formal organizational process because even though it sounds like a conceptual exercise, it is a critical resource allocation issue. Failure to define properly the systems scope will result in improper coverage and security breakdowns or a waste of resources.

Therefore, unique and meaningful boundaries have to be established for each processing, communications, storage, and information-related component under the control of the information assurance system. Logical interrelationships have to be made explicit. Since scope is always tied to the resources available, the standard approach to tailoring is to detail the responsible parties and their roles for each item under control.

Defining roles and responsibilities is a critical step in building the assurance system since it ties personnel and financial resources to functions. It is an often-overlooked part of the process because participants carry assumptions about who is responsible into the process. They rarely make those assumptions clear. Thus important aspects can fall through the cracks because everybody thought someone else was responsible.

Roles and responsibilities are assigned by designating accountability for performance of each function as well as all of the organizational reporting lines. If third parties or contractors are responsible for any aspect of information assurance, the responsibilities of both the contractor and the organizational unit must be defined. The definition should specify measurement standards.

System Operation

In addition to identifying and relating the components that make up the information assurance system, each of component should be categorized in terms of their role within the operation. It is important to designate the specific purpose of each asset to understand how it has to be secured because each element plays a different role in the overall assurance process.

The first consideration is the specific applications that ensure security. For example, the firewall, the IDS, and the password control system have different assurance requirements than the elements of the system that support the operation. Consequently, protection has to be aligned with purpose.

Since the security applications perform clearly defined actions, their importance can be understood in terms of the specific functions that they underwrite. Therefore the specific threats associated with each of these have to be analyzed, understood and addressed. The elements of the system that operate in a supporting role have a different set of needs. Supporting elements typically serve a broad range of purposes. These include the operating system utilities and network management functions common to any information system operation. The role of supporting systems is to enable, or support, a variety of system components that require their services. They are not dedicated strictly to information assurance or security.

However, since support systems ensure that data are neither altered nor damaged during processing they require some form of assurance. It is hard to define the assurance requirements for supporting systems because they have a variety of purposes. The definition of measures to assure supporting system functioning is sometimes overlooked because the assurance process focuses on protecting those elements of the system that have a direct information protection role.

General Purpose

Purpose and criticality are related. It is important to know the function of each component to decide how important it is to the system purpose. The determination of purpose entails a simple description of each element. That description should convey the importance of the element. This satisfies two goals. First, it allows managers to make informed assignments of priorities for the protected components. Second, it allows managers to coordinate the implementation and management of the information assurance functions assigned to them.

Environmental Considerations

Environmental considerations are a factor that must be specified for the system. This specification should describe all technical and environmental factors that might cause impact the assurance process. For example, if the system operates in an environment where a high probability for attacks exists—if it is Internet-based versus a LAN, for instance—then that is an important information assurance consideration and it has to be made explicit.

Sensitivity Requirements

It is essential to specify the sensitivity of each item of information within the system to determine the extent and rigor of the controls to be imposed. It forms the basis for the assurance controls that will be assigned. Minimally, the specification of the sensitivity of the item should detail the policies, laws, and any relevant constraints that affect the confidentiality, integrity, or availability of information within the system. That specification should not be a listing of technical standards and protocols. The specification should be a detailed recommendation of how the particular requirement will be addressed by a particular control. In addition it should provide a justification for why that particular approach was taken. The intent is to indicate the type and relative importance of the protection needed.

The sensitivity of the information determines the levels of confidentiality, integrity, and availability required. Each type of data and information processed by the system should be classified based on the severity of potential negative effects (financial and otherwise) on the organization and the degree to which the ability of the organization to perform its mission would be degraded, were the information compromised. The sensitivity of information should be characterized based on which of the following risk categories it falls into:

- **High Risk**—a loss of confidentiality, integrity, and/or availability would compromise information characterized as critical and would result in loss of life, significant financial loss, threats to national security, inability of the organization to perform its primary mission, and so on.

- **Medium Risk**—a loss of confidentiality, integrity, and/or availability would be an important concern but not necessarily critical to the organizational functioning.

- **Low Risk**—some minimal level of risk is associated with a loss of confidentiality, integrity, and/or availability; however, this would not be vital to organizational functioning.

It is important to establish the consequences of failure for the assurance system. This type of assessment has to be done for each category of threat, to understand what the consequences are. The cost to the organization or the inability to perform a specific function is a **consequence**. Therefore the consequences of any loss of confidentiality, integrity, or availability should be spelled out in concrete terms.

Types of Controls

Information assurance control procedures fall into four categories. These are 1) management controls; 2) developmental, or implementation, controls; 3) operational controls; and 4) technical controls. Figure 4-3 outlines the concentric environments in which each of these operates.

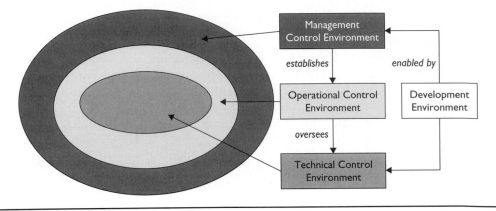

Figure 4-3   Relationship of control categories

The controls for each environment differ in their purpose and specificity. Keep this in mind when designing effective control processes because the people who will execute each control activity must understand how to perform all of the tasks required. Consequently, it is important to ensure that managers are not presented with highly technical specifications of procedure. It is equally critical that technical people are not asked to perform managerial or control activities. In both cases there is potential that the control will either be misunderstood or misapplied if focused inappropriately. Therefore, it is important to know the environment for which the specification is designed.

In addition to application, it is important to understand the **operational status** of the control. It is important in the design process because some controls will exist while others will need to be established. It is essential to have a complete understanding of where procedures have been implemented already and where it must be developed. This classification is based on a decision about whether each necessary control item is:

- **In Place**—In this category, a measure must be both operational and judged to be effective by whatever measures of effective performance that have been specified for it in the design.

- **Planned**—This category includes specific control functions planned, but not actually operational. The description of this category of measure would include an estimation of the resources involved and the expected operational dates.

- **In Place and Planned**—It is common to have part of the control in place while other parts are still missing. If some parts of the control are implemented and others have been planned, there should be an explicit statement of which is which. Where there are planned measures, this description should also include a list of resources required to make them operational and the expected date.

- **Not Feasible**—Situations exist where control measures would be desirable but it is neither cost effective nor feasible to implement them. This should be noted for future planning as well as potential long-term monitoring of the vulnerability that the measure was meant to manage.

Management Controls

Management controls are behavioral. They are based on and implement information assurance policies and procedures. They regulate access to protected information through procedures rather than technology. These controls are typically assigned based on a risk analysis, which references the cost of the applicable controls to the value of the information resource they are designed to protect. Management controls are always deployed based on the assessed impact of the threats that they have been designed to address.

Development and Implementation Process Controls

Development and implementation process controls are important because they ensure that information assurance protection is designed into the system from inception. These controls are used primarily during the system development phase. They ensure that appropriate technical, administrative, physical, and personnel security requirements are satisfied. The controls are based on the verification and validation review process. The organization must ensure that tests are performed during the development process to confirm that the information assurance specifications have been met. This is discussed in further detail in Chapter 9, "Security in the Development Process."

Operational Controls

Operational controls are the day-to-day procedures that protect the operation from a wide variety of physical and environmental threats. Operational controls fall into six categories:

- Physical and Environmental Protection
- Production and Input/Output Control
- Contingency Planning
- Installation and Update Controls
- Configuration Management Control
- Documentation Control

The first type—*physical and environmental protection*—includes the common safeguards designed to shield the ordinary information processing function. The primary focus of these controls is on threats to the physical equipment or space, such as physical attacks and intrusions, natural or manmade disasters, and utility outages or breakdowns. Controls of this type include physical barriers, such as locks on doors, grills on windows, and locks on terminals.

The second category is *production and input/output controls*, which include all safeguards that ensure the proper handling, processing, storage, and disposal of data and media. Where physical media are involved this category includes access controls. That involves a full range of actions and procedures from labeling to distribution procedures.

The third category is the *contingency planning controls*, which safeguard against the failure of the processing function by specifying procedures for continuing essential functions in the face of major disasters or simple interruptions. The controls are based on formal plans and are monitored through reviews and audits. These reviews and audits are designed to detect and react to departures from established policies, rules, and procedures. This is discussed in much detail in Chapter 10, "Continuity."

The fourth category, software *installation and update controls*, includes the control procedures designed to maintain the ongoing integrity of software. The intent of these controls is to ensure that the software will function as expected and that a historical record of changes is maintained. Among other things, these controls ensure that only authorized software is allowed on the system.

The fifth area of control is *configuration management control*. This is the means to ensure that systems remain in a known configuration and that a record of system changes is maintained. Configuration management control may apply to hardware and system configuration security.

Configuration management describes the conventional management process that is traditionally part of the software engineering discipline. This control is important because many information assurance and security vulnerabilities are introduced during the change process. Configuration control is driven by status assessments and enforced by management authorization of modifications.

The sixth control focuses on *documentation control*. This is an important aspect of information assurance because most of the organization's awareness of proper procedure is based on documentation. Accordingly, the integrity of the documentation has to be preserved; it is accomplished by controlling the documentation set the same way as the technical components of the system. This includes rigorously controlling documentation of changes to the system as well as performing systematic backups and planning for contingencies.

Technical Controls

Just as with the management process, the procedures that affect technical controls should be well defined, understood, and followed. The most obvious **technical controls** are those that make up the automated access control system. In addition to controlling access, there is also a need to authorize the rights of the user to various parts of the system.

These are *authorization controls*. They provide the appropriate level of access to each entity and restrict users to authorized transactions and functions. They may also detect unauthorized activities. Another type of technical control is *integrity control procedures*. They protect data from accidental or malicious alteration or destruction. These controls provide assurance to users that data has not been altered and assure that the data meets defined expectations about quality.

Technical controls are important and should be monitored closely. That is an essential aspect of management accountability as well as a technical issue. Consequently, the monitoring of technical controls is associated with audit procedures. A complete audit trail and a chronological record are evidence of adequate monitoring. The use of system log files is an example of this type of control.

Chapter 4 Review

Chapter Summary

- Formal procedures are justified because information is a resource.

- Satisfactory assurance requires that the resource is organized and administered.

- The organization must deliberately and in a disciplined fashion perform the information assurance function as a systematic and sustainable process.

- The organization must define and enforce a substantive set of procedures and work practices, as well as assign roles and job responsibilities, and enforce accountability.

- The five practical steps involved in building a secure organization force the operation to think through the detailed requirements of its particular situation.

- Defining an attendant set of procedures and work instructions, which constitute the functional system, operationalizes these steps.

- The purpose of the **status assessment** activity is to characterize the precise information assurance needs of each individual item in the inventory.

- The successful development of an information assurance system depends on the ability to tailor the right set of controls.

- The approach to this is hierarchical. Higher-level items are decomposed into smaller and more precisely defined subfunctions to establish an understanding of the required procedures and controls.

- The practical day-to-day mechanism for establishing information assurance practices is documentation.

- Documentation captures three characteristic types of things: policies, procedures, and work instructions.

- The policies provide direction, while the procedures and work instructions provide the details.

- By convention, policies are documented and communicated through an organizationally standard and generally accepted information assurance manual.

- The primary mission of the information assurance manual is to record a formal statement of the organization's specific information assurance policies.

- The information assurance manual states the organization's policy toward information assurance. It also itemizes the set of best practices for each policy element.

- The information assurance manual specifies all relevant control objectives and provides an overview of the process that will be used to judge whether these objectives have been satisfactorily achieved.

- The only way that an organization can conduct a sustainable process is if it has documented procedures in place.

- Once the manual has been prepared and approved, a complete set of operating procedures is written to implement each policy.

- The purpose of procedure is to define what specifically has to be done to meet an individual information assurance requirement.

- Work instructions itemize the standard operating steps that will be taken to allow the organization to execute a security procedure.

- The development of the procedures and their work instructions represents most of the effort required to create a functioning information assurance system.

- The outcome of the documentation process is a complete and fully defined information assurance scheme.

Key Terms

accountability (93)
assurance specification (100)
authentication (91)
authorization (91)
availability (91)
confidentiality (90)
consequence (103)
context (101)
development and implementation process controls (105)
documentation (89)
documentation set (98)
information (90)
information assurance infrastructure (90)
infrastructure (90)
information assurance manual (97)
information assurance procedures (93)

information assurance process (92)
integrity (91)
management controls (105)
management specification (100)
non-repudiation of origin (91)
operating procedure (98)
operational controls (105)
operational status (104)
operations specification (100)
procedure (89)
status assessment (107)
tailoring (93)
technical controls (106)
work practices (92)

Key Term Quiz

Use terms from the Key Terms list to complete the following sentences. Not all terms will be used.

1. Information assurance responses must be _____ to fit the specific circumstance.

2. The _____ describes the precise approach to information assurance.

3. The information assurance manual is embodied by a _____.

4. Procedures are substantiated through _____.

5. The information assurance scheme is communicated through _____.

6. If a control is currently operating properly, it is said to be _____.

7. The ability to provide proof of sender and recipient is called _____.

8. The quality that reflects the logic and correctness of data is called _____.

9. The proper safeguard to an emerging array of threats is called a(n) _____.

10. If a system can interact with other systems, it is said to be _____.

Multiple Choice Quiz

1. Procedures define _____.

    A. specific practices

    B. general concepts

    C. work instructions

    D. details

2. The documentation process starts by defining _____.

   A. work instructions

   B. top-level information assurance requirements

   C. who is responsible

   D. text

3. Each procedure must be _____.

   A. traceable to work instructions

   B. supported by a work instruction

   C. illustrated

   D. complete

4. The information assurance scheme must specify the _____.

   A. overall owner of the asset

   B. specific system being secured

   C. resources

   D. schedule

5. Information assurance manuals demonstrate _____.

   A. due diligence

   B. understanding of information assurance

   C. knowledge

   D. political factors

6. Human factors are important to a sustainable assurance process because:

   A. people are important

   B. people are malicious

   C. disciplined practice is important

   D. people can be evaluated

7. Context determines the:

   A. controls

   B. procedures

   C. threats

   D. approach

8. Scope is tied directly to:

   A. resources

   B. protection

   C. effectiveness

   D. documentation

9. Behavior can be:

   A. technical

   B. managerial

   C. process

   D. both technical and managerial

10. Procedures specify:

   A. costs

   B. sequence and timing

   C. controls

   D. the work practices to be performed

Essay Quiz

In your own words, briefly answer the following questions.

1. What is the role of policy in formulating the information assurance manual?

2. Why is it useful to have a template for documenting the information assurance system?

3. Operational controls are important to security—what purpose do they serve?

4. Why is it necessary to follow a hierarchical decomposition process to define information assurance procedures?

5. Why do the various types of information in the system have to be described? What outcome does this activity support?

6. What is the reason why the security applications have to be specifically identified in the process of security system formulation?

7. What are infrastructures composed of? What purpose do they serve?

8. What is the role of the configuration management process? What other type of function does it serve?

9. Why is it hard to secure information? Why are concrete procedures necessary?

10. What is the purpose of the estimate of operational status? Why is this an important element of real-world security system formulation?

Case Exercise

Complete the following exercise as directed by your instructor:

Refer to the Heavy Metal Technology Case in Appendix A. You have been assigned the task of preparing a information assurance manual for the Jackson Street facility. Prepare a complete and coherent set of procedures to address the following issues identified for that facility.

1. The entrance to the meeting rooms is not controlled.
2. The hallways are not monitored or controlled.
3. No documentation tracking exists.
4. There are no documentation assurance practices.
5. The loading dock is not secured.
6. Access to the IT facilities is not controlled.
7. Access to the employee facilities is not controlled.
8. IT staff can come and go through their own entrance without control.
9. Documentation staff can come and go through their own entrance without control.
10. Administrative staff can come and go through their own entrance without control.

Then trade work with another member of the class and perform a management review of their response. Is this a complete and coherent solution? Can you see any areas that might require additional policies to cover them?

Maintaining Security of Operations

In this chapter, you will learn how to:
- Establish routine security of operation
- Create a dependable operational security process
- Ensure operational response to incidents

Security of operations is a critical part of the information assurance lifecycle. The security of operations function ensures the integrity and performance for the remaining organizational information assurance and security processes. Information assurance and security of operations ensure the consistent execution of policies and procedures. It monitors and evaluates day-to-day performance of the continuity, compliance, physical security, and personnel security processes. They make certain that all technical counter-measures are in place and operating properly.

If any of those processes experiences a problem, security of operations is responsible for initiating and coordinating the proper **corrective action**. As a result, security of operation is the **process** guaranteeing the long-term viability of the information assurance capabilities of the organization. The security of operations process involves actions such as

- Ensuring that current operating procedures are properly aligned with the organization's security policies
- Monitoring the performance of assigned security duties to confirm that they correspond to proper processes
- Defining and executing **operational housekeeping** processes to ensure that the security function continues to operate properly

Aims: Aligning Purpose with Practice

Every organization has information assurance goals. Those goals must be satisfied for the organization to be secure. However, the overall environment is always changing, so, the information assurance goals have to change accordingly. Factors that can affect this process include changes in

- People who use the system or their motivations
- The types of systems interconnected with the organization's systems
- The type or sensitivity of data flowing to, through, or from the organization's systems
- The way the organization does business or the type of business the organization conducts.
- The rigor and extent of the information assurance objectives
- The organizational risk model and risk tolerance approach

If it is found that an information assurance goal is not being met, the organization has to perform a risk assessment/risk mitigation process to decide how to meet it. The typical response would be to change the practice or to change the requirement.

Changes to requirements might include reclassification of information to a different sensitivity level or making an alteration in the access rules for a facility. Factors that might lead to changing the requirement, rather than the practices that satisfy it, would be the lack of availability of time and resources or the existence of feasible alternatives. In each instance, however, the outcome of the risk assessment/mitigation process is an alignment between information assurance requirements and information assurance and security practices. Figure 5-1 illustrates this continuous balancing act.

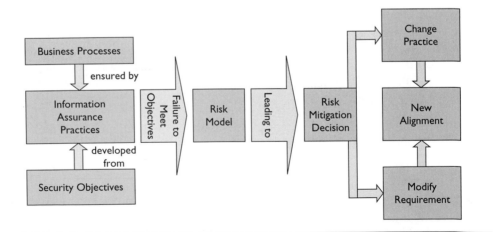

Figure 5-1   Execution cycle for the security of operations process

The duty of the security of operations function is to maintain a correct alignment between the organization's information assurance goals and its information assurance practices at all times. To ensure this alignment, security of operations is responsible for monitoring the execution of each of the other processes. The focus of the monitoring activity is the detection of meaningful deviations from correct practice.

Because the information assurance environment and the organization itself are constantly changing, confidence in the correctness of the information assurance response has to be renewed. Therefore, security of operations must also verify periodically that security practices remain aligned correctly with information assurance goals. In highly secure settings, this responsibility involves occasional re-certification of the information assurance system. In every situation, however, the security of operations function is to routinely review, inspect, test, and audit the diverse requirements of the response, to ensure their continuous secure performance.

Threat Response: Keeping the Organization on Its Toes

Threat response is either proactive or reactive. *Proactive* activities include identification of threats and vulnerabilities; the creation, assessment, and optimization of security solutions (within a generalized information assurance architecture); and the implementation of controls to protect the software and the information that it processes. *Reactive* activities include detecting and reacting to external or internal intrusions or security violations in a timely manner.

Staying Alert: Elements of the Operational Security Process

Operational security process is composed of four principles. These principles represent the primary functions of the operational security process: *sensing, analyzing, responding,* and *managing.*

In the case of sensing, it is essential to monitor continuously (sense) the operational environment for threats. That is because those threats can arise at any point in time and can create a range of unanticipated problems. Monitoring the operational environment is done through a standard, regularly scheduled and disciplined process.

Threats arise from the environment. It is a requisite of good practice to *analyze* the environment regularly, to identify and decide how to *respond* to potential security threats, exposures, vulnerabilities, or violations. The aim is to respond as quickly and effectively as possible to these incidents.

To be effective the security of the operations process must be standardized, fully documented, and coordinated continuously. To ensure the effectiveness of the process, the security of the operations function must be defined by standard procedures (discussed in Chapter 4) and the infrastructure must be *managed.*

Management of the security of operations process involves organizing the required assurance activities and routinely evaluating the policies, procedures, tools, and standards of that function to ensure effectiveness. The details of how to do that are discussed in the following subsections.

Sensing: Understanding the Threat

The first required assurance activity is the sensing function. Operational sensing is proactive. It must be performed continuously because it serves as the eyes and ears of the organization where threats are concerned. The operational sensing function is implemented and run by defined policies, procedures, tools, and standards. The aim of the sensing function is to *monitor, test,* and *assess* the organizational environment, to detect vulnerabilities and security violations as they arise. Because threats can appear at any time, operational sensing is executed continuously in the background of the day-to-day operating environment. This function is so important that the only limitation to operational sensing is the availability of resources.

Operational sensing *identifies* and *resolves* threats as they arise within the information assurance environment. Because threats can be associated with almost any activity from contract violations to hurricanes and malicious employee behavior, operational sensing is not limited to oversight of the information technology. Instead, it extends far into the operating environment.

Reviews monitor and **evaluate** management and end-user behavior. The review process includes walkthroughs, inspections, or audits. These can be either managerial, or technical. The reviews are periodic activities scheduled, as appropriate, to **assess** the effectiveness of everything from personnel security to technical configurations. Subsequent threats, vulnerabilities, or violations that are identified are documented and reported through a defined problem reporting/problem resolution process. The problem resolution process must be designed to allow decision makers to authorize corrective action based on assessment risk.

Ideally, tests and reviews should be compared against established benchmarks. An operations security **benchmark** is taken at the time when the organization was known to be secure. To establish operational assurance, the organization must be able to confirm that it is in a secure state, that all required security elements are understood and documented, and that all information assurance functions are enabled. At a minimum, this assurance requires documentary evidence of

- A feasible information assurance and security perimeter

- An overall concept of standard operating procedure

- A generic operational testing and review plan

- Policies to ensure appropriate response to unexpected incidents

- A secure site plan

- A Business Continuity and Disaster Recovery Plan (BCP/DRP) with Recovery Time Objectives (RTO), Network Recovery Objectives (NRO), and Recovery Point Objectives (RPO) fully established for every item within the information assurance perimeter

- Assurance that all staff members are adequately trained in secure operation

- Assurance that all staff are capable of utilizing security functionality relevant to their position in the organization

Analyzing: Making Smart Decisions

To make a good decision about a given threat, it is essential to understand the consequences and impacts. Therefore, everything involved with the threat must be documented in the analysis, not just the impacts on technology. It is not sufficient to list the information assurance implications of a change without explaining what each represents in terms of potential impacts on people, the organization's operations, and general information assurance.

Threat Assessment: Understanding the Consequences   It is essential to understand the implications of a threat. Complete understanding requires the identification of all affected elements and the ability to characterize the impact of prospective responses. Impacts on existing policies, procedures, and countermeasures must be understood and characterized along with any cascading or ripple effects that might take place within the organization. In addition to the obvious technical or procedural implications, this could also involve understanding legal, regulatory, and forensic requirements.

Impact Analysis: Evaluating the Strategy   To implement the correct response, all feasible alternatives must be evaluated and understood. A comprehensive and detailed impact analysis is necessary. This analysis should be based on a formal method. The method should ensure comprehensive understanding of the operational implications of a given response, its requirements, and the changes required.

To understand the strategic issues, classify threats by type and criticality, the scope of the threat as it affects resources, and finally the remediation option that fits within the known constraints. Once these have been fully understood, results and recommendations are communicated to the proper decision maker for authorization.

Reporting: Understanding the Alternatives   To evaluate alternatives intelligently, identify the type and extent of the impacts and respective risks for each option as well as the likelihood of each risk. From that identification process, it should be possible to estimate the information assurance, security, and resource implications of responding, as well as those of *not* responding.

That judgment includes an estimate of the implications for policy and procedure, the business continuity/disaster recovery strategy, and finally the return on investment. Return on investment should include a feasibility estimate along with resource estimations.

Authorizing: Getting the Go-Ahead   The results of the analysis must support decision-making about the response. Therefore, it is essential that the body of evidence be communicated in an easily understood form to the senior system manager (SSM) or designated approving authority (DAA) for authorization.

To support that decision it is necessary to provide a full explanation of the implementation requirements for each option presented. Consequently, the report must clearly outline all of the effects of each option and the recommendation must be traceable to the business case.

Responding: Ensuring a Disciplined Response

The responding function implements the authorized corrective action. In some instances, there might be a good operational justification for not responding to a threat or for not responding to it as soon as possible. Factors that might influence the decision are resource constraints, difficulty, or infeasibility of the response required.

It is essential that all threats and vulnerabilities are *tracked* and the resulting responses are *overseen*. Consequently, whether a decision to respond is authorized or not, the security of operations function must continuously monitor all known threats within the operational environment to be able to react appropriately when required.

The organizational component actually responsible for modifying the protection scheme must understand the requirements and restrictions involved in making the change. That rule applies whether it is a technical issue or a change in policy. Therefore, a process must exist to communicate the technical and contextual requirements to the change agent. There must also be a defined process to ensure that this is done accurately.

The security of operations staff should continue to monitor and analyze the outcome to verify that the intended results have been achieved. This is supported by a comprehensive testing, review, and audit program. The assessment certifies that the threat has been successfully addressed and the desired protection has been re-established. The assessment program should be specified when the authorization is given.

To ensure confidence in highly secure settings, it might be necessary to perform a third-party assessment or audit. In those cases, a third-party agency must be identified to conduct the certification audits using standards specified by regulation or contract. Finally, properly certified auditors must perform assessments for certification/recertification.

Managing: Maintaining an Effective Process

To ensure a secure organization, all information assurance processes have to be planned, designed, administered, and maintained as routine organizational functions. The administration and maintenance of standard, routine information assurance processes is the province of security of operations. The duty of security of operations management is to ensure that effective leadership vision and expertise is exercised at all times.

As we said earlier, infrastructure is always aligned to maintain a proper and timely response to potential threats through correct alignment between information assurance objectives and information assurance responses. The alignment involves the development and continuous maintenance of appropriate effective countermeasures. The operations security management function oversees and coordinates the alignment process to maintain the best response to threats and changes in a dynamically changing situation.

Implementation: Setting Up the Security of Operations Process

Security of operations is founded on organization-wide policies, procedures, and countermeasures. In Chapter 4 we called this an information assurance infrastructure. Security of operations maintains the relevance and effectiveness of that infrastructure. A comprehensive, cross-organizational planning process is needed to ensure that the security of operations process is established because the infrastructure encompasses the entire organization. The security of operations should be embedded as part of day-to-day workplace functioning because this planning effort must reach across the entire organization.

The security of operations process specifies the organizationally approved methods and processes that will be followed to ensure security performance. In addition, since operational assessment is critical, the specific methods and metrics used to track this performance must be specified as well as certifications used to judge proper execution.

Operational Planning

Security of operations is established by a plan that delineates the requirements necessary to ensure a robust and persistent process. It specifies the standard practices and the schedule or timetable to be followed.

A formal security of operations plan is an important **baseline** document. It is a point of reference in the evolution and day-to-day management. The plan operationalizes and coordinates the elements of the security of operations function as well as guides the resource allocation for its conduct.

The operational plan is a useful support to the budgeting process because it allows decision makers to align their safeguards with available resources. The operational plan organizes and focuses the effective deployment of those resources.

The operational plan makes the organization's security objectives explicit. These objectives are the basis for the deployment of the overall security function and they are an excellent way to gauge performance. The plan serves as a good mechanism for assessing whether the contractual and regulatory obligations of the organization are being met because it details the performance criteria.

The operational plan organizes the technical and management response so that the right set of countermeasures is always in place. As with the strategic plan, which guides the deployment of the overall information assurance function, the operational security plan should be a simple document that is easily understood by all participants. It should leave all members of the staff knowing what activities they need to carry out and the timing requirements for performance.

The operational security plan is built and maintained through eight stages, shown in Figure 5-2 and discussed in the following subsections.

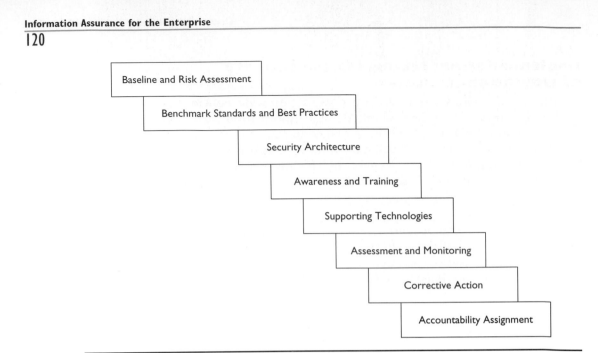

Figure 5-2 Steppingstones to a secure operation

Step 1: Document the Baseline

The first step in the operational planning process is an assessment of the status of the organization. This assessment is done (usually annually) to describe the near-term security situation and specify the resulting security requirements. The outcome of this process is a baseline or benchmark status.

The baseline documents the current security situation and specifies the requirements needed to ensure security. The actual identification process used to establish that status is derived from and is similar to the asset identification and risk assessment process described in the first two chapters.

Step 2: Determine the Benchmarks

After the current status has been established and documented, change requirements are defined. These could be focused internally and apply only to a particular unit. On the other hand, they might be global recommendations. This provides a roadmap for executing the security of operations function.

This roadmap documents all issues and priorities that define the conduct of the operational security process during the planning period. The roadmap also provides a management framework for the technical and procedural countermeasures to be adopted. To determine the feasibility of these approaches and the resources required for carrying them out, the decision process rests on a thorough understanding of the risks involved filtered through the threat prioritization process.

Step 3: Establish a Security Architecture

The roadmap is used to develop the security **architecture**. Once the direction is decided, planners document an appropriate infrastructure of **operational procedures** to create a secure and stable day-to-day operational security function.

The outcome is a set of defined practices and work instructions detailing the operational security practice. The aim is to ensure understanding among all participants of the procedures required to support every aspect of day-to-day security functions. This is communicated through a **policy and procedure manual**. Because that manual publicizes the security of operations function to the organization at large, it must be kept current.

Step 4: Build Awareness

Once security procedures and technical countermeasures have been captured and publicized in the policy and procedure manual, the organization uses that manual to build awareness involving focused employee awareness, training, and education programs.

It is not sufficient to provide a set of procedures without making the user community aware of their individual responsibilities for any defined practice. Therefore, proper awareness, training, and education is a cornerstone of the implementation process.

The awareness, training, and education program is deployed and administered as part of operational planning and is a continuous responsibility.

Step 5: Deploy Supporting Technology

The security of operations plan contains the technologies and other off-the-shelf products used during the planning period. Technology alone will not secure the organization, but it is a critical part of the process. The operational security plan should specify the security-related products that will be used and their application.

These technologies are varied and must be itemized and related to the security procedure supported. They should be traceable to an element of the business case. In addition, the method for installing, maintaining, and operating them on a secure basis must be specified.

Step 6: Assess Performance

Once the supporting technology has been identified and the system implemented, there is an obligation to perform ongoing status **assessment** and **monitoring**. Every security process has to be assessed, monitored, and controlled. To ensure this, the right information has to be collected and distributed to the decision makers. The distribution should include the top- and mid-level managers responsible for process oversight and the technical participants.

Communication is a critical part of the tracking function, because all significant stakeholders have to be tied together by coordinated information. The definition and design of the information exchange process is an integral part of the operational planning process and has to be revised and updated as the information assurance environment changes.

Step 7: Specify How Corrective Action Will Be Taken

Corrective action brings the operational security plan into line with changing conditions or other unanticipated circumstances. Because conditions are always changing, the steps involved in the execution of corrective action function have to be established by the annual operational plan.

The method for reporting the requirement for corrective action and the procedures for responding to each report must be specified. The plan must establish the protocols that managers, the technical staff, and end users will follow to respond to environmental changes or new circumstances.

Step 8: Enforce Accountability

It is impossible to guarantee that procedures will be followed correctly without formal **accountability**. The organization must assign personal responsibility for execution of the steps in the plan. Those responsibilities have to be itemized and assigned to individual participants. Once itemized, measures have to be defined to enforce them.

Enforcement is a critical success factor. To ensure security, explicit enforcement requirements and the consequences for non-compliance have to be designated for every job title. The consequences have to be communicated and personally agreed to in order to ensure that individual employees will carry out their assigned security duties dependably. Strict enforcement has to be practiced on a continuous basis and as an organizational commitment from the top of the organization.

Operational Response

The organization's continuity planning process establishes the overall approach to ensure operational continuity. It is the responsibility of the security of operations function to make certain that all pre-planned responses remain appropriate and that the organization is able to identify, report, and respond to incidents in a timely and effective fashion.

An important duty of security of operations is to ensure that the organization is always protected by an effective operational response. The operational response process resolves problems as they appear. The response is established and maintained by a plan. The plan integrates the sensing, analyzing, and responding principles into a set of procedures that meet the security needs of the organization.

The operational response function follows the same sensing, analyzing, and responding steps fundamental to the security operations process. These principles apply regardless of whether the organization is reacting to foreseen or unforeseen events. The only difference is that if the event were anticipated the response is determined in advance.

For example, there is always a set of operational contingencies aimed at responding appropriately to a fire and most facilities execute a regular fire drill to make certain that the response is executed properly. The presence of that pre-defined response ensures that an optimum solution is provided in a timely fashion.

However, many events are unforeseen and can be the most dangerous. If the incident is unforeseen, the security of operations process continues to ensure a coordinated and appropriate response. The difference is that, because the incident was unforeseen, there is a greater emphasis on timely analysis leading to a rapid and intelligent response. Timeliness is underwritten by effective **incident reporting**.

Ensuring Effective Reporting and Response

Incident reporting triggers the operational response process and ensures that every event that might threaten the organization's information is identified and reported. These incidents are not limited to events that make the six o'clock news, like the occasional Internet-wide denial of service attack. They include everything from major time-sensitive attacks all the way to routine reports of vulnerabilities spotted by the staff during the execution of their routine duties.

Whether the event has a foreseen response attached to it or was unforeseen, all incident reports require a reliable incident response function. A formal **incident response team (IRT)** or **operational response team (ORT)** establishes effective incident response. These entities operate like the fire department. They are called as soon as possible after the event and follow a disciplined process to ensure the best possible resolution.

Ensuring Timely Reports

The incident-reporting function is initiated when an incident is identified. It provides a description of both the type and estimated impact of the incident. The critical success factor for effective incident reporting is *timely* detection. A successful incident reporting function is founded on a range of sensing functions.

These functions are measurement based and are placed throughout the organization, both on the perimeter and embedded within operations. The goal is to identify security violations, or attempts to exploit security vulnerabilities, or inadvertent breakdowns in security functions in as timely a fashion as possible.

The sensing and measurement process itself can be as varied as automated intrusion detection (IDS)/intrusion prevention (IPS) systems through simple software-driven scans for malware and virus checking to low-tech items as tips or direct reports from guards, law enforcement officials, or other outside sources.

Ensuring Timely Response

If the incident has been foreseen, the incident report recommends the approved management and/or technical resolution specified in the incident response plan. This recommendation would be transmitted to the operational response team for implementation and coordination.

Proper security practice dictates that incident reports go to a single central coordinator or facilitator for confirmation analysis and subsequent action. Central coordination is necessary, because attacks and compromises do not present themselves in a single neat package. Instead, a series of suspicious events begin to form the signature of an impending attack. Consequently, a single coordinating entity has to be responsible for collecting and analyzing the sensing information.

Once an incident can be confirmed, its impacts must be (at least minimally) understood to set the right response in motion. The staff's role of the central coordinating agency is to work continuously to connect the dots. In practice, incidents are either *potential* or *active*.

Anticipating Potential Incidents

Potential incidents include such things as pre-attack probes, unauthorized access attempts, denial of service attempts, or vulnerabilities in the infrastructure identified by the staff. One other potential source could be the formal notification by an outside entity, such as the Computer Emergency Response Team (CERT®) Coordination Center (CERT/CC) at Carnegie Mellon University that a potential incident has been identified.

The reports of potential incidents are frequently generic and usually result from routine data-gathering activity and analysis. For instance, there might be a wide array of similar reports that a virus incident has taken place or is likely to occur. Potential incident reports also result from analyses performed by the software themselves. For instance, manufacturers can send out a notice that vulnerability has been identified during the operational use of the product.

Most potential incident reports are generated by the intrusion detection devices. These methods will be discussed in much greater length in Chapter 6. Since detection is also a critical aspect in the identification of potential incidents, one of the most common methods will be discussed here.

That method is *operational event logging*. It is critical to security of operations because it monitors events taking place within the system itself. Most operating systems provide an event-logging function implemented in a software sub-system that captures and record events as system services are requested. This information is recorded and stored for retrospective analysis by people who oversee the system's operation. They determine whether the services are being used as prescribed. It helps them diagnose undesirable events such as security violations and intentional or unintentional misuse.

Event logging in most systems generates a range of records. These records capture and document all events taking place within the system. They record auditable events such as administrator actions, errors or faults that have occurred, and suspicious end-user behavior. In addition to capture and storage, system administrators may view events in real time as they are generated. This feature allows the security staff to identify and respond to incidents as they happen.

Alternatively, the event logger can allow auditors and other system security personnel to review system history. History records provide an audit trail containing evidence about system performance. This evidence is a critical component of the overall security of operations process, because it allows managers to make decisions about the security functioning of the system that are based on concrete actions.

There may be many conflicting or unclear incident reports because cyberspace is complex and confusing. If the reports are consistent, the operational response team will continue to gather data. If there is enough valid evidence to support the conclusion that an attack is taking place or a compromise has been identified, the incident is moved into the active category.

Working with Active Incidents

Active incidents always require an operational response. If it is possible to confirm that an unauthorized access, denial of service, or successful vulnerability exploitation has occurred, then the appropriate corrective actions must be implemented. Those actions are dictated by circumstances and range from applying a technical patch, reconfiguration, or reinstallation of the system, to a change in policy and procedure or the implementation of new enforcement mechanisms for the entire organization.

The operational response team initiates that process. The operational response team contains the harm from an incident and prevents its reoccurrence. When a technical recommendation is required, the operational response function supervises the change to the target system through the organization's configuration management process. Configuration management then ensures that the recommended change has been properly requested, analyzed, authorized, executed, and assured.

When a change to organizational policy and/or procedure is needed, the operational response team performs the coordination and documentation activities needed to ensure that the change has been persistently established within the target system and is being followed.

Ensuring Continuing Integrity: Configuration Management

The requirement to ensure the integrity of the configuration of all operational systems is another responsibility of the security of operations function. Whether it is part of conventional IT, or a security function, this process is usually called **configuration management**.

Configuration management is a formal procedure undertaken for the change management. Configuration management refers to the evolution of change to objects such as hardware and software components. Its objective is to control those changes to preserve system integrity.

Configuration management is a critical component of security for two reasons. First, it ensures the predictable day-to-day functioning of system hardware and software. Second, it offers the ability to detect unauthorized changes, by establishing "day one" knowledge of what the system *should* look like. With that knowledge, it is possible to perform audits or other inspections to confirm that the system is functioning as intended and does not contain unauthorized or potentially malicious objects.

A configuration management system maintains the integrity of the items under its control and allows for the evaluation and performance of management changes. To do that properly, configuration management follows the sensing, analyzing, and responding principles discussed throughout this chapter.

Configuration management establishes the integrity of the system because it maintains and enforces traceability among components making problem identification, tracking, and resolution possible. Besides ongoing configuration control, the organization also conducts audits of the configuration baselines to ensure continued correctness.

Because of its advantages for security, configuration management is practiced organization-wide. The organization should be responsible for ensuring the uniform participation of subcontractors in the configuration management process. All organizational contractual agreements should apply to the subcontractors and be included in the plan that establishes the overall configuration management function.

The following subsections discuss the human-based roles that are involved in configuration management.

The Configuration Manager Role

Configuration management is assigned to specific managers or a management team. The *configuration manager* ensures that the change management requirements are carried out. The role of the configuration manager is to

- Process all requests for change
- Manage the change authorization (responding) process
- Verify that the change is complete.

The Baseline Manager Role

The organization must assign a manager who accounts for the status of the baselines under configuration control. This manager ensures that all configuration items are identified, accounted for, and maintained with the identification scheme. This individual establishes a baseline management ledger (BML) for each controlled entity. The baseline management ledger provides a complete accounting for the configuration items in each controlled baseline. The baseline manager records all changes and promotions to baselines in this ledger and maintains the libraries associated with it.

Since items not in the ledger are not secured, the baseline manager is responsible for keeping the ledger current, maintains accounts to reflect the current state of all baselines, and is responsible for authorizing new baselines.

The Verification Manager Role

The Verification Manager ensures that integrity is maintained during and after the change process. The role is to

1. Confirm that items in the change management ledger conform to the identification scheme

2. Verify that changes have been carried out

3. Conduct milestone reviews and audits

The verification manager maintains full documentation of the audit and review recommendations. The Verification Manager guarantees that items in the baseline management ledger reflect the true status of the configuration at any time.

Status Accounting

The status accounting function ensures the continuing correct status of each baseline. The configuration identification scheme is the cornerstone of status accounting. This scheme is a prerequisite for a configuration management process because it establishes the "day one" baseline, which is maintained throughout the rest of the life cycle. All components within the baseline are identified and labeled uniquely. These are organized based on their interrelationships and dependencies and represent the structure (*configuration*) of the system.

Precise baselines are pre-requisite for the overall information assurance process, since software and information items are intangible. Therefore, the *representation* of these items is what is actually secured. Once the configuration has been established and documented, that scheme is continuously maintained. Changes at any level in the structure must be maintained at all levels.

The Configuration Management Plan

Finally, the configuration manager (or team) builds a plan that lists the activities in the configuration management function including the procedures to be followed during the configuration management process and the schedule for routine activities. In addition, it includes the procedures for performing configuration management activity involving other organizations. This can apply to either an internal unit or external entities (that is, subcontractors).

All organizational roles, responsibilities, and interrelationships are defined and assigned in the plan. The management level authorized to approve changes is also defined in that plan. The outcome of this process is a complete and fully documented description of how the configuration management process will be carried out.

This plan should itemize the change management, baseline management, and verification management functions, as well as how the configuration identification scheme will be conducted and ensured. A mechanism must be specified that will monitor baselines and provide timely information to managers for decision-making integrity.

Operational Housekeeping

Operational housekeeping is a humble but necessary aspect of the security of operations function. Operational housekeeping ensures that routine information processing activities are performed securely.

Operational housekeeping is responsible for ensuring that the organization's information is protected from common threats. This is not a simple matter of preventative maintenance. It includes proactive measures such as periodic inspections and compliance audits. Housekeeping includes managerial concerns such as making sure that visitors do not casually wander around the premises without an appropriate badge or tracking device. It also involves ensuring that routine patches and repairs to equipment and facilities are performed.

The frequency with which an organization carries out its operational housekeeping tasks differs based on integrity requirements, the criticality of the information, and the nature of the extent of the housekeeping task. The following section explains some of the most common operational housekeeping chores.

Preparing an Operational Procedure Manual

Every organization has to compile, distribute, and update a procedure manual. This manual details all required procedures to ensure continuous security of operations. The manual should contain simple checklists providing clear direction for employees performing routine housekeeping.

The checklists prevent the people executing a security process from omitting something important and it specifies remediation options. For example, if there were frequent instances of equipment failures, a recovery procedure might be specified as a corrective action. Every documented procedure should ensure that the required steps are listed, as well as the expected results, and some way to determine that those results have been achieved. Finally, there should be a clear statement of the interrelationship between related procedures.

Managing Security Patches

It is important to have a set of defined practices in place ensuring the operational security of software. Software has to be consistently updated and maintained to close vulnerabilities. The common way to do this is through security patches. These **patches** are important safeguards and are a routine part of the security maintenance process.

All software needs to be patched. Consequently, there is a continuous struggle between the software vendors and the "black hat" community to identify and patch security vulnerabilities as they are detected. The usual solution is a free security **update**. From a system management perspective, any operating system security update should be verified, tested, and installed immediately. Remember, if the manufacturer knows about the breach, then there are hackers out there with the same knowledge.

Back Up Your Data, Back Up Your Job

From a security standpoint, **backups** are important housekeeping functions. **Operational backups** have many purposes. In the case of security, they support the recovery function and backups are essential prerequisites for business continuity. It is impossible to restore system functionality to a specified recovery point, called a recovery point objective (RPO) in business continuity planning, without a record of the contents of the system. Subsequently, if the data processing facility should burn down, having a complete backup available means that the organization's information was safe, even if the equipment that generated it was lost

Of course, there are many less dramatic reasons to provide reliable backup. Hard drives are mechanical and can fail; the system could suffer a serious virus attack or other accident. In each case, the system can be rebuilt without a safe backup, it could not be restored to its most recent state.

In large installations, backups are still done using magnetic tape, since this is an exceptionally high-capacity, stable, and easy-to-store medium. Magnetic tape has always been the traditional backup medium of large DP operations and it is still a practical (although slow) way to store massive amounts of data in a low-cost, reasonably secure medium.

Early mainframes used reel-to-reel, seven-track or nine-track magnetic tape drives. However, various types of high-speed, removable, direct access drives and much greater capacity quarter-inch cartridge (QIC) tapes have superseded the older methods. Because of the much greater speed, efficiency, and ease of use of these newer technologies, there is no excuse for not performing routine backups.

Backups are based on a schedule dictated by operational circumstances. If the organization accumulates many transactions or data in a given day, then it needs a backup schedule that is executed more frequently. If it does not, then the frequency of backups can be decreased. Scheduling is a consideration because backups of even lightly loaded systems take time. Consequently, the optimum run time for backups is the middle of the night, as opposed to the middle of the day, when they would slow the operation down.

Enforcing Personal Security Discipline

Personal security **discipline** implies that the staff members routinely follow approved security procedures. Steps need to be taken to ensure that routine activities are performed in a continuous and repeatable way. This might be as simple as ensuring that workers lock the door, or it could involve more elaborate or controversial steps, such as asking individuals to monitor co-workers' activities for proper behavior. The essence of this requirement is that workspace security discipline must be established as a deliberate consistent practice.

Proper workspace security discipline is a critical function because the staff is often the first line of defense. Therefore, it is important that all staff members are properly trained and able to respond to threats as they occur. That means that personnel should at least have an established process that will let them immediately report problems.

Discipline is the key to ensuring that routine behaviors, such as backups, or hardware and software maintenance is performed. Proper discipline hinges on people understanding the value and importance of their routine security practices. Thus, the education, training, and awareness function are as critical to maintaining proper operational housekeeping as the plan that installed the function in the first place.

Maintaining Your Software

Because information processing is software-driven, proper security demands that software must be configured and operate without conflict. The visible part of that process includes activities such as ensuring that registry and file system utilities are correctly aligned and interacting properly, running disk cleanups, and performing hardware checks. However, there is also a requirement to ensure that security utilities are operating properly.

Security utilities are built into the system. That includes such things as virus and spyware checkers and spam **filters**. These are software-based applications that work with the operating system to ensure safe and secure operation of the computer. They provide essential automated security service and must be installed and configured properly.

The criteria that underlie their functioning are usually installed during the initial set-up process. These criteria are used to gauge and monitor performance, detect anomalies, and ensure consistent performance. However, their effectiveness has to be monitored and maintained continuously as an operational security function. Operational security has been traditionally responsible for maintaining this.

Making Your Software Behave

Finally, there is also a need to address **conflicts** that might arise from improper or inefficient use of the system. Software function may seem like a system engineering issue. However, conflicts between running programs degrade or destroy the overall information-processing capability and threaten the integrity and availability of the system. Therefore, it is also a security concern.

Software functionality is difficult to assure since software interactions occur within the computer itself and therefore are frequently hard to monitor. Even when everything seems to be working properly, it is still necessary to perform integrity checks on the system to assure that the registry files, applications, and system utilities are installed properly and working as designed. Because this is an integrity and availability concern, this preventive maintenance should be routinely scheduled, coordinated, enforced, and reported through the information assurance function, not system programming.

Watching Your Back

Because of their importance to information processing, it is necessary to have a set of operational procedures in place to secure application systems. The procedures include system management responsibilities such as ensuring that security functions are enabled on both user and administrative accounts at the time the application is launched, to software engineering procedures such as routine operational testing, down to the simple process of regularly ensuring that passwords are changed.

From the standpoint of the system and application control, system event logs should be checked periodically to determine whether they contain suspicious activity on that application. This is also important in order to ensure that events have been captured and logged correctly.

Disposing of Assets in a Secure Manner

In conjunction with the need to assure the security of applications, a critical part of the day-to-day integrity of information is the **secure disposal** of media. The process makes certain that unauthorized persons will not be able to read residual documentation or electronic records after they have been discarded.

It is a common misconception that electronic information is destroyed when a user deletes it. In fact, it is easy to recover deleted files from a system. Consequently, there must be rules for the secure erasure or destruction of electronic storage media. It is an important routine to clear out temporary files and temporary Internet cache files for the same reason. This part of the operational security process is easy to forget but media that has not been actively disposed of could contain important information that is easy for an intruder to access and read.

Modern shredders are an inexpensive and effective way to dispose of paper copies. In the case of especially sensitive material, some organizations make use of contracted destruction services. In addition, magnetic storage media such as floppies should be routinely degaussed or shredded prior to disposal. This should be done to the hard drives in discarded workstations if they contain classified or sensitive material.

Locking Down Electronic Office Systems

The systems associated with day-to-day business are among the most difficult to secure because so many people use them. They are, by their very function, most open to unauthorized use. As a result, frequent abuses—both inadvertent and intentional—are associated with e-mail and electronic office systems.

For example, a nationwide survey conducted in 2002 by their Department of Trade and Industry in the United Kingdom, found more e mail and Internet abuse than any other type of security violation. The difficulty with these systems is inappropriate use, which arises from a range of unrelated motives, which vary from criminal intent to innocuous and inadvertent violations.

For the operational assurance scheme to be effective, it has to ensure that e-mail and office automation systems are tightly controlled. Unlike other systems, the first step in establishing that control is not the performance of a classic risk assessment. Instead, there is a need to develop and formalize an organizationally sanctioned statement of what is and is not **acceptable use**. This is called an **acceptable use policy** and it serves as the formal basis for subsequent control.

Because it is central to the entire control scheme, the acceptable use policy has to be communicated to everyone within the organization from executive managers to line workers. The definition of acceptable use varies from organization to organization, but all personnel in an organization must be made aware of how it is defined. That baseline then serves to enforce compliance and it dictates the sanctions that will be taken for violators.

Defining Good Security Practice for an E-Mail System

The unique problem with e-mail is its volume. In the good old days, security people had to ensure that sensitive physical documents were not leaving the building. Now, just by hitting the send key it is possible for people to transmit information that they would need a forklift to deliver if it were physical documentation.

Defining, communicating, and enforcing good security practice in the daily operation of the e-mail system can prevent most violations. For instance, most companies allow staff to use the e-mail system for "reasonable" personal purposes. The requirement is to have a formal yardstick available for each employee to use to judge what "reasonable" means. The monitoring of acceptable use is frequently used in larger organizations and can be embedded in a software utility.

Chapter 5 Review

Chapter Summary

- Security of operations is responsible for maintaining continuous security functioning within the routine daily operation. In addition, it ensures that an appropriate set of best practice policies and procedures is properly implemented and followed.

- Security of operations is built around behavioral rather than technical practices, which are aimed at monitoring and controlling the performance of specific operational tasks that the organization considers important.

- The role of security of operations is to maintain the operational procedures needed to secure network and application systems and media.

- The security of operations function is a management process, not a technical one. It is embodied through a procedural plan like other critical management functions.

- The correct operational response is always initiated by a plan or protocol.

- The point of operational response is to contain the harm from an incident and prevent its reoccurrence.

- Operational housekeeping safeguards the day-to-day information processing operation of the organization.

- Good standard housekeeping practices are essential in preventing the most common types of potential security problems.

- Housekeeping procedures should be expressed in a procedure manual for the operational security function.

- All the workers in the organization have to be given individual responsibility for the integrity of their own workspace.

- **Controlled space** describes the commitment to ensure that each worker's individual space is routinely secured.

- Operational maintenance is aimed at ensuring that the system is properly tuned.

- It is necessary to follow operational procedures in order to secure application systems.

- It is essential to develop and formalize a detailed, organizationally sanctioned statement of what is and is not acceptable use.

Key Terms

acceptable use (131)
acceptable use policy (131)
accountability (122)
active incidents (125)
assess (116)
architecture (121)
assessment (121)
backups (129)
baseline (119)
benchmark (116)
configuration management (125)
conflicts (130)
controlled space (132)
corrective action (113)
discipline (129)
evaluate (116)
filters (130)
incident reporting (123)
incident response team (IRT) (123)
monitoring (121)
operational backups (129)
operational housekeeping (113)
operational procedures (121)
operational response team (ORT) (123)
patches (128)
policy and procedure manual (121)
process (113)
secure disposal (131)
update (128)

Key Term Quiz

Use terms from the Key Terms list to complete the following sentences. Not all terms will be used.

1. The rules for operational housekeeping are contained in a _____ .

2. Identifying and cataloguing all relevant areas of concern is called _____.

3. There are essentially _____ types of risks: _____,_____, _____, _____, _____.

4. Maintaining the system so that its components are running within correct operating parameters is called _____.

5. The purpose of _____ is to describe the proper way to operate office systems.

6. ___ _____ procedures are necessary because electronic information is not erased when it is deleted

7. Rapid response to incidents is the responsibility of the _____ or the _____.

8. _____ is one of the most important practices that underwrite the Continuity process.

9. The primary mechanism for capturing the status of an item under configuration control is the _____.

10. _____are the way that a vendor ensures that the security of the software product is maintained as _____ are identified.

Multiple Choice Quiz

1. Operational maintenance ensures that the system is:
   A. operated properly
   B. properly tuned
   C. kept spotless
   D. accessible

2. Active incidents require a:
   A. plan
   B. schedule
   C. timely response
   D. document

3. Operational security is less involved with strategy and more with:
   A. isolation
   B. detection
   C. long-term
   D. day to day

4. The operational procedure manual is usually built around a:
   A. check list
   B. strategy
   C. control
   D. enforcement mechanism

5. A baseline is a report on the current security:

   A. plans

   B. status

   C. model

   D. procedures

6. The evidence about the need for a change must be communicated in simple terms because:

   A. people making the decision are not technical

   B. people making the decision are not very smart

   C. people making the decision want simple answers

   D. feasibility rests on a simple communication

7. The role of the security roadmap is to:

   A. document the security plan

   D. document the security requirements

   C. document the security situation

   D. document the security functions

8. The overall duty of security of operations is to maintain alignment between security goals and:

   A. the security situation

   B. the security requirements

   C. the security objectives

   D. the security communication

9. Applications are important elements of security functioning because they:

   A. do the actual information processing work

   B. perform routine functions

   C. ensure backups are performed

   D. are part of system engineering

10. The role of the baseline manager is to:

    A. record and manage the assurance

    B. record and ensure the day-to-day functioning of the software

    C. record and manage the overall process of configuration management

    D. record and ensure the status of formal baselines

Essay Quiz

In your own words briefly answer the following questions:

1. Why is security of operations useful to overall information assurance?

2. Backups are an essential part of operational security. What other element(s) of information assurance do they support? Are there other activities within operational security that are part of other aspects of the information assurance process?

3. How would you differentiate operations security from incident response? Is there a difference?

4. How does discipline relate to secure housekeeping?

5. Why should the issue of free patches or fixes be controversial? What element of the overall IT/organization process makes it that way?

6. Why is there a need to perform routine sensing of the environment? How does the regular staff figure into this?

7. What is the role of operational testing? Why is it needed to ensure security?

8. What is the function of the verification function in configuration management? What would happen if this function was not performed?

9. Why is a corrective action function necessary? What would happen without one?

10. What are the vulnerabilities associated with secure disposal? Name the two considerations that must be kept in mind when doing secure disposal?

Case Exercise

Complete the following exercise as directed by your instructor:

Heavy Metal Technologies (HMT) is a defense contractor headquartered in Huntsville, Alabama. HMT was recently contracted by the Army to upgrade the fire control system for the MH64-D Apache Longbow attack helicopter. This is a high-security project. All legal, regulatory compliance, fiscal, and DoD reporting work will be handled at the Sunnyside Street Main building. This is the nerve center of the HMT operation and it is the workplace for the executive managers. It provides the management oversight services for the other units as well as interfacing with DoD in terms of the details of management and accountability.

It is the central repository of all administrative data for the entire corporation. It has a large and highly professional mainframe-based IS unit as the central part of its operation. In addition, it provides the operational support for the administrative systems at the remote HMT corporate sites. Finally, the project management staff is located there. When DoD projects are ongoing; the DOD has representatives headquartered in this building. The layout of Sunnyside Street Main looks like Figure 5-3.

Because the contracted enhancement is so important to the continuing success of the main ground attack helicopter program and thus because of its importance to national defense, the Army wants a total commitment from HMT that the operational integrity,

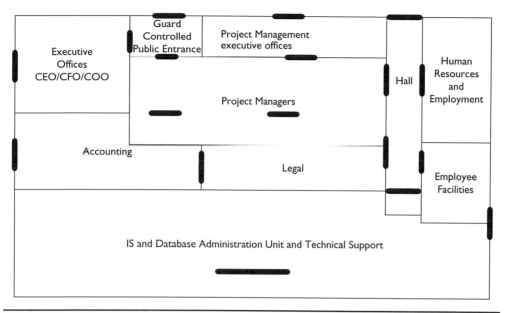

Figure 5-3   Building layout

confidentiality, and availability of the project information will be assured. From this case make a list of 14 operational countermeasures that may be developed to address potential area of operational security concern. Include specific controls to address the following:

- The Army requires a procedure to ensure that control of IS functioning will be continuous.

- The Army requires a procedure to ensure that the control processes will be cost efficient.

- The Army requires a procedure to ensure that all storage and transport of data will be secure.

- The Army requires a procedure to ensure that all security incidents will be responded to effectively.

Ensuring Controlled Access

In this chapter, you will learn:
- The fundamental principles of access control
- How to structure and conduct the authorization process
- Common access control models

To make a system secure, it is essential to regulate access. Consequently, the entire range of information assurance countermeasures—from physical and personnel, to software and network security—involves some form of *access control*.

The term "access control" describes the regulation of interaction between *subjects* and *objects* within a given environment. The degree of regulation will determine how comprehensive and robust the overall protection scheme will be. The countermeasures within that scheme must be able to guarantee that access to the resources of the system is granted to properly authorized individuals and entities.

The definition of what a legitimate subject might be can be very broad. Generally, with information assurance the subjects are *people* or *processes*. Processes can be either *managerial* or *technical*. Objects can be anything appropriately accessed by a valid subject. Therefore, in the case of information, objects might be anything from physical space, to computer files, to a hardware device.

Principles of Access Control

In the largest sense, access control is a multifaceted process that regulates the right of access to a computer, its attached network, or the physical facilities. Implementing and managing the access control process can be a very complex activity. The access control process centers around three principles. These are

- **Identity**—Asserts and verifies the user's identity
- **Authority**—Authorizes user access privileges
- **Accountability**—Tracks user actions, analyzes and reports

The principle of **identity** is composed of two functions. These are **identification** and **authentication**. Their purpose is to assert the subject's identity. Once a subject's identity has been established, the **authority** principle determines the **access rights** that have been assigned to that identity.

Authorization underwrites access based on the rights assigned to each individual subject. That is, authorization allows access only to those areas of the system, resources, and operations that the subject is permitted to access. Authorization enforces organizational authority by implementing only those rights granted to each subject.

Accountability enforces authority. It tracks usage to ensure that access rules have not been violated. The other function of accountability is to ensure that undesirable incidents are identified and responded to appropriately.

Identification and Authentication: Establishing Identity

The identification function establishes the identity of every person or process that seeks access to organizational assets. Once identity is confirmed, the authentication function confirms that it is valid. These two functions hinge on a single requirement. They both rely on the ability to discern and validate unique properties of the subject, which are not shared by any other person or thing.

With information assurance, the chief means of making that differentiation is through something that the subject alone knows something that the subject solely possesses or a unique characteristic of the subject. As such the three customary factors for establishing identity are

- Something you know (a password for instance)
- Something you have (a credit card for instance)
- Something that you are (a physical attribute)

Passwords: Something You Know

Passwords are the simplest and most economical means of identifying an individual subject to the system. Identity can be established by asking subjects to provide an answer to a question that only that individual should know (challenge and response). With information assurance, the typical means of implementing that is by assignment of a unique subject ID and a password. Then the access control system simply asks the subject to present those credentials every time identification is needed. This is an efficient and relatively straightforward way of proving identify. This is why most identification processes rely on good **password management**.

Passwords are easy to assign and maintain and, if proper information assurance practice is followed, they can be very effective. A capable password management system will consistently

- Allow legitimate users to directly register for access
- Allow forgotten passwords to be authenticated and reset by user
- Allow IT support staff to authenticate callers for password management

- Synchronize users across a range of platforms (also known as single sign-on)
- Provide for immediate cancellation of passwords of individuals who leave the organization

The Problem With Passwords: Memory and Usage Vulnerabilities

In simple systems, the goals of a properly managed password scheme are easy to achieve. However, commercial systems are usually very large and highly complex. The size and complexity creates a serious problem with password management because the subject is forced to keep track of many unique identifiers to navigate between different applications or to move from platform to platform.

Thus, the information assurance and security vulnerability most often associated with multiple passwords originates in the limitations of human behavior. It is practically impossible for an individual to remember all the passwords that they will need to navigate a complex system. Therefore, they will write them down somewhere. If that is done, it is a serious violation of information assurance or security protocol, because the minute that a unique password is committed to paper its secrecy is potentially compromised.

Short passwords are easily compromised by brute force, guessed or obtained through surreptitious means. Therefore, a system can be compromised through a legitimate password that has been gotten through illegitimate means. The tendency for the secrecy of passwords to degrade over time implies that they should not be allowed to remain valid for any significant period. Nevertheless, users will have the same memory problems with a single constantly renewing password as they would if they had to juggle multiple ones, and they will take the same avenue to address that problem, which is writing them down.

As such, in order for passwords to remain a feasible information assurance mechanism, something has to be done about the problems associated with limitations of human memory. The two most common solutions to this problem are the **single sign-on** and the **one-time password** embedded in hardware. We will provide a short discussion of these here, since they are significant current trends in password management.

Single Sign-On: Coordinating Identities Across Platforms

Single sign-on is an important concept because it coordinates passwords across a range of platforms and applications. Thus, it is an extremely effective way to authenticate a subject in the sort of user situation typified by modern system architectures.

In an organization with multiple systems and even authentication points within a single enterprise system, single sign-on can be a very cost-efficient method of password management. As the old adage says, "Time is money." With single sign-on, users authenticate once to a central authority. In effect, they log on once to the entire system and access additional authorized resources based on that single authentication. Figure 6-1 illustrates this.

Single sign-on systems operate by storing every subject's login ID and password on an authentication server. Single sign-on is directly linked to the applications (objects) that the user is permitted to access. Thus, authorized applications for that ID and password can be launched through a single identification and authentication process.

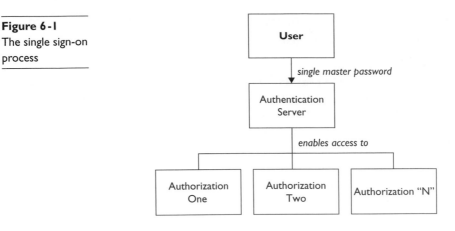

Figure 6-1
The single sign-on process

Users can create stronger, more complex patterns, to serve as the single sign-on ID because there is no need for multiple passwords. The system has to track only one identity and password combination, making it easy to enforce information assurance criteria across the entire range of managed objects. Finally, a single sign-on approach allows for centralized administration of passwords, so they can be renewed more frequently.

Single sign-on has had limited success in large organizational environments due to the high costs of deploying and integrating the complex software functionality required to seamlessly implement it. Additionally, there are other drawbacks to its use. For example, single sign-on becomes a point of failure if a single sign-on password were breached; since that compromised password would allow unauthorized subject access to all authorized system resources. In addition, because accesses are controlled through a supporting secondary server, a failure of that server affects the availability of system services for the entire organization.

One-Time Passwords: Shortening the Period of Use A password is an excellent way to control access as long as nobody but the user knows what it is. However, history shows that most passwords are easy for unauthorized people to obtain and use. One-time password schemes are innovative in the sense that they allow the password to be more robust because the actual password function is handled in hardware.

One-time passwords reduce the unauthorized access problem by authenticating only the current session. They are changed after every use. The one-time-use rule prevents third parties from returning to the system later to use a fraudulently obtained password. Figure 6-2 illustrates this.

Since issuing and using a one-time password is a very complex task, the actual process is token or hardware-based where the password resides within an object such as a smart card, a USB flash-drive, or even a memory chip built into the sending device. The actions to change password, such as one-time pad encryption, take place between the object and its target, and are transparent to the user.

Figure 6-2
The one-time
password

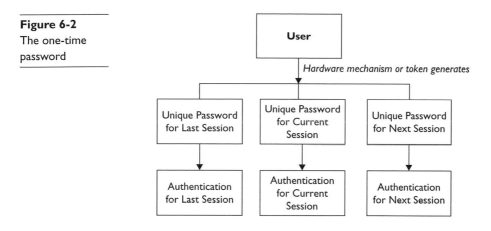

The primary advantage of a one-time password is that an eavesdropper (man-in-the-middle) who might capture it could never use it again. However, the eavesdropper could capture the remaining session connection and view data, so there still is an obligation on the part of users to control their current access.

Token-Based Security: Something You Have

Another way to establish identity is by asking for something that only a valid user should possess. The most common example of this method is the ubiquitous driver's license. Identification and authorization devices presented at the time of access are normally called **tokens**. The token functions in the same way as a key works with a lock. That is, the keys in your pocket belong only to you, and therefore they should only open your locks. Debit or credit cards are another example of a token-based access device.

In secure settings, the most frequently used authentication device is the *smart card*, or *swipe card*. Smart cards are credit-card-sized plastic tokens, which are kept attached to a cord worn around the subject's neck or clipped to their clothing. These cards work in conjunction with a "reader." They have an embedded semiconductor chip that accepts, stores, and sends information. The card can keep personal information with a high degree of security and portability.

Token-based authentication devices provide secure enterprise-wide access control. However, because of their utility and size, smart cards and security flash-drives are applicable not only there. They provide tamper-resistant storage and transport for critical data and they can be used in encryption systems, to store digital keys, and to create one-time passwords.

Theft and loss of tokens are the chief vulnerabilities associated with using smart cards as the only means for access control. Even if the cards are hung around their neck, people will lose them, which means that they will be prevented from accessing the system. Worse, if an unauthorized individual finds the card, the finder will be able to gain access under the legitimate user's authorizations.

That is why smart cards and other authentication tokens are combined with passwords to increase the strength of their protection (two-factor authentication). If a party only knows the password but does not have the token, or vice versa, they will be excluded. If they have both, however, access will be granted.

Biometrics: Something You Are

A third method of authentication uses something that is unique about the individual. Authentication using physical characteristics is known as *biometrics*. In *biometric authentication*, the subject asserts identity by presenting a unique personal characteristic such as a fingerprint to a reader.

Biometric authentication access control processes are highly secure because they confirm identity by means of physical characteristics that cannot be duplicated such as fingerprints, hand geometry, iris patterns, retinal scans, facial recognition, or behavioral characteristics. Biometric authentication is very effective, since physical characteristics might change slowly over time but they are impossible to lose.

The problem with biometric technology is that it is still in its infancy and since it is dependent on advanced processing capabilities, it can occasionally fail. When it comes to the identity process, false positives and negatives are possible failures. False positives inadvertently allow unauthorized individuals to access system resources while false negatives deny authorized people access. As the technology improves, biometric authentication methods can be expected to become more popular.

Combining Approaches: Multifactor Authentication

The combination of two or three different approaches to create a single access control function is called **multifactor authentication**. With the advent of biometrics, this is an important aspect of access control.

The most secure way to ensure sound authentication processes is by using multiple authentication mechanism at the same time. Multifactor authentication increases the level of security, because more than one factor would have to be compromised in order for an unauthorized individual to gain access.

Your typical automatic teller machine (ATM) provides a good example of simple multifactor authentication. Obviously, the security of your bank accounts is important to you and so access to those records is secured by more than one factor. To access your account you must present a valid token (the ATM card). However, ATM cards can be lost or stolen and so you are required to know something that only a valid user would know. That is the role of your personal identification number (PIN). Access to your accounts is only granted once the validity of *both* the token and the password is confirmed.

A biometric factor might be added to increase security further. That would make the authentication three-factor, rather than two-factor. Three-factor authentication is a common requirement in highly secure settings. In that instance, the subject would have to present a valid authentication token, tied to a PIN. In addition, the subject would validate their identity by means of a personal characteristic such as a fingerprint. Since it is very difficult for an unauthorized subject to compromise all three factors at once, this usually ensures secure access control.

Approaches for Establishing Identity in Cyberspace

Since identities also have to be established in cyberspace, there has to be a means to uniquely identify and authenticate the identity of electronic communications. The most common approach to this is the use of the digital signature and the **digital certificate**. These two methods have become the primary mechanism for establishing identity and authenticating electronic communications.

Digital Signatures: Asserting Identity Using Cryptography

The ordinary means of authenticating the integrity of an electronic message is the digital signature. These "signatures" are generated from the message itself by mathematical means. The process is discussed at much greater length in Chapter 13.

Although in August 2005 the The MD-5 algorithm was reported to be broken, it is the most widely used mechanism for generating a digital signature. MD-5 produces a unique 128-bit "signature" value from any message of arbitrary length. Because that value is substantially smaller than the text, it is often called a *message digest*. Moreover, since the value is calculated from an encryption key that only the user possesses (called a *secret key*), the digest can be attached to a message to prove the identity of the sender.

Message digests also ensure non-repudiation of creation. The receiver knows the message is from the sender because the digest can be validated mathematically against the message. If the digest values calculated by the receiver are the same as the values sent with the message, then it was not altered in transit. If they are different, then the message was compromised.

Digital Certificates: Utilizing Trust Infrastructures

A digital certificate can also be an attachment to a message. That is third party confirmation that verifies that the message did indeed come from the entity it claims to have come from. It may also contain a key to encrypt further communication. Because electronic messages are important in today's commerce, this certification process is supported by large commercial entities commonly called Public Key Infrastructures (PKIs).

PKIs provide the administrative infrastructure to support the encryption needed to produce digital signatures and digital certificates. They do this by verifying, enrolling, and certifying users. A digital certificate is a public document that contains information that identifies a user, as well as the user's encryption key, the validity period for the certificate and other information. The digital certificate is unique to the individual user. That allows identity to be validated based on the ability to present a valid certificate.

PKIs serve as the trusted third party in any secure electronic transaction or communication process. PKIs usually entail a Certificate Authority (CA), a key directory, and associated management rules. Their function is to verify and register the identity of users through a Registration Authority (RA). Once they are registered, each user is given a digital certificate. That certificate is maintained through a CA. A number of companies offer PKI services. One of the largest and most popular of these is VeriSign; however, there are numerous other commercial PKI vendors.

Mutual Authentication: Ensuring Identity During Transmission

Mutual authentication is a more sophisticated approach to electronic message authentication. The term describes a process in which each side of an electronic communication verifies the authenticity of the other during the transmission of the message. Mutual authentication is a critical aspect of access control because it ensures the integrity of the transmission process as well as the message sent.

Many security breaches occur because one of the parties to the transmission is not properly authenticated. This failure could allow an unauthorized subject to gain access during the transmission process under the guise of a legitimate sender. Because they are tied so closely to Internet communications, **mutual authentication** processes are especially important when remote clients are attempting to assert their identity to servers.

There are a number of possible approaches to securing electronic communications, some dating back to the 1970s. Right now, two products are used for mutual authentication. These are Kerberos and CHAP.

Kerberos   The Kerberos network authentication protocol is an example of mutual authentication. Kerberos uses encryption, so a client can prove its identity to a server and the server can in turn authenticate itself to the client within a secure transaction.

The basis for identity in a Kerberos environment is a ticket granted by a separate authentication server. An authentication server is a system designated and agreed on as trusted by both the client and the server that the client is trying to access. PKIs provide this function. The client presents the ticket to the server that it wishes to access as a proof of identity. The receiving server knows that the incoming message is authentic if the ticket is valid. The tickets are time-stamped so attempted reuse will not be successful. Figure 6-3 illustrates this process.

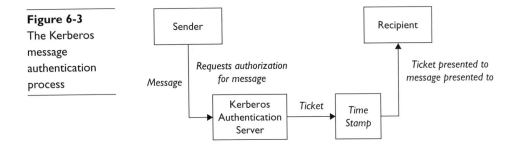

Figure 6-3
The Kerberos
message
authentication
process

CHAP   Challenge Handshake Authentication Protocol (CHAP) is another example of mutual authentication. CHAP provides authentication services across a point-to-point link employing the Point-to-Point Protocol (PPP) part of the Internet.

PPP does not maintain authentication after the link has been established, which could create a vulnerability should a third party enter the session after the original authentication has been confirmed. Instead, CHAP uses a periodic authentication process to ensure that only authorized parties are involved in the transmission. Figure 6-4 illustrates this.

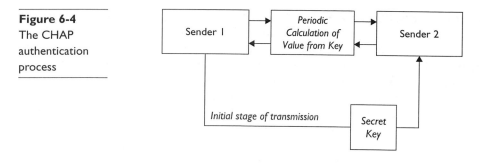

Figure 6-4
The CHAP
authentication
process

Periodic authentication uses a secret value only the client and host share. The shared value is sent to the client when the transmission is opened. The client periodically calculates the appropriate response and sends it to the host. The host compares the response it received with the correct value. If it matches, the session continues. If the two values do not match, the connection is terminated.

Authorization: Controlling Access

Once subjects have been identified and authenticated, they are granted access. Upon entry into the system, the subject will be authorized to perform a specified set of functions. The authorization is based on the level of trust that has been assigned.

Authorization asserts specific rights to use the system, which have been granted to an individual (subject). The term describes both the process of granting those rights and the process of ensuring the subject's access to the authorized objects. Therefore, in some respects the authorization function might be considered the most important aspect of the larger requirement for access control.

In large multi-user systems, authorization describes the formal management process by which access rights are granted to subjects. In this part of the process, users' specific rights of access are established and enforced. These rights are referred to as **permissions** or **privileges**, and are based on the concept of "trust." *Trusted subjects* are allowed access to specified objects. Authorization involves the determination that an authenticated subject has attained the required level of trust to access a given object. Untrusted or unknown subjects will be denied access until authenticated.

The determination, assignment, and monitoring of access has to be based on some systematic point of reference. In the case of information assurance or security, that reference point is called a **security domain**. A security domain incorporates all related objects, with common protection needs, into a single manageable entity. The real-world term for a security domain is a clearance or sensitivity level.

Each individual clearance or sensitivity level is composed of a highly interrelated set of subjects and objects. As such, every sensitivity level encapsulates a common set of information assurance or security properties, which are guided by a single information assurance policy. Sensitivity levels constitute logical categories of protection. Operationally each sensitivity level is assigned a level of required trust needed to allow access to the objects placed within it.

In application, sensitivity levels are arranged hierarchically based on the degree of trust required to access them. Every level implements well-defined rules and parameters to guide that access. These rules are designed to limit access only to those subjects with the right identify. Confirmation of a valid identity will allow a subject right of access to the data or system resources that lie within a particular clearance level.

Since admission to each sensitivity level is based on the identity of the subject, the most critical requirement for control of access is that the subject's identity is accurately determined and its authenticity validated. As such, the overall access control process is composed of identification and authentication functions, which assert that a subject's identity is valid, based on individual characteristics, or membership in various pre-defined groups. Once a subject's identity is validated then access privileges are *authorized* and *monitored*.

Types of Permission: Methods for Granting Access

In modern operations, authorization is established by three generic methods:

- Policy-based access control
- Discretionary access control
- Mandatory access control

These three different approaches serve as the basis for implementing practical access control. In operation, each of these has a distinctive focus and different level of complexity. We are going to discuss each of these in detail since these methods provide an excellent summary of the practical issues associated with access control.

Policy-Based Access Control

Policy-based access control is the most frequent example of a policy-based access control method is the **access control list (ACL)**. An ACL is a list that specifies the authorized users of the system and their access rights. The list identifies not only the individual subject, but also the access that that subject has for each particular object. Access control lists (ACLs) regulate access to each software object within the system. Figure 6-5 illustrates this.

The list is automatically referenced each time a service is requested. It controls the subject's access to the objects and services by subjects. By specification of the individual access rights of each person on the list, ACLs can control the access permissions of multiple users or groups. Although ACLs provide the most popular means to protect information stored in a computer, they are not limited to computer resources. A variation of an ACL is the checklist that the guard uses to control the physical access of individuals to the facility. The advantage of an ACL is that it allows the administrator to designate access rights separately, for every individual. Access is based on the permissions granted to the individual subject.

From an information assurance standpoint, the flexibility that an ACL provides is greatly preferable to the other simple alternative, which is to maintain one level of permission. A one-size-fits-all approach is dangerous because all users of a single permission level system have the same rights to access resources, independent of their security status.

Figure 6-5
Access control
lists

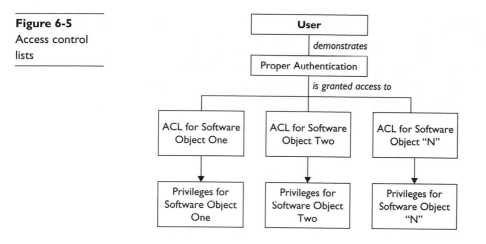

The security permissions of the night janitor would be the same as those of the CEO. An ACL allows the organization to make the proper differentiations of the rights among the various types of users.

Discretionary Access Controls

Discretionary access control (DAC) is by far the most common model for access control in large systems. In systems that employ DAC, the owner or manager of each data file assigns users' rights. DAC lets the owner of a file or physical object selectively grant or deny access to users.

DAC centers on the assignment of privileges. The owner of the protected object decides which users get access, and what access rights they can have. DAC uses identity and the associated "need to know"—which every subject, process, and/or group must have—to regulate the type and level of privilege that each entity receives. This assignment applies to a given object at a given time. Figure 6-6 outlines this.

Figure 6-6
Discretionary
access control

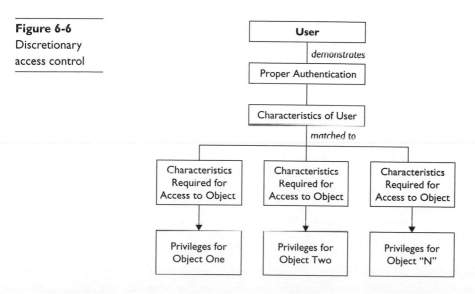

The controls are discretionary in that privileges are assigned based on subject characteristics. Therefore, that assignment may not necessarily be direct. In the case of group permissions, every member of a group assumes the access rights that the group has been given. So in effect, the individual's rights in this case are derived from the group. The access rights of all of the subjects in an organization will vary based on the groups that they are assigned.

The owner of an object assigns permissions for that object to the subject or the user group to which the subject belongs. In order to maintain flexibility, the discretionary access process also includes an "other" category. Rather than using a group assignment of privilege, the owner specifies the permissions for each individual by using an access control list.

That gives the owner explicit control over the rights of additional users and groups who might be transitory within the system. A good example of a transitory group are contractors. Using this technique, access rights that are granted to project managers in the organization can be temporarily extended to cover the project managers of subcontractors working on the same project. That of course assumes that these managers have been given the same security clearances as the prime contractor's staff. The authentication characteristics in that case would be both membership in the project management group as well as their assigned project's status. Then, once outside people stop working on a project, their permissions can be revoked using the same process.

Typically, discretionary access control is implemented by three different approaches. These models allow the owner of information to flexibly assign privileges and evaluate access rights based on three global criteria. These criteria are *role*, *content*, and *time*. These are not mutually exclusive factors. Therefore, in actual application these three approaches can be combined to support an extremely efficient and highly secure specification of the privileges that will be granted users in the organization.

Role-Based Access Control   **Role-based access control (RBAC)** is a common form of discretionary access control. It is a specialized technique involving the assignment of access permissions to objects that are associated with given roles. RBAC is an effective means to secure access in large or complex networks because of its simplicity and flexibility. Figure 6-7 illustrates this.

Figure 6-7
Role-based
access control

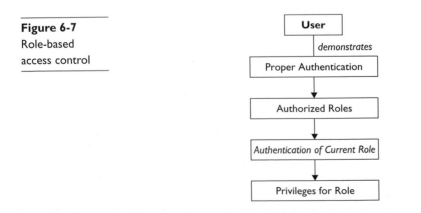

The principle behind an RBAC system is that access permissions are assigned based on the specific roles that the user fulfills. In application, users are associated with a set of roles they may perform. Those roles are assigned the specific access permissions necessary to perform the duties associated with them. Thus, the subject's access rights to objects are determined strictly by the role he or she fulfills at a particular point in time.

Users and programs (subjects) are granted permission to access system objects based on the duties that they perform, not by their security classification, which makes the process of assigning the authorizations more straightforward. In addition, it allows for greater flexibility in the day-to-day management and enforcement of the protection policies.

Individual workers can be assigned to roles and easily reassigned from one role to another without modifying the fundamental security control structure of the system. Those roles can be modified and permissions can be granted or revoked centrally in response to the changes in technology and processes of the organization.

Content-Dependent Access Control As its name implies, **content-dependent access control** uses information that is provided by the object being accessed and is considered a form of discretionary access control. This approach is commonly used to control access to record-intensive applications, such as databases. The system determines the rights of individuals attempting to access the record and then permits them to access only the content that their privileges allow.

For instance, the various roles in a hospital see different types of patient records. Hospital administrators see the financial and treatment history of the patient without seeing the actual medial records. Doctors, on the other hand, are permitted to see medical information without the attendant financial data. Ward clerks would be limited to nothing more than information about what patient is in what room. The point of this example is that, while the source record is a single entity, the content is accessed based on the security rights of the individual seeking access.

The same rules apply to the right to access and execute certain processes (objects). For instance, only doctors could execute a process that performs a medical diagnosis, while only administrators could run the financial reconciliation program—but not the patient diagnostics. Ward clerks, in contrast, would not be permitted to run processes. A constrained interface, which is presented by the program itself, controls who can run what. For instance, the doctors' role would have a button on the interface that would let the doctors run patient diagnostics, whereas administrators would have one that lets them perform the financial operation. Ward clerks would not have buttons on their interface. Clearly, it is critically important to ensure that people in dissimilar roles do not have access to each other's interfaces.

RBAC is effective if it is based on a capability table. These tables of identifiers specify the access rights that are allowed a subject possessing that capability. In a capability-based system, access to protected objects is granted if the user possesses a capability (ticket) for the object. An *Authorization Table Matrix (ATM)* manages the assignment of access privileges. The advantage of this approach is that it achieves a greater level of granularity in the authorization process and it is both simple and intuitive. The disadvantage is that the process itself is machine-intensive, so this type of access control has to be supported by a very high level of computer performance.

Temporal Access Control   This type of control is also a form of discretionary access control. It is temporal, in the sense that events, rather than type of specific designations, drive it. Consequently, it is dynamic. Whether access is granted, and the type of access given, is determined by such things as the time of day, the point of origin, how many times the individual identity attempted to access the system, and even the number of password attempts.

For instance, if an individual user attempts to log on five times and fails, the access control system should be instructed to shut off the port until the identity of the person is confirmed. This is one of the oldest forms of access technology with roots in the early mainframe days. However, there are other elements of real-time evaluation that can be included in this approach that make it among the most advanced and high-tech approaches.

The system continuously monitors user actions against set policies. For instance, there might be certain IP accesses that are automatically denied based on time of day or where they originate. There might be a policy that says users may not execute a given application more than twice without resubmitting their password.

The advantage of such an approach is that it allows the organization to anticipate and protect itself from some types of known undesirable events, such as hacker attempts late at night. The disadvantage is that the chain of events that lead to a given decision is not always predictable. This creates a high potential for false positives and negatives in a context-based system. That is why it is often used in conjunction with other approaches, such as RBAC.

Mandatory Access Control

Mandatory access control, which is also known as **MAC**, restricts a subject's access to objects based on a set of security attributes. MAC mechanisms are used when the information assurance policy of a system dictates that protection decisions must not be decided by the object owner or that the system must enforce the protection decisions over the wishes or intentions of the object owner. MAC is a required function for some levels of the Rainbow Series, which is a series of government specifications for how to secure critical systems, and for Common Criteria conformant systems. However, because of the complexity of assigning rights, it has not been widely used outside of the federal government and the military

Security attributes are attached to the subject, system processes and files or other objects. MAC prevents users from sharing objects arbitrarily and uses a specific set of policies or security rules to define the sharing of data within the organization. These rules list subjects and state the access permissions that are allowed for each subject. For instance, the system can be set to ensure that "Only users with a 'classified' access level can access classified data." The assignment is always enforced in addition to discretionary controls that be implemented for groups within that clearance level. Figure 6-8 illustrates this.

Access is controlled automatically by the system using set criteria. For instance, someone with a top-secret clearance could only read a document in a file that is labeled "top secret," or any lower classification. In addition, the system actively controls what can

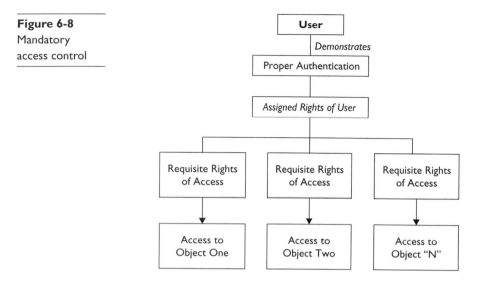

Figure 6-8
Mandatory
access control

be done with a given protected object. For example, even if subjects were permitted to read a top-secret document, the system would not allow them to grant access to another subject else unless the recipients were appropriately cleared.

Having the appropriate level of clearance does not mean by itself that a subject will always be allowed to view a top-secret object. The concept of "need to know," which is actually a form of discretionary control, is used to determine who is allowed to access a given piece of information at a specified time. The user has a label or clearance and an object has a label or classification, which are compared to determine whether access to the object is allowed.

MAC also associates the programs a user is running with his or her session security level. This is based on the level of clearance of the user and/or the sensitivity label of the program. MAC permits access to information, or programs and devices at the same or lower level only. To underwrite and enforce information integrity requirements MAC will also prevent users from writing to files at lower levels.

In application, MAC cannot be overridden without special authorizations or privileges. Unlike discretionary access controls, the programs that a user employs cannot modify these controls. Instead, MAC is enforced by the system. The operating system uses characteristics the user cannot control, like IP address, to decide about the actual authorizations. Then it uses such things as clearances and sensitivity labels to enforce the appropriate security policy.

Real-World Access Control: Automating the Process

It is impossible for humans to monitor accesses in a complex system environment. The actual monitoring is done by automated means. The most common mechanism for establishing an automated monitoring capability is through a reference monitor implemented either operationally or within the operating system.

Operationally, an automated system is usually the only alternative because of the volume and complexity of real-world traffic. In the same way as the operating system, this reference monitor keeps and reference a valid list of authorized identities and their associated individual permissions and respond to each correctly. This is always a problem because users can approach the system under different identities. All of these might be legitimate depending on their role and the time that they access the system.

For example, the CEO would possess that specific identity and the associated permissions. That same person might approach the system under the identity of an employee, a customer, and even an outside visitor (for a phone number, for instance). These roles are appropriate, but have different access rights and permissions that must be assigned at the time access is requested. This has to be determined based on the identity that is presented, irrespective of the person who is presenting it.

Real-time and dynamic allocation of access privileges is an important system capability because in a complex organizational environment, there may be hundreds of people in different roles, including executives, employees, vendors, customers, and other external visitors, seeking access at any given time. The situation can involve internal and external processes and applications. That accesses must be managed securely in real time for the system to meet its required confidentiality, integrity, and availability objectives. This means that the system must be able to distinguish instantly and correctly assign the rights for each individual identity, as well as determine what each can and cannot access.

Automated **identity management** systems involve an integrated set of processes and technologies bundled into a continuously evolving solution that must be coordinated and deployed across the entire enterprise in order for it to be effective. These systems require five basic conditions:

- Identity infrastructure
- Privilege setting
- Identity reference
- Enforcement of privileges
- Continuous maintenance

Identity Architecture: Establishing the Identity Infrastructure

The identity infrastructure affects the key processes, applications, and information assets of the organization. This infrastructure is a complete and coherent set of processes for identity management, which must be linked directly to organizational goals, information assurance policy, and the business case. Therefore, identities, roles, sensitivity levels, and access rights must be established.

Privilege Setting: Establishing the Rights of Each Identity

Managers can then define the permissions and security settings appropriate for each individual and role within the corporation. Once the infrastructure is established, the organization has to define and enforce the privileges explicitly assigned to each person or process seeking access.

This involves an analysis and assignment activity to designate the data, applications, and services that each individual identity (subject) will be permitted to access, along with the operations that they will be allowed to perform. It includes specifying a procedure for maintaining the correct permissions over time, as well as selectively revoking those privileges when required. The actual determination of privileges is part of the Personnel Security function, which will be discussed in much greater depth in Chapter 7.

Identity Reference: Automating the Process

It is the unenviable task of an access control system to distinguish and validate the identity of every attempt to access protected information. In commercial applications, this involves high volumes and the decision about each request has to be made on a split-second basis. Once required permissions are established and assigned, a central reference function has to be established to maintain them. The aim of that function is to let the access control system determine the privileges of anybody seeking access to the system in the shortest time possible

This automated function is implemented through a *reference monitor*. The monitor is an operating system function that is interposed between all subjects seeking to use the system and system objects. It permits or denies access to objects based on the subject's level of trust. The monitor employs an authorization database to store the criteria to make decisions. This requires storing individual subject's information and establishing an automated means to perform the look-ups. This database then becomes the driver for the access management function.

The reference monitor supports two classes of functions: *reference functions*—for accessing authorization information, and *authorization functions*—for making changes to the authorization database. A properly functioning reference monitor involves three factors.

1. Completeness—The reference monitor must be invoked for every reference of an object by a subject.

2. Isolation—The reference monitor and its database must be protected from unauthorized alteration.

3. Verifiability—A critical design issue. If the reference monitor is not well structured, simple, understandable, and small, it cannot be fully analyzed, tested, and verified to determine if it performs its function properly.

In complex organizations, development of the reference database is likely to be an involved engineering project, which can be very resource-intensive. However, an effective reference monitor is perhaps the single most essential requirement for implementing real-world access control. It is also one of the most frequent points of failure, since identities can be compromised in many ways.

Compromise through spoofing involves the unauthorized use of legitimate identification and authentication data to gain access to a system and its information. E-mail spoofing, IP spoofing, piggybacking, and mimicking are all recognized examples of this. Spoofing is not a modern problem; everybody is familiar with classic tales where characters disguise themselves as other people to gain unauthorized access. It is just that the information age has made detection of spoofed identities all the more difficult.

Enforcement of Privileges: Guarding the Door

Enforcement of privilege is the primary driver behind any automated access control system. It is in effect the real-time element of the access control process. Privileges are granted or denied based on the system's ability to authenticate the identity of an individual (subject) seeking access to an object. This has to take place at the point where access is requested. Enforcement techniques can vary widely both in their complexity and in their level of rigor. However, this is always facilitated by automation of the actual privilege assignment process.

Continuous Maintenance: Keeping the System Current

The final function in identity management involves the ability of the system to modify user identities and access rights on a continuous and dynamic basis. This involves maintaining correct and valid interconnections among the various user identities and the applications, data and services associated with them.

There always is the probability of both false positives and negatives during the authentication process because of the many guises that an individual might use to approach the system. Therefore, this maintenance process has to be performed on a continuing basis. The generic term for this maintenance activity is account management.

Setting Up the System: Account Management

Account management is the day-to-day face of any automated access control system. This may be something as simple such as allocating passwords to users or as complex as storing their fingerprints for biometric readers. Account management ensures that identity data are accurate and up to date and that the monitoring and enforcement system is operating as intended.

The term **account management** describes the process by which user access is administered and supervised. The role of account management is to link user identities to the specific applications, databases, and services they are permitted to access. It is not possible to identify and authenticate user identities and their associated access rights without building an effective account management function into the access control system. The account management function is built around three related processes:

1. Creation of new system access
2. Modification to system access
3. Termination of system access

Account management creates, maintains, and deletes user accounts, as well as manages changes in access rights. In addition, user authentication procedures and tokens, such as user name and password, are assigned and administered by this operation.

Account management is the function that implements the personnel security process. It does that by detailing each individual's access rights in an account management structure, which is the central element of the identity reference function. Because IT personnel requirements change frequently, the specific account information stored and retrieved in that account management structure has to be reconfigurable, based on the specific situation. For example, if the security requirements are raised for a particular application or database, it might be necessary to increase authentication factors and sign-on protocols to the user account structure accessing it. If the change is significant, it may be necessary to delete some users because they no longer have the proper clearances.

Proper account management implies that a subject's access rights are both dynamic and extensible. That is, the privileges that are assigned to an individual should be evaluated at execution time to grant or revoke access to specific objects within the system. This run-time decision is based on factors such as time of day and origin of request. For instance, the account management function could be configured to make it possible for a user ID to gain access during working hours, if the request is from a client located inside the building. It should prevent access from the same ID—or at least set off an alarm—if the access request originated at 3 A.M. from a foreign country.

The process of evaluating access rights dynamically is usually an automated function within the account management structure that flags attempts that do conform to parameters set for a given account and responds accordingly. In addition, good account management ensures that users who are no longer part of the organization are barred from access. As we will see in Chapter 7, this is a critical requirement, as there is nothing more dangerous than an unhappy ex-employee, who still has full access to the system.

Intrusion Detection: Backstopping Access Control

Access control is backstopped by intrusion detection. Since intrusion detection is an operational necessity for incident response, that function could have been discussed in Chapter 5. On the other hand, intrusions are a dangerous type of access and they are focused differently than routine attempts to gain access to the system. Therefore, we have chosen to include intrusion detection with access control.

Overall, the information assurance has four general goals.

1. **Preventive**, where the goal is to avoid the occurrence
2. **Detective**, where the aim is to identify characterize the occurrence
3. **Corrective**, which seeks to remedy the circumstance
4. **Compensating**, where alternative control is provided

Intrusion detection is a purely detective activity, while general access control involves all four of these functions. However, intrusion detection is an essential pre-requisite for overall access control assurance because it is the function that detects access attempts that are out of the ordinary.

The distinction has to be kept in mind between the measures needed to identify and authorize routine access, versus those required to detect a potential attack or exploit. In essence, access control is responsible for identifying and authorizing users as they routinely attempt to access the system. Since the vast majority of these access attempts are from legitimate sources, access control serves a primarily management function.

However, there are also occasional attempts from clearly illegitimate sources. These must be actively controlled because they are more often than not launched with malicious intent. Therefore, it is essential to have an access control system with a robust intrusion detection function built into it.

Intrusion Detection Systems: Keeping the Perimeter Secure

Intrusion detection systems are designed to sit on the perimeter and detect, characterize, and report on any suspicious attempts to access a protected space. Thus, intrusion detection systems are built around boundary sensors.

A boundary sensor is a software utility that is located at the perimeter of the protected space and monitors traffic into and out of the system to identify potential attacks or malicious attempts to intrude. The term that is commonly used to describe this utility is **intrusion detection system (IDS)**.

However, there are also utilities called *intrusion prevention systems (IPSs)*. These are different from intrusion detection systems in that they have the ability to both monitor access as well as respond appropriately in the case of an attack.

Types of Intrusion Detection: Automated Versus Human Centered

Intrusion detection can be approached in two ways depending on how timely the necessary response. If an instantaneous response is needed, intrusion detection is usually automated. However, if time will allow for a more considered response, intrusion detection can be built around a human-centered audit process.

The most common detection system deployed in commercial environments is the intrusion detection system because of the short time horizon involved in network attacks. The function of an IDS is to identify and isolate attacks. It does that by monitoring access attempts or assessing other types of performance data. There are two types of IDSs:

- **Network-Based IDS (NIDS)**—These detect attacks by capturing and analyzing network packets. NIDSs monitor network packets and traffic on transmission links in real time. They analyze electronic protocols and other relevant packet information and can send alerts or terminate an offending connection, if a problem is detected.

- **Host-Based IDS (HIDS)**—These operate on information collected and analyzed by an individual computer system. HIDSs reside on a host and detect apparent intrusions through the audit function. They accomplish this by examining event logs, critical system files, and other auditable resources to identify unauthorized change or suspicious patterns of behavior. Properly configured, HIDS will communicate an alert when unusual events are discovered. Multi-host HIDSs are capable of auditing data from a number of hosts at the same time.

Common Network-Based IDS (NIDS)   There are five common approaches to network-based intrusion detection. These are

1. Pattern matching
2. State matching

3. Analysis engine

4. Protocol anomaly

5. Traffic anomaly

The first two rely on patterns within the data. The other three are driven by anomaly identification and statistical process control techniques. The simplest approach by far is the **pattern-matching IDS**.

Pattern-Matching IDS

Pattern matching offers a simple defense. It scans incoming network packets for specific byte sequence signatures stored in a database of known attacks. They function in the same way as a standard virus checker. They can identify and respond to common-place attacks using data from known approaches.

Because pattern-matching IDSs have to use previous patterns to respond, an attack can be modified to avoid detection. Therefore, it is essential to update the attack signature file frequently.

State-Matching IDS

A **state-matching** approach is more reliable than pattern matching because it scans for attack behaviors in the traffic stream itself rather than the presence of an individual packet signature.

As a result, state-matching IDS can detect an incoming attack that is spread across multiple packets. The IDS requires frequent updates of the behavioral signatures to be effective because it still relies on known patterns.

Analysis Engine Methods

Analysis engine methods are data based. At their heart, they are anomaly detection systems. That is, they use anomalous behavior, such as multiple failed logons or users logging in at strange hours, or unexplained system shutdowns and restarts, as the basis for their response. **Statistical anomaly-based IDSs** are a common example of this method.

Statistical anomaly-based IDSs get around the limitations of signature files because they have a heuristic engine. They are capable of making decisions about access events based on prior experience. Analysis engine techniques develop baselines of normal traffic and then center their alerts on deviations from these baselines.

These systems can identify previously unknown attacks as well as such dynamic attacks as denial of service floods because anomalous behavior serves as the basis for the baselines. The problem with these systems is their complexity. They are complex and can be difficult to tune properly. Because they are reliant on their baselines to judge responses, it always has to be ensured that the system has a good picture of what the "normal" traffic environment looks like.

Protocol Anomaly-Based Methods

Protocol anomaly-based systems are another form of analysis engine. They are also heuristic, which means they are capable of using feedback from prior attempts to refine their approach. In some respects, they are very close to the pattern-matching IDSs; however, the anomalies they seek are defined based on an international rulebook.

That is, anomalies in a protocol anomaly-based system are identified from criteria that have been established by the Internet Engineering Task Force. Because these systems are based on standard definitions of what constitutes a deviation from normal, they can identify specific types of attacks without a signature and do not have the problems of an analysis engines. However, the protocol analysis modules that drive these systems take a lot longer to deploy than a signature file and must be monitored continuously.

Traffic Anomaly-Based Methods

Traffic anomaly-based systems are analysis engines. These systems watch for unusual traffic activities, such as a flood of TCP packets or a new service suddenly appearing on the network.

These types of IDSs can identify unknown attacks and denial of service floods, but they suffer from the same problem as the statistical anomaly-based approaches with the requirement to ensure that the "normal" traffic environment is properly understood. Table 6-1 summarizes the five common network-based methods for intrusion detection.

Method	Based On	Analyzes	Advantages	Disadvantages
Pattern Matching	Signature files	Byte sequences	Simple	Must update signature frequently
State Matching	Signature files	Attack behaviors	Detects more sophisticated attacks	Must update patterns frequently
Analysis Engine	Anomaly	Anomalous patterns	Can identify previously unknown attacks	Complex and difficult to manage
Protocol Anomaly	Anomaly	Standard criteria	Identifies attacks without signatures	Protocols take too long to deploy
Traffic Anomaly	Anomaly	Anomalous Behavior	Can identify previously unknown attacks	Complex and difficult to manage

Table 6-1 Common Network-Based Methods for Intrusion Detection

Host-Based IDS (HIDS) HIDSs do their work through the audit function and monitoring audit trails. An audit trail is a record of system activities usually generated by the system. Alternatively, it can be kept in paper logs maintained external to the system. The audit itself can be performed to capture data generated by system, network, application, and user activities.

Audit trails alert the human staff to suspicious activity. The outcome of this alert is usually further investigative activity. The aim is to secure all evidence needed to understand intruder activity and provide information for proceeding with remedial action. The types of events captured in an audit trail include

- Network connection event data
- System-level event data
- Application-level event data
- User-level event data
- Keystroke activity

The primary issue arising from audit trails is the volume of data that must be examined for this understanding to be adequate. This is based to some extent on the degree of event filtering or the clipping level that is imposed on the detail captured in the logs. There are automated auditing tools, which can alleviate the volume demands.

However, whatever the approach to address the volume problem, the most important success factor in auditing is to establish and maintain a set of best practices to ensure the process itself is secure and being executed in the most effective possible manner. That includes such things as securing the logs from unauthorized access, preventing the logs from being disabled or cleared, protecting them from unauthorized changes, and storing and archiving them securely.

Security Assessments: Penetration Testing

No discussion of intrusion detection would be complete without a visit to the topic of **penetration testing**, which is called "pen" testing by people in the field. Pen testing denotes activities undertaken to identify and exploit security vulnerabilities. We have chosen to discuss this topic here because penetration testing is a common means used in industry to test the access control system.

Penetration testing is often referred to as "ethical" or "samurai" hacking. It is the act of simulating an attack on the system at the request of the owner. To be ethical, pen testing must adhere to clearly defined methods and goals, which are established up front. To be effective, it must use the methods or techniques of the adversaries.

Pen testing evaluates system security by attacking it. It is aimed at the security conditions that are the most common targets of intruders such as the Internet connection or the intranet, extranet and remote dial-in connections. The types of pen tests include

- **Zero-Knowledge**—where the tester has no relevant information about the target. It is performed by an independent third party.
- **Partial-Knowledge**—where the tester may have some information about the target.
- **Full-Knowledge**—the tester has intimate knowledge of the target environment.

Pen-testing methods are based on four activities. The first of these is *discovery*, which is where the target is identified and documented. This is followed by *enumeration*, where the tester attempts to gain more knowledge about the target through intrusive methods. *Vulnerability mapping* takes place after that, and is where the tester maps the profile gained in the test environment to known vulnerabilities. Finally, testers attempt to gain *user and privileged access* using the knowledge they have gained.

The final phase in the process is the documentation of findings in the form of a final report. The results of this report can help an organization to identify

- Vulnerabilities of the system
- Gaps in security measures
- IDS and intrusion response capability
- Whether anyone is monitoring audit logs
- How suspicious activity is reported
- Potential countermeasures

Various types of penetration-testing strategies can be used. Those strategies include:

- *Application security testing,* where the goal is to evaluate the controls and the application's process flow;
- *Denial of Service (DoS) testing,* where the purpose is to assess a system's susceptibility to attacks that could render it inoperable
- *War dialing,* where the purpose is to identify, analyze, and exploit modems, remote access devices, and maintenance connections.
- Where they are in use, there also might be *wireless network penetration* testing, which seeks to identify security gaps or flaws in the design, implementation, and operation of wireless technologies.
- However, by far the most common of these techniques is simple *social engineering,* where the tester uses social interaction to gather information in order to penetrate the organization's systems.

All of these can originate from both external and internal sources. The procedures that are performed from the outside seek to exploit the Internet or extranet connections. Internal procedures focus on identifying anomalies in the internal IT environment.

That includes *blind tests,* where the tester uses only publicly available information about the target. The most rigorous of these types of tests is the double-blind approach. This obeys the rules of a blind test except the security staff is not notified that it will be conducted. Double-blind testing is an effective method of testing the operational monitoring, incident identification, incident escalation, and response procedures of the staff. Finally, there are *targeted tests.* These involve both the internal IT team and penetration testing team, who work together to identify or resolve some focused objective or problem. This requires a preidentified issue.

Remember that penetration testing may involve techniques that are unethical or illegal in certain jurisdictions.

Common Access Control Models

Finally, any discussion of access control should describe the common models that are used to implement the process. In practice, access control models enforce policies.

The access control method adopted must be specifically designed to embody the organization's overall approach to security. This approach is driven by the organizational requirements, or the business case. The access control system enforces those requirements by controlling access to information based on the security requirements. In most situations, this is based on limiting the flow of data between clearance levels.

There are three types of models in common use in the industry today. These are all designed to specifically implement and enforce a desired level of confidentiality or transactional integrity:

- **Confidentiality/Classification-based models**—Bell-LaPadula
- **Integrity-based models**—Biba
- **Transaction-based models**—Clark-Wilson

Classification-Based Security Models: Bell-LaPadula

A common confidentiality/classification-based security model is **Bell-LaPadula** was developed by the United States government in the 1970s. The Bell-LaPadula model is a framework for managing different classification levels intended to limit the disclosure of information between dissimilar levels.

Because Bell-LaPadula uses a hierarchical classification structure, this type of model is known as a multilevel security system. The model uses the classification level of the data and the access rights of the subject to decide what data a particular subject can access and what it can do with it. Figure 6-9 illustrates this.

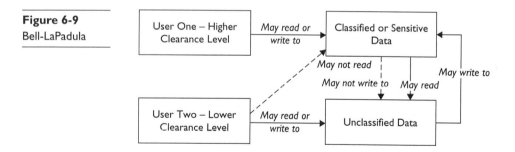

Figure 6-9
Bell-LaPadula

The aim of Bell-LaPadula is to make it impossible for data to be disclosed to a subject at a given security level without the appropriate security clearances. Because it revolves around classifications of sensitivity and clearances, it is commonly used by governmental or military organizations. However, it can be used in any hierarchical security system. It employs both mandatory and discretionary access control mechanisms to implement its two security rules—"no-read-up" and "no-write-down."

The model centers on the definition of a set of subjects along with data objects and their relative security levels. Authorization for access rights between a subject and a given object is based on their individual security levels. A security level is a security classification and the set of objects associated with it. One security level may be considered higher than another if, and only if, its sensitivity requirements are greater than the other level and its object categories include every object in the lower-level category.

The classification level of the object and the access rights of the subject determine what data the subject is authorized to access and then independent from that, what they may legitimately do with it. The actions that under a DAC system subject can perform with a given piece of data are

- Read-only, which means that the subject can only read the object
- Append, which limits the subject to writing but not reading the file
- Execute, which allows the subject to execute an object but not read or write
- Read-Write, which allows the subject full permission to the object

When Bell-LaPadula is applied, the security levels that determine which one of these actions is performed are *unclassified, confidential, secret,* and *top-secret.* Two rules define the mandatory access control policies for Bell-LaPadula: the simple-security property, which states: "A subject can only read an object if the security level of the subject is higher than or equal to the security level of the object (no read up)." The second is the "***" property (pronounced "star property"), which dictates that "A subject can only write to an object if the security level of the object is higher than or equal to the security level of the subject (no-write-down)."

The logic behind these two rules requires some explaining. There are five assumptions that underlie them. First, there is the assumption that there cannot be a breach of confidentiality if a subject at a higher-level "reads-down" to objects that are either equal to or lower in security level. Consequently, the highest security level in a Bell-LaPadula system will always have (at least) read-only access rights to all objects in the system.

The second assumption is that a lower-level subject should never be allowed to "read up" to higher-level objects. This is simple common sense. There would be no security if low-level subjects were allowed to read objects that required a higher level of security.

The third assumption is that it should be possible to provide the greatest degree of access (for example, read-write) when the security requirements of both the subject and the object are aligned at the same level. Again, this is simple logic. If both subjects and objects have the same level of sensitivity, there is no implicit vulnerability in the access. Furthermore, it would be dysfunctional, from the standpoint of operational efficiency to limit accesses between entities that are by definition working at the same level of sensitivity.

The fourth assumption is that a lower-level subject should always be able to "write-up" to objects of equal or higher levels of classification. That is because, by definition, the subjects at the higher level should be able to read material that has been classified at a lower level.

Finally, the last assumption is that a higher-level subject should never be permitted to "write-down" to lower-level objects. That is because those lower-level objects are by definition not at the same level of security as the higher-level subject. Therefore, it would be possible for sensitive material to be leaked to a lower level from a higher source. Therefore, writing to the lower level could pose a breach of security.

There are a number of problems associated with Bell-LaPadula. These are primarily related to its hierarchical classification structure. The model does not apply in realms where hierarchical security classifications are not in use, which describes many conventional commercial operations. Second, if these rules are rigorously enforced (by automation, for instance) subjects at higher levels are precluded from EVER passing information down to an object at a lower level, even though this might be necessary. The most significant problem, though, is the fact that the model only ensures confidentiality. It does not specifically ensure integrity and so it does not guarantee that the data that is passed is reliable. However, there are models that are focused on integrity that DO allow that.

Integrity-Based Security Models: Biba

The **Biba** security model is also from the 1970s. It is a formal approach centered on ensuring the integrity of subjects and objects in a system. However, integrity levels are used to define the access rights, instead of security classifications. Integrity levels indicate the level of "trust" that can be placed in information kept at different levels. Thus, the primary objective of Biba is to limit the modification of information, rather than its flow between levels.

Bell-LaPadula is useful for an organization like the military, where the preservation of confidentiality at all levels is the prime directive. Biba is more applicable in business organizations because it is aimed at ensuring the integrity of the data that is passed. Figure 6-10 illustrates the Biba approach.

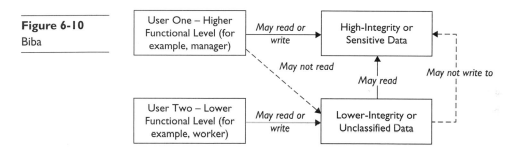

Figure 6-10
Biba

Biba operates on two simple rules, which are specifically designed to ensure the integrity of the data at a given level of trustworthiness—not its confidentiality. The assumption behind Biba is that data with a higher integrity level is more accurate or reliable than data of a lower integrity level. The first rule in Biba is that a subject with a lower classification cannot write data to a higher classification. The second rule is that a subject with a higher classification cannot read date from a lower classification.

You will notice that both of these are an exact reversal of the rules embodied by Bell-LaPadula. That is because Biba is intended to ensure that cleaner higher-level entities cannot be corrupted by potentially dirtier data from lower level entities. To ensure the integrity information, it may only flow downward.

This reverse orientation does not make sense at first, but the logic behind it is impeccable. For instance, when you go to the bank, you do not ask the janitor what your account balances are; you ask the teller. Moreover, if you have questions about some particular bank policy, you ask the bank manager, not the teller. That is because in each case the people providing the information have to be in the right position to answer the question. The janitor is not authorized to answer questions about your accounts; if he did, you would likely get incorrect information, because he is not at a high enough level in the bank to access valid data.

Likewise, the teller can only tell you what the balances are, not what bank policies made them that way. The same is true for writing data. You would not write a check and give it to the janitor. That is because the janitor is in no position to record the transaction accurately. Accordingly, in order to ensure the integrity of the data, both as it is read and written, a subject should never read or write data at a lower level of reliability. Because it deals with the flow of information through different level of classification, like Bell-LaPadula, the **Biba model** is called an *information flow model*.

The first two rules in Biba's model are the opposite of the Bell-LaPadula model in that what it enforces are "no-read-down" and "no-write-up" policies. It also embodies a third rule that prevents subjects from executing programs of a higher level. This third rule states "A subject can only execute a program if the program's integrity level is equal to or less than the integrity level of the subject." This rule ensures that data modified by a program will only have the level of trust (integrity level) that can be placed in the classification level of the individual who executed the program.

If this were not the case, potentially corrupt data created by a program after reading data of a lower integrity level could end up being recorded at a higher level of trust then it should.

Combining Biba and Bell-LaPadula provides both integrity and confidentiality in a single system.

Transaction-Based Security Models: Clark-Wilson

Unlike the other two, the **Clark-Wilson** security model uses transactions as the basis for its access control decision making. Like Biba, this model is designed to ensure the integrity of data. However, Clark-Wilson uses the personnel security concept of separation of duties to ensure that authorized users do not make unauthorized changes to data. To do this it defines two levels of integrity (rather than four). These are

- **Constrained data items (CDI)**—which are the controlled assets
- **Unconstrained data items (UDI)**—which are not deemed valuable enough to control

The handling of constrained data items is subject to integrity controls, while **unconstrained data items** are not controlled. The model then defines two types of processes to control CDIs:

- **Integrity verification processes (IVP)**—which ensure that the CDI meets specified integrity constraints.
- **Transformation processes (TP)**—which changes the state of data from one valid state to another.

In concept, the data in a **Clark-Wilson model** is not actually manipulated by the user. A trusted transformation process (TP) does the actual handling and, accordingly, the access control centers on those TPs. **Transformation processes** are software functions, or other types of trusted procedures whose only role is to ensure that the subject has the proper classification.

The **validation** of integrity is done to ensure that the data item being modified is valid and that the results of the modification are valid. Thus, the user's access to the transaction processes is that is restricted. In that respect, the ability of a user to perform certain activities is what is actually constrained. That/allows a greater level of precision in assigning access rights. Figure 6-11 illustrates this.

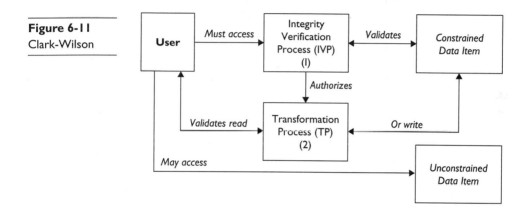

Figure 6-11
Clark-Wilson

Critical functions can be split into multiple transformation processes using this model. In this way task can be divided into different parts and different subjects can each do different things. The idea is to assign and control the necessary transformations in such a way that control over that function is not given to a single individual, which is the essence of the separation of duties principle that we will discuss in Chapter 7. This ensures that multiple individuals will be required to perform certain critical tasks.

Chapter 6 Review

Chapter Summary

- All of the operational processes, like physical security and network security, have to establish the specific access rights of authenticated parties.
- The concept of access denotes the ability of a subject to interact with a target object.
- Access control enforces authorizations.
- Identification asserts the user's identity.
- Authentication verifies who the user is and whether access is allowed.

- Authorization defines what the user is allowed to do.

- Accountability tracks what the user did and when it was done.

- Access controls define what actions a user can perform or what objects a user can have access to.

- Authentication is the function that ensures that the proper information gets to the right object to permit or deny an access request.

- There are three generic factors that be considered during the authentication process. These are: something you know, something you have, and something that you are.

- Authorization is the right that is granted to an individual to use the system and the information that is stored on it.

- In modern operations, the authorization process is embodied through four generic control approaches: policy-based access control, discretionary access control, mandatory access control, role-based access control.

- Account management describes the active process by which user access is operationally administered and supervised.

- The role of account management is to link substantively user accounts to the specific applications, databases, and services that they are permitted to access through this process.

- Identity management is perhaps the single most essential requirement of account management because, in order for the system to provide proper authorization, it has to be able to distinguish and validate the identity of every attempt to access a protected object.

- Identity management embodies five generic principles: infrastructure, privilege setting, identity reference, authentication, and continuous maintenance.

- Intrusion detection systems are the perimeter sensors in access control systems.

- There are two main types of IDSs: network-based IDSs (NIDSs), which detect attacks by capturing and analyzing network packets; and host-based IDSs (HIDSs), which operate on information collected and analyzed from within an individual computer system.

- Network-based IDSs monitor network packets and traffic on transmission links in real time. They analyze protocols and other relevant packet information and can send alerts or terminate an offending connection, if problems are detected.

- Host-based IDSs reside on a host and detect apparent intrusions. They do this by scrutinizing event logs, critical system files, and other auditable resources.

- Pen testing describes the activities that are undertaken to identify and exploit security vulnerabilities.

- The purpose of pen testing is to assess directly system security by attacking it.

- There are three types of standard models that are currently in common usage in the industry. These are: classification-based models, integrity-based models, and transaction-based models.

- The most common classification-based security model is the Bell-LaPadula model.

- The Bell-LaPadula model employs two security rules—"no-read-up" and "no-write-down."

- The Biba Security Model is a formal security approach that is centered on ensuring the integrity of subjects and objects in a system.

- The first rule in Biba is that a subject with a lower classification cannot write data to a higher classification and the second rule is that a subject with a higher classification cannot read date from a lower classification.

- This is an exact reversal of the rules embodied by Bell-LaPadula.

- The Clark-Wilson security model uses transactions as the basis for its rule making.

- Clark-Wilson uses the personnel security concept of separation of duties to ensure that authorized users do not make unauthorized changes to data.

- To do this it defines two levels of integrity: constrained data items (CDI) and unconstrained data items (UDI).

Key Terms

access control list (ACL) (148)
access rights (140)
account management (156)
accountability (140)
analysis engine methods (159)
authentication (139)
authorization (140)
Bell-LaPadula (163)
Biba model (166)
Clark-Wilson model (167)
digital certificate (145)
discretionary access control (DAC) (149)
identification (139)
identity management (154)
intrusion detection system (IDS) (158)
multifactor authentication (144)
mutual authentication (146)
one-time password (141)
password management (140)

pattern-matching IDS (159)
penetration testing (161)
permissions (147)
policy-based access control (148)
privileges (147)
role-based access control (RBAC) (150)
single sign-on (141)
state-matching (159)
statistical anomaly-based IDSs (159)
tokens (143)
traffic anomaly-based (160)
transformation processes (TP) (167)
unconstrained data items (UDI). (166)
validation (167)

Key Term Quiz

Complete each statement by writing one of the Key Terms from the list in each blank. Not all terms will be used.

1. One password to a range of applications and platforms is a _____.

2. Assigning access based on identity is a form of _____.

3. There are essentially _____ types of intrusion detection: _____ and _____.

4. Biometric devices confirm identity based on _____ and _____.

5. In access control, the goal of _____ is to designate what the subject has a right to access.

6. _____ access control is based on classifications

7. _____ is the access control model that ensures the integrity of data

8. Rights to access information are assigned based on the user's level of _____.

9. Unlike the other two, there are three types of _____.

10. Classifications are based on _____.

Multiple Choice Quiz

1. Discretionary access control:

   A. lets the owner define the access

   B. cannot be changed

   C. prevents arbitrary sharing of information

   D. can be shared

2. Bell-LaPadula:

   A. is based on transactions

   B. prevents leakage between security levels

   C. is not hierarchical

   D. prevents writing data up

3. Access control implements this type of control:

   A. compensating

   B. detective

   C. preventive

   D. corrective

4. The practical outcome of the identification process is the _____ security principle.

   A. authentication

   B. authorization

   C. access control

   D. accountability

5. Accountability is based on security:

   A. plans

   B. analyses

   C. models

   D. procedures

6. Pen testing involves:

   A. writing instruments

   B. livestock

   C. hacking

   D. security evaluations

7. Multifactor Authentication will involve:

   A. no more than one factor

   B. no more than two factors

   C. no more than three factors

   D. no factors at all—that is why it is called multifactor

8. Protocol based anomaly methods are based in:

   A. statistics

   B. standards

   C. protocols

   D. anomalies

9. An authentication token is:

   A. something you have

   B. an access control device

   C. a small coin

   D. a means of monitoring security accesses

10. Temporal access control is based on:

   A. time

   B. time of occurrence

   C. access control lists

   D. mandatory privileges

Essay Quiz

In your own words answer the following questions briefly:

1. Why is the identity management function necessary?

2. Bell-LaPadula is hierarchical. What does this achieve and what is it based on?

3. Differentiate content-dependent versus context-dependent access control methods. What are the advantages of each?

4. How does account management relate to the overall access control process? Specifically, what would be missing without it?

5. Why are analysis engine methodologies potentially more effective than signature file approaches?

6. Why is social engineering part of pen testing? Why is it important there?

7. What is reason for content based access control techniques? Why is it particularly important for large corporations?

8. What is the purpose of a classification scheme? How does it apply to access control?

9. Why are transaction processes controlled rather than data itself in the Clark-Wilson model?

10. Where does the "no-write-down" rule apply? What does it ensure?

Case Exercise

Complete the following case exercise as directed by your instructor:

Heavy Metal Technologies is a defense systems contractor headquartered in Huntsville, Alabama. It has been granted a contract that involves work with highly sensitive national security data. Because the work is so important to national defense, the Pentagon wants a total commitment from HMT that access to the project information will be highly controlled. As the security analyst for this project, please suggest a substantive area of access control to address these five concerns:

- The Pentagon requires a procedure to ensure that access to applicable IS functions by identities at all levels of clearance will be controlled.

- The Pentagon requires a procedure to ensure that the integrity of the network systems will be maintained.

- The Pentagon requires a procedure to ensure that all people attempting to address the system will be authorized to do so.

- The Pentagon requires a procedure to ensure that all intrusion attempts will be identified.

- The Pentagon requires a procedure to ensure that all third-party work will be maintained at the same level of control.

Personnel Security

In this chapter, you will learn about:

- Ensuring secure behavior
- Controls for the personnel function
- The role of human resources in ensuring personnel security
- Contractor control

If current statistics are an indication, most security incidents do not originate with technology. In fact, security problems do not even originate within the IT function. The people who operate the technology are the main source of security breaches and violations. People cause information assurance programs to fail.

Predictability is the key. The information assurance process involves technology, processes, and people. Any of these can cause a breakdown in the security of assured systems. Nevertheless, technology is predictable and well designed processes are, at least, consistent. On the other hand, human **behavior** is hard to predict and control.

Worse, security systems are typically designed to detect and prevent attacks originating from outside the perimeter, not within. Frequently there are no substantive safeguards set to observe the insiders and employees. It takes only one disgruntled worker with system-level access, or a system manager with a financial or a drinking problem, to compromise the entire security infrastructure of the organization.

Consequently, the disastrous effects of employee-based actions should encourage organizations to have mechanisms in place to ensure the secure behavior of the employees. Commonly accepted practices used to achieve that goal are the topic of this chapter. This chapter offers a comprehensive explanation of the problems the organization faces and the steps that must be taken by the organization to protect its information against employee misconduct and mistakes.

First Steps First

This section presents several critical issues that have to be mastered before thinking about establishing a **personnel security** process. It starts with a discussion of how threats associated with human behavior affect the overall security of an assured system and it concludes with issues regarding continuous execution of the process.

Origination of Threats

Threats that center on people can be classified into two categories, *outsider* and *insider*. Threats posed by attacks from outside the organization are commonly recognized. When the average manager thinks about the kind of people who threaten their system, they think about hackers and cyber-criminals.

Statistically, malicious actions by an organization's own personnel are more likely to occur and difficult to prevent. Consequently, insider attacks pose a more serious threat to information assets than actions by outsiders. Insider attacks include such things as *fraud, misuse, theft*, and *human error*.

Access and Security Control: Establishing Secure Space

Control of human behavior begins by establishing secure space defined by perimeters. Perimeters are important because they define the boundary where behavior must be controlled. The area of control is called **secure space**. Secure space implies that approved controls have been established to ensure the confidentiality, integrity and availability of the information assets. Once secure space has been established, the trustworthiness of every person who crosses the perimeter must be evaluated to determine the access rights and ensure correct behavior.

Strict perimeter control is important because every individual who seeks access can be granted only the rights matching their individual level of trust. For instance, a visitor would not have the same access privileges as the Chief Executive Officer. However, once both are in the secure space, it is difficult to know what rights each individual has. Therefore, to ensure appropriate behavior within a secure space, privileges should be assigned specifically; badges should be visible and clearly reflect the access rights. These badges should not be worn outside the secure space since it signals to outsiders the wearer's access rights. In physical security, assignment and monitoring of privileges is usually done by people. While in cyber-security, that function is the job of the system's controls.

Secure space is both logical and physical. It is important to understand that distinction because the physical boundaries of secure space are three-hundred-and-sixty degrees, while the cyber-boundaries are established by the system connection points.

Those connection points might be hard to secure but at least they are known. The problem is that, it is critical to ensure timely access from cyberspace while everyone approaches the system anonymously. Each connection point has to be able to grant appropriate access, in the shortest possible time and with high reliability. Unlike physical security, this requirement applies to everyone every time that person approaches the system. The requirement includes people who could be easily authenticated or who are known to be trustworthy, the CEO of the organization for instance, but who must be reliably authenticated and authorized every time they attempt to cross the system perimeter or **boundaries**.

Access control across the physical boundary is not as time-dependant as it is with cyber accesses and once the access rights of a person are validated they can later be validated by tokens like badges. Unless barriers are established and closely monitored, anybody can cross the physical perimeter at any point. Therefore, access to secure physical space is controlled by restriction mechanisms that force all individuals seeking access to be cleared at a checkpoint.

These old-fashioned approaches are resource intensive. As a result, the physical security perimeter has to be feasible within available resources. Accordingly, the physical security perimeter is normally limited to the space that the security team feels they can efficiently ensure with passive boundaries and checkpoints.

Because of the issues involved in controlling human access across two perimeters, cyberspace and physical, it is important to have a set of rules to define and enforce how people gain access to secure space. Those rules have resource implications and will dictate how personnel policies will be set.

Ensuring Continuous Practice

Information assurance requires the reliable and repeatable performance of approved security requirements. To be effective, the assurance process must ensure continuous and disciplined execution of all security tasks. That means that all employees in the organization must be motivated to ensure they will follow correct procedure continuously.

The requirement for **disciplined practice** implies that attention must be paid to motivation. The value of executing day-to-day security tasks consistently must be communicated clearly and understood broadly to be certain that each member of the organization will carry out their information assurance and security duties. That is true in the case of practices that add to individual workload—security requirements are frequently viewed this way.

Therefore, people have to know both the importance and reason for their expected behavior. That insight motivates employees to perform their information assurance and security tasks reliably and continuously. **Motivation** requires **awareness**, and nobody can be fully aware without understanding why specific behaviors are required.

Ensuring Personnel Security Behavior

Personnel security behavior falls into three categories: *routine activities, operational functions,* and *management responsibilities.*

Routine activities are actions that an individual takes to secure the space that they control from any threats arising during everyday work. Routine activities involve such things as safe housekeeping procedures designed to protect information assets, computer equipment, or media from theft. They can also involve technical duties, such as ensuring that the operating system and network connections are properly configured.

Operational functions are the activities that are performed to ensure the security of the entire system during day-to-day operation. These activities are not a matter of preventive maintenance. Operational functions involve such things as regularly monitoring staff activities to ensure that prescribed work practices are carried out, and continuous analysis of system operations to ensure that the system is being used safely and securely. This involves a more complicated set of behaviors than the individual, personal ones.

Finally, there are overall management responsibilities. The security operation must be managed properly to be effective. That requires a broader set of security considerations. Actions that fall into this category guarantee that the information assurance and **security strategy** is implemented properly. These actions range from simple tasks that establish the supervision needed to ensure that individuals and organizational units follow required security procedures, to complex tasks, such as developing strategic plans aimed at securing the organization's entire array of information assets.

Documenting Security Procedures

The way that an organization establishes a repeatable set of security procedures is through documentation. Documentation ensures that security activities are recorded and properly understood. The mechanism employed to communicate procedures to the entire organization is the personnel security manual. That manual specifies the actions required for ensuring personnel security.

Once the manual has been prepared, it is circulated to everyone in the organization. The manual serves as a basis for feedback as well as a mechanism to build and reinforce awareness of what has to be done. Each individual in the organization should be able to contribute to the creation of security procedures. The personal participation and subsequent buy-in will underwrite and motivate proper execution.

Every employee in the organization must be informed about what behavior is expected. If adequate awareness has been ensured, then the organization can hold individuals personally accountable for the proper performance of their assigned information assurance and security tasks.

Accountability does not imply that every individual should be forced to memorize the **procedure manual**. It means that all members of the organization must be aware of the recommended practices that apply in their particular case. The organization must ensure that all information assurance activities, or security management procedures, are performed satisfactorily in the employees' daily routine.

A procedure manual also documents the corrective actions to be taken if a problem occurs. The recommendations for corrective action can be provided only for known problems, but since those are the most likely to occur, the recommendations will usually ensure that a solution is available.

For example, if there were frequent instances of network failures, the availability of a well-understood recovery procedure would ensure that the network was restored to operation in the shortest possible time. At a minimum every documented procedure should specify the

- Required steps to be taken and by whom
- Expected outcomes and some way to determine that they have been achieved
- Interfaces with other security procedures

Assignment of Individual Responsibility

Because consistent performance of security tasks is important, selected managers should be responsible for ensuring that assigned information duties are carried out. That oversight and enforcement function involves assigning individual accountability to each worker and the regular monitoring of routine information assurance and security operations to ensure that responsibilities are performed.

The rule of thumb in assigning of responsibility is that specific accountability for security duties must be delegated in writing to each individual involved with the creation, handling, or use of information assets. Then, every designated worker must be trained and knowledgeable in all aspects of the technology used to perform those duties. In addition, they should be kept up to date for all related practices used to ensure organizational information assurance and security processes. It is important to include the management control processes in the update.

The assignment of individual responsibility hinges on the development of a set of rules. These are called rules of behavior. It is essential to have these rules of behavior in place to monitor and enforce compliance with security requirements.

Rules of Behavior

All users must be aware of what **acceptable behavior** is. In particular, users must understand the consequences of **noncompliance**. These consequences should be spelled out and enforced through a detailed set of *rules of behavior*. Such rules convey the expected actions and **accountabilities** applicable to each user.

These rules are the basis for security awareness and training operations and should be in writing. They should delineate the responsibilities and expectations for each individual clearly. Everyone should understand the rules before they are allowed to access the organization's information assets.

Rules of behavior should be aligned with system-use requirements and overall information assurance and security policies. It is important to define the thresholds of acceptable risk to fit the behavior to the duty requirements of each worker. To ensure that individual behaviors are sufficiently aligned with the actual risk environment a risk analysis should be undertaken before the rules are written.

Rules of behavior include all the information assurance and security requirements for individuals who use the system as well as the people it serves. The rules have to be rigorous enough to ensure security, while giving each user the flexibility to perform their jobs properly. Rules of behavior should define the organizationally sanctioned response to such concerns as

- Individual accountability
- Assignment and limitation of system privileges
- Networking and use of the Internet

The rigor of these rules should be related directly to the type and degree of security required. This means that highly secure operations will use a different rulebook than operations where less security is required.

Both the rule and the reason for each rule must be explicit, particularly where technical constraints are involved. Confusion arises when a particular password length or form is mandated for obtuse technical reasons. That confusion happens because users like to use passwords that are meaningful to them. When the name of an employee's favorite dog is no longer valid due to new password rules, the potential for security breaches increases because the employee will write down the password. Nevertheless, it can be assumed that if the information assurance justification for restricting the user to a specific format is explained, the user will be more likely to adapt to the constraint.

Rules should be enforced. Employing system-based sanctions such as the temporary or permanent loss of privileges helps ensure this behavior. In extreme cases, rules can be enforced through the organizational disciplinary system. Sanctions such as fines or dismissal can be imposed, in the same way as they would for violating any other formal code of conduct.

The Role of Awareness and Training

Users of a system should be trained properly in their information assurance duties; this should occur before they are allowed access to information assets. This prerequisite is important because training is an effective countermeasure, which ensures that users are well versed in the system's technical and procedural controls.

It is human nature for interest—even in vital topics—to diminish over time. Therefore, the importance of information assurance has to be reinforced. In addition, any substantive change to a system or application requires changes to user procedures or rules. These new procedures have to be taught. Employees should have scheduled, periodic refresher training to ensure they continue to understand and abide by the applicable conditions. To enforce this requirement, it is acceptable to make continued system access contingent on taking periodic refresher courses.

Specialized training should be required for staff members who are responsible for maintaining the information assurance functions. This training should include targeted programs centered on how individual responsibilities relate to ensuring the fulfillment of the security conditions. The training guarantees that the people who are responsible for system security features are aware of their responsibilities.

Training should also support the user community and should help them understand how to obtain help when security incidents occur. Because they are on the front lines, users are frequently the first to detect problems. Therefore, some awareness or training activity for users should be focused on making all employees part of the information assurance solution. Topics range from steps to ensure the general awareness of information assurance issues, such as viruses or malicious code, to more formal topics such as technical functions that support information assurance.

Both types of training ensure the information assurance activities of the work force are focused correctly. But the need for ensuring understanding of information assurance should not preclude the administration of mandatory training in specific information assurance or security topics as they become relevant. The goal of an awareness or training program is to ensure an acceptable level of knowledge about information assurance practice for all people who work in the secured space.

Training is most effective when presented in logical modules or learning stages with a specified scope and sequence. Traditionally, training revolves around classroom instruction. However, cost effective training can frequently be delivered in the form of interactive computer-based training (CBT) sessions or through well-written handbooks. Modern training philosophy for information assurance leans toward "just-in-time" and "blended" learning approaches because of constant, rapid change. The level of depth and intensity of training should always be linked to the potential risk and degree of associated harm.

Planning: Ensuring Reliable Control over Personnel

The success of the information assurance function rests on the organization's ability to guarantee a minimum level of formal control over personnel. That control is defined by a plan. Decision makers evaluate information about the threats posed by personnel and prepare concrete strategies to mitigate them.

Those strategies must ensure that all aspects of personnel behavior that threaten security, are anticipated and controlled. In large corporations, this analysis and planning function may be a major human resources initiative. With smaller organizations, it might require nothing more than listing the anticipated threats and investigating whether any worker behavior pose threats in those areas.

For instance, in large organizations if there is a potential for costly employee theft, there might be a need to install monitoring systems. Whereas, in a two-person shop the only rule might be that the employees monitor each other. If that is the case though, the behavioral requirement must be made explicit. Whether it is an expensive project or a simple investigation, the aim is to ensure that adverse personnel actions are anticipated and reliably controlled by establishing a clearly recognized and understood safeguard.

Control Principles

It is a fact that the greatest harm will be caused by the properly authorized trusted individual who chooses to engage in improper acts. That is the case beause authorized individuals have trusted access. Their harmful actions can be intentional, but they may be accidental. In either case, the organization must establish a set of technical, operational, and managerial controls to detect, prevent, and mitigate harm caused by trusted employees.

Protecting the organization from employee error or **misuse** can be difficult, because human behavior is unpredictable. There are, however, three principles that make that job easier. They are **individual accountability, least privilege**, and **separation of duties**.

Individual Accountability

The individual accountability rule states that everyone should be held responsible for his or her actions. Adverse actions that take place on the system must be traceable back to the initiating user. The process of identifying and authenticating users of the system and subsequently monitoring their activities is the mechanism by which individual accountability is assigned and ensured. This is usually enforced through a periodic examination of the automated system logs that record the action of individuals, to identify any malicious or inadvertent harmful actions.

Least Privilege

The concept of least privilege describes the principle of restricting a user's access to the minimum level of access needed to perform his or her job. This principle ensures that the system does not accidentally violate confidentiality and integrity requirements, by providing too much access.

Privileges for each user category are established by the access control policy and controlled by the system. The assignment of privileges is contingent on knowing the access requirements for each job type and individual. Making sure that those requirements are up to date is part of the human resources function.

Designated managers may grant exceptions to access rights, if necessary. However, the principle of least privilege still applies for any exception. That is, the particular user may only be granted access to the additional functions required to carry out a task; no other additional privileges are allowed and the exception should be time limited.

Separation of Duties

Separation of duties entails the distribution of the actions to perform a single function among a number of individuals. This is a checks-and-balances principle. The separations prevents a single individual from controlling a critical process. It is a common-sense way to ensure that people are able to monitor each other in the execution of routine processes. The simplest example of separation of duties is the standard business practice of not allowing the person who has authorized a check to write it and vice versa. This ensures that two people responsible for disbursing funds monitor each other's behavior.

The definition of the separate elements of each function requires that tasks involved in the execution of a process are understood. Therefore, each function in the organization must be analyzed, characterized, and logical control points must be established. Once this has been done, it is possible to identify the logical areas of separation. The assignment of individual responsibility for a subset of tasks within a larger function establishes the actual separation of duties.

Personnel Screening

Personnel screening assures that the individuals with access to protected information are not security risks. The personnel security screening process supplements the separation of duties, least privilege, and individual accountability principles. Personnel screening is employed where the information is considered sensitive enough that controls cannot assure security.

Screening trusted individuals is critical where there is a risk of significant harm from enhanced access. Minimally sreeening applies to the system staff and the information assurance and security specialists within the organization because they may be able to bypass technical and operational controls. They represent a greater degree of risk.

In addition, personnel who have any access to critical systems and information assets should be screened. This may not be done as rigorously as it would for system staff, but there should be routine procedures to determine that individual access fits the policy guidelines. Screening should be done prior to authorizing use of the system and should be conducted periodically after that.

Because it is resource intensive, **personnel screening** should be done proportionate to the potential risk and magnitude of harm that might originate from a violation of a classification requirement. Personnel screening is labor intensive. It involves background checks, which can be extensive and time consuming in the case of the higher levels of classification. It might also involve invasive activities such as stress interviews and lie detector tests that are often conducted on a periodic basis for each individual in positions of trust.

Planning for Personnel Assurance

The personnel security function is most effective if the selected controls and related procedures are embedded in day-to-day operations. This integration is achieved by making personnel security planning part of the overall strategic planning function. Doing so ensures that the level of personnel security control corresponds to the likelihood of harm.

The cost of establishing and maintaining control has to be balanced against the risk. The damage that may result from loss, misuse, or corruption by employees must be assessed and a priority must be assigned for protection.

Two areas must be addressed by personnel security plans. First, the plan should define the procedures required to ensure security through the staffing function. Second, the plan should provide procedures to ensure that the access for each type of employee is always monitored and controlled.

Security and the Human Resources Function

In many organizations, the responsibility for personnel security falls within the human resources function. The aim is to ensure that security is considered in the overall staffing process.

The control points for employee hiring can be divided into four stages in the process. (See Figure 7-1.) The rules for each of these apply equally to managers, system engineers, users, and even information assurance personnel. The four critical staffing stages are

- Job definition
- Clearance
- Applicant screening and hiring
- Employee training

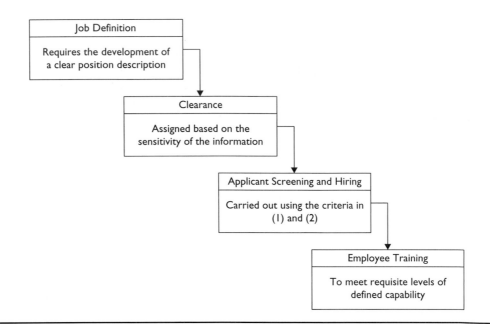

Figure 7-1   Security stages in the employee hiring process

Job Definition

Job definition allows the organization to embed a set of information assurance and security requirements into the standard task requirements for the position. This ensures that information assurance is always a consideration in the hiring and job assignment process.

The first step is to decide where each position fits in the hierarchy of the organization. Spell out the degree of authority and responsibility that each position will have. That authority will then determine the access rights and the level of trust required for every individual holding that position.

Then the type of sensitivity and associated level of access required for the work are documented. That documentation supports the definition of privileges for the position and it ensures the requirements associated with separation of duties have been addressed.

Because the requirements will apply to anybody who is holding that position the sensitivity and access rights definitions have to be stated carefully which means that they should fit the requirements of the position, not those of any particular individual.

As we saw in the prior section, the principle of separation of duties requires that the work should be segmented so that no one job position has complete control of protected processes. The example we used was that in most companies, the person initiating the request for a check is precluded from writing it. Instead, the party responsible for **authorizations** approves the other party's request. This control is established as a deliberate *modus operandi* within each position to ensure that necessary checks and balances are maintained in the process.

Also as noted earlier, least privilege dictates that individual employees should only be granted sufficient access to perform their duties. For instance, a clerical position should not run database integrity checks. So access to the system-level functions would not be available to that individual. On the other hand, a clerk might have to query the database, and that right should be built into the privileges granted to that position.

Least privilege must not restrict an individual's access to necessary functions because such a restriction violates the principle of availability. The goal of least privilege is to control accidents, errors, or unauthorized use. It is assumed that such damage is most likely to occur if workers access functions they are not familiar with or unauthorized to use.

Least privilege rights are set for the specific position, not determined by the level of privilege of the individual who occupies it. It is important to keep this in mind when assigning least privilege access rights because people move from job to job within an organization and it would be unproductive if the access rights for the position had to be re-established every time a new person filled it. Instead, it is better to set those rights and then only allow workers to move into the position with a level of trust that matches the required privileges.

Assignment of Required Trust

Most individuals are familiar with security clearances, if not from television and the movies then from experience with the government or military. The same set of principles that guide the management of security clearances in government agencies also apply in industry. The only difference is the terminology.

Trust or trustworthiness is frequently used in an industrial setting. The next step in the staffing process is the specification of trust requirements for each position. These requirements are based on the level of trust that must be given to the position. In government terms, this would be termed a **clearance level**. In the civilian world, this is communicated by specifying the sensitivity of the information that each position can access.

It is important to specify the **sensitivity** requirements for every position. That is because access to different information assets implies different types of restrictions. Therefore, different types of screening activities have to be carried out to identify the individuals who meet the access requirements for a given position. Individuals filling roles with high sensitivity requirements should always be screened extensively to determine if they exhibit sufficient trustworthiness to fit defined information assurance and access criteria.

The specification of sensitivity levels for each position is based on factors such as the type and criticality of information handled by that position, as well as traditional criteria such as managerial level and fiduciary responsibilities within the organization.

Information assurance and security controls should be assigned to regulate each position. This assignment is based on the potential risks and damage likely to ensue if there were a information assurance breakdown associated with that role. It is important to find a proper balance of information assurance controls to ensure the efficient day-to-day functioning of the position. Too much control makes the worker unproductive and uneconomical. Too little control imposes an unacceptable risk of compromise.

Background Screening and Hiring

Background screening helps the organization confirm that prospective employees fit the information assurance criteria for a given position. In the case of extremely sensitive positions, this background check could be a formal investigation carried out by professional investigators. For most other positions, however, the check might be as simple as an electronic record scan to confirm the basics of the individual's credentials.

Typical background checks examine things such as criminal history, which is easy to learn from a number of record services. Other factors that should be examined include such things as

- Work history
- Credit history
- Educational history
- Interview or psychographic data
- Any public evidence of addictive behavior, such as hospitalizations

With sensitive positions, this check could include examination of legal history, financial and/or credit history, medical history, immigration and/or other government records, and any recorded observations about overall personal or organization behavior. This level of inquiry is necessary because employees who have a personal vulnerability are easier to compromise and it is important to ensure that people who hold sensitive positions are not susceptible to blackmail.

The screening process is driven by information assurance criteria adopted by the organization. Requirements for the rigor of the screening should be based on the level of sensitivity of the work. Rigor should be driven by sensitivity to make the process as cost efficient as possible. For instance, an employer is not likely to conduct an extensive background check for a janitor's position—unless, of course, that position is located within a highly secure site, in which case rigorous checks might be justified and necessary.

Another rule on background checks is that the position supervisor should not be involved in the screening process. Instead, third parties, human resources, or information assurance security specialists should be involved. The point of the check is to learn whether the prospective employee has met the information assurance criteria for the position, not to learn anything else about him or her.

Employee Awareness Training and Education

Once an individual has been hired, it is important to provide information assurance and security awareness, training, and perhaps even formal education to allow him or her to get sufficient understanding of the organizational policies and expectations that apply to the position. In addition, it is important to communicate an understanding of the procedures required of that position to ensure the routine behavior of the employee.

From the standpoint of enforcement, accountability is based on the assumption that the employee has knowledge of the consequences of inappropriate behavior. The lack of knowledge of policy and procedure is one of the primary causes of breakdowns in personnel security. While often treated as human error, ignorance of policy and procedure is in fact a failure on the part of the information assurance function to ensure sufficient assurance.

United States Government Training Standards

In the early 1990s, the United States government undertook a major project to implement the training requirements of PL 100-235. This act required that *"each Federal agency shall provide for the mandatory periodic training in computer security awareness and accepted computer security practice of all employees who are involved with the management, use, or operation of each Federal computer system within or under the supervision of that agency."* This has been reiterated in the Federal Information Security Management Act (FISMA), which was established under PL 107-347. These two public laws motivated the establishment of training standards by the National Institute for Standards and Technology (NIST) and the Committee for National Security Systems (CNSS).

These standards serve as the basis for the identification of National Centers of Academic Excellence in Information Assurance Education (CAE/IAE). These designated universities function under the joint aegis of the National Security Agency (NSA) and the Department of Homeland Security (DHS). Their aim is to foster the development of academically based education and research based programs for the field of information assurance.

FISMA The E-Government Act (Public Law 107-347), passed by the 107th Congress and signed into law by the President in December 2002, recognized the importance of information security to the economic and national security interests of the United States. Title III, The Federal Information Security Management Act (FISMA), requires certain government personnel categories to obtain professional qualifications appropriate to their role or function, including both training and experience. To comply with FISMA, United States government agencies routinely use personnel training standards developed by NIST and CNSS.

NIST Standards   The National Institute of Standards and Technology (NIST) has developed several standards to guide personnel training programs, as follows:

- SP 500-172 Computer Security Training Guidelines, November 1989—Superseded by SP 800-16—These specify a basic set of security principles and topics for federal government applications.

- SP 800-16 Information Technology Security Training Requirements: A Role and Performance-Based Model (supersedes NIST Spec. Pub. 500-172). This updated SP 500-172 and shares components and a common body of knowledge with CNSS standards.

- Special Publication 800-53, Recommended Security Controls for Federal Information Systems. This is still a draft publication but its aim is to specify a minimum set of concrete controls for information security applications. Knowledge of the purpose and application of these controls could serve as the basis for additional professional certification.

CNSS Training Standards   The CNSS was established to provide a forum for the discussion of policy issues, set national policy, and promulgate direction, operational procedures, and guidance for the security of national security systems. They have provided detailed documentation of the training content in the following standards:

- Information Security Professionals—NSTISSI 4011
- Senior Systems Manager—CNSSI 4012
- System Administrators—CNSSI 4013
- Information System Security Officers—CNSSI No. 4014
- System Certifiers—CNSSI 4015
- Risk Analyst—CNSSI 4016
- System Security Engineer—CNSSI 4017

DHS and NSA Academic Certification   The Department of Homeland Security (DHS) and National Security Agency (NSA) sponsor a program to certify that the curricula of academic institutions meet required standards. This program is called the National Information Assurance Education and Training Program (NIETP), and it is designed to support improvements in information assurance (IA) education, training, and awareness. The NIETP is national in focus, future-oriented, multidimensional, and tied to technology and business. It encourages and recognizes universities through its Centers of Academic Excellence in IA Education (CAE) program. The CAE program is supported by the national Colloquium for Information Systems Security Education (CISSE) and the National Information Assurance Training and Education Center (NIATEC).

Under the CAE program, four-year colleges and graduate-level universities may apply to be designated as a National Center of Academic Excellence in Information Assurance Education. Each certified institution passes a rigorous review demonstrating its commitment to academic excellence in IA education. CAEs receive formal recognition from the United States government and students attending CAE schools are eligible to apply for scholarships and grants through the Department of Defense Information Assurance Scholarship Program and the Federal Cyber Service Scholarship for Service Program (SFS).

Private Sector Security Certification Standards

In 2005, Ryan and Schou pointed out that the trade of "security practitioner" is more or less in the same state as medical practitioners were in the 1800s. There are technicians, systems architects, policy experts, mathematical theorists, and a host of others. However, until recently there is not a recognized common body of knowledge to use as a point of reference in the development and refinement of accepted practices for any of these roles.

As a result, a range of organizations has sprung up to promote their own view of proper practice. Most represent a particular perspective or a philosophy about the way the assurance process should be structured and conducted. Some are commercial organizations specializing in training for particular technological applications. Others are non-profit organizations, whose certifications are broadly based, such as the Information Systems Audit and Control Association (ISACA) and the International Information Systems Security Certification Consortium [(ISC)²].

In addition, private sector training organizations, academic institutions have begun to offer a range of certifications spanning everything from two-year degree programs through doctoral research. The challenge for hiring managers, as well as certificate holders, is to make sense of the choices and understand what they mean.

Assigning Value to Certification

Assessing the value of a certification is not easy. Certification is the result of a process. In most cases, successful completion of the process is indicated by a certificate attesting that an individual has passed a test, attended a sequence of classes, performed some task, worked for a number of years in a skill field, or any combination of these.

Some certifications are awarded at the end of an apprenticeship, while others are awarded after a period of academic preparation. Establishing the value of each certificate means understanding the process and deciding how rigorously it was followed. It is also important to know the time dependencies of the capabilities. For instance, a certification that attests that an individual is competent to manage version 1.4 of a firewall becomes obsolete when version 1.5 is released.

In many respects, the certifications that are the most valid teach critical thinking rather than a particular skill. A certification that attests that an individual has been taught how to consider complex options against a set of requirements will never be obsolete: The certification attests not to a specific technological ability, but to the overall capability to think critically about an identified problem space. Each approach has value—firewalls have to be managed competently, for example—but there is no easy answer to this question: "Which certification should I include in my personnel plan?" The answer is, "It all depends."

The following are some of the decision criteria that would help provide an accurate picture of the value of a certification:

- How long has the certification been in existence?
- Does the certifying organization's process conform to established standards?
- Is the organization ISO/IEC 17024 certified?
- How many people hold the certification?
- How widely respected is the certification?
- Does the certificate span industry boundaries?
- What is the probability that 5 or 10 years from now, the certificate will still be useful?
- Does the certification span geographic boundaries?

Controlling Access of Employees and Contractors to Restricted Information

A sound personnel security program must define the rules that regulate the access of employees to restricted information. For computerized information, this activity centers on the management of user accounts.

User account management establishes the policies and procedures to identify, authenticate, and authorize individual access to the system and information assets. That requires mechanisms to both establish and periodically audit the way accounts are accessed and authorizations given. Accompanying those practices is an associated set of rules to ensure that **access privileges** are modified or removed in a reliable and timely fashion for any employee reassigned, promoted, terminated, or retired.

Effective management of the access of every user is essential to maintaining security. Therefore, the personnel security process must ensure that user access is properly defined and controlled. Most of the techniques associated with this process were discussed in Chapter 6, "Access Control"; however, it is appropriate in this chapter on personnel security to touch on the process by which access to the system is assigned, managed, audited, and modified or removed. The following six factors determine the shape and outcome of that process:

1. User account management
2. Audit and management review procedures
3. Detection of and response to unauthorized activities
4. Friendly termination
5. Unfriendly termination
6. Knowing your contractors

User Account Management

User account management encompasses the practices that an organization employs to

- Establish, issue, and close the accounts of individual employees
- Track employee access behavior
- Track individual employee access authorizations
- Manage the employee access control operation

User accounts are established and documented by a formal request, which should state the level of access to be granted and may be specified by function. Sometimes it is specified by documenting a user profile. To ensure management oversight, the employee's supervisor, rather than the employee, should make that decision. This determination is sent to the part of the operation that oversees the technical configuration and operation of the system—e.g., IT management and operations.

The actual assignment process within each area will vary depending on access privileges requested. For instance, if the request is for general access, the assignment of privileges may be assigned by the system administrator. If the employee is to be given special access to a critical application, the manager of that application might be involved in the assignment process.

This phase ensures that the appropriate managers in the technical or systems operations have provided input. It is important to note that this access and authorization decision-making process is a continuing responsibility of personnel security. Within the course of day-to-day operation, new user accounts are always being added, while others are deleted. To ensure proper access integrity, the turnover has to be controlled through a formal and systematic process.

The conventional IT function establishes the approved access privileges by creating an account for the new user. It is particularly important for the technical side to double-check through their own security operations, whether the access levels enabled for that account are consistent with those requested by the user's supervisor and approved by system management.

This is one of the most likely points of failure where critical applications are concerned, or where there are variations from the normal privileges. Consequently, it is important, to ensure and enforce accountability that the level of privilege that has been approved is communicated properly to the systems staff and that a manager supervises the implementation process.

Once the account has been created, the access information is communicated to the employee. Access information includes the particulars that user will need to use their account, including the identifier (the user ID number) and the means of authentication (the password or the PIN, if a smart card is involved). To confirm the security elements, users should be given an acceptable use policy, account rules, and applicable regulations document. They should be asked to study these and demonstrate competence through a test or performance criteria.

Do not forget that the employee would still need some form of training. For instance, one of the primary points of failure in access control comes from sharing passwords.

So the security ramifications of password sharing need to be emphasized. If the organization does not take active steps to reinforce the importance of security issues, it is hard to blame an employee who causes a security breach by inadvertent violations of procedure while performing routine tasks.

A similar process must be followed when a user is no longer authorized to access the system. The employee's supervisor should be responsible for informing the system administrator when a change in employment status has occurred. The appropriate technical manager should be responsible for supervising removing employee access principles. Removal of access privileges must be done as rapidly as possible to prevent a disgruntled employee from taking out frustration on the system.

Access permissions may change permanently or temporarily, based on employee movement in the organization. So, another significant aspect of user account management involves keeping user access authorizations up to date. Access authorizations are changed based on two conditions, a change in job role or termination.

Changes in role can be temporary, for instance while covering for an absent employee. They can also be permanent, for instance after a transfer or promotion. In the first instance, users are required to perform duties outside their normal scope during the absence of others, which might require some sort of change to their access authorization. Although necessary to keep continuity in the workplace, an *ad-hoc* change to access authorizations should be granted sparingly and monitored carefully. That monitoring and control must be consistent with the need to maintain separation of duties for internal control purposes. Also, access privileges should be removed promptly when no longer justified.

Permanent changes take place when an employee moves to another position within the organization. In that case, the process of granting account authorizations will have to be carried out as if that individual were a new employee. At the same time, however, it is important to remember to remove the access authorizations of the prior position.

This is another point of failure in the security process. Because of problems enforcing this requirement, there have been many instances of "authorization creep," where employees have continued to maintain access rights for previously held positions within the organization. This practice is inconsistent with the principle of least privilege and it is the cause of serious breakdowns in information assurance and security.

Finally, there is the issue of maintaining appropriate personnel access if applications change. Since the criticality of applications is always subject to changes, maintenance of access rights is important. In day-to-day organizational operation, functions are always being added, upgraded, or removed, which might radically alter the access privileges and number of authorized users for a given application.

None of these changes should take place outside of the control of the information assurance operation because access control is a critical security function. The tracking and control of aspects of systems functions and the maintenance of access control changes to allow employees to carry out assigned responsibilities is an important duty of the personnel security management function.

User Account Audit and Management Review

Regular and systematic **reviews of user accounts** are a necessary part of personnel security practice because the use of those accounts has to be monitored and personal inspection is the only way to do that. These reviews should verify five user characteristics:

- Level(s) of access for each individual employee are appropriate to assigned level of privilege for each application

- Level(s) of access assigned conform with the concept of least privilege

- Accounts assigned to an employee are active and appropriate to the employee's job function

- Management authorizations are up to date

- Required training has been completed

User account reviews should be conducted on at least two levels. First, they should be done system-wide. Second, they should be done on an application-by-application basis.

In the first instance, the system administrator should be able to verify that employees have been granted the access rights their managers specified. However, access requirements can change over time; it is good practice for application managers and the owners of the information asset to review the assigned access levels of the users of applications under their control.

This type of review should be performed on a routine basis. It is important to involve application managers in the review process because they are the only people who are able to tell whether the currently defined access rights are appropriate for every user.

Detecting Unauthorized/Illegal Activities

A good security system must have procedures in place to address employee fraud or misuse. Countermeasures employed in this area are frequently based on **software-enabled monitoring** functions. These are installed as part of an overall security system. However, the solution does not lie with the software. It revolves around a set of personnel policies that specify what is permissible within each employee's role. Moreover, along with these policies there should be a clear understanding that disciplinary processes will be enforced if violations are discovered.

In light of the critical need to enforce disciplined and secure use, policies must also establish a clear understanding of what constitutes an unauthorized or illegal use. As discussed earlier, this should be documented in the Acceptable Use Policy. If clear definitions of misuse and violation are available, then the organization can install software-based monitoring/enforcement systems to do the actual detection and even policing. These systems are commercially available under the generic title of intrusion detection systems (IDSs). IDSs are high-level hardware/software utilities that sit on the network end of the system and monitor network traffic for unauthorized access.

As we saw in Chapter 6, IDSs perform that monitoring function by either matching system behavior with known patterns of misuse or violation (pattern matching), or they can be set to detect anomalous behavior with respect to a baseline of normal operation (anomaly detection).

- Pattern Matching—With pattern matching the system looks for actions that fit well-recognized patterns. Pattern matching is easier to do, since patterns can be defined. However, it is impossible to distinguish when an action is illegal if there is no pattern.

- Anomaly Detection—With anomaly detection, the utility is essentially looking for actions that do not fit well-recognized patterns of system usage. This type of monitoring, which is called heurism, must have a robust picture of acceptable user behavior as a point of reference.

Essentially, these types of systems take defined policies and enforce them throughout the organization by monitoring individual accesses. The policy enforcer software prevents common forms of misuse by not allowing the action to be taken, and it can report other violations that it detects.

In addition to software solutions, there is a range of procedural methods to detect **unauthorized or illegal activity**, including mechanisms such as direct auditing of system logs and procedural analysis using audit trails to detect fraudulent actions. There might also be periodic rescreening of personnel. Finally, there is the simple expedient of rotating employees in sensitive positions. Regular rotation of responsibilities should expose any violation that requires a particular employee's actions in order to be effective.

Friendly Termination

With a **friendly termination**, there is no reason to believe that the employee is leaving the organization under anything other than mutually acceptable terms. The IT workforce is fluid, and these terminations are common. However, the security element always has to be considered, no matter how friendly the separation appears.

Assurance under the conditions of friendly termination requires a set of standard procedures are available to guide outgoing or transferring employees. The guide is implemented as part of the standard human resources function. In the case of information assurance, the only purpose of a friendly termination procedure is to ensure that user account privileges are removed from the system in a timely manner. This includes the

- Removal of access privileges, computer accounts, authentication tokens
- Assurance of the continued integrity and availability of data in accounts that each access privilege was granted for
- Briefing on the continuing responsibility for confidentiality and privacy
- Securing cryptographic keys
- Return of organization IS property

In the case of critical information, employees might be instructed to "clean up" or completely wipe their electronic storage media prior to leaving. If an employee has access to cryptography keys or other types of tools, those keys must be secured and the integrity of the encryption system should be verified.

Unfriendly Termination

A different set of procedures applies when an employee leaves the organization under unfriendly circumstances. In such cases, there is a greater potential for mischief, and careful attention must be paid to the security considerations. The issues involved in friendly terminations still apply to **unfriendly terminations**, but because of the conflict that is implicit in a dismissal, the steps to address them are considerably more complicated.

The greatest threat from an unfriendly termination comes from the system or programming staff, because they are capable of altering code or modifying the system. Technical personnel are ideally positioned to disrupt the normal functions of the system or damage its assets. Without the appropriate safeguards, people with direct system access can set logic bombs or backdoors that will let them get the personal paybacks they feel they are owed. In the past, this has amounted to self-indulgent acts such as wiping hard drives and even, in some cases, holding whole applications hostage.

The potential havoc that the system staff can wreak should be obvious, but one other personnel category should be carefully controlled in the case of unfriendly terminations. That is the ordinary user. Any employee with access, such as a general user account, can create serious problems that would demand significant resources to repair.

For example, organizational data, such as accounts under their control, can be altered. Critical documentation can be destroyed or "misplaced," and other "accidental" errors related to system operation can occur, such as the destruction of media. It is possible to copy terabytes of proprietary data prior to dismissal and walk out the door with valuable organization property in a briefcase.

Given the number of adverse consequences associated with an unfriendly termination, the organization should at least consider the following steps:

- When an employee notifies an organization of a resignation and it can be reasonably expected that it has occurred on unfriendly terms, system access should be terminated immediately.

- If the organization decides that an employee is to be fired, then system access should be removed immediately after that decision is made. In no case should the employee be allowed to have access to the system after they have been notified that they have been dismissed.

- If the employee continues to work for a period after they have been notified they will be terminated, then good practice dictates that they should be assigned duties that do not require system access. Even though it might not be productive, this rule applies especially to system and application programming staff, because of their potential to do serious harm.

- Where terminations are extremely unfriendly or where the employee has immediate access to critical functions or information, it is advisable to expedite their physical removal from the area.

Contractor Considerations

In addition to instituting the procedures to control an organization's own employees, the personnel security process should also establish a system to ensure the security of contracted and outsourced work. The objective of that system should be to establish sufficient control over the personnel in all of the organization who are involved in performing work or delivering specific work products.

This is not as simple as just writing security into a contract with a supplier because there is a wide range of tasks that might be outsourced and outsourcing is done in many strange places. The fact that the term outsourcing is frequently used to describe both local subcontracted work and work that is done offshore, for which the proper term is "off-shoring," indicates the chief problem that outsourcing represents. The problem is that outsourcing is a broad and diverse topic, which is hard for most people to understand.

The size and diversity of the outsourcing trend creates confusion and management problems for the information assurance and security function. For instance, the safety and security requirements for an outsourced call center across town or even in the basement of the building are going to be different from those associated with critical software development in another country. The variation of situational requirements has to be taken into consideration when an organization sets out to control outsourced work.

Since outsourcing expands secured space into unfamiliar or unknown places, it is essential that all steps to ensure perimeter integrity have been followed. This is essentially a vertical integration process. That is, the information assurance systems of all organizations involved in the outsourcing arrangement, from prime contractor through various sub-subcontractors, have to be aligned into a single integrated virtual entity, which forms logical secured space.

Given the spatial and organizational complexity of outsourced arrangements, this is an unbreakable rule. To ensure proper integration it is necessary to follow a rigorous design process. The outcome of that process is an information assurance architecture incorporating the processes and accountabilities of the participating organizations into a single approach. Given the importance of information assurance and security in outsourcing, the process followed should be no less formal than the process that was followed to design the work product.

The first step in the process from a personnel security standpoint is to establish a picture and understanding of the work. The understanding of the work required, roles, and responsibilities, has to be obtained in advance of any contract. A commitment to impose the degree of interorganization rigor to ensure security has to be baked into the contract from the beginning of the process.

A thorough job-task analysis of all the outsourced work must be performed. In some respects, the requirements for this analysis are no different from those we discussed in the section "Security and the Human Resources Function." However, the job definition and assignment of trust must be driven by a detailed assessment of risks involved with each outsourced task category, and the screening process must be much more meticulous.

The depth of analysis required to do this can be costly but it is necessary to establish control. In most instances, access to the system is a necessity for outsourced workers to carry out their assigned duties. Therefore, each individual's access has to be assigned and accounted for by the personnel security scheme. Accountability includes all extra monitoring and supervision steps conducted through audits and reviews of the work, as well as the implementation of rigorous control functions within automated processes.

In addition to defining the monitoring and control functions, an outsourced relationship must be governed by measurable performance criteria. These criteria fine-tune the process and ensure that participants live up to their commitments. In an information assurance or security setting, the most common measure of performance is incidents and associated losses, typically expressed as a dollar cost and is reported vertically through the outsourcing management hierarchy.

Another feature that makes sense for the outsourced arrangement is the establishment of an incident reporting function. This is most commonly known as a computer emergency response team (CERT). Centralizing the incident-reporting function allows the involved organizations to respond effectively and in a coordinated fashion to events as they occur throughout the supply chain. However, the chief advantage is the insight and attendant control that the data feeding into a CERT will establish over the overall process.

The requirement to extend the job-definition and personnel-screening process outside the organization can be an expensive additional step in the development and implementation of an outsourced work arrangement. The cost of the additional vetting and control features needed for information assurance could erase the financial advantages of outsourcing. In fact, this might lead an organization to decide not to spend the money on the project. On the other hand, the organization could also decide not to spend the money to assure their information assets. At a minimum that would be an unethical decision and at worst it could lead to major information assurance breakdowns and disastrous losses.

Chapter 7 Review

Chapter Summary

- The primary cause of security breaches originates with the people who operate or use information systems.

- Personnel security entails all of the policies and procedures necessary to control the activities of the individuals who work within an organization.

- Because of their potential impact on organizational success, all of the threats to personnel have to be understood and the appropriate countermeasures have to be deployed.

- That requires an organizational risk assessment process.

- It is important for each organization to develop an information assurance strategy for itself.

- This scheme has to stipulate the actual amount of protection that the executive managers consider acceptable.

- The boundaries of personnel security must be set.

- To be effective, information assurance and security discipline has to be continuous and it should be carefully planned and executed.

- Every planned response requires disciplined practice.

- People have to know both the reason and importance of what they are doing in order to properly motivate themselves to perform those tasks in a reliable and continuous fashion.

- The purpose of information assurance procedures is to define what has to be done by each individual in order to achieve satisfactory levels of information assurance.

- The only way that a organization can establish and execute a repeatable set of actions is through the **documentation process**.

- The idea is to prevent requisite procedure from being omitted by accident when an individual is carrying out his or her daily duties.

- Given the importance of critical systems, it is particularly essential that the organization is able to ensure the effectiveness of the security technology as well as the assurance methods on an ongoing basis.

- It is particularly important to designate a management role that is solely responsible for the safety and security of critical functions.

- All users of a system should be made aware of what constitutes acceptable behavior.

- In particular, users must understand the consequences of noncompliance with procedural requirements.

- These rules should be in writing and be able to serve as the basis for information assurance awareness, training, and education.

- Rules have to be enforced.

- The level of depth and intensity of the training is always referenced to the potential risk and degree of associated harm.

- Least privilege is the practice of restricting a user's type of access to the minimum necessary to perform his or her job.

- Separation of duties is the practice of dividing the steps in a critical function among different individuals.

- Personnel screening is a process that is employed to assure the security of the individuals who are involved in an information assurance process.

- The primary personnel countermeasures in the area of incident response are awareness and training.

- For personnel security to be most effective, the planned controls and their related procedures must be embedded into day-to-day operations.

- The clearance level delineates those requisite information assurance and security behaviors as well as the officially authorized access levels for the position.

- It is necessary to communicate a sufficient understanding of the relevant procedures in order to ensure proper behavior with respect to each policy.

- This is particularly important from the standpoint of enforcement because accountability rests with having a clear knowledge of the consequences of noncompliance.

- User account management dictates the policies and procedures that are used to identify, authenticate, and authorize individual access to the system.

- This requires mechanisms to both establish and periodically audit the way accounts are accessed and authorizations given.

- Assurance is based on a set of standard procedures that are formally defined for outgoing or transferring employees.

- Personnel security planning should establish a set of rules to ensure the security of **contractor and outsourced work**.

Key Terms

acceptable behavior (179)
access privileges (190)
accountabilities (179)
authorizations (185)
awareness (177)
behavior (175)

Key Term Quiz

Complete each statement by writing one of the terms from this list in each blank. Not all terms will be used.

1. It is necessary to stipulate _____ in order to ensure control over the human resources of the organization.

2. _____ is used to ensure that the human resources of an organization meet the proper security background requirements.

3. The assignment of user privileges to access data is part of _____.

4. Clearances are based on the _____ of the data.

5. Employee terminations can either be _____ or _____.

6. Automated monitoring of human behavior is called _____.

7. The definition of _____ is the first step in enforcing accountability.

8. Making sure that no single person is responsible for a function is called ____.

9. The definition of ____ is the first step in creating secure space

10. Providing access to only the information needed to do work is called _____.

Multiple Choice Quiz

1. Rules of behavior are:
   a. threat based
   b. consistent with policies
   c. ineffective
   d. enforced by laws

2. Access control centers on
   a. software
   b. auditing controls
   c. training
   d. user account management

3. Discipline is important to ensure
   a. performance
   b. repeatability
   c. motivation
   d. behavior

4. Separation of duties involves
   a. segmenting
   b. increasing authority
   c. limiting control
   d. limiting access

5. Least privilege involves:
   a. segmenting
   b. limiting authority
   c. limiting control
   d. limiting access

6. Training is most effective when:
   a. presented in logical modules
   b. done by a professional
   c. administered at work
   d. accompanied by incentives

7. Personnel screening should be done:

   a. for everybody at the same level

   b. only when the information is sensitive

   c. proportionate to the risk

   d. never because it bothers the staff

8. Control is always defined by:

   a. accident

   b. designated employees

   c. infrastructures

   d. plan

9. In the case of friendly terminations, the only purpose of termination procedures is to:

   a. get the employee out of the building

   b. ensure user access privileges are removed

   c. wipe out all affected documentation

   d. ensure that the employee is happy

10. Subcontractor control is based on:

   a. argument over contracts

   b. constant monitoring and control of outsourced staff

   c. vertical integration of security functions

   d. incentives

Essay Quiz

1. Why is the assignment of individual responsibility an essential part of personnel security?

2. Why might ergonomic considerations be part of a personnel security program? How do they affect security in the personnel area?

3. What is the purpose of personnel screening? Does it apply to everybody in cases?

4. How are people involved in incident response? What is the proper method for involving them?

5. Why are contractor considerations important elements of personnel security in today's industry?

6. What types of security procedures are there? How do these differ in terms of their application?

7. What is the contribution of documentation to enforcing personnel security?

8. Why is the assignment of personal responsibility important? Why is this especially essential for critical systems?

9. What is the contribution of rules of behavior? What would be hard to enforce if these were not made explicit?

10. Why is training an important countermeasure when it comes to personnel security?

Case Exercise

Complete the following case exercise as directed by your instructor:

Refer to the Heavy Metal Technology Case in Appendix A. You have been assigned the responsibility for planning the human resources control policies for the Oceanside Main building. Prepare a complete policy manual to secure the personnel who work at this building. Here is some background that might help you do this.

The actual manufacturing takes place at Oceanside Main. The project managers in the Oceanside Main facility teleconference daily with the managers in Buffalo from the time that the project is completed until the time that it begins operational testing. Because the intent is to move the final product into immediate deployment, these teleconferences will include the production managers from the Jackson street facility as soon as the project passes its initial acceptance audit. Where a signoff is required to validate that the project has passed, a critical stage DoD project managers will sit in on teleconferences. It is assumed that these project managers will be located in Washington, D.C., rather than Fort Walton. After an initial inspection seven areas of concern were identified. Factor these into your plan. In order of relative priority, the concerns are

- IT, production, and testing staff have not obtained security clearances.
- There are no rules of behavior.
- Accountability is not assigned.
- There is no personnel planning process.
- The password system is not monitored. Expired passwords are allowed to remain on the system.
- There are no provisions for least privilege or separation of duties.
- There is no formal clearance structure to define and control diverse levels of security.

Physical Security

In this chapter, you will learn how to:
- Manage the problems of dispersion and diversity
- Factor the concept of secure space into a physical security scheme
- Construct a security process using a security plan
- Mitigate physical security threats

Physical security safeguards assets from nondigital threats. Unlike the rest of the information assurance process that protects intangible assets, physical security protects information processing **facilities** and equipment from deliberate or accidental harm. Some physical security technologies like biometrics and microwave intrusion detection are complicated. However, most physical security concepts such as secure areas, layered defenses, and defense in depth are intuitive and have been in place since early mainframe days.

Because physical security protects tangible things like computer equipment, rather than abstract things like computer files and information assets, it may appear to be less "refined" and less important. Many E-organizations separate the responsibility for physical security and information assurance. That separation is unwise, since the ability of an attacker to gain physical access poses a serious threat to the information that facilities and equipment contain.

An uncontrolled physical space makes it easy for an attacker to subvert most security measures; proximity to the equipment allows attackers to mount attacks more easily. If the attackers can sit next to a server and run intrusion software against a network, the job is easier since they are inside the defensive perimeter. That location makes them invisible to security measures established to protect the network. Remember that high-capacity memory sticks allow anybody who can touch a USB port to transfer gigabytes of information in seconds or upload unapproved data or harmful code to a system.

It is possible to violate physical security at many places in many ways. Therefore, the process of physical access control is more involved. For instance, it is easy to monitor the comings and goings of electronic users through a firewall; it is a different matter to ensure the perimeter integrity of every door and window in a skyscraper.

It should be clear that physical security is complex and essential to protecting the information asset base. This chapter examines each of the areas of concern and suggests fundamental safeguards.

The Problems of Dispersion and Diversity

Physical security accounts for and controls tangible assets. That control has become more difficult with the advent of distributed systems. It difficult to secure these resources effectively because network resources are diverse and widely distributed.

For example, Internet access originates from outside the building and the secure perimeter. Therefore, the telephone, cable lines, and broadband interfaces in uncontrolled space are as much a part of your physical network as your protected modem or router. These external parts are more susceptible to attack.

Most broadband connections come into a building in unobtrusive places such as the basement. It easier to access and tamper with a broadband connection in a basement than an access point located in the main lobby. The potential for covert access created by physical dispersion, should lead one to ask, "Where do you draw the line in defining the physical security perimeter?"

There is another attendant problem of distributed systems. It is easy to assure obvious targets such as hardware, facilities, equipment, and storage media from attack. However, less obvious repositories of information containing potentially critical items such as contracts, plans, and agreements also need protection.

Non-computerized repositories are frequently a more valuable storage resource than electronic ones because the organization is not likely to put critical documents such as legal contracts on the network. These will invariably be stored them in physical holding places, like file cabinets. If the information in those contracts were lost, compromised, or stolen, the organization could suffer financial or legal harm. Yet the deliberate security of simple repositories such as filing cabinets is rarely part of the information assurance scheme.

Collections of assets have different protection requirements and the organization must consciously decide how to protect each. It is important to think through the safeguards that will be set for each asset because each has a role and priority in the overall process.

Establishing safeguards begins with physical asset accounting framework that itemizes the physical records and resources of the organization. The framework requires maintaining a perpetual inventory of tangible assets as well as **rules for controlling** each asset. In physical security, the combination of a defined set of assets and the associated controls is called **secure space**. This is not unlike the process described for intangible information assets.

The Joy of Secure Space

Safeguarding a facility requires deliberately creating a secure space. The first step in creating secure space is to define physical perimeter or boundary. Once the boundary is established, deploy countermeasures to assure the security, confidentiality, and integrity of the items contained. The management objective is to make certain that access to resources within a secure space is carefully monitored and the ability to react effectively to intrusions at the perimeter is established. Clearly delineate the boundary of all controlled locations; if there is no established boundary, the likelihood of compromise in the grey areas will increase.

The organization should consider three factors in establishing a secure space. These are *location, access,* and *control.*

Factor One: Ensuring the Location

Location dictates the type of physical access control and is a primary consideration in **physical security planning**. For example, if the computer is located in a locked office, the organization will have to plan less to ensure physical access than if the computer is in an unattended reception area. Remember, secure physical assets proportionately to the risks resulting from **unauthorized access** to that facility.

Location dictates the characteristics of the security solution. For instance, do not locate computer facilities in a prominent location in the building and do not conspicuously mark the location. The principle is that authorized individuals will know where the computer facility is and unauthorized people will not. Thus, the placement and signage serve as a *de facto* control technique

Factor Two: Ensuring Controlled Access

Access and security go hand in hand, since access control regulates the privilege of entry to the secure space. Physical access control is a significant security factor and can be complex. Physical access to secure space is granted using the same principles as electronic access. Remember, **access** is a *privilege*, which is individually assigned and enforced, rather than a *right*. Consequently, it is important to enforce all rules regarding violations of secure space.

Securing physical space is a 360-degree problem since the physical perimeter can be accessed at any point in its circumference. The number of places on the perimeter to be secured is large. Granting and monitoring of access privileges and the confirmation of **authorizations** is complicated. Intentional or unintentional physical threats are likely to appear for the first time at the perimeter; this makes the problem of ensuring physical access substantial. Electronic space is easier to defend since it has defined access points.

For example, computerized patient records at a hospital can be accessed only through the access points established by the network information assurance plan. Hypothetically, these records are relatively easy for network security to identify and control. However, those same records can also be accessed in by anyone who gains physical entry to the building. That includes everyone from authorized employees entering through a security checkpoint to somebody breaking a window in the basement of a 30-story building in the middle of the night. The broad range of access points creates a larger set of considerations and it represents a large number of places to be monitored and controlled.

Factor Three: Ensuring Control of Secure Space

Control is the mechanism that enforces security. Control is based on the specification and enforcement of a set of behaviors that can be objectively monitored. The active element of physical access control is monitoring to keep track of the behavior of people within a secure space. The monitoring activity ensures that behavior within the controlled space complies with all requirements and rules.

There are simple mechanisms available to allow organizations to enforce physical monitoring at assigned spots, such as **gates**, guns, and **guards** (G^3). For the rest of the perimeter, there is a range of electronic monitoring and control mechanisms that can be used. Examples of these devices are passive microwave monitoring, closed circuit TV (CCTV), and access control biometrics.

The Physical Security Process and Plan

The physical security process guarantees that the effective safeguards are in place. The effectiveness of these controls is ensured by making certain that threats have been identified and that the associated vulnerabilities have been accurately characterized, prioritized, and addressed appropriately. The physical security process is implemented through planning and is supervised and enforced by consistent and ongoing management.

The Physical Security Process

The first step in the process is to identify the items to be protected. There are three classes of items requiring assurance: *equipment, people,* and *the environment.* Each requires different safeguards and different mechanisms to assure them.

The first class includes tangible things associated with the computer itself. Items in this category include hardware and network connections. The second class involves threats from the people who use the computer. The human resources aspect is part of the *personnel* security process discussed in the previous chapter. However, where physical access considerations are involved, the "people" factor has to be addressed using physical access control countermeasures. Therefore, we will also discuss personnel issues here from a different aspect.

The final class is composed of those things that are a part of the environment. This is probably the most bewildering aspect, since it is hard to list all items in this class. The class includes hazards associated with the environment as well as the safety requirements of the physical space. To complicate the problem further, threats like the weather (which is a consideration in this category) are constantly changing. As such, environmental security revolves around scanning the horizon to try to identify and respond appropriately to threats as they emerge.

Physical Security Plan

The physical security plan should be developed once an understanding of the threat environment has been developed. The physical security plan establishes a response to events that represent potential harm and that have a reasonable probability of occurrence. Harm and probability are equal factors in formulating a physical security plan.

The assurance plan responds to a threat by recommending the deployment of a set of countermeasures. Defining that set requires broad spectrum planning rooted in a complete and thorough understanding of the situation. For instance, if the facility is located in an earthquakes prone area, such as San Francisco or Los Angeles, then defining steps to ensure the structural integrity of the building, tethering the equipment, and reinforcing the housings is essential. If the facility is in the Gulf Coast, then hurricanes are the focus rather than earthquakes. Consequently, planning has to center not only on wind proof buildings but it also has to consider the effects of floods. Effective planning for all contingencies ensures efficient disaster recovery.

Ensuring Effective Planning

Physical security protection is implemented through a formal, organization-wide plan aligned with both the business and information assurance goals. The actions recommended should be directly linked to the organizational assets they protect.

The team responsible for developing the plan should specify the threats associated with the protected items in the secure space and specify countermeasures to address those threats. The top echelon in the organization has to be committed to underwrite the physical security planning and execution process because of the relatively high cost of security countermeasures.

The physical security plan should be able to respond to all credible threats in advance. The plan must include the mechanisms for re-evaluating and reclassifying known threats and redeploying the measures to respond appropriately because the circumstances of a security event are unpredictable.

There should be controls in place to ensure that the secure space is not susceptible to intrusion and that sensitive materials are stored in secure containers. Physical security access measures make certain that only the people with a legitimate need are granted access. Finally, physical security planning should ensure that the organization responds effectively to natural disasters.

The implementation plan is overseen by the audit function that monitors and enforces accountability. The harm arising from a breakdown in physical security is significant, so accountability must be assigned during the planning phase and subsequently enforced. Management roles have to be designated to enforce accountability through continuous monitoring.

Physical security plans might be—and often *are*—developed separately from the information assurance planning function because physical security is not always perceived as part of information assurance. Whether physical security planning is done separately or as part of the information assurance function, it is essential that the plan ensures a fully integrated, continuous, and effective protection against physical threats.

If the actions to assure the physical space and equipment are not coordinated with measures taken to protect the information itself, the system may be vulnerable. In fact, physical and electronic safeguards are inseparable because many assets that physical security protects such as computer equipment and network cables are part of the overall information infrastructure.

Defense-In-Depth Countermeasures

Like everything else in the information assurance and security process, physical security relies on the ability to identify and prioritize the threats and vulnerabilities. The threat assessment process was discussed in detail in Chapter 2. In this chapter we will discuss the aspects of physical security to be considered in a general threat assessment process.

The purpose of the physical security process is to safeguard equipment, facilities, or infrastructure by preventing or delaying damage to assets under its control. The planner should recognize that physical security threats may be slowed down; they cannot be prevented entirely. Therefore, the physical security process is built around measures to extend the time it takes for a threat to cause harm. This is called a **defense in depth** strategy.

Defense in depth involves design of the steps to detect, assess, and report physical threats or intrusions that might occur. Because circumstances are always changing, the only way to ensure reliable threat assessment is through regular and systematic evaluation of the physical environment. During that process, all possible occurrences should be identified and catalogued and their probability estimated. In that respect, this activity is no different from the process outlined for cyber-threats. It simply focuses on threats in a different dimension, physical space.

In the threat assessment process, a decision has to be made about the probabilities of occurrence and harm. The goal is to develop and prioritize a list of hazards that represent both a high degree of potential for damage as well as a high likelihood of occurrence because physical countermeasures are expensive to implement. As a result, the threat assessment process has to be driven by cost-benefit analysis.

The outcome of that assessment should produce a manageable set of threats, which are likely to occur for that particular space.

Physical Security Targets and Threats

It is important to factor four threat types into a comprehensive physical security plan. Although some may seem trivial at first glance, all are sources of threat:

- Facilities
- Equipment
- People
- Environment

Threats to the Facility

The first category of threat involves the physical infrastructure and protecting that infrastructure against operating failures. Two common examples of infrastructure threats are power outages and breakdowns in building systems. These are critical security considerations, because the information processing function relies on clean and steady power, as well as the integrity of its physical support systems.

Ensuring Clean and Steady Power

A common facility threat is a loss of power. This happens more frequently than one would think. According to IBM, the average computer operation experiences over 120 power events or problems a month. These events include voltage spikes, sags, and brownouts. These may be minor irritations in the middle of the night or if they happen intermittently. However, loss of power poses a major operational hazard if it interrupts work in the middle of the day or takes an organization's website out of service.

Power disruptions have an economic effect in information dependent organizations. For instance, most assembly lines are computer controlled, so a power failure affecting the computing function may cause a costly production disruption, even if the organization itself has all necessary labor and parts available to operate. Therefore, factor in the cost of downtime across the organization when deciding about the importance of avoiding **power interruptions**.

A complete loss of power lasting from one to five minutes has significant operational impact; however, a catastrophic incident, is the blackout—the loss of commercial power for a significant time. There are also building-related problems such as sags and dips (short periods of low voltage), surges (sudden rises in voltage), and **brownouts** (deliberate reduction of voltage by the utility company). These produce momentary and sometimes indistinguishable problems in the short term but they may damage computer equipment over time.

Power problems affect computers in three ways. First, they can damage the hardware, causing downtime for the equipment. They can affect network availability, which translates into lost productivity across the system. Finally, power problems may result in a loss of data. The latter happens when a sudden outage corrupts open databases or unsaved documents. Power problems stem from many sources within the facility. High demand electrical devices such as air conditioners, space heaters, and copiers on the same circuit can cause chronic power sags or surges. These sags and surges typically account for up to 60 percent of the 280 potentially disruptive interruptions. A primary consideration to mitigate power interruptions is having backup power sources available to allow an orderly shutdown. Devices designed to eliminate fluctuations are hardware items, such as surge suppressors and Uninterruptible Power Supplies (UPS). A simple safeguard like a UPS is an important protection against significant data loss or damage from a power failure. The UPS also reduces or eliminates power fluctuations.

For the area to be secure, the best solution is a fully integrated infrastructure for power assurance. Careful planning is necessary because there are so many things—both natural and manmade—that could go wrong with power supply. Potential infrastructure hazards to look for are:

- **Voltage swings**—the installation of automated power line monitors that detect, record, and respond to fluctuations in frequency and voltage is best. These devices should note swings in voltage and set off alarms. They are important safety features because fluctuations can be indicative of serious power problems.

- **Drains**—drains are a more substantial form of swing. Because of drains, computers should never be placed on the same circuit as high-capacity items that require a lot of current to operate properly. The threat may come from simple home equipment, like electric dryers and microwaves. Even if a power distribution system is perfectly healthy, starting a copier on the same circuit induces sags that over time are damaging to mechanical components like hard drives.

- **Hazardous wiring**—Simple wiring considerations, as low-tech as they seem, are an important part of engineering a clean and steady power supply. Because the growth of the information processing is tied directly to power demands, the building wiring should be designed to accommodate the demands of a growing organization. For example, if the organization is planning to engage in a new area of work, it is important to build the power demands into the initial planning and design.

- **Alternate power sources**—backups must be readily available in the event of a failure of the primary resource. A UPS meets that requirement in the case of temporary interruptions, but with major outages it might be necessary to have some sort of dedicated feeder line or circuit that attaches to an on-site generator or an alternative utility substation.

Any solution beyond installing a UPS might seem dramatic for the small business. However, for situations like the three-day outage experienced in the Midwest in the summer of 2003 these precautions could be the difference between business survival and failure.

Finally, because power is so important, it is prudent to locate rooms that contain power distribution panels, master circuit breakers, transformers, and feeder cables within the security perimeter. This ensures that access to the physical controls is enforced.

Ensuring Other Building Systems

While ensuring the power source is important, it is equally important to ensure that other critical building systems are reliable. This includes the *heating, ventilation*, and *air conditioning* (HVAC), *plumbing*, and *water supply* systems.

Computers are electrical devices that should not get wet. It is vital to ensure that leaks in the building's water or plumbing system do not cause flooding in the machine room. Therefore, it is important to ensure that water supply and plumbing systems are designed and installed to ensure that a failure will not threaten the information processing and storage facilities.

Clearly, data center or server rooms should not be located adjacent to or directly below water sources. This common sense rule is why the placement of the information processing function in the basement of the building is a design flaw. While a subterranean location may make access control easier, remember, water flows downhill.

In addition to common-sense water handling design precautions, it is also good practice to inspect the water and plumbing systems on a routine and regular basis and have a contingency plan if a failure happens.

Temperature extremes can cause long-term harm to computer equipment; temperature and humidity should be strictly regulated. The operating temperature for electronic devices might not meet the same criteria for comfort as the other occupants of the building. Therefore, it is best to isolate controls that regulate the temperature for the computer equipment away from the temperature controls for the rest of the building.

Although the HVAC ensures ideal operating temperatures it also introduces the hazard of dust and airborne pollutants particularly in industrial and manufacturing facilities. Therefore, it may be necessary to isolate the air intakes for the heating and air conditioning system for the computer facility, away from of the intakes for the rest of the building. Routine accesses for maintenance should be monitored because the equipment control rooms are the primary points of vulnerability for the system.

Safeguarding Equipment

In the computer industry's first 25 years equipment was easy to protect. Critical items such as mainframe CPUs and peripheral devices were locked in controlled environments and were not portable. Few workers had access to the space and they could be carefully monitored and controlled.

Computers containing critical information are now the size of a small notebook and a seemingly infinite amount of data can be stored and carried in memory devices the size of your thumb. Keeping this in mind is important to the physical security process.

The physical security process safeguards tangible items from theft. This includes communication, processing, storage, and input or output devices in the secure physical space. The countermeasures must assure the safety and security of all equipment, media, supporting systems, and supplies that resident within the physical space.

Conventional **physical access control** measures establish the integrity of controlled spaces. These measures include locks, passcards, RFID, and swipecard readers, video cameras, and safes. They may also include human-based monitoring and control methods, such as security guards and badges as well as simple administrative mechanisms and visitor escort.

Because systems must be distributed to fulfill their mission some equipment, media, and supporting equipment cannot be secured using a controlled space method. Examples of these would be network devices and easily portable equipment. Problems associated with these items are discussed in the following sections.

Protecting Networks: Ensuring Integrity over a Wide Area

The steps needed to ensure the integrity of the physical components of a network are a crucial part of the assurance process because information processing is indivisible from network operations. Protection of networks is a separate and critical concern in the protection of information technology because network equipment is a primary point of access to any system. It may be more vulnerable than the other components because they are distributed. Remember, parts of a network such as physical transmission connections and cables are outside of the security perimeter.

Protection schemes prevent unauthorized access to network assets and components. Network devices and transmission media are tempting targets because they are exposed beyond the security perimeter and their physical security is more difficult to guarantee. Technical countermeasures such as interruption sensors, line monitors, and emanations security can be adopted to increase security of network equipment. These ensure continuous monitoring of the network's operation or detection of interruptions and suspicious behavior. They may also shield the transmission from surreptitious access.

Security failures on networks happen in two ways. A conventional failure occurs when unauthorized users intercept information by physically accessing the network equipment and compromising the integrity or confidentiality of the transmission through remote facilities. Conversely, a failure can occur if the network is unable to carry out its transmission functions; this is a violation of the availability principle.

The simple solution is to locate network equipment unobtrusively and either bury cables or route them out of reach. Cables are particularly vulnerable to damage. The best response to the vulnerability of cables is to route them in such a way that they are away from common hazards such as backhoes and falling trees. Once that is done, cables should always be monitored for suspicious variation in the transmission characteristics.

If network transmissions are particularly sensitive, the military for example, the cables must be physically shielded to prevent external parties from "reading" the electromagnetic impulses and other signals that go along them. This type of countermeasure is called **emanations security**.

One of the oldest examples of an emanations security standard is TEMPEST, which is a classified set of U.S. government standards aimed at restricting electric or electromagnetic radiation emanations from electronic equipment.

The standard is necessary because computers and electronic devices emit radiation, called "emanations." These emanations are not difficult to intercept, read, and record. Since emanations can be read from some distance—including space—in the 1950s and 1960s the federal government developed a series of specifications for how to shield sensitive transmissions. These TEMPEST standards specify measures to eliminate electronic "leakage" from the processing, transmission, or storage of information. Security is based on shielding the device, or even an entire room, with materials that will absorb emanations. Originally, shields were based on metals such as copper to establish a Faraday Cage. However, with the advent of high-tech polymers the shielding is much more sophisticated. Emanation standards are not confined to the United States; there are similar standards worldwide including Great Britain, Germany, and NATO.

Protecting Portable Devices

Physical protection of equipment has become more difficult with the advent of portable devices including laptops. The ultimate physical access attack is simple theft of the equipment. Therefore, it is pointless to talk about other forms of security if the device can be stolen easily. The most effective countermeasure against theft is to lock up machines containing sensitive data. Fifteen years ago, the rule was easy to enforce because it was hard for an employee to walk out the door with a bulky CPU under an arm.

To complicate matters further, it is a simple matter of popping a memory stick, a removable hard drive, a notebook computer, or a PDA into a briefcase and disappearing with the confidential data. The problem of ubiquitous portability requires that organization should adhere to the following principles:

- First—ensure that the device itself is always controlled—assign individual responsibility and enforce accountability for all portable devices.

- Second—ensure that the data on the device is secure—in the case of sensitive data ensure that it cannot be transported nor displayed without authorization and accountability.

- Third—ensure controls that are provided to ensure the security of a portable item are easy for end-users to follow. Otherwise, they will be subverted.

The last of these three principles is the most important since these principles depend primarily on systematic and disciplined execution. Remember, the security procedures for the protection of portable devices must be easy to execute.

Ease of use can be increased by automation such as installing tracking devices on either the protected mechanism or its storage location. In addition, organizations have turned to RFID- and GPS-based monitoring systems to make sure that controlled items are where they are supposed to be. Organizations should make sure that data on portable devices is secured by encryption to prevent access even if the device is lost.

Finally, positional technology and software controls are augmented by procedural safeguards such as storing the protected device inside an easy to access secure space when it is not in use. Of course, all rules for secure access and storage must be enforced.

Controlling Access by People

The third type of physical control protects the system from malicious human acts including theft, industrial or state-sponsored espionage, and sabotage. Most of the serious damage to computers and information assets comes from the intentional or deliberate acts. The most common of these acts are criminal—theft of computer equipment or documents and **vandalism**.

These problems were discussed in the chapter on Personnel Assurance. Recall the detailed steps that should be taken to create and enforce trust and confidence throughout the organization. We will now detail the safeguards included in physical access control.

People are the weakest link in both the personnel and physical security chain. Therefore, access control mechanisms have to be established to ensure that only the right people have access to the facility and its equipment and information assets.

As you go through the following subsections, you will find that effective access control requires designing a **layered defense** in the physical environment with continuous monitoring and control of access built in.

The planning process for establishing physical facility access controls involves identifying and countering the vulnerabilities open to a thief. One should be mindful of the roof, basement, and window access points. In addition, fire escapes and service access areas such as loading docks are a problem, since they must less restricted when needed, but highly restricted when they are not. For example, an unsecured loading dock creates a point of vulnerability. However, initiating extensive security procedures on a loading dock can restrict the access of authorized individuals and make deliveries harder. This would increase cost. The design process involves finding the proper balance between security and availability.

The heart of **access control systems** is the ability to grant convenient physical access to authorized people and at the same time completely denies access to unauthorized ones. Therefore physical access control measures include mechanisms to ensure that people access the security perimeter only at authorization checkpoints. Mechanisms for restricting physical access include **perimeter controls** designed to channel access into specific places. Controls include restriction devices such as *natural barriers*, **fence systems**, *walls*, and they may be supplemented with *mechanical barriers* such as secure windows, **doors**, and **locks**.

Perimeter Controls: Barriers

Of the three primary physical controls, perimeter security is the first line of defense. Devices to secure the perimeter include natural or structural protective **barriers**. *Natural barriers* include high ornamental shrubs, decorative streams, and long grassy lawns. A grouping of shrubs or trees provides a barrier to access as well as defines a point of entry. They might look as if they were placed there to enhance the attractiveness of the site, but their primary purpose is to provide terrain that is difficult to penetrate or cross without detection. Many facilities use dense prickly shrubs like boxwood or spiny shrubs such as Spanish bayonet, holly, or cactus, around the building as an eco-friendly fence.

Structural barriers are a larger category of defense. These include such devices as *fences, gates, bollards,* and facility *walls* and *doors*. **Fences** are critical to physical security because they define the secure areas and enforce entry only at designated points. They are composed of a barrier material like chain link, which meets gauge and fabric specifications. High-security areas may use a "top guard" of barbed or razor wire. Some security environments require multiple concentric fences—triple wire.

Once a fence is installed, good security practice centers on proper maintenance, including regular patrols around the entire boundary. Factors that need to be considered with fences include assurance that the fence fabric is securely attached to the poles and that vegetation or adjacent structures cannot serve as a "bridge." Once the fence line is established, electronic monitoring using fiber optic systems such as FOIDS increases the security.

Gates and **bollards** (concrete posts or barriers) are part of the restriction system. They ensure controlled access persons or vehicles from a secured area. Gates define the entry and exit points and bollards control traffic and protect property by preventing vehicles from being rammed through the access point in the security perimeter.

If the site is particularly sensitive, there might be a need to install additional fence controls. These controls are usually termed a *perimeter security system* and typically include technical elements such as photoelectric, ultrasonic, microwave, passive infrared (PIR), and pressure-sensitive sensors.

One of the most effective and cost-efficient **intrusion detection** devices along a perimeter is closed circuit television (CCTV). CCTV uses dedicated cameras to monitor a fence and send pictures to a central location over a secure transmission medium. There are three main components of a CCTV. The first is the camera—either fixed or zoom-capable. Cameras may have remote controls that allow them to be panned and tilted. The transmission media typically are based on coaxial cable, fiber optic cable, or wireless technologies. Finally, there are the monitors, which provide three levels of control:

- **Detection**—The ability to detect the presence of an object

- **Recognition**—The ability to determine the type of object

- **Identification**—The ability to determine the object details

The ability to observe is limited by the system design. For example, the success of a fence-line CCTV system depends on two factors—*placement* and *lighting*. To get placement right it is necessary to understand the surveillance requirements of the facility including such things as the size of the area to be monitored. Once the height, width, and depth parameters are established, a camera can be selected.

Lighting ensures continued visibility in darkness. Because it is passive, lighting should be used in conjunction with other controls, such as **patrols** and alarm systems. The type of lighting required is important because different types of lamps provide different effectiveness. Good lightning creates a good contrast between the object and background. Lamp types offer different features, such as continuous-on, glare projection, flood, trip, standby, and emergency lighting.

Perimeter Controls: Intrusion Detection

Perimeter-based intrusion detection systems ensure the integrity of a physical space. As their name suggests, they detect intrusion into secure areas and provide real time warning of perimeter violations. The system monitors for suspicious traffic, tracks intruders, and subsequently marks security holes discovered.

In real time, perimeter detection is based on monitoring sensors and observing actions along the perimeter. It can also be retrospective. Retrospective monitoring uses security logs or audit data to detect unauthorized accesses. Intrusion detection on the facility boundary is as important as the more sophisticated network IDS techniques because threats from physical intrusions, such as malicious damage and theft, are as real and valid as the cyber threat posed by hackers.

Sensors installed at each access point such as windows, doors, ceilings, and walls, establish perimeter protection. In addition to the obvious locations, sensors should be installed on less obvious access points including ventilation openings or air conditioning vents. Physical intrusion detection sensors are frequently designed around alterations of electrical circuits, electrostatic fields, and light beams as well as sound, vibration, and motion detection.

Perimeter Controls: Guards and Patrols

Most human-based measures including guards and patrols date to prehistory. They are a low-tech, labor-intensive approach to access control. However, human-based security systems can provide an effective deterrent to unauthorized entry if the guards are properly disciplined and adequately trained in security procedures.

A good security guard is less expensive and no less reliable than automated systems. Guards are not passive and cannot be disconnected or sabotaged as with high-tech solutions. However, they are subject to error. Thus, effective human-centric security relies on well-defined procedures and constant discipline coupled with clear, commonly understood rules accompanied by constant oversight and motivation by security managers.

Perimeter Controls: Structural and Mechanical Barriers

Doors and windows have to be strictly controlled since they are the most likely point of access to a facility. There are numerous considerations in determining which type of door structure should be used. These include:

- Whether to employ a hollow-core versus solid-core technology
- How to identify and address hinge and doorframe vulnerabilities
- Whether to monitor use through contact devices such as switches and pressure plates

To ensure maximum security, doors should be solid-core construction with sufficient and appropriate lock mechanics. The hinges should be securely fixed to the frames and the frame should be securely attached to the adjoining wall. Finally, the door hinge pins should be concealed or secured.

Windows are important since they are points of illicit access to the secured perimeter. Since they are compromised by breaking, window material makes a difference to the level of security. Windows can be made of standard plate glass, tempered glass, and acrylic materials such as polycarbonates. Polycarbonate windows are glass and polymer combinations that combine the best quality of glass and acrylics. For special applications, other types of glass may be employed including laminated and wired glass. These are particularly effective where breakage is likely. In any case, critical windows should be have breakage sensors and alarms.

Finally, security should also be considered in the design of the building itself. For instance, computer facility walls should not be external building wall. In addition, walls should extend from the floor to the underside of the above floor—slab to slab. Unused places such as attics and crawlspaces should be equipped with alarms to monitor both unauthorized access and the presence of smoke or fire.

Mechanical Barrier Devices: Locks

Locks are the most widely accepted and employed mechanical barrier devices. They are composed of a lock body and a cylinder, a bolt, a strike plate, and a key. Locks are "pick-resistant," not "pickproof," and should be used in conjunction with other controls in a physical security scheme

All locks are subject to force and if a more elegant solution is required, special tools can be used to gain entry. Locks can be opened by anything from a special-purpose electronic "pick" to a tension wrench. Consequently, they must be considered a delay device rather than a foolproof barrier. Types of locks include

- Cipher locks contain buttons that open the lock when pushed in the proper sequence.

- Combination locks use a sequence of numbers in a specified order.

- Deadbolt locks use a separate bolt not operated by the primary door handle inserted into the doorframe for added security.

- Smart locks permit only authorized people into certain doors at certain times. Most use some form of time-sensitive radio frequency or smart card for access.

Keys are the **authentication tokens** for most locks and therefore, one security element rests with the control of keys. Key control procedures must be established, adhered to, and documented. Conventional keys have several limitations. They are hard to change, easy to copy, and difficult to invalidate. Therefore, the organization must employ sound practices for the issuance, sign-out, inventory, destruction, and immediate replacement of lost keys. Knowledge of the combination is the key with combination locks, so it must be changed at specified times and under specified circumstances.

There are also more modern types of keys. For instance, radio frequency keys and readers are becoming high-end items on some brands of luxury automobile. This technology uses radio frequency chips in the keys to send out a code to the vehicle. The code is read and used to validate the user in the authentication database. Because keys can be lost or stolen, this technology is most effective when used in a **two-factor authentication** system (with a door PIN for instance). That ensures that a lost key cannot be used to steal the vehicle and that any key that is lost is deleted from the database.

Biometric Systems

Biometrics is an emerging authentication tool in physical access control and represents a leading edge in physical perimeter protection. Through advancements in smart cards and cheaper reader prices, biometrics is catching on as the primary security alternative to passwords. It makes use of "something you are," for example, fingerprints or a retina scan, signature dynamics, voice recognition, and even hand geometry, to authenticate "who you are." The process is based on exclusive physical attributes, which can be read and digitized. The user is scanned and the data are compared. In theory, only a match should allow access.

Depending on the sensitivity of the information and value of the facility and its contents, biometrics can be used in conjunction with **smart cards**. These "smart" cards are credit-card-sized plastic items issued to authorized individuals with a special chip embedded in the surface. The chip stores information in an electronic form that can authenticate a user. An example of a smart card is the plastic card that is used as a key in some hotel rooms; it is replacing the plastic card with magnetic stripe. However, this is also an example of the limitations of a simple smart card. Since the authentication is built into the card (just like a simple key), unauthorized individuals who want to gain access can also use a lost card. Thus, a biometric reader can ensure that only the authorized holder of the key is attempting to gain access and the presence of the key can help counteract biometric errors by minimizing false positives.

A problem with biometric systems is that scanning errors occur leading to false positives and false negatives. A false positive permits access to unauthorized people. False positives can be generated using illicit approaches such as using stolen fingerprints. With a false negative, the system denies access to someone who is authorized. These false results can be based on several factors such as physical changes to the individual's actual biometric signature over time.

Doubling the Assurance: Multiple Factor Authentication

Most high secure facilities make use of more than one form of authentication to control access. This is called a **multiple-factor authorization** based on three broad categories:

- What you are (for example, biometrics)
- What you have (for example, tokens)
- What you know (for example, passwords)

Simple multiple-factor authentication requires confirmation of at least two factors before granting access. For example, biometrics can be used with a smart card to authenticate the user. In this form of authentication, the user's biometric information is stored on a smart card, the card is placed in a reader and a biometric scanner collects its data. That data is matched against the information stored on the card to authenticate that the user of the card is indeed the person who is authorized to use it. If the two match, then access is granted.

Three-factor authentication combines three types, for instance a smart card reader that asks for a PIN before enabling a retina scanner. Multiple factors reduce the probability that an attacker would have the correct materials for authentication. Multiple factor authentication a is fast, accurate, and secure method that is gaining popularity due to its ease of use and effectiveness.

Ensuring Against the Well-Intentioned Human Being

Finally, a good physical security system accommodates the "people" factor. In the section on physical access control, we discussed ways information assets can be safeguarded against malicious individuals. Nevertheless, accidents and not intentional acts are the most frequent cause of human-based harm. Because they are unintentional, they are harder to anticipate and difficult to prevent.

There are many ways humans cause accidental system damage. The practical safeguard is training and a sound set of common-sense procedures aimed at preventing the common errors. For instance, because spilling liquids onto computer equipment can cause irreparable damage, most computer rooms have signs saying, "No food or drinks allowed." This demonstrates that the best procedure to prevent accidental damage is by eliminating the cause.

A proactive way to address human error is through training and drills. The primary purpose of routine drills, exercises, and testing is to keep people continuously aware of their security responsibilities. To be effective, the training has to be continuous to be effective. The basic rule of thumb is a corollary to Murphy's Law: *A disaster plan is an appropriate countermeasure.* This leads directly to the last category.

Mitigating the Effects of Natural Disasters and Fires

Response or disaster planning is the primary means of assuring against the broad category of **natural disasters**. An effective response plan is essential for dealing with disasters because things like earthquakes and hurricanes are hard to predict and impossible to prevent. The response to them *can* be planned. Therefore, most secure facilities have a disaster planning team. Disaster response countermeasures center on awareness, anticipation, and preparation:

- **Awareness**: It is essential for the responsible parties in the organization to be kept continuously aware of the need for physical disaster planning because information systems are susceptible to natural events. These events have to be accounted for in the information assurance plan. It is essential that the organization maintain and continue to support the development of up-to-date and appropriate plans for all contingencies that affect the facility adversely.

- **Anticipation**: Involves the development of a set of contingency plans to respond to anticipated natural or environmental disasters. Anticipation involves specification of the procedures to be followed to safeguard facilities and information assets against a given natural disaster. Natural disasters are less likely occurrences than facility failure or malicious action. However, when a natural disaster occurs, it is frequently extremely destructive and costly.

- **Preparation**: In addition to the plan, it is also important to have measures in place to respond to anticipated natural events. If a facility is located in a place susceptible to earthquakes, safety measures ought to be in place to ensure that earthquake damage is minimized. These measures would be irrelevant in a place that is not likely to have an earthquake. However, some type of natural disaster occurs in every place in the world and so physical measures to ensure reasonable protection should be available to counter the effects of foreseen event.

Planning for Fire Prevention

When it comes to physical disaster, fire is a common event. Although loss of power is the most frequent source of physical harm to computers and information, the second largest cause is fire according to a national study done by KPMG. The primary difference between these two incidents is their level of destructiveness and loss. If a fire happens, it is usually results in total loss. Earlier, we discussed how loss of power can be mitigated. There is little mitigation for fire, consequently, we will discuss the physical threat of fire as a separate category.

Computers and their components are extremely flammable devices. Some experts speculate that a contributing factor in the collapse of the World Trade Center was the tons of burning computer equipment inside. Fires are hard to control because they may occur in unsecured parts of a building and a fire does not respect secure space boundaries. They can originate from a number of external sources both natural and human, such as wildfires and accidents; they destroy the entire space rather than just selected parts.

Computer electronic components are a combustion source, extremely flammable, and most computer equipment is housed in hydrocarbon-based plastic. Tests have shown that a computer keyboard subjected to nothing more than a candle flame will begin to burn after only 20 seconds. Thus, rooms full of computer equipment are extreme fire hazards and this has to be considered in creating an effective physical security plan. There are three primary issues associated with fire protection:

- Prevention—Reduction in the causes and sources of fire
- Detection—Receiving a warning of fire before it becomes a problem
- Suppression—Extinguishing and containing a fire to minimize damage

Preventing Fires

A good building design improves the chances of prevention. That includes the use of fire-resistant materials in walls, doors, and furnishings. Reduce the number of combustible material in the surrounding environment.

A proactive approach to fires protection is fire-prevention awareness for employees. Because computers are fire hazards, employees have to be aware of the consequences of smoking and the use of open flames and they have to know what to do if computer equipment ignites. Recall that a burning computer may emit poisonous gasses.

The immediate danger that a computer fire poses requires that employees know how to react. Thus, it is important to conduct response drills, such as a fire drill, so that personnel know how to react safely if a fire breaks out.

Fire Detection

Another essential of fire safety is **fire detection**. Fire detection provides warning as close to the fire event as possible. Large computer operations have many electrical parts, any one of which can because of a malfunction heat up and start a fire. Given the flammability of computer equipment, it is critical to have the capability to identify and deal with a hot part before it becomes a disaster.

The means of providing warning is through passive monitoring devices, of which there are a number of types. The most common are the ionization-type **smoke detectors**, which detect charged particles in smoke (Figure 8-1).

Figure 8-1
Operation of
an ionization
smoke detector

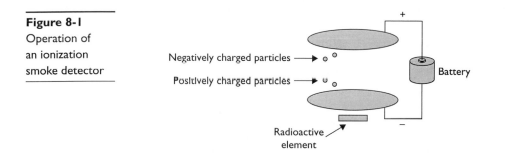

Negatively charged particles ⟶

Positively charged particles ⟶

Battery

Radioactive
element

Because smoke is frequently the first symptom of a computer fire, smoke detectors are effective when maintained properly. Some kinds of non-equipment-related fires do not produce smoke; however, ionization detectors will work in most cases.

Two related types of detectors are photoelectric and heat sensing. Photoelectric or optical detectors react to light blockage caused by smoke particles; however, the down side is that the fire has to be advanced enough to produce enough smoke to change the lighting situation. Finally, there are fixed or rate-of-rise temperature sensors. These are heat detectors that react to the heat of a fire. They suffer from the same problem as the optical devices; fire has to have been burning for some time in order to activate them.

Most facilities use some combination of these devices to get a layered covering (defense in depth) of the space. Deploy the most effective array of sensors to cover all types of fire. Early detection reduces damage since fire is a real and present danger. There is a strong economic justification for a thorough risk analysis followed by implementation of a broad set of operational sensing devices.

Fire Suppression

If the fire occurs, the first line of defense is the **fire suppression** system. Effective fire suppression depends on having the right type of fire extinguisher available. There are various types of fire extinguishers each effective in different situations. The internationally approved designation of different fire extinguishers is a lettering scheme. Each extinguisher type is lettered "A," "B," "C," or "D". Each is designed to suppress a different type of fire based on the materials involved.

The range of effectiveness of extinguishers goes up with the lettering. The "C" type extinguisher will be effective against "A" and "B" fires; however, an "A" type extinguisher should not be used to fight a "B" or "C" class fire. The "A" type extinguishers fight common material fires, such as wood or cloth. The "B" type extinguishers are designed for liquid fires, such as oil. Type "C" extinguishers should be used on computer fires, because they suppress fires associated with electrical sources including faulty wiring, fuse boxes, energized (electrified) equipment, and other sources of electricity.

The most common "C" type extinguisher contains pressurized carbon dioxide (CO_2), which displaces oxygen and provides a colorless, odorless chemical blanket for the fire. It leaves no residue that might cause additional damage.

It is important to have fire extinguishers on hand for immediate fire suppression; however, know that fire extinguishers have limited use. They are not designed to fight advanced fires. Attempting to put out a large or spreading fire with a hand fire extinguisher may make the situation worse. The correct response to large scale firefighting is a fire suppression system. In the machine rooms of the 1980s and 1990s these were built around a substance called Halon, which is a compound consisting of bromine, fluorine, and carbon.

Halon is effective and it was the fire suppression agent of choice in most computer rooms and other protected spaces. It was deployed through both built-in systems and handheld portable fire extinguishers. Halon displaced oxygen in the space and was dangerous for humans in the room. However, the Montreal Protocol on Substances That Deplete the Ozone Layer banned Halon in 1987 because it contributes to ozone depletion. The European Union requires removal of Halon from implementations, even those installed prior to 1987.

After 1992, new fire suppression systems had to use alternate chemicals. The common agent now is FM200 (FM-200/heptafluoropropane), which is sometimes referred to as HFC-227ea. FM200 extinguishes a fire by both robbing it of oxygen and by its physical suppression effect. It is a colorless gas, which is stored as a liquid in pressurized tanks and dispensed from the fire suppression system as a vapor spray. It is electrically nonconductive and environmentally inert. It is active on fire but inert on people, so it is also not hazardous.

The oldest and by far least effective way to put out a computer fire is the water sprinkler system. While these are useful to fight class "A" fires and as such are often deployed throughout a building including secure computer spaces, they are dangerous for two reasons. First, water can be a conductor of electricity, which will compound the problem in a computer room fire. Moreover, unlike the more sophisticated products such as Halon and FM200, water damages electrical equipment.

Chapter 8 Review

Chapter Summary

- Physical security centers on the definition of coherent measures to safeguard against direct physical attacks.
- The classic purpose of physical security is to account for and control tangible information and IT assets.
- Physical security can only be assured by procedures.
- Assets should always be protected with several perimeters. This is called a layered defense.
- Location is the primary determinant for physical security because it dictates the requirements of the access control system.

- Access has to be granted and monitored.

- Authorization needs to be continuously monitored.

- Defining a logical set of control objectives and then confirming compliance establishes control.

- The basic mechanisms that are used to underwrite physical security are designed to control access and detect intrusion.

- The process is instituted through a strategic planning activity and it is monitored and enforced by a consistent and ongoing security management function.

- The only sure way to protect facilities is to define a finite physical space and an effective set of countermeasures to assure the integrity of the area.

- Secure workspaces evolve from a comprehensive threat analysis and subsequent prioritization process, which leads to a carefully arrayed physical security plan.

- The process of establishing physical security rests on the ability to distinguish the threats and vulnerabilities that apply to a given situation.

- The most frequent cause of human-based harm is accident.

- Controls are an essential part of physical security.

- Most highly secure facilities usually make use of more than one form of authentication to control access.

- In the domain of physical security, there are three primary issues associated with fire protection: prevention, detection, and suppression.

- Perimeter intrusion detection methods and technologies should be used to ensure the integrity of a computer facility.

Key Terms

access control systems (216)
authentication tokens (219)
authorizations (207)
barriers (216)
biometrics (219)
bollards (217)
brownouts (211)
doors (216)
facilities (205)
fence systems (216)
fire detection (222)
fire suppression (223)
gates (208)
intrusion detection (217)
keys (219)

layered defense (216)
location (207)
locks (216)
multiple-factor authorization (220)
natural disasters (221)
perimeter controls (216)
perimeter-based intrusion detection (217)
physical access control (213)
physical security planning (207)
power interruptions (211)
rules for controlling (206)
secure space (206)
sensors (218)
smart cards (220)
smoke detectors (223)
three-factor authorization (220)
two-factor authentication (219)
vandalism (215)

Key Term Quiz

Complete each statement by writing one of the terms from this list in each blank. Not all terms will be used.

1. Physical security is the area of information assurance that protects tangible resources from intentional acts and _____ by people.

2. _____ controls make use of biological properties to differentiate "what you are."

3. The point of "clean and steady power" is to avoid _____.

4. An access control technique based on biometrics and a PIN is called _____.

5. Secure areas are delimited by a _____ that is assured by a range of _____.

6. Physical security schemes are defined by a _____.

7. Authentication the might include biometrics and a smart card is called _____.

8. _____ are impossible to prevent, but they can be anticipated.

9. The perimeter is defined by _____.

10. Physical security is also based around deployment of _____.

Multiple Choice Quiz

1. Physical access negates:

   A. perimeter control

   B. disaster plans

C. other measures

D. plans

2. Physical security controls center on access control and

A. monitoring

B. intrusion detection

C. training

D. planning

3. Doors have to be controlled for good building defense; the other aspect is

A. windows

B. gates

C. network components

D. behavior

4. Disaster impact classification involves assessing the impacts of each

A. weakness

B. vulnerability

C. threat

D. contingency plan

5. Layered defenses involve

A. segmenting

B. defense-in-depth

C. limiting control

D. limiting access

6. The problem of dispersion is important because

A. information is dispersed to everybody

B. it influences access control

C. network equipment extends outside the secure space

D. it is impossible to protect against human error

7. The essential elements of access control in a physical space are

A. the same as they are for electronic access control

B. important to ensure least privilege

C. necessary for separation of duties

D. barriers, gates and bollards

8. Water and fire disasters are a particular problem because

   A. they are more destructive than any other type of disaster

   B. they happen more frequently

   C. they are impossible to prevent

   D. they can happen anywhere and neither respects secure space

9. Power problems are

   A. rate

   B. frequent

   C. physically destructive

   D. impossible to prevent

10. Location is an important factor because it dictates the form of the:

    A. solution

    B. risk assessment

    C. access control

    D. security policy and procedures

Essay Quiz

In your own words briefly answer the following questions:

1. Why is it particularly dysfunctional if the responsibility for physical security is assigned separate from the information assurance function?

2. What typical business functions might power problems impact?

3. Why are multiple-factor authentication techniques more effective than single authentication measures?

4. What is the purpose of sensors in perimeter and building security?

5. Why might it be harder to ensure against physical access?

6. What are the implications of inadvertent damage? How can inadvertent damage be prevented?

7. What are the implications of uncontrolled physical space? What can happen if it is not properly controlled?

8. Explain defense in depth in the physical universe. What are possible components of a layered defense?

9. How is the physical security process implemented? What are the factors that go into successful implementation?

10. What is the proper response to a threat? What are the elements of that response?

Case Exercise

Complete the following case exercise as directed by your instructor:

Heavy Metal Technologies (HMT) is a defense contractor headquartered in Huntsville, Alabama. It has been granted a contract that involves work with highly sensitive national security data. The bulk of the initial design work will be done at the Sunnyside West building. The layout of Sunnyside West is shown in Figure 8-2.

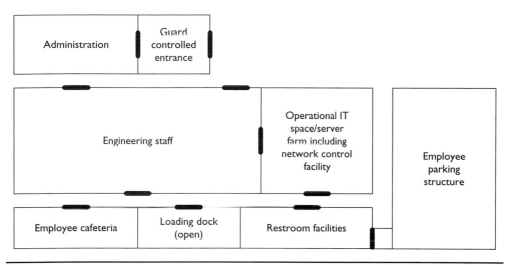

Figure 8-2 Building schematic

1. There are at least five physical vulnerabilities. What are they?
2. Describe the countermeasures you would deploy to counter these.

Assuring Against Software Vulnerabilities

In this chapter, you will learn how to:
- Assure against software vulnerabilities
- Evaluate commercial hacking attempts
- Quantify the software assurance process
- Assure outsourced work

Compromises of information assets are commonly caused by the exploitation of programming defects. Exploitable defects in programs allow attackers to affect the confidentiality, integrity, and availability of information assets processed by the program. Security of information assets rests on the integrity and security of its software.

Minor defects and flaws in programming lead to adverse consequences, such as the exploitation of buffer overflows and the execution of remote procedure calls. These flaws give attackers access to information on a target systems and may open the door to malicious code attacks.

Software defects raise information assurance and security issues; therefore, any programming failure found in commercial software after release can be very costly. A 2005 Department of Homeland Security study found that the announcement of a vulnerability in a product release led to an average $860 million reduction in the vendors' stock value. According to ZDNet, in 2005 the losses from programming and design errors approached $55 billion per year; the cost has been doubling every year since 2001.

In this chapter, we will learn how a meeting of the minds (contract) and other methods are used to deal with software defects. We will see how the process of developing or acquiring software causes defects and we will learn how to identify and remediate these defects before they create a compromise or vulnerability.

Hacking for Profit

A recent report from the FBI's Computer Intrusion Section points out that attempts to exploit defects in software are becoming more purposeful and organized because money is now the primary motivation for hackers, not curiosity as it was in the old days.

There are organized Internet groups who target companies in the financial sector for profit.

Frequently, these groups of hackers are as capable and well-financed as their targets and many of their attacks succeed. The number of successful targeted attacks represents about 40 percent of the total recently *reported* attacks. Since many organizations do not report an attack or compromise, the situation may be worse than it appears. The ability to ensure that software is free of security flaws is a national priority and policy.

Software Assurance as National Policy

Improving software assurance practice is a national priority because of the widespread problems that defects pose for protection of the critical information infrastructure. Remember, software enables everything from our national defense and financial systems to the controls that regulate our pipelines and nuclear plants. Presently there is no way to guarantee that software is free of exploitable defects.

To illustrate this point, the President's Information Technology Advisory Committee (PITAC) has issued a report that found that "Commonly used practices permit dangerous errors, which enable attackers to compromise millions of computers every year." Consequently, the National Strategy to Secure Cyberspace requires the Department of Homeland Security to "promulgate best practices and methodologies that promote integrity, security, and reliability in software." The term for the process that addresses that problem is **software assurance**.

What Are the Aims of Software Assurance?

Software assurance identifies and eliminates exploitable defects in the **development**, **acquisition**, and **operation** of software. Due to complexity, this task has been compared to "finding a needle in a haystack;" however, a more accurate analogy might be "finding a particular needle in a stack of needles." Short of failure, it is almost impossible to tell the difference between **secure code** and **insecure code** in a running system.

In practice, software assurance guarantees that all instances of a software product are

- **Trustworthy**—there are no exploitable vulnerabilities, either maliciously or unintentionally inserted.

- **Predictable**—there is justifiable confidence that software, when executed, functions in the manner for which it is intended.

- **Conformant**—organized, multidisciplinary practices are in place to ensure that software processes and products conform to all **requirements** and applicable standards.

Given the complexity of modern computer systems and the increasing tendency for organizations to develop software by global **outsourcing** or through un-vetted supply chains, ensuring these qualities is difficult. The solution is to perform software acquisition and development work using a systematic and disciplined process. The means for establishing this process is a set of well-defined, highly structured, and secure assurance practices.

A Pair of Distinctions

It is necessary to draw a distinction between activities that characterize the discipline of software assurance and those that logically part of information assurance. This distinction rests on the need to eliminate *exploitable* defects. Not every defect is exploitable. Therefore, the activities that assure that the software functions properly are *not* directly a part of the information assurance process. The body of knowledge that is oriented toward finding and fixing all software defects is part of **software engineering**.

Vulnerabilities in software result from defects in specification, design, or programming. The elements of software assurance relevant to information assurance are those aimed at identifying and remediating defects that constitute *security vulnerabilities*. Because the focus is identification, not remediation and repair, the information assurance component of software assurance is part of the testing and review process. Whether or not information assurance professionals actually perform tests and reviews themselves; the testers must understand the methods and concepts of those processes to meet their security obligations.

Given that responsibility, the goals of the software assurance professional and the information assurance professional differ only in the testing and review process objective. For software assurance professionals, the aim is to ensure properly running code that meets the user requirements. For information assurance professionals, the aim is to identify and remediate only the defects that may lead to the compromise or exploitation of information assets accessed the software.

The distinction implies a difference in the type and amount of work performed by these professionals and will be discussed in greater depth in the section entitled "The Software Process." This distinction seems minor, given that both processes are assurance oriented. Nonetheless, the difference between assuring the overall function of software versus ensuring against exploitable defects should be kept in mind when establishing an information assurance process. Assuring that software runs properly and meets user requirements is a large and separate area of concern that drains resources from any information assurance effort.

In addition to the distinction between software assurance and information assurance one should understand that there is a difference between the process of building software and maintaining it. Vulnerabilities are introduced at three points in the process:

- Design and Development
- Distribution
- Updates and Patches

These three fall into two areas of the discipline, *development* and *use* (sometimes called *sustainment*). The development process always results in new code, while sustainment remediates, repairs, or enhances existing instances of code.

Security should not be a late binding activity—one should think security while designing and building the function. Design and **development** involves the activities that create new code. In practice, design and development is the actual construction of a program. However, it also includes the modification, re-use, or re-engineering of existing code into new products. Defects in code represent vulnerabilities that should be easier to recognize and eliminate because the development is controlled using proper practices. Given this, it is possible to build the case for assurance as the software is being built.

Sustainment activities include the correction of defects, the optimization of existing code, and the implementation of minor changes. Code might be written but the aim is not to produce a new entity. Ensure that currently existing software operates as intended.

Code maintained by sustainment is *legacy code*. It is difficult to ensure that legacy code does not introduce exploitable defects because the code has been maintained over a long period typically without adequate record keeping, documentation and testing. It is likely that information assurance and security were not issues throughout its lifecycle. Without an unjustifiable expenditure of resources, it is difficult to confirm that legacy software is secure. Consequently, the problem of exploitation of hidden vulnerabilities in legacy code is one of the most serious facing information assurance professionals today.

Development and sustainment process defined by a set of commonly agreed-on practices intended to build or enhance a software product is called the **software process**.

The Software Process

Software is a set of instructions that make the computer useful. Programmers write those instructions for the computer using a **coding** or programming language.

Studies make it clear that defects originate not only during the code-writing stage. Problems with software originate from a failure to specify the product correctly; incorrect design; poor programming practice; or ineffective or inadequate review and testing.

The Stages of the Software Process

Software development has five stages—*specification, design, coding, testing,* and *use.* The first stage, specification, defines the product and can be accomplished through various means including classic specification, prototyping, or even extreme programming. Whatever method is used however, the outcome is an in-depth documented understanding of the functional requirements of the software.

In the design stage, the blueprints for the software product are created and decisions are made about how to build it. There are numerous ways to do a design. Recall that the purpose of the design stage is to conceptualize and communicate the structure of the product to the programmers who execute the plan.

The programmer translates the design into a computer program. A programming language is used to do this, hence the name of the stage, **programming**. The outcome of the programming stage is a correctly functioning code component.

Frequently, the programming stage is the source of defects. They can be accidental, like buffer overflows, or intentional, like the installation of Easter eggs, back doors and Trojan horses. The defects result from incorrect practice, human error, or malicious intent. The entire discipline of *secure coding* has been established to assure this area. The best place to assure against programming defects is during the programming stage when they are created. Despite the recommendations of experts like Fred Brooks in his book the *Mythical Man Month* who would encourage a focus on design, the actual programming work is so difficult and involved that it consumes all of the time.

Some testing is always done during the programming stage to confirm proper functioning. However, from an information assurance standpoint, if those tests are done by the programmer they violate the principle of least privilege and separation of duties. It is good practice for third parties to perform all assurance work while the programming is still going on.

Programming and testing should be done in parallel to confirm that the code is defect-free and functions properly. Since this is primarily a quality control function, it identifies the sources of the defects that create vulnerabilities. Therefore, the next stage in the process is the point where it is logical to directly identify and remediate defects. That stage is **testing** and is an appropriate place for information assurance professionals to be involved in software assurance.

Accordingly, that is the place where we will begin this discussion. As we said earlier, defects are not necessarily vulnerabilities, but from a software perspective, all vulnerabilities are defects. Thus, any vulnerability that might cause a loss of availability, confidentiality, or integrity must be identified and remediated. Figure 9-1 provides a roadmap of the major stages involved in assuring the development of vulnerability-free software.

Figure 9-1
Ensuring security in the software that you build

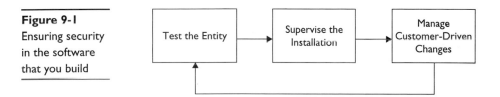

Preconditions: Establishing the Point of Reference

Testing makes use of documentation generated during prior stages in the software development process. The documentation is a point of reference that guides subsequent testing work. The tester must have a detailed description of what the software is intended to do. That description should include a definition of the system boundaries, as well as the behaviors the software should exhibit. It is essential to have a clear definition of the boundaries and behaviors to be able to judge whether the software contains the correct set of functions.

Significant problems can occur if the organization loses its understanding of the functions to be contained in the software. That understanding is easy to lose because the eventual form of the product is easy to change. Remember, that users will request new functions at the slightest whim and the designers and programmers can change course to accommodate unanticipated problems as they are encountered.

These *ad hoc* changes lead to the introduction of unintentional defects or malicious code segments that will never be tested or inspected because their existence is unknown. These types of problems are called *hidden vulnerabilities* and are a serious threat to code security. They may be created and inserted for the explicit purpose of causing mischief later.

Testing must have a point of reference to confirm that the functions in the finished product align with the specified functions. From an information assurance standpoint, testing should confirm that nothing exists in the code that should *not* be there. It takes a documented point of reference called a *software requirements specification (SRS)*, or more often simply a "specification." to achieve that level of control.

Vulnerabilities: Ensuring Nothing but Required Behaviors

The specification provides a complete, comprehensive, and unambiguous statement of the behaviors that the system must exhibit. This statement is developed at the beginning of the design process and it steers the construction of the product. Since much of testing is oriented toward confirming that the software functions as intended, this document also serves as an important support for the testing phase.

The required functions are detailed in the specification that prescribes a set of functions to be validated. Each function is described in terms of the behaviors that it must exhibit. To confirm these behaviors, the specification should provide an objective set of concrete assessment criteria. These criteria provide an observable description that can be used to confirm the existence and proper operation of the function. That allows the tester to validate that the software is performing as intended and is free of known vulnerabilities.

Vulnerabilities: Ensuring Nothing Extra

A testing process that focuses on confirming the behaviors required by the specification does not guarantee that hidden vulnerabilities are not present. Since hidden vulnerabilities may be placed in code for malicious purposes, it is important to identify and eliminate them. In addition to testing for conformance to the required behaviors, three additional categories of functionality should also be considered. These are

- Unintentional software defects—currently the most common source of vulnerability in software.

- Intentional extra functionality—particularly unused or hidden functionality; hidden elements are usually malicious.

- Easter eggs—Code placed in software for amusement of developers or users—at best, this is inefficient and may introduce accidental vulnerabilities.

Testing usually does not look for added functionality; therefore, everything from Easter eggs to malicious items like backdoors and Trojan horses may become part of the final product. The challenge of identifying potential vulnerabilities hidden either by accident or by malicious intent is a problem facing security testers today.

The only way to identify hidden vulnerabilities is through code inspection, which is a resource-intensive and a painstaking process involving reading the entire program. Since modern programs can easily range between one hundred thousand to millions of lines of code, that is an impossible task unless a specific approach is adopted to focus the code inspection.

Best Practices and Methodologies

Over the past 40 years, the software industry has developed a range of best practices and methods that dictate how software is to be assured given the rapidly increasing constraint of size and complexity. These techniques are executed through a set of sequential stages discussed next.

Phase 1: Module Testing and Integration

The module testing and **integration** phase is the first place where vulnerabilities arising from defects in code are easily identified and remediated. Modern software is composed of small logical chunks of programmed code called *modules*. By definition, each module encapsulates one function. That restriction by rule to a single function ensures that modules are small and easy to work with. The size and function restriction is an important precondition for the accurate identification of vulnerabilities.

The modules that make up a program are defined during a **design phase**. That phase defines the relationships among modules and with the program structure. The defined modules are then coded. If the design process is rigorous enough, each module will be inspected using a process called a *code inspection* after the coding is finished

Code inspection is a formal testing procedure during which an inspection team composed of internal or external experts examines the code line by line to determine if it meets the specified coding criteria. Passing the code inspection is usually the last step in the programming phase. In systems analysis and design, this is called a structured walkthrough.

The First Line of Defense: Code Inspections

In a code inspection, the module is studied by expert peers to determine whether the code was written correctly. The syntax, logic, and coding practices are assessed. This procedure is sometimes also termed a *white box test*.

A rigorous code inspection is a valuable tool for information assurance and security because it lets independent reviewers inspect the assumptions and work that underlies a program. Serious attacks on software frequently begin with an exploitation of assumptions made by the programmer; challenge every assumption made while designing and writing the program.

Common examples of poor programmer assumptions are: *"there is no need to specify every buffer size"* or "explicitly *specifying string termination conditions is a waste of time."* Both assumptions are faulty and after the attack has occurred, it is easy to see why; however, before the attack takes place it is easy to justify both of these assumptions based on time and efficiency. It is important to test each underlying assumption using a standard method based on a checklist of common programming errors.

Standardizing the Inspection: Code Review Checklists
Code review checklists ensure that common code based security flaws are identified in a given piece of software. Examples of common flaws that might be looked for during a code inspection include:

- **Buffer Overflow**—caused when a program tries to store too much data in a temporary storage space. The resulting overflow into unauthorized memory locations allows malicious or arbitrary code to be executed.

- **Command Injection**—allows an attacker to inject illegal commands into a running program, which makes the program do something that it should not.

- **Cross-Site Scripting**—allows access to a trusted environment through code originating from untrusted sources. The attack is launched from the trusted context.

- **Path Manipulation**—attacker may specify an illegal path for an operating system function. Attackers gain unauthorized access by being allowed to specify an unauthorized path.

- **Process Control**—allows an attacker to make an actual change in the commands that the program executes, which gives control of the computer to the attacker.

- **String Termination Errors**—allow data to enter a program because the termination conditions of a string function were either unspecified or not properly specified.

- **Unchecked Return Value**—the failure to validate a return value can allow the program to overlook return states and conditions that could be malicious.

These examples are not an exhaustive list. The National Institute of Standards and Technology (NIST) has identified 28 categories of programming errors representing more than 1,400 potential flaws. An organization should compile a standard list of coding errors that apply to their programs. Buffer overflow and string termination are likely candidates since they account for a majority of programming flaws. Remember there are also specialized conditions that must be considered and accounted for in each organization.

The Second Line of Defense: Integration Testing
After each module has passed code inspection, it is integrated into the programming system. Assuming the code was properly verified and validated during the module-testing phase, integration testing ensures the components have been properly integrated and their subsequent interactions do not create potential information assurance and security flaws.

Modules are usually integrated in a top-down, incremental manner. All combined parts are tested to determine if they function correctly together. This testing is relevant to the security of client/server systems because the vulnerabilities that allow the cross-site scripting, command injection and process control attacks are more easily identified during **integration testing**. Since these attacks affect distributed systems, rigorous integration testing is an essential element of ensuring network software is secure.

Integration tests validate the flow of data among modules to ensure the integrity of communication process. Both the programmed procedures that pass data and the procedures that ensure data integrity while in transit are tested and validated. Integration tests also validate the structure of the program, the integrity of the global data structures, and the correct functioning of the internal pointers.

The integration test confirms behaviors attributable to the interaction of two (or more) components within the larger system. Integration tests analyze every conceivable link between a given module and every other module within the program structure.

The call test is an example of the process of confirming proper interaction between two modules. In programming, a "call" is an instance where data are passed between modules. In a call test, it is assumed that Module 1 should be able to call Module 2. The test would therefore identify only those instances where Module 1 calls Module 2 and tests to see whether that calling process functioned as expected.

The call test also checks to see whether Module 1 calls Module 2 reliably based on a given input; this confirms the predictability of the call. This second examination would be done independent of the question of what Module 2 does with whatever it is passed. The combined validation of the integrity of the calling function and the confirmation of predictable execution, given a specified input, constitutes the bulk of the integration testing process.

Ensuring a Systematic Testing Process: The Integration Testing Plan

Because its complexity, the process of integration testing has to be formally planned, controlled, and coordinated. The plan is drawn up at the beginning of the testing process and is a checklist for all activities performed during the integration testing phase.

The integration-testing plan documents actions to be taken during the testing process and specifies the test requirements, anticipated outcome, procedures, testing responsibilities, and schedules. The plan specifies the acceptance criteria for each validation test. Moreover, it must provide **qualification** criteria allowing the organization to confirm that all components have been successfully integrated.

Testers construct a set of tests cases appropriate for each software module. They assure the qualification criteria including appropriate inputs, outputs, and test criteria needed to confirm and ensure proper integration. Sufficient testing should be performed to ensure that the finished product is both complete and ready for **qualification testing**.

Integration testing is important to the information assurance process, because it is the only place where the integrity of the inter-operation among components is examined in detail. Remember the complex communication process involved and the interactions among components are likely security flaws. So, the best place to look for security flaws is during the integration testing phase.

Phase 2: Qualification and System Testing

The next phase is globally oriented. It determines whether the final product has met all of the qualification criteria formally specified for the project. Qualification or "system" testing never focuses strictly on the security issues.

Instead, qualification testing focuses on the project's requirements to determine whether they represent a meeting of the minds (**contract**) and certify that the project's procedures have been executed as specified. This examination must be rigorous because it is the point where the developers make the determination that the product finally meets requirements prior to customer acceptance testing.

Qualification reviewers examine each processing and security function individually to determine if it complies with all criteria for traceability, external and internal consistency, and appropriateness of methods and standards. The inspection uses prior code and integration test results as a reference. A rigorous examination should be conducted by a "**third-party**" assessment even if the third parties are actually members of the developing organization. The third-party assessors in a development organization are frequently termed "*software quality assurance*" personnel.

Qualification reviews determine if the process elements comply with the plan and contract. To document this determination the project's plans, schedules, requirements, and the approach used to satisfy each is reviewed. Reviewers may legitimately examine at least 37 different artifacts from the actual development process ranging from source code to contracts.

Qualification reviews are an essential control element because they determine whether the process complies with secure practice. Information from qualification reviews supports individuals with direct responsibility for ensuring the security of the entire project.

Qualification reviews are sponsored by the individual with direct responsibility for the assurance of the project. The reviews involve the sponsor as well as management and technical reviewers; customers may be also involved. A qualification review generates a report identifying variations from plans or defined procedures. The report documents decisions about corrective action to be taken as well as the allocation of resources. The report leads to changes in the project scope to accommodate identified variance from contracted requirements but are uncorrectable.

Qualification reviews trace initial requirements to implemented features. In addition, qualification reviews examine all procedures to ensure the safety and security of the product and project. The objective is to identify and report noncompliance. Consequently, qualification reviews always incorporate a defined analysis, reporting, and feedback process, involving the following:

- *Formulation of team and assurance of competent personnel*—Qualification reviews must be staffed by people who can do the management, security, and technical inspections.

- *Assignment of roles and responsibilities for review*—to ensure the proper depth of analysis, specific areas of focus and accountabilities for outcome have to be assigned.

- *Distribution of review materials to reviewers*—based on the least privilege principle, reviewers should be given only the material needed to make their assessment.

- *Training and orientation of review team*—is necessary to ensure that the review team is oriented to the task. This cannot be left to chance. If additional training is required to ensure a proper depth of analysis, it is provided here.

- *Review, documentation, and classification of defects*—this is where the qualification work is done. In this phase, the software is evaluated against specifications and the project status is reviewed for compliance with all **contractual requirements**. Reviewers must ensure objectivity. Defects are compiled and classified for subsequent remediation and action.

- *Review of defects with development team*—to ensure understanding. The objective is to get the development team's take on any identified variances to determine their underlying assumptions and responses.

- *Generation and documentation of action items*—Action items are recommendations that have not been prioritized yet and state the remedial action needed to bring the item into compliance with requirements or proper procedure.

- *Risk assessment and recommendations based on action items*—once the action items are compiled, they are prioritized based on risk into a set of specific recommendations for remediation.

- *Assurance that recommendations have been addressed*—there must be a defined procedure and accountabilities assigned to each recommendation including a statement of how each recommendation will be satisfied and closed out.

- *Generation of documentation certifying compliance*—provides documented certification that a recommendation has been met. The method for obtaining formal certification of compliance must be specified.

Qualification reviews are scheduled during initial project planning and are tied to milestones representing the terminal phase of the project. However, this does not exclude *ad hoc* qualification reviews held to certify the status of the project.

Once the qualification phase is passed, there are standard delivery requirements stipulated in the contract. These require the developer to update and prepare the software product for the final phase—installation and support. At the end of the qualification process, the developer transitions the software to the final phase by defining the formal baseline for the software asset. This is the asset baseline discussed in Chapter 1 and is the entity secured by the information assurance scheme.

Phase 3: Installation and Operational Testing

In the final phase, the contractual requirements that the software code and databases initialize, execute, and terminate as required have to be confirmed and accepted formally by the customer. The testing process is called **acceptance testing**. The activities within acceptance testing essentially duplicate those of the qualification phase. However, the customer sponsors and conducts the testing exercise.

Once the software has been accepted by the customer, it is installed in the target environment as a planned process. The developer prepares the plan and it is approved by the customer. The developer identifies the information and resources needed to ensure proper installation; installs the product in conformance with the plan and tests the installation.

The installation process is a source of security vulnerabilities because the system is in transition from the control of the developer to the customer organization. The product must be tested in the operational environment after the installation and subsequently to ensure the required security properties are present.

Continuous operational testing is important to identify security threats, vulnerabilities, or control violations in the software as it is implemented and operated. Identified incidents must be reported through a standard process to respond as quickly as possible to trouble arising from exploits, known vulnerabilities, or malfunctions. The reporting process should be established as part of the incident reporting functions discussed in Chapter 5, Security of Operations.

Operational testing practices include intrusion detection, penetration testing, and violation assessment using boundaries called clipping levels. Periodic reviews are performed to evaluate operating policies and procedures as well as operation against established standards. Identified threats, vulnerabilities, or violations are reported using a formal problem-reporting and problem-resolution process defined during the qualification phase.

It is important to ensure that operational assurance is performed effectively and efficiently. The functioning of the operational assurance process must be continuously monitored to identify and report deviations from proper practice. Good practice requires assessment and audit of the policies, procedures, tools, and standards used for operational assurance.

In addition to maintaining software integrity, operational testing ensures that the software continues to operate within a secure environment throughout the operational lifecycle. This requires periodic validation of the

- Correctness of the concept of operations
- Policies to ensure appropriate response to unexpected incidents
- Security of the physical site
- Recovery Time Objectives, Network Recovery Objectives, and Recovery Point Objectives
- Capability of staff and users to use the embedded **security functionality**

Quantifying the Process: Software Assurance Measurement

So far, we have discussed the methods employed to review and test software. In this section, we examine the methods used to turn the knowledge obtained into quantitative information used to support decision making.

Due to the worldwide importance of computer systems, the generation and use of quantitative information to support decision making is an important responsibility of the United States government. Authoritative entities like the Software Engineering Institute (SEI) and their Computer Emergency Response Team (CERT®) Coordination Center (CERT/CC) and the Department of Homeland Security's US-CERT provide extensive processes and data to support a qualitative and quantitative understanding of software defects.

The information needed to establish control over vulnerabilities is situational. There are two measurement approaches. The regular measurement activity is called *software assurance*. Where critical systems are concerned, the software measurement activity is termed *software reliability*. The term "reliability" implies the use of a more rigorous process to generate the control information. Integrity requirements of the software dictates whether regular assurance measurement or reliability measurement activities are required. We will examine the measurement question from a software assurance standpoint.

Software assurance measurement develops a quantitative understanding of hazards. The term **hazard** denotes conditions that could cause software to malfunction. There are three types of hazards: data hazards, programming hazards, and equipment hazards any of which may contribute to information assurance failures. The unit of measure that quantifies hazards is usually the number of incidents, errors, defects, faults, and failures. This is expressed as a simple count of the data, programming, and equipment malfunctions that occur either by category or as a total in a given period.

Models, Metrics and Data

The three building blocks of the software measurement process are *models, metrics,* and *data.* The complexity of the model, the intensity of the measurement, and the level of depth of the data are tailored to meet specific assurance requirements. **Tailoring** decisions are based on the criticality criteria discussed in the pervious section. Criticality is based on assumptions about considerations such as complexity of the software development work itself, the required performance levels, and the specific reliability requirements. Figure 9-2 outlines this.

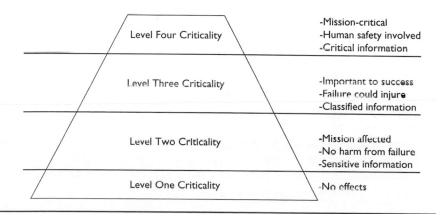

Figure 9-2   The criticality pyramid

Building an Effective Metrics Program

Every measurement program depends on effective metrics. A metric is composed of two or more independent measures, frequently expressed as a ratio, such as miles per hour. **Metrics** identify factors that are measured rather than the measurement process. Examples of metrics used for software measurement are things such as defects per lines of code, number of reported security failures per day, or number of tests per module.

Metrics may be quantitative or qualitative but are always describe a specific characteristic of an object or activity. The measures a metric produces are derived using a consistent method, applied at consistent intervals. A metric is as a standard of measurement for performance. For example, if there were a contract requirement to maintain defects within a certain level of acceptability, the metric would be the number of defects identified and accounted for within a given period. The number of defects in that case could be compared to previously established standards to determine whether contractual requirements were met.

Nine attributes or qualities are part of effective **metrics programs**. The measures developed from these attributes form the basis of the quantification scheme. The data produced can be used to support decision making with respect to the level of software reliability:

- **Suitability**—a set of measures can be specified to describe each function.
- **Accuracy**—the measurement produces verifiably correct or agreed on results or effects.
- **Interoperability**—measures apply across a range of functions.
- **Compliance**—measures adhere to standards, conventions, regulations, or laws.
- **Security**—unauthorized access can be characterized, for example, incidents.
- **Maturity**—decreasing frequency of failure can be used to judge acceptability, for example declining defect ratios.
- **Fault tolerance**—a minimum level of performance can be specified, for example, number of failures.
- **Recoverability**—the ability to recover data can be measured, for example, RTO, RPO.
- **Criticality**—the degree of criticality of the software can be measured.

Tailoring a Set of Reliability Measures

The successful execution of a software measurement program depends on the organization's ability to tailor appropriate metrics to gauge performance accurately and support decision making. The method follows a three-level approach.

The process begins with the definition of a set of top-level information items. These items should include the nine attributes listed previously. They constitute the specific information provided to users and management. The high-level items are converted into substantive measures appropriate to provide quantitative information.

For instance, a metric such as mean time to failure might be used to provide a direct measure of security performance (fault tolerance).

Once the top-level phase is complete, each set of measures is decomposed into the sub-factors representing the monitored attributes. These measures satisfy the information needs of the system operators. At this level, rather than using mean time to failure as the metric, performance might be expressed as the time required for detecting and recovering from specified attacks.

Operational sub factors are refined into metrics used to benchmark the continuous assurance of the project performance. An ideal software measurement program feeds information back to project managers to identify priority areas for action. For instance, the ability of software to detect and recover from a certain high-probability attack can be used to judge the subsequent allocation of maintenance resources.

Now that we have discussed the various elements of assurance in the process of building software, we are going to move on to an aspect that falls more appropriately into the realm of the business. That is the question of how to acquire a secure piece of software.

Acquiring Software

People focus on development when they think about the way software is embedded in their organization. However, that focus is incorrect. Since the 1980s, the world's software inventories have been built using by acquisition. In fact, today companies rarely actually build the applications they use. Instead, they purchase the applications as completed systems or in the form of components that are integrated into other systems. The **commercial off-the-shelf (COTS)** approach is cost effective, but there should be specific consideration of the security aspects of acquisition outlined in Figure 9-3.

Figure 9-3
Ensuring security
in software that
you buy

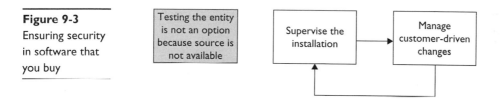

Software that is purchased rather than built gives the organization no way to ensure that security is built into the software other than by contract. Because the source code, the actual computer code of the product, is typically the sole property of the vendor, the customer has no access. Therefore the customer has no ability to do intensive code testing for defects. In its place, the vendor identifies and prepares the remediation for flaws in the product. These remediations are called *patches* and the vendor issues them to its customers as security updates.

There are standard recommendations about how to ensure security for a purchased product. Because security is increasingly important where COTS products are concerned, standards are available that define the requirements for conformance testing. These standards are applicable in both the public and private sectors.

Examples range from DoD 5200.28, to more focused efforts, such as NIST FIPS 140-2 and ISO 15408, better known as the *Common Criteria*.

Conformance testing or type testing is carried out to determine whether software meets a specified standard. As an aid to conformance testing, many test procedures and systems have been developed. These are issued both by standards bodies and other organizations. Conformance testing itself is usually done by external organizations; however, sometimes the standards body will do the testing. Products tested in this manner may then be advertised as certified in compliance with the standard giving the product greater credibility.

Because of the importance of conformance testing for COTS products, Common Criteria certification will be discussed in the final section of this chapter.

Installation and Maintenance: Ensuring Long-Term Performance

Eventually the supplier will be ready to deliver and install the completed product; the acquiring organization must be prepared to conduct a formal acceptance review. The customer conducts as many acceptance reviews and tests as needed to ensure that the product conforms to the contract requirements. The product is accepted when contract conditions are certified complete.

Acceptance tests and associated criteria should be specified in the contract. Items such as the test cases, test data, test procedures, test documentation, and test environment—as well as the extent of the supplier involvement in the acceptance testing—are defined in that contract. This serves as the primary point of reference for the final validation of the product.

Acceptance testing has a range of specific tests. These include obvious tests like security testing, where the security and information assurance features of the software are exercised and evaluated. In addition, acceptance includes tests for the usability of the software, its stability during operation, and its conformance to contractual requirements. Acceptance should always be based on a third-party audit of conformance with requirements, including security and authorization functions. Users of the system are usually involved in acceptance test procedures.

Acceptance testing is based on a formal test plan drawn up prior to the acceptance testing process start. It should specify a range of severity levels for defects and remediation options. Severity levels range from simple problems, such as cosmetic or simple performance errors, through to defects that cause major functional problems or security vulnerabilities. The successful outcome of an acceptance test supports both customers and developer confidence in the product correctness.

Once acceptance is certified, the acquiring organization conducts installation tests. During development, the system is under control of the supplying organization's configuration management system. After acceptance, arrangements have to be made to transition the system from the supplier's control to the acquiring organization's control. Installation tests are performed to ensure that the product is satisfactorily installed in the customer environment. Such testing frequently occurs on the actual hardware where the software product is embedded.

Secure Management of Outsourced or Third-Party Services

The acquisition process adds to the software asset base and may be used to procure software services also. These services range from the operation of a network to outsourced project management work. For outsourced software development, the form of the product, as well as **operational requirements**, security, and service levels required, are defined by a contract that documents details of roles, responsibilities, and requirements. This is particularly true where the requirements involve work across different languages and cultures.

Outsourcing and subcontracting magnify security problems, since there is no direct control over the developer processes except by agreement. Therefore, it is necessary to implement security procedures for both outsourced or subcontracted work followed by exacting acceptance reviews.

These relationships are specified using a legally enforceable **service level agreement (SLA)**. A service level agreement is a statement of the services that the supplier will provide. The SLA should be written in measurable terms that define security performance as well as operational security during development.

Using an SLA approach managers can substantiate the degree of assurance required and evaluate the options for compliance. Some of the qualities specified in an SLA might include:

- The specific criteria used to benchmark performance
- Metrics that will be used
- Accountability for instances of noncompliance
- Methods of remediation/problem resolution

Security functions required by the organization should be defined using a systematic process within an SLA. To support this process, the organization should use a standard template of security requirements tailored into a SLA contract. The **protection profile** discussed later in this chapter is a popular example of how a reusable template works. In addition to the functions specified in the profile, state minimum requirements for each function within the SLA.

Once the range of service requirements is stated in the SLA, review the performance periodically to fine-tune and enhance the execution level of the entire process. Drive the refinement process by a formal review, audit procedure, or an ongoing automated feedback. The critical outcome of the process is that the items within the SLA are aligned with the organizational security requirements that is checked and maintained on a continuous basis.

It is important to ensure that outsourced work has the same security level and information assurance as in-house work. The protection profile also ensures that security is maintained as specified is by periodically executing a rigorous audit and review. The standard protection profile provides a set of common criteria to benchmark the security performance of in-house and outsourced work.

The difficulty with outsourced work is not in defining the requirements it is in enforcing them. To do that properly, the contractor's control system must be aligned with the customer's and all accountabilities must be enforced. Enforcement requires the identification of third-party and supplier interfaces in the project plan.

In addition to the identifying interface among parties, it is necessary to assign and document the information assurance related roles and responsibilities in both the contractor and customer organizations. Accountability is assigned based on ownership. So, it is essential to assign and document the relationships and responsibilities for deliverables and process execution. It is also important to assess the qualifications of the third parties participating in the work from the standpoint of ensuring competency as well as security clearance.

The vendor assessment process must be established by a plan that provides a road-map for developing and maintaining third-party relationships. It is the benchmark used to determine if the requirements of the contract are being adhered to. The plan should provide formal mechanisms allowing both organizations to adapt on the fly to maintain continuity of services because security requirements change due to circumstances. This plan is kept current and updated by a periodic review of the status and effectiveness of the relationships.

A Common Criteria: Basing Security Functionality on a Protection Profile

The software assurance elements of information assurance should define and embed adequate automated safeguards into the final product. To ensure they have been implemented properly, these behaviors must be traceable, testable, and consistent with the defined level of system criticality. The behavior is expressed as a specific set of software functions, usually within a **specification of requirements**.

The specification of requirements is an itemized list of **security behaviors** to be implemented for a product. This would be difficult were it not for the fact that most security requirements are common across the applications operated within an organization because those applications all serve the common purposes of the organization.

Commonality of purpose makes it possible to use standard profiles of the functions required to protect the information assets. A reusable profile summarizes the standard organizational security functions and is a point of reference for comparisons to ensure the security functions of an application conform to the information assurance strategy. The comparison is possible because the approved set of functions to implement that strategy is captured in the profile.

The security environment has to be clearly understood to specify information assurance and security functions. Understanding the security requirements environment means that organizational policies and assumptions must be factored into the protection scheme. These conditions are documented as a set of reusable *security objectives*, which communicates the organizational information assurance and security requirements.

Standardized organizational security profiles serve as a consistent and reliable reference point for necessary behaviors to assure software.

The protection profile is reusable because it contains the common policies, assumptions, and requirements. It is developed based on an assessment of the security requirements of the organization, environmental considerations, policies, and assumptions that guide the organization.

The profile facilitates and directs the tailoring of software and environmental security functions for a secure system. In most cases good information assurance ensures a consistent set of safeguards. The use of a reusable protection profiles to guide the specification process is an effective way to ensure security. A standard profile guarantees that the software, security functions, and the attendant procedures originate from a single clear source. Properly referenced, a protection profile establishes a comprehensive and seamless software security function.

The Common Criteria: Form of the Standard

The ISO 15408 standard, the "Common Criteria," is a useful model for developing that protection profile. There are three parts to the standard: Part 1: Introduction and General Model; Part 2: Security Functional Requirements; and Part 3: Security Assurance Requirements. The security functional requirements that are used in preparing the protection profile are itemized in the Common Criteria, Part 2.

Security **functional requirements** are a catalogue of attributes that could be included in any security application. The Common Criteria provides the security advice needed to address most ordinary threats. As such, the standard is an effective reference point for selecting and embedding detailed security best practices within an application development process.

The Common Criteria provides advice about commonly accepted functions used to create trusted systems. The standard is considered complete and it is assumed to satisfy overall organizational security requirements.

The Common Criteria enumerates known software security attributes confirmable through direct observation and provides an encyclopedic collection of standardized adaptable security properties. They may be adapted to particular situations depending on the specific policies and assumptions in place.

The Common Criteria support the evaluation of software products by listing attributes to benchmark security behaviors. However, the application of the Common Criteria provides a universal set of desirable behaviors that might be present in any security situation. The advantage of the Common Criteria is that, because of its focus on observation, these behaviors are understandable and easier to implement.

The level of understanding can be employed to develop the security process. Managers can use the properties itemized by the Common Criteria to verify that the security objectives and dependencies in a software design represent best practice. These security properties represent the state of the art in information assurance. Remember, the standard substantiates requirements that are considered valuable.

Advantages of a Protection Profile

A protection profile based on standard security requirements ensures uniformity in the security capabilities assessment. A profile has other advantages including the software security requirements can be updated at a single point in the organization.

An organizationally sanctioned statement of desired behaviors expressed by the profile can be used to perform type testing of commercial off-the-shelf (COTS) products. The protection profile can be used as a point of reference to guide the process of acquiring software and service products for secure systems.

Developing a Protection Profile

The generic profile is developed top-down, by involving the largest group of stakeholders possible. This is a human-centered process allowing people who use the system to make decisions about embedded security functions.

The availability of a profile supports a trade-off process. It allows the organization to decide what constitutes "good enough" security for each application or product and helps line managers assess whether they have implemented appropriate security requirements. It allows decision makers to compare alternatives by providing a common visible assessment and trade-off analysis capability.

That assessment and trade-off process applies to both external vendors and in-house developers of software. Using this profile, organizations can guide development and ensure that the resulting applications will meet the security needs of the organization. Doing so establishes trust in the development process.

Chapter 9 Review

Chapter Summary

- Information assurance is linked to software because security functionality is enabled by it and software processes organizational information.

- It is essential to assure that the software within that asset base incorporates the required **information assurance functionality**.

- That body of discrete requirements includes the security functions incorporated in the software.

- Specifications define the form of the final product as well as dictate the testing and assurance procedures used to warranty that it meets requirements.

- The challenge lies in ensuring that the correct set of requirements are specified and built.

- By that convention, acquisition and development are the two global processes that an organization might use to expand its software assets, acquisition, and development.

- The most important and traditional approach to bringing software into an organization is the development process.

- The development process stipulates the "complete set" of activities that might be undertaken by an organization that fulfills the role of **software developer**.

- The comprehensive set of software functions that must be included in a particular software application are identified and described in the requirements and design phase.

- The overall goal of the development process is to deliver a satisfactory software solution.

- The first item that is decided is the specific **development strategy**.

- What is determined in this phase are the **criticality requirements** or, as they are sometimes called, the **system integrity requirements** of the project.

- The aim of information assurance is to define and embed adequate safeguards into the eventual software product or service.

- The protection profile summarizes the security aims of the organization.

- The protection profile is reusable for a number of applications because by definition, it embodies the requisite policies, assumptions, and requirements of the organization.

- The complete set of functional and **nonfunctional requirements**, including the desired security functionality, is communicated through a formal software requirements specification (SRS).

- The specification of requirements contains a valid set of functional and non-functional (qualitative) requirements.

- Software reliability management is a technical security concept that seeks to identify hazards that can lead to system failure and resolve or ameliorate them prior to their occurrence.

- All **software reliability management** and **software safety programs** depend on the existence of an effective metrics program.

- There are nine generic attributes or qualities that an effective reliability measurement program must embody: suitability, **accuracy**, **interoperability**, compliance, security, maturity, fault tolerance, **recoverability**, and **criticality**.

- The acquisition process originates with the formal expression of the need to obtain a product or service, which leads to a plan for obtaining it.

- Outsourced or subcontracted work is controlled using a legally enforceable service level agreement (SLA).

- Security functions are defined within service level agreements through a standard organizational procedure.

- This is best supported by having a protection profile.

- Besides service levels, it is important to ensure that outsourced work embodies the same levels of security functionality as in-house work.

- The plan is the roadmap for developing and maintaining the third-party relationship.

Key Terms

accuracy (251)
acquisition (232)
coding (234)
contract (240)
contractual requirements (241)
commercial off-the-shelf (COTS) (245)
criticality requirements (251)
design phase (237)
development (232)
development strategy (251)
functional requirements (249)
hazards (243)
information assurance functionality (250)
integration (237)
integration testing (239)
interoperability (251)
metrics (244)
metrics program (244)
nonfunctional requirements (251)
operational requirements (247)
outsourcing (232)
protection profile (247)
qualification (232)
qualification testing (232)
recoverability (251)
requirements (232)
security behaviors (248)
security functionality (242)
service level agreement (SLA) (247)
software developer (251)
software reliability management (251)
software safety programs (251)
specification of requirements (248)
system integrity requirements (251)
tailoring (243)
testing (235)
third-party (240)

Key Term Quiz

1. Outsourcing is done by _____.
2. The document that describes the functions required in a piece of software is a _____.

3. The document that tells how a piece of software works is called a _____.

4. Agreements in software are enforced by a _____, which is negotiated during the project _____ phase.

5. The _____ defines a generic set of security requirements for the organization. It is _____ because most of those requirements are generic across the organization.

6. At the acceptance level, assurance is best underwritten by _____.

7. If the assurance requirements are especially rigorous the form of the testing is called_____.

8. The aim of the qualification phase is to certify the _____ that is built into the product.

9. The integration testing phase confirms all _____ requirements.

10. The type of software that is acquired rather than built is commonly called _____ or COTS.

Multiple Choice Quiz

1. The specification of software requirements states applicable
   A. functions
   B. laws
   C. regulations
   D. standards

2. Suppliers are always chosen based on
   A. three P's
   B. formal selection criteria
   C. specifications
   D. whether they are relatives

3. Service level agreements are specifically important to define the provision of
   A. products
   B. deliverables
   C. services
   D. hardware

4. Security can be
   A. both a functional and a nonfunctional requirement
   B. only a nonfunctional requirement
   C. unmeasurable
   D. never embedded in software

5. With software developments, contracts define and enforce

    A. roles and responsibilities

    B. rules

    C. regulations

    D. accountability

6. The essence of measurement is the identification of relevant

    A. models

    B. metrics

    C. data

    D. resources

7. Formulating a Common Criteria Protection Scheme requires understanding of

    A. software functionality

    B. security practice

    C. environmental requirements

    D. policy and procedure best practice

8. The difference between software assurance and information assurance is that the former

    A. is a lot harder to do

    B. involves metrics

    C. starts with integration

    D. encompasses all defects

9. Qualification reviews support

    A. the person responsible for the entire project

    B. development project managers

    C. software standards

    D. the common criteria

10. The aim of the information assurance element of software assurance is to

    A. eliminate all defects

    B. eliminate exploitable defects

    C. eliminate programming defects

    D. predict exploitation

Essay Quiz

In your own words briefly, answer the following questions:

1. How are security requirements elicited?

2. Why are protection profiles reusable?

3. Why are rigorous audits essential at the acceptance phase?

4. Why are coding, testing, and use immaterial to ensuring that the right set of security functions are in place?

5. Why is software reliability management reliant on quantitative measurement?

6. Why should a distinction be made between information assurance and software assurance?

7. If most defects are injected at the coding phase, why are they not all caught there?

8. What is a module and why does it provide a practical place to do code inspections?

9. Why is operational testing periodic? What would happen if it was not conducted that way?

10. What is the difference between a vulnerability and a hidden vulnerability? Why is the latter so potentially dangerous?

Case Exercise

Complete the following case exercise as directed by your instructor:

Refer to the Heavy Metal Technology Case in Appendix A. You have been assigned the responsibility of planning the overall development process for the project to upgrade the target acquisition and display (TADS) for the AH64-D Apache Longbow attack helicopter. You know that in order to start the process you must first create a project plan. Therefore, using the materials outlined in the case, perform the following tasks:

1. Identify the software items.

2. Define a step-by-step process for either developing or integrating these into the final build.

3. Define an assurance approach for each of the approaches you described in item two (2).

4. List issues that might be associated with outsourced work and then define a process for assuring those software elements.

Devise a software safety plan to validate the performance of the integrated TADS system.

Continuity Planning and Disaster Recovery

In this chapter, you will learn how to:
- Develop an effective business continuity approach
- Manage an effective incident response
- Plan for disaster recovery

Business continuity functions preserve essential organizational assets and protect resources from damage, destruction, and loss. The function includes information assets and the systems that contain them. Business continuity serves as an information assurance lifeboat.

The key term with continuity is *essential*; business continuity does not preserve everything the organization owns. It seeks to preserve only those things essential to continue business operations. Preservation processes use a plan to identify and safeguard the assets needed to return to a predefined operational status.

The business continuity process develops and maintains an up-to-date, comprehensive strategy to ensure that the organization can recover critical information assets after a disaster. Further, it ensures that designated critical systems and the information they contain will be available to resume operation within a specified period. Successful recovery follows a prescribed sequence; therefore, planning and scheduling are essential to business continuity.

Business continuity planning mitigates the interruption of essential services and seeks to re-establish full operations as quickly as possible by focusing on critical functions rather than the entire information system. Business continuity relies on contingency plans that itemize the steps to follow when needed. The first step in building the plan is to identify and prioritize critical assets through risk analysis.

Business continuity frequently centers on offsite storage and recovery facilities because the worst possible contingency is the loss of the primary site. Continuity plans seek to ensure the continuing availability of the physical components and the assets they contain by maintaining redundant systems. The plan includes the maintenance of everything from networks, servers, and storage media, to the information that they contain and process. The term "continuity" also implies the requirement for a mechanism to ensure the continuous integrity of the information during offsite transmission and storage. Finally, continuity describes the processes for assigning and notifying key personnel needed to re-establish operations.

Business continuity has evolved from its original purpose, which was to salvage what was left of the business's data after a catastrophe. Continuity processes now involve all strategies and steps necessary to ensure that the information infrastructure will survive a disaster. This chapter discusses many of these aspects of the continuity function. It details the procedures by which business continuity is ensured, as well as the common mechanisms for providing that assurance.

Continuity and Business Value

Business continuity is a planned response implemented if other safeguards fail. The methods and techniques adopted to ensure continuity extend of the assumptions of the information assurance process. Continuity differs from the assurance process is in its orientation. Other assurance processes focus on prevention and response while continuity focuses on *preserving business value after assurance fails*.

Continuity processes can be both proactive and reactive; however, the goal is to ensure the quickest possible resumption of operation if an *interruption* occurs. It makes no difference whether the reason for the disruption was hacker penetration or a force 5 hurricane; the consequence is that business value is lost for the duration of the stoppage. As such, the continuity process seeks to guarantee that, no matter what the cause, the extent and effect of a shutdown are minimized. Good planning ensures this.

Continuity Planning

The continuity process prescribes a set of actions taken if a disaster occurs. The steps are documented in a *preparedness plan* that itemizes the approach to prevention and minimization of damage as well as the steps to secure or recover information after a disaster.

The plan is developed through a strategic planning process because of the critical value of information. The plan characterizes the operational measures followed to prevent avoidable disasters. It enumerates the contingency measures to be adopted, should a disaster occur. It itemizes the replacement and restoration procedures used to ensure the integrity of the information assets.

Contents of a Continuity Plan

The continuity plan itemizes the steps the organization takes to ensure its vital functions survive a disaster. An effective continuity plan is uses the same threat modeling and risk evaluation process used to implement the overall assurance scheme.

Developing a unique, tailored continuity plan should be kept in mind when the information assurance process is established. A separate planning effort is needed because the activities to ensure continuity are different from those that are required by routine operational security. Unless the organization undertakes a specific contingency-based, disaster-planning process, those requirements may be lost in the larger aims of securing the information base from routine threats.

The continuity planning process has two goals. The first is to avoid loss of critical information in a disaster. The second is to return critical information functions to operation as quickly and efficiently as possible. Most continuity programs use a range of measures to prevent or minimize damage from anticipated events. To do this, the continuity planning function targets the three components of an IT operation:

- Systems
- Personnel
- Facilities

These elements fail in many "interesting" ways. Plans must be established to respond to every possible threat. Since there are many potential threats and limited resources, the key concept in contingency planning is *feasibility*.

For example, an organic virus that prevents the support staff from showing up for work can be as dangerous to critical systems as widespread Internet attacks. Since computer viruses affecting servers are more common than a flu epidemic, they should be anticipated and addressed actively. One might justifiably leave a flu shot to chance.

The continuity planning process employs ongoing threat modeling and risk assessment processes to identify and prioritize threats because of the need to identify and address only the feasible options. The planning process establishes a risk analysis procedure to decide the order in which the threats should be addressed by a formal **preparedness response**.

Since an active response is resource-intensive, one should limit the development of responses to likely events and the ones with the largest effect. In Chapter 2, we said that a likelihood estimate is usually a "best guess" since it involves too many factors to ensure reliability. However, if the planner focuses on developing standard responses to categories and types of harmful events, it is possible to ensure an appropriate and effective response for a range of events, some of which could seem quite unlikely on the surface.

For example, the total loss of the physical space is an eventuality that must be anticipated independent of cause. Therefore, a plan should be in place to accommodate the catastrophic loss of the structure. The same planning mitigates a range of similar occurrences. For example, the extensive plans to accommodate the loss of the physical space in the World Trade Center may have mitigated an economic disaster that 9/11 would have caused. This was true despite the fact that total destruction of the building by terrorist act was low on the probability list at the time.

Contingency planners were not thinking about an aircraft being flown into the building when they established mirror sites and secondary facilities. They planned for the possibility of the catastrophic loss of the building. Their response was successful because the plan fit the model of the disaster. This epitomizes good contingency planning.

Proactive Response: Ensuring "Continuous" Continuity

To ensure continuity if you cannot avoid disasters, build real-time survivability into the overall information function. Whether this is part of the information assurance scheme or the continuity plan, resilience and immediate "recoverability" implies integration of protection strategies with a range of proactive recovery technologies such as hot sites. The result should be a dynamic assurance solution that blends protection elements, such as firewalls and intrusion detection systems, with effective response procedures and the technologies. Make certain continuous operation occurs under circumstances given all known contingency.

Rigor is essential since the survival of critical information technology processes is inextricably linked to the continuing effectiveness of organizational function. To illustrate the criticality of recovery time in continuity planning, recall that global markets are always open and stock trading is done worldwide. The required data must be available 24 hours a day, 7 days a week because global operations never cease. In the middle of the night on Wall Street, the computers at the Stock Exchange are still in the middle of the action. If any systems fail for a significant period, even at 3 a.m. New York time, the impact on the world's financial markets could be significant.

Recovery Time

To understand the continuity process, it is necessary to understand recovery time. That is because the fundamental aim of the business continuity process is to ensure the shortest realistic recovery time possible.

The estimate of recovery time is calculated by determining the **Maximum Tolerable Downtime (MTD)** for each critical function in the operation. MTD might be an old-fashioned data processing term, but it is applicable to continuity management because the organization has to know how long it can survive without a particular function. This metric allows one to estimate what should be invested to ensure continuous operation. The estimate is based on three concepts:

- Recovery Time Objective (RTO)
- Network Recovery Objective (NRO)
- Recovery Point Objective (RPO)

RTO

Recovery Time Objective (RTO) is a business concept based on the processing requirements of the organization. RTO states the maximum operationally acceptable period of time that a system can be out of service without causing harm. RTOs are often linked to the degree of harm. Remember, the RTO for hospital equipment is near zero; production line operations may be measured in hours while the RTO for payroll might be measured in weeks. The latter is true since payroll can be manual.

NRO

Network Recovery Objective (NRO) is an adjunct to RTO that specifies the greatest amount of time a network can be out of service. It is driven by the same requirements as RTO but it is independent of the system recovery estimate. Users access systems through networks and there are different operational and timing requirements associated with restoring or reconfiguring the network.

For instance, there might be less pressure to restore network processing because the users might be able to work offline during network downtime. NRO requirements are part of the continuity scenario independent of the RTO.

RPO

Recovery Point Objective (RPO) has a different premise. It is describes the principle of data integrity; every continuity plan should specify the RPO. The RPO identifies the point in time to which data can be restored after a failure. RPOs dictate the time between backups.

Data created or modified outside of the parameters set by the RPO will not be recoverable after a disaster and will have to be re-created. Re-creation may be expensive and frequently RPOs are developed after information asset valuation exercises. The RPO is normally set at the shortest, economically feasible interval.

Ideally, the RPO would be positioned exactly at the point of failure, meaning that no data would be lost. However, to maintain that level of assurance it would be necessary to have a continuous mirror backup site. This might not be economically or technically feasible.

Frequently, organizations make a conscious decision about the most effective RPO within their business context. This is a tradeoff between business value of the information asset and the cost of ensuring it. For instance, it is the RPO that drives the decision making about whether to adopt the hotsite, warmsite, or coldsite solutions that will be discussed in the next section. Obviously, criticality of the information affects the setting of the RPO criterion; however, availability of resources is an equal factor.

Determining RTO, NRO, and RPO for one Environment

RTO/NRO and RPO are mutually supportive, but they are different concepts and support different set of decisions and protection requirements. For instance, a highly automated automobile assembly plant sets the shortest RTO/NRO possible for their assembly lines due to high labor costs. Perhaps they could afford to lose some of production data without significant financial impact. They might be willing to modify the RPO to meet that requirement.

In contrast, banking systems credibility requires they ensure customer transaction records of data are maintained to the exact point of failure, even if the actual time it takes to bring the system back online is extended. Therefore, the RTO/NRO uptime might be extended in order to ensure that critical RPO objectives are met.

Alternative Sites

Ideal continuity plans ensure a continuous processing capability with no loss of data. In the event of a disaster, systems should being able to switch processing functions efficiently to alternative sites. The resources to establish and maintain this capability are dictated by the degree of assurance required. The relationship between criticality requirements and alternative processing models introduces the topic of **hotsites**, **warmsites**, and **coldsites**.

Data Recovery Hotsites

At the top of the cost and assurance hierarchy are bare metal recovery sites. Here the system and its data are deemed so critical that the capability must be provided to restore them to their original state at the time of the disaster. Examples of this would be the critical systems in places like the Pentagon or major financial institutions like the New York Stock Exchange. Figure 10-1 outlines the factors involved in determining whether to use this approach.

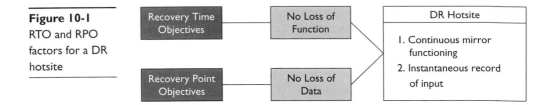

Figure 10-1
RTO and RPO factors for a DR hotsite

Bare metal recoveries require a **Data Recovery Hotsite (DRH)**. These facilities mirror the real-time processing at the primary site. They provide near instantaneous backup since they operate in parallel. They have the same hardware, data communication, and environmentally controlled space that the primary site has and they are in linked real-time communication. That ensures the optimum potential for total recovery of the data resource and continuity of operation.

This approach involves maintaining a redundant operation, so the cost of running a DR hotsite can be prohibitive. To reduce costs, commercial services may provide a shared hotsite capability for several business clients.

Data Recovery Warmsites

The next step down the assurance ladder is the **Data Recovery Warmsite (DRW)**. These provide the equipment and communications interfaces for establishing an immediate backup operation, but they do not mirror the real-time processing at the target site. This leaves a gap between the contents of the operational resource and the backup site. Warmsites cannot ensure that all the data will be preserved if a disaster occurs. Figure 10-2 outlines the factors involved in determining whether to use this approach.

The RPO depends on the routine backup procedures specified as part of the continuity plan. Backup parameters are set by the organization and may change based on the criticality of the situation. Sometimes the RPO causes a momentary pause while the

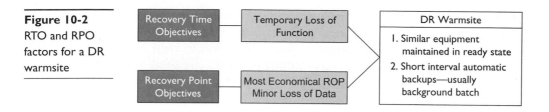

Figure 10-2
RTO and RPO factors for a DR warmsite

target site automatically "batches" transactions in the background before sending them to the backup site. Sometimes this gap will be the time between the disaster and the last time the primary system was backed up to stable media, like tape. This may be a day or so in some operations.

Backup processing parameters are established based on a "best economic estimate" of the RPO. The RPO is set by estimating the value and criticality of just the missing data. It optimizes the cost/risk factors for information that may be lost.

Because warmsite backup parameters can be tailored to the exact circumstances and changed if the situation warrants, warmsites are usually the most practical approach. They are extremely cost efficient; so, shared warmsite services are increasingly popular.

Data Recovery Coldsites

The **Data Recovery Coldsite (DRC)** option is the lowest rung on the ladder. It provides a degree of protection and therefore many large data processing operations implement some sort of **coldsite** option. This involves maintaining a back-office facility with the hardware, system, and environmental controls to assure only the most critical processing functions continue if processing at the primary is interrupted. Figure 10-3 outlines the factors involved in determining whether to use this approach.

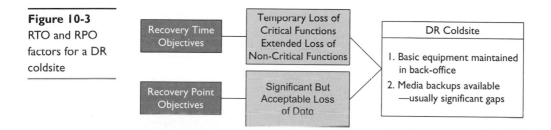

Figure 10-3
RTO and RPO factors for a DR coldsite

A DRC has the equipment and the communications links to accommodate the **migration** of critical staff from the primary site and perhaps copies of regular backups. The value of a DR coldsite is that the organization can resume business operations as soon as the staff is moved. The disadvantage lies in the fact that significant data from the primary site might be lost or have to be rebuilt, because of the delays in getting processing functions back online.

Coldsites are effective for functions that have a built in time lag. Payroll is an example, because paychecks are only issued in weekly or monthly increments and the amounts do not change frequently. A weekly backup is sufficient to keep the data near current. Coldsites do not work well for organizations with critically short-term RPO, such as an assembly line or a stock trading system, because significant time is wasted and lost time is costly.

Analysis Processes

A regular operational risk assessment should be performed to ensure that the assumptions and estimates that support the design of the continuity system continue to be valid. In addition, continuous assessment helps monitor and refine the system. A commitment to assessment obligates each organization to identify the risks to its critical systems and the effect of their failure has on overall business processes. Two kinds of analyses are associated with continuity plans development: **business impact analysis** and **risk analysis**.

Business Impact Analysis

Business impact analyses are carried out to determine the effect that a potential disruption might have on a function or information asset. When addressing the problem these analyses consider a range of eventualities in a threat model. The range includes everything from the inability to perform a critical business function to broader factors such as financial or legal and regulatory affects. Other considerations included in a business impact study include revenues and expenditures, application and hardware recovery influences, and even the potential for fines or other of regulatory penalties, if critical information were lost.

For example, a business impact study assesses how daily production goals would be affected if there were downtime in a particular assembly line subsystem such as engine components. The study factors in contextual considerations, such as the effect on the relationship with the labor union if the organization were unable to access production information for a time during a labor negotiation. A business impact analysis might even factor in global questions, such as how downtime in the brake assembly system might affect overall cash flow.

Risk Analysis

Risk analysis examines the critical functions and resources that support the operations detailed in the impact study. Once the elements of information and processing constituting the core functioning of the organization are identified, risk analysis estimates the likelihood that those elements will suffer harm or disruption. This assessment determines the degree of risk for each item. Once the risk is determined, it is possible to develop a strategy to eliminate or minimize the effect.

Since risks usually exceed available resources, the list of critical business functions and assets are prioritized to ensure that strategies to prevent and/or recover from disruptions match the resources available.

Risk analysis is driven by an estimate of the overall criticality of the system. A major component of risk analysis is disaster tolerance that describes the affect that a major disruption to a system or process would have on the overall organization. It is important because the margin for safety must be known in order to formulate the actual response.

Disaster tolerance requirements are different for an in-flight avionics system than for the game program on your home PC. In the first case, there is little room for failure and the disaster response should be established accordingly. In the second instance, the worst outcome might be inconvenience and so the consequences of failure are less dramatic.

Criticality estimates determine how rigorously the **disaster planning** and response process will be applied. Because disaster tolerance implies various levels of criticality, there are varying degrees of associated responses, which form four categories:

- **Minimal criticality**—Lost data or a lost processing will have no meaningful impact or the effect will be offset by other systems. The continuity solution takes the form of conventional backups with little additional planning or monitoring beyond routine operation.

- **Average criticality**—In this case, the system performs a unique function or it is the only system supporting a specific business operation. In that case, any lost processing time affects the overall performance of the functions it supports. Therefore, the continuity solution has to provide some means to restore operations as quickly and correctly as possible. Nevertheless, if an economical RPO can be tolerated, that solution can be based on a DRC.

- **High criticality**—Here, the system supports the overall operation and any lost processing time seriously affects the organization's long-term health. Alternatively, a failure might affect the health or safety of workers. Therefore, the continuity solution ensures the restoration of functionality as close to the event as economically feasible. Given the importance of the data, maintaining an RPO of the highest level of integrity is a factor. At a minimum, a DRW will be required.

- **Mission-critical**—The system contains irreplaceable functions essential to the continuing financial health of the business, or to the health and safety of the workers. Lost data or processing would be catastrophic. At a minimum, the loss of data would lead to imminent failure of the organization; at worst, the loss might have a cascading affect on other operations. Failure may cause death or injury. The continuity solution must provide high availability and no known points of failure. It must be assured **redundant** through a real-time, mirror, DRH for mission-critical applications.

Ingredients of a Continuity Plan

Continuity plans have two steps:

- the assumptions about the circumstances of the plan and the events that could change or affect those assumptions.

- the second is the strategy for maintaining continuity, based on those assumptions.

Step One: Assumptions

Assumptions are derived from an understanding of the threats and the associated threat modeling. Assumptions are dynamic since the threat picture changes constantly and the assumptions have to be periodically updated.

As new risks emerge, assumptions have to be made about their affect on critical functions. The assumptions should include the timing and extent of the threat and the areas of potential harm. Note, that the formal activity supporting this is the risk assessment process, explained in detail in Chapter 2.

Step Two: Priorities and Strategy

The second element is more conventional. In the *continuity strategy*, organizations develop continuity strategies from their particular philosophy and the priorities assigned to their assets. There is no such thing as a uniform method. Each organization approaches the challenges of prioritizing and developing continuity responses in its own way. The only given in the process is that the strategy adopted and the philosophy that drives it must be understood and accepted throughout the entire organization. Remember, there cannot be confusion about how to respond to a disaster. It is important for the organization to adopt and communicate a single common continuity approach. To make the approach acceptable to employees, the strategy should originate from and align with the stated organization strategy and philosophy.

In addition to a common approach, it is important to know exactly when, where, and how the plan applies. For instance, an effective disaster plan would not be designed to start when a hurricane reached an installation. The organization should build in lead-time to initiate its emergency procedures. The plan should state when the response is to start and when it will stop. In the case of a hurricane it would be hazardous to have the disaster plan end the minute the wind stopped blowing since wind damage is only part of the disaster. Floods, power outages, and civil disruptions may accompany hurricanes. However, it would be inefficient to continue to follow a hurricane disaster plan a year later. Therefore, it is important to embed in the plan a set of criteria that dictate when it applies and when it will end.

Instituting the Business Continuity Management Process

The management goal of the business continuity process is to keep critical systems operating and to react to failures as soon as possible. The response must be established within operating parameters—that is, business continuity solutions have to be carefully planned. The planning process may be the single point of failure in a continuity management effort.

The management plan for the business continuity process protects the maximum number of assets with the highest degree of assurance. This is accomplished by minimizing the recovery time for each process within the process. Time is the tool for judging the success of the plan. As we saw, recovery time is based on the following related but independent factors:

- The time it takes to restore the operational business processes to the RTO
- The time that it takes to recover the IT processes to the RTO/NRO
- The time it takes to recover the data to the RPO

Each factor is independent since they are determined by many functions. Five common sense questions need to be answered to ensure that the plan has the right set of elements. These are:

1. What are the critical business systems?
2. What is the business impact of each of these systems?
3. What risks are associated with each system?
4. What is the level of integrity required for each system?
5. What are the RTO and the RPO for each system?

The Four Phases of the Business Continuity Planning Process

Business continuity planning is a difficult task; so, it is best done in phases. There are four phases:

- Identify critical business functions
- Establish Recovery Time Objectives
- State the explicit work (SOW)
- Ensure acceptance and understanding of the solution

This process is diagrammed in Figure 10-4.

Phase 1: Identify the Critical Business Functions

The first step identifies the critical business functions. The continuity process ensures these target functions. Critical functions are those essential to the continued fulfillment of the business purpose. Failure of these functions results in one or more of the following:

- Permanent interruption of the process
- Unrecoverable loss of data
- Significant financial loss

Function criticality is always based on centrality to the business purpose. This assessment is derived from a characterization of the explicit value (to that purpose) of

- Products
- Services, including supporting functions
- Governance or administration factors

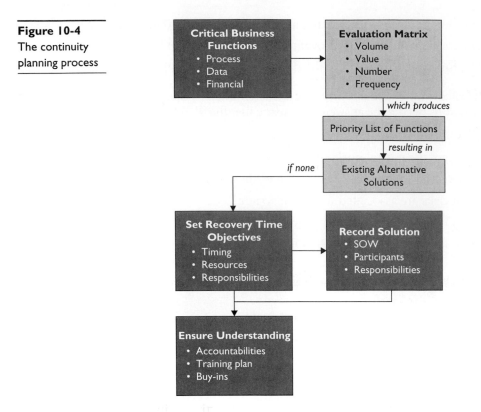

Figure 10-4
The continuity
planning process

Once these have been identified and evaluated they are assessed based on their over-all contribution. Volume and load factors are measures employed to describe the contribution. It includes performance items, such as the actual

- Volume of deliverables produced in a given time
- Value of those deliverables in a given time
- Number of customers processed in a given time
- Frequency of other services provided in a given time

This information is organized in an evaluation matrix similar to that in Table 10-1. This matrix allows the organization to understand the relative contribution and value of its products, services, or functions.

Planners develop a perspective on the relative criticality of each individual product, service, or function using the data from this array. Once the productivity patterns have been established, the organization can characterize the effect of failure. This second examination identifies high-impact functions that otherwise have scored low on the productivity estimate. For example, a function like the continuity planning operation itself does not involve actual production, but it is central to the success of the overall operation.

	Delivered	Value	Customers	Frequency
Products				
P_1				
P_2				
P_3				
P_n				
Services				
S_1				
S_2				
S_3				
S_n				
Functions				
A_1				
A_2				
A_3				
A_n				

Table 10-1 Evaluation Matrix of Critical Functions

Once these two passes are complete, each item is labeled in terms of its level of criticality. The following classification characterizes the activities in the evaluation matrix:

- **Critical Activities**—Activities essential to the business

- **Included Activities**—Activities not directly essential, but which should be continued

- **Non-Essential Activities**—Activities not essential to the immediate operating needs of the business, or that may be temporarily discontinued without significant loss of value

It is possible to develop a prioritized list of the functions from these criteria. Assign priority based on the estimates of productivity and impact, with essential activity assigned priority number one. Once priority is established, derive a quantitative impact estimate for any disruption of critical functions. Since this estimate depends on more factors than criticality, it also requires an understanding of the organization's ability to provide a feasible substitute for each priority function.

Determining Feasible Alternatives The organization should determine whether there are other ways to perform a given operation or whether it could be carried out by a similar set of tasks. This determination must consider all **redundancy** provisions. This is not a simple list-making exercise. It requires consideration of operational factors such as geographic location and organizational and communication linkages.

For instance, the same function might be available in another data center. However, it would be pointless to base an alternative solution on that fact, if there were significant logistical problems in using the center.

It is important to designate functions that could be carried out temporarily by a contractor or outsourced during a disruption. The designation is based on the ability of contractors to bring their services to bear on the problem immediately. It is not sufficient to point to a list of contractors who could do the same kind of processing; the contractor must have a working relationship with the organization already and must understand the continuity requirements of functions. In common sense terms, the organization should already have a plumber on retainer who knows their pipes before the leak happens.

Know That It Is an Ongoing Effort It takes significant time and effort to understand and address continuity needs at the highest level of response. Perform needs assessments on a continuous or regular basis because organizations change constantly. This level of analysis and understanding is practical only for critical functions since they are time- and resource-intensive. Nonetheless, depending on factors such as the organizational size, the level of assurance expected, and resources available, it is possible and acceptable to encompass the categories Include Activities and **Non-Essential Activities** into in the plan.

There are no established rules to limit elements covered by the plan. There is one requirement, however; activities designated as "critical" must be addressed appropriately, and it must be possible to validate them by direct observation. If confirmation is not possible, the assignment of criticality must be adjusted to drop that activity into the **Included Activities** category.

Phase 2: Set Recovery Time Objectives (RTO)

Once the **critical activities** have been designated, set the Recovery Time Objectives for each function. RTOs are specified in the order of their criticality after considering redundancy and contract alternatives.

Each critical product, service, or administrative function is assigned a value describing how soon it must be operational. These values include conditional descriptors such as "immediately," as well as time designations expressed in seconds, minutes, or hours.

The RTO timing must be accompanied by an estimate of the resources required to achieve it. This list is a detailed itemization of the personnel, equipment, and timing requirements for each RTO in the plan.

Once a list of requirements is prepared for each RTO, establish a mechnism to ensure the resources will be available. The list must be agreed to and cross-referenced to the resource estimate. Depending on the situation, the resources to achieve a given RTO can come from both internal and external sources.

The organization should first identify the internal resources to be provided and then any external sources and contractors. Once this analysis is done, the organization should be able to identify any potential shortfalls in either resources or capabilities. Itemize and cross-reference **shortfall areas** to the RTO, using the same categories that used to estimate the requirements.

It is important to identify the shortfall areas, because these are potential failure points. Consequently, this part of the process is a critical element to continuity planning. It benefits management because it identifies the places where they should direct their attention, as well as providing a target for developing the organization's disaster response capabilities.

Phase 3: Identify and Record Solution in a Statement of Work

This information is recorded on a **statement of work (SOW)** for each RTO in the plan. The statement of work is a specification itemizing the steps to be taken to meet each RTO and details the procedures followed to address foreseeable problems. The SOW identifies areas of shortfall in personnel, work area, equipment, supplies, or service capability identified previously. It includes a set of recommendations for how that shortfall will be addressed.

The statement of work specifies the organization's assumptions about continuity and it should be based on a careful analysis of the circumstances and contingencies for a given situation. It provides clear guidance for each foreseeable contingency.

To ensure the applicability of these recommendations, it is good practice to audit plans regularly to determine if they still apply. Audits are also important to determine whether the plan has been documented adequately. There are commercial services that perform routine third-party assessments of the applicability and capability of a continuity plan.

The collective body of these recommendations, made up of applicable statements of work for each RTO, expresses the organization's continuity strategy. Consequently, the people responsible for implementing and managing the process have to be aware of their accountabilities. A final step is required; make the members of the organization aware of their personal requirements.

Phase 4: Ensure Understanding

Developing the continuity plan is complete once the organization is prepared to make sure everyone understands it. There should be detailed procedures available for each RTO. If they have been prepared capably, these procedures should assure the persistence of the organization's critical functions and services.

A plan is only as good as the people who implement it. The organization must ensure that all participants in the process clearly understand their role and accountability. The plan states the assumptions about dependent or subsequent complications. Examples include complications beyond the actual disaster, such as responsibility to families and the human resources as well as public relations issues.

As the organizations that experienced anthrax scares after 9/11 found out, it is hard to restore continuity if the workers are afraid to go back to the building. Therefore, any dependent contingencies associated with the disaster must be identified, and during the planning process responses must be implemented to address that contingency.

The organization must make appropriate parts of the plan available to each stakeholder to ensure an awareness of roles, responsibilities, and accountability. The categorization of the participants in this process should have taken place when the critical functions were identified. The managers responsible for implementing and overseeing the continuity function have a list of the key people designated for each function. These lists serve as the basis for the assignment of tasks, as well as the estimation of **resource requirements**.

It is important to instill continuity concepts in active projects because much of an organization's information processing function involves project work. Once the assignment of roles and responsibilities is complete, the organization should plan and execute a focused, organization-wide, awareness, training, and education program. The program should bring the entire organization to the required level of capability. Everybody essential to the success of the continuity plan must be aware of their role and adequately trained to respond correctly as the plan is executed.

Finally, all levels of management, from senior managers down to team and project leaders, have to understand and support the process. Remember, as with every other information assurance principle, management support is an important requirement.

Continuity is resource-intensive and like car insurance, it only really makes its true value evident after the fact. It is an ongoing challenge to maintain the management discipline required to ensure an effective continuity process. Without strong endorsement and support from the top-level management, discipline becomes nearly impossible to maintain.

Managers have to be convinced that the resources invested in a continuity program are justified. That buy-in is obtained by giving them an active role in the process. Involve managers in the process of creating the overall information assurance infrastructure (discussed in Chapters 1 and 2). This leads to an acceptance of the purpose and value of the plan. It will be endorsed by everybody from executive management to the first line managers responsible for implementation.

Disaster Recovery Planning

Disaster recovery planning or **crisis management** is the aspect of business continuity management that applies after a disaster. Business continuity planning and disaster recovery planning require different orientations and activities.

Disaster planners focus on a narrower aspect of continuity. They recover assets after a disaster. They identify every disaster contingency and offer a prescription that allows the organization to respond effectively to each. This thinking is captured in a **Disaster Recovery Plan (DRP)**.

The DRP is oriented toward restoring the technical operations with the aim of bringing an identified set of critical systems back to a desired level of operation. Since most disaster recovery plans are triggered by a major disruption at the target site, the DRP goal requires migrating damaged systems or applications to an alternate site. Accordingly, the DRP comes into effect only when a catastrophic event such as a major fire or a natural disaster denies access to normal processing facilities.

Timing and the DRP

Timing is important in the design of the disaster strategy and the implementation of the recovery plan. The DRP is activated only if there will be an extended disruption.

The rule of thumb is that the estimated time to return the threatened system to normal operation at the damaged site must be significantly greater than the time it would take to migrate it.

Consequently, a disaster recovery plan requires understanding of the affect that the downtime has on business processes. In addition, it should to be possible to confirm through analysis that it will be impossible to satisfy the Recovery Time Objective (RTO) with any other type of response.

The Elements of Disaster Planning

Disaster planning has both a long-term and a short-term perspective. In the long term, effective disaster planning centers on anticipating disasters and ensuring the proper solution. To do that it is necessary to be aware of the risks and their likelihood.

Because practically anything is possible, and associated likelihoods are often hard to determine, building disaster-planning scenarios entails a degree of "blue-sky thinking," and feasibility of threats is a key concept.

Although the possibility of life on earth being extinguished by an asteroid is conceivable, it is less likely than fire or flood. Therefore, one must establish and maintain a balanced perspective on threats that may cause loss of business value and not waste time planning for improbable threats.

The assumptions in the planning process are based on selecting the most likely **disaster scenarios** and regularly updating their probability. In the short term, crisis planners have to specify the steps taken if a particular disaster occurs. Anticipated events associated with a given scenario have to be clearly understood, laid out, and cross-referenced to the procedures. This is based on a plan implemented through clear instructions for each circumstance.

Disaster planning involves raising the level of awareness and preparation organization wide through normal human resource procedures such as assigning staff responsibilities for implementation. This requires itemizing of the specific roles and responsibilities of the participants. The personnel process requires motivating and educating executive managers and other stakeholders who are accountable for ensuring that the plan is updated and maintained.

To implement crisis management, disaster plans have to be tested. Testing requires planners to refine, operationally exercise, and assess their assumptions. The goal is to prove that selected strategies adequately address the operational requirements.

Types of Disasters The goal of a disaster response plan is to minimize interruption of work and loss of information, should a disaster occur. The types of disasters that must be planned for vary based on the situation and factors such as geographic location.

One of the initial requirements is the compilation of a prioritized list of possible disasters. Plans should be based on the most probable disasters. Disasters can be broken down into three categories: natural, site, and civil. For illustration, here are some examples in each category:

Natural Disasters

- Localized or area floods
- Tornadoes
- Hurricanes
- Earthquakes

Site Disasters

- Fire (both structural and natural, like forest fires)
- Water and sewer emergencies
- Gas leaks
- Telephone or cable service interruptions
- Chemical leaks or spills (both in the building and external)
- Explosions (both in the building and external)
- Failure of the building (including local or complete collapse)

Civil Disasters

- Car, plane, or train crash
- Civil disturbance

Elements of a Disaster Recovery Plan   A disaster recovery plan should be able to respond to all credible threats. The range of disasters may vary; however, the plans that cover them always have the same three elements:

- **Disaster impact** description and classification
- **Response deployment** and communication processes
- **Escalation** and reassessment procedures

These are diagrammed in Figure 10-5.

Disaster impact classification requires understanding and describing of the threat implications. For instance, knowing that a hurricane is coming does not address its consequences. One must determine the probable consequences of a hurricane coming ashore. Will floods occur? Will buildings collapse? Will there be looting? Once the threats have been identified and described and their likelihood of occurrence assessed, the preplanned response can be described.

Not all disasters are same; therefore, responses are based on assigned roles rather than fixed procedures. The response designates the right people to react in the case of a disaster, rather than the steps they should follow. For instance, since it is impossible to dictate in advance how to fight a building fire, it is sufficient to know that the local fire

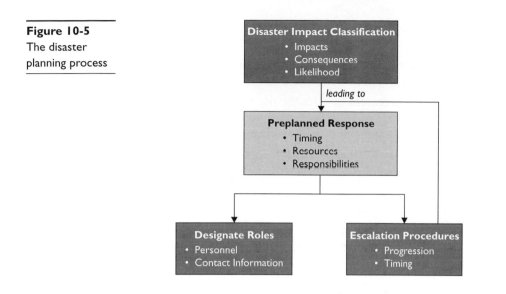

Figure 10-5
The disaster
planning process

Disaster Impact Classification
- Impacts
- Consequences
- Likelihood

leading to

Preplanned Response
- Timing
- Resources
- Responsibilities

Designate Roles
- Personnel
- Contact Information

Escalation Procedures
- Progression
- Timing

department is the proper agency to call. Likewise, a proper plan designates which fire station to call, along with its detailed contact information.

In high-security situations, the required contact information includes contact information for responsible parties for every hour of the day. In addition to designating the point of contact for the responder, the plan provides the contact information for other stakeholders.

Finally, because disasters are characterized by the unknown, there must be a defined set of **escalation** and re-evaluation procedures. These are helpful if the situation turns out to be worse than anticipated, or was not properly understood in the first place. Thus, the plan must include mechanisms for re-evaluating and reclassifying the threat and redeploying the appropriate roles to respond. It must have a mechanism for contacting or recontacting a new set of concerned parties.

Chapter 10 Review

Chapter Summary

- Business continuity management lays out the critical steps that the organization needs to take to ensure that its essential functions are preserved in the event of a disaster.

- Business continuity plans are developed based on the threat identification and risk assessment process.

- The first aim of continuity planning is to avoid the complete disruption of critical information services in the event of a disaster.

- The second aim of continuity planning is to get information functions back in operation as quickly and efficiently as possible.

- Continuity management focuses on developing concrete safeguards for systems, personnel, and facilities.

- Continuity management implies the use of a continuous risk evaluation process to identify and list threats and then decide which ones are acceptable and which ones have to be dealt with by a formal response.

- The procedures for business continuity planning are based on achieving realistic recovery time objectives.

- These are formulated by determining the Maximum Tolerable Downtime (MTD) for each organizationally significant function.

- The answer to that question is expressed as a Recovery Time Objective (RTO), Network Recovery Objective (NRO), or a Recovery Point Objective (RPO).

- RTO is a business concept. It is a timing goal that is established to define the maximum operationally acceptable time that a given system can be out of service.

- An adjunct to RTO is the Network Recovery Objective (NRO). This term indicates the maximum time that the network can be out of service.

- RPO is the integrity principle. It defines the point to which data can be restored after a failure.

- Any data that is created or modified outside of the parameters that are set by the RPO either will be lost or must be re-created.

- Businesses make a conscious decision about the most effective RPO within their business goals.

- The aim of business continuity plans is to ensure continuous processing capability with no loss of data.

- Where the system and its data are deemed so critical that the capability must be provided to restore them to their original state at the time of the disaster, recoveries are based on the use of a Data Recovery Hotsite (DRH).

- A Data Recovery Warmsite (DRW) has equipment and communications interfaces to provide immediate backup functioning, but they do not mirror the processing at the target site.

- Warmsites cannot ensure that data will be preserved in the event of a disaster.

- Backup processing parameters are usually established based on a "best economic estimate" of the Restoration Point Objectives (RPO).

- A Data Recovery Coldsite (DRC) involves maintaining a small reserve facility with all of the necessary hardware, system, and environmental controls in it to take over quickly only the most critical processing functions, should the main site be lost.

- Coldsites are effective for functions that have a time lag built into them, like payroll. That is because paychecks are only issued in weekly or monthly increments and the amounts do not change frequently, so a weekly backup is sufficient to keep the data current.

- The trade-off process that underlies decision making about continuity strategy is supported by business impact analysis and risk analysis.

- Business impact analyses are carried out to determine what impacts a potential disruption might have on a function or data asset.

- Risk analysis estimates the impact that a major disruption to a particular system or process would have on the overall situation.

- There are various levels of criticality associated with risk. These can be categorized at four levels.

- The aim of the business continuity management plan is to protect the maximum number of processes with the highest degree of practicable assurance.

- It does that by minimizing the recovery time for the business processes within the scheme.

- Business continuity planning is broken up into four phases: identify the critical business function set, establish recovery time objectives, identify the solution, and ensure understanding of the solution.

- The business should reliably ensure that all of the participants clearly understand their roles and accountabilities.

- Disaster planners are focused on recovering the information asset after a disaster has occurred rather than preventing that occurrence in the first place.

- The tangible representation of this thinking is captured in a Disaster Recovery Plan (DRP).

- DRPs are aimed at bringing an identified set of critical systems back up to a level of desired operation.

- The assumptions that underlie a DRP are based on identifying the most likely disaster scenarios and keeping a regularly updated estimate of the return on investment of alternative approaches for responding to them.

- DRPs always have the same three generic procedural components: disaster impact description and classification, **response deployment** and communication process, and escalation and reassessment procedures.

Key Terms

business continuity planning (257)
business impact analysis (264)
crisis management (272)
critical activities (270)
Data Recovery Coldsite (DRC) (263)
Data Recovery Hotsite (DRH) (262)

Data Recovery Warmsite (DRW) (262)
disaster planning (265)
disaster recovery (272)
Disaster Recovery Plan (DRP) (272)
disaster scenarios (273)
escalation (275)
Included Activities (270)
Maximum Tolerable Downtime (MTD) (260)
migration (263)
Network Recovery Objective (NRO) (261)
Non-Essential Activities (270)
preparedness response (259)
Recovery Point Objective (RPO) (261)
Recovery Time Objective (RTO) (260)
redundancy (269)
resource requirements (272)
response deployment (277)
risk analysis (264)
shortfall areas (270)
statement of work (SOW) (271)

Key Term Quiz

Complete each statement by writing one of the terms from this list in each blank. Not all terms will be used.

1. Information assurance and continuity planning ensure the same organizational _____.

2. One of the most serious steps in disaster recovery is ensuring that there are no _____.

3. The _____ is established based on maximum allowable downtime

4. The _____ is established based on the integrity requirements of the data.

5. The steps that will be taken to meet a given RPO are contained in a _____.

6. The _____ strategy is always based on business considerations

7. A _____ is the least effective way to ensure continuity.

8. A _____ is the most effective way to ensure continuity.

9. Continuity is always based on a reliable _____ analysis.

10. The objective that defines the optimum point where the data should be _____ after the disaster is called the _____.

Multiple Choice Quiz

1. Information assurance and continuity management are similar because

    A. different assets are involved

    B. they implement the same policies

    C. one continues the other in-depth

    D. they are the same process

2. Recovery Point Objectives

    A. are never exact

    B. are based on economic RTOs

    C. are based on unfeasible RTOs

    D. are essential parts of media protection

3. The process of formulating the RTO should be based on

    A. MDT

    B. the NRO

    C. cost

    D. priorities

4. Bare metal recoveries rely on

    A. warmsites

    B. hotsites

    C. coldsites

    D. eyesight

5. Disaster planning always involves

    A. best guess

    B. best practice

    C. limited roles

    D. communication

6. Business Continuity solutions have to be implemented within

    A. realistic boundaries

    B. operating parameters of the business

    C. expectations

    D. feasibility

7. Maximum Tolerable Downtime is an estimate of

   A. MTBU

   B. RPO

   C. NRO

   D. RTO

8. Continuity is in effect the assurance processes'

   A. escape hatch

   B. firewall

   C. lifeboat

   D. defense in depth

9. Continuity Plans are always based on:

   A. information identification

   B. risk assessment

   C. access control

   D. legal compliance

10. Continuity plans communicate an organizational

   A. best guess

   B. estimate

   C. risk estimate

   D. strategy

Essay Quiz

1. Why is the formulation of the RTO and RPO a trade-off process?
2. What is the relationship between impact and likelihood in disaster planning?
3. Why might planning be the single point of failure?
4. What is the relationship between assumptions and strategies?
5. Why is organizational buy-in so important to continuity management?
6. What makes continuity important? Why is continuity an important goal?
7. Why is continuity sometimes not thought about during the overall information assurance process? Why is that a critical omission?
8. How does the concept of categories of disaster make it easier to accommodate potential harmful events? What is an example of how that works?

9. What is the point of the statement of work? Why is one necessary? What would happen without one?

10. Why is it so important to define roles for disaster response? What would happen without this specification?

Case Exercise

Complete the following case exercise as directed by your instructor:

Heavy Metal Technologies (HMT) is a defense contractor headquartered in Huntsville, Alabama. HMT was recently contracted by the Army to upgrade the fire control system for the MH64-D Apache Longbow attack helicopter. Because the contracted enhancement is so important to the continuing success of the main ground attack helicopter program and thus because of its importance to national defense, the Army wants a total commitment from HMT that the program will be delivered as contracted. In order to do that, it is necessary to develop a disaster plan that will ensure vital functioning no matter what occurs. Therefore, the Army would like HMT to address the following organizational control concerns. Please provide a written solution for each of these.

1. The Army requires a plan to ensure that the information that currently resides at Jackson Street will be protected from any foreseeable disaster,

2. The Army requires a plan to ensure the same conditions for the information at Sunnyside Main.

3. The Army requires a procedure to ensure that a management team will be put in place if a disaster occurs.

Because Ft. Walton is on the ocean, the Army requires a hurricane/flood response plan.

Laws, Regulations, and Crime

In this chapter, you will learn how to:

- Work with legal issues associated with computers and information
- Work with the laws and regulations governing the security of information
- Consider the various aspects of cyber-crime
- Work with the elements of ensuring contract compliance

It is necessary to factor legal issues into an information assurance scheme. Failure to comply with the requirements of a particular law, regulation, or contract brings a significant organizational exposure. For information assurance professionals, *compliance* is a critical topic.

Compliance describes a formal process to ensure fulfillment of the terms of a law, regulation, contract, or standard. Compliance process describes the overall approach to ensuring conformance with applicable laws, regulations, and contracts. Compliance processes are an important part of day-to-day operation; the consequences of non-compliance are severe.

Information itself is not affected by compliance failure. The failure affects the whole organization. For example, an organization that violates an intellectual property law, like the 1998 Digital Millennium Copyright Act (DMCA), is both criminally and civilly liable. In the case of individuals, violation of the DMCA may lead to jail time. Including of a few lines of stolen code into a product can lead to millions of dollars in fines, plus civil penalties.

Whether a violation is intentional or not, individuals and companies that break laws and violate contracts are legally bound to pay the consequences. Prudent organizations have a duty to establish a formal identification process for legal problems associated with information and ensure compliance.

This duty requires wrestling with conflicting concerns such as ensuring intellectual property rights where there is no tangible or **real property** and investigating data theft.

In this chapter, we are going to discuss the things that you need to think about to establish a compliance process. We focus on the laws as well as the questions they raise. We discuss some of the common issues associated with compliance as well as the evolving legal environment.

Protecting Intellectual Property

It is a very difficult task to assure **intellectual property** in cyberspace. With cyberspace, the legal problems center on two concepts, *intangible value* and *international enforcement*.

Intangible property has no actual *form* but it has *value* and is an asset. In most organization's, intangible property is everything from patents, designs, copyrights, and trademarks, to trade names, licenses, and contracts that they own. In the case of information, intangible property can include everything from proprietary methods, programs, systems, procedures, and technical data, to business forecasts, industry estimates, survey data, and customer lists (Treas. Reg. § 1.482-4[b]). Since these are mainly intangible, the legal test for determining possession is whether the ownership is documented and tangible value can be assigned.

For example, the existence and value of the copyright to a piece of software is established by law. If that software were pirated, its relative economic value can be calculated and that value allows a court to determine damages and penalties for violating the copyright. This is possible even though the software program is intangible. This ability to document ownership and assign real value to intangible things makes enforcement of intellectual property rights possible.

On the other hand, it is a greater challenge to enforce intellectual property rights for assets where the value is unknown and/or the ownership cannot be legally documented. To prove that a theft has occurred, it is necessary to demonstrate that a possession of value was stolen. The problem that the **legal system** faces with cyberspace is how to judge ownership of property that neither exists nor has commonly accepted value.

Traditional mechanisms for assigning value to intangible assets, like copyrights and trademarks, allow protection under the same assumptions that guide the courts in tangible assets. However, the ownership and value of the other important items residing in cyberspace has to be consciously indicated for those items to be protected by law. It is an ongoing responsibility of the assurance function to ensure that legal designations of ownership are placed on all important intellectual property items in cyberspace. It is also important that a formal valuation property is attached.

It is possible to steal intangible assets and property from anywhere on the Internet so it is important to make sure that all provisions for international regulation of intangible property are understood and obeyed.

This is essential since it is possible to prosecute foreign nationals for intellectual property theft. Although the first prosecution, *United States versus ElcomSoft*, resulted in a "not guilty" verdict, enforcement agencies like the Business Software Alliance (BSA) and the Recording Industry Association of America (RIAA) see the Digital Millennium Copyright Act (DMCA) as the tool of the future.

Enforcing Protection Rights:
The Digital Millennium Copyright Act

The quantity of material electronically accessible and anonymous access makes it difficult to track down and prosecute intellectual property thefts. Individuals and companies frequently have to enforce ownership rights in foreign courts because the Internet is global; however, geopolitical realities make this difficult.

The best hope for enforcing worldwide intellectual property rights is the Digital Millennium Copyright Act of 1998 (DMCA) that implements the World Intellectual Property Organization's (WIPO) Copyright and Performances and Phonograms treaties signed in Geneva in 1996. The intent of the DMCA is to protect and criminalize copyright infringement by increasing the penalties. The DMCA makes it criminal to circumvent software anti-piracy measures or produce illegal copying of software.

Numerous gray areas of definition of intangible property lead to strong opposition, by scientists, librarians, and academics while it was enthusiastically supported by the software and entertainment industries. The DMCA provides obvious exemptions, for instance nonprofit libraries, archives, and educational institutions. The DMCA also relieves Internet service providers (ISPs) from copyright infringement liability for just transmitting information over the Internet. This exemption was important for ISPs during the Napster trial.

Although the DMCA strengthens legal protection internationally, currently enforcement of intellectual property ownership rights does not extend much outside of the U.S., Canada, and Western Europe. This is particularly true in the case of software piracy.

Software piracy is a worldwide phenomenon. According to the Business Software Alliance (BSA), about 25 percent of the software used in the United States is pirated. The problem is more serious in the Pacific Rim. The estimated piracy rate in China ranges between 92 percent and 97 percent. The rate in Eastern Europe ranges from 71 percent to 84 percent, while rates in the rest of the world are close behind.

The software industry estimates that it loses more than 10 billion dollars per year to piracy. Therefore, software piracy prevention is the best-organized international property rights enforcement area. Companies have banded together to create their own enforcement mechanism in the Business Software Alliance (BSA).

International Prevention and the Business Software Alliance

The BSA is one of the most influential players in international piracy prevention. The BSA counts Microsoft, Symantec, and Adobe among its members. It works with law enforcement agencies in over 30 countries to identify and prosecute **licensing agreement** violators.

The BSA functions as a quasi-legal international entity. A single call to the BSA from any country, reporting licensing violations, may trigger a costly investigation leading to hefty fines and criminal penalties.

Companies need to develop robust processes ensuring compliance with all licensing agreements. The enforcement work of the BSA and similar national enforcement organizations such as the Washington D.C.–based Software Publisher's Association (SPA) and the Canadian Alliance Against Software Theft (CAAST) makes compliance important.

The work of the BSA is limited to countries where piracy is discouraged because it depends on the good will of local law enforcement. The BSA does *not* include several large software markets including China and Thailand.

Software Piracy

Deliberate theft of software is piracy. Computer programs are **copyrighted works**; when you "buy" software, you do not actually own the product. You have a license or permission to use it. One must be able to produce valid proof, called a **software license**, to demonstrate that you are using the software on your system with permission.

Various types of **permissions** accompany these licenses. Some limit installation to a single computer. Others provide a site-wide authorization, or **site licenses**, that let the organization install it on every computer. This is usually explained in fine print on the licensing agreement. Users blithely click on to "accept" the conditions of the sale without reading and understanding their obligation. Once these conditions are accepted, the user is bound by a contract that establishes specific rights and penalties for violations.

Consequences of Piracy

Piracy is important corporate America because there are millions of computers in cubicle-land that make it hard to track the software running on every machine at any time. Without proof of due diligence in enforcing licensing agreements, the piracy conditions applicable to an individual also apply to the organization. Organization may be liable for violating licensing agreement terms even if an individual worker actually caused the problem.

To show due diligence, the organization must document a conscientious effort to enforce licensing restrictions in its day-to-day operation. The proof of this is a comprehensive, formally documented control system that strictly monitors and enforces all contracts and agreements.

Regulating Piracy

There are two federal regulations addressing software piracy. First is the Computer Software Rental Amendments Act of 1990 specifying that rental, lease, or lending of copyrighted software is forbidden without copyright owner authorization.

Second, and more important, is copyright law (Title 17 of the U.S. Code), which is interpreted to mean that the creation or distribution of copyrighted software without authorization is illegal even if there is no express copyright given to the owner. The only requirement is to document original ownership. Under this law, the unauthorized duplication of copyrighted material including software can lead to fines of up to one hundred thousand dollars and jail terms of up to five years per incident.

Laws Affecting Computer Use

Most contemporary computer-use laws deal with protecting privacy and regulating commercial transactions. There are four categories:

- Governmental regulations
- Privacy regulations

- Laws that define computer crime
- Laws that regulate classified or sensitive information

Each has different compliance requirements and each will be discussed below.

Governmental Regulations

The first regulatory actions having application to computing were actually passed before the official birthdate of the commercial computer in 1950. The laws included 18 U.S.C. 1005 (1948) prohibiting false entries in bank records and falsifying credit institution records; 18 U.S.C. 1362 (1948) prohibits malicious mischief to government property; and 18 U.S.C. 2071 (1948), prohibits concealment, removal, or mutilation of public records. In 1952 18 U.S.C. 1343 prohibited wire fraud using interstate communications systems.

Although these laws were passed in the Jurassic era of computing, they served as a framework for the laws passed in the 1980s, when the computer had become the primary instrument for communication in government, business, and industry.

New laws were passed in the 1980s to respond to legal problems developing arose around information processing and communication. Based on the earlier laws that public records could not be tampered with, 18 U.S.C. 1029 (1984) prohibited fraudulent use of credit cards, passwords, and telephone access codes. 18 U.S.C. 2701 (1986) prohibited unauthorized access to electronically stored information. 18 U.S.C. 2778 (1989) prohibited illegal export of software or data controlled by the Department of Defense (DoD) while 18 U.S.C. 2510 (1989) prohibited the illegal export of software or data controlled by the Department of Commerce.

Privacy Regulations

While theft of intellectual property is an identifiable breach of common legal principles, the concept of privacy has proven harder to pin down. Privacy centers on the acquisition and use of personal information as a commercial product. It is unpleasant that most personal information is as much a commodity as manufactured goods and services. The ethics of privacy will be discussed in Chapter 16. The legal ramifications will be discussed here.

A range of good and potentially malicious institutions collects and maintains most vital personal information available about people in the United States. This information includes information that people already know about themselves, as well as things that they might not know—such as conclusions that people have drawn about them recorded in data warehouses.

The accumulated information is harmless as long as it is not obtained or used with malicious intent. However, as demonstrated by identity theft and online fraud, the effort to keep information private is a serious and growing concern.

Privacy is closely related to the information assurance principle of confidentiality. However, the misappropriation of personal information may lead to more than privacy loss; it may lead to financial damages. For example, if an inside employee embezzles credit card information and sells it to identity thieves; there are economic consequences, both for the victims and the organization.

As the amount of personal information kept in corporate databases continues to grow, identity theft can be expected to increase. According to a recent study by Javelin Research, approximately 8.9 million people became victims of identity theft in the past 12 months. That amounts to 24,386 people per day, 1,015 per hour, or 17 per minute. As reported by the Interactive the Identity Theft Center a Harris study found that victimization rate increased from 11–20 percent, in the period 2001–2002, and by 80 percent between 2002 and 2003. The fallout from the civil litigation substantiates the idea that it is essential to keep personal data secure.

Notwithstanding possible criminal activity, privacy violations occur because of **human error**. In fact, according to a 2003 nationwide survey by CompTIA, human error was most likely cause of problems with personal information. The study found that only 8 percent of the computer problems information could be blamed on purely technical causes; the remaining 92 percent involved some form of human error.

Legal consequences can be severe and apply even if the error was inadvertent; prudent organizations will try to anticipate the threats that possession and handling of personal information represent by instituting routine assurance procedures and controls. In addition to risks of litigation, there are also a number of laws regarding privacy. Many define the rights of individuals to know and control their personal information while organizations must implement adequate safeguards. Violations of these laws lead to specific penalties; organizations must factor compliance into the equation.

Laws to Protect Privacy

Individuals have the right to control some, but not all, of their information. This is based on laws and common law precedents developed over the past 40 years. Most are all derived from the first and directive provided to support the confidentiality of individual information. That is the Bill of Rights to the U.S. Constitution (1791). The *Fourth Amendment* guarantees individual protection against unreasonable search and seizure by the government (note that it does not offer an explicit guarantee of a right to privacy except as noted in *Griswold v. CT*). Figure 11-1 illustrates the timeline of these laws.

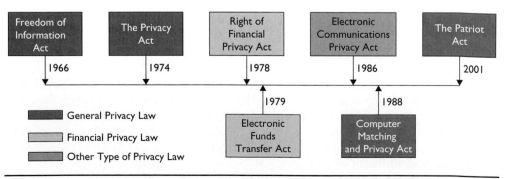

Figure 11-1 Timeline of public acts related to protection of privacy

The Freedom of Information Act

The Freedom of Information Act (FOIA) (5 U.S.C. 552 PL 890554) enacted in 1966 offers the first electronic-age privacy protections. Prior to this act, individuals had to demonstrate the need to know if they wanted to see personal records kept about them by the government. Under FOIA, the burden of proof shifted to the government; the "need to know" standard was replaced with a "right to know."

FOIA guarantees access to documents held by Executive Branch agencies and cabinet departments. FOIA does not apply to records held by elected federal officials, the federal judiciary, private organizations, individuals who receive federal contracts or grants, tax-exempt organizations, or state and local government.

FOIA requires federal agencies to provide full public disclosure of information. It sets standards for determining which records should be made available for public inspection and which records can be withheld. It provides administrative and judicial remedies for those denied access.

In 1986, amendments to FOIA gave agencies some authority to deny access to a record or refuse to confirm its existence. There are specific instances where this applies:

1. Records that might interfere with an active law enforcement investigation

2. Records from confidential informants

3. Records that pertain to foreign intelligence

The Privacy Act

In 1974, PL 93-579, The Privacy Act, defined the rights of individuals with respect to the computerized information kept about them. This act is the first instance of the omnibus regulation of electronic information. The Privacy Act requires the U.S. government to safeguard the integrity, confidentiality, and availability of all of the personal data that is processed by the computer systems that support federal agencies. In addition, agencies are required to offer ways for individuals to determine what information is being recorded about them, and it mandates that a process must be in place to correct inaccuracies.

The Privacy Act safeguards individuals from invasion of privacy by the federal government by regulating the way the government collects, maintains, uses, and disseminates personal information. It ensures that the personal information collected is for a necessary and lawful purpose. It prohibits personal records from being used for purposes other than those intended or where the owner did not provide express consent.

Under this act, federal agencies or specified organizations such as ISPs or credit-reporting organizations are subject to penalties for willful or intentional action that violates individual rights. Criminal penalties may be applied if prohibited information is disclosed or where the maintenance of the record was in violation of the law.

Acts Related to Financial Privacy

The Privacy Act was expanded by the Right of Financial Privacy Act (1978), which establishes that a depositor's bank accounts are private and can be accessed only by court order with due and proper notification. The Electronic Funds Transfer Act (1979) that followed specifically safeguarded the privacy of transmissions related to funds using electronic funds transfer (EFT).

The Electronic Communications Privacy Act of 1986 (PL 99-508, 18 U.S.C. 2510) enhances the protections provided by the preceding two laws by offering single clear statement of individual rights with respect to electronic information. It expressly prohibits the unauthorized interception of communications independent of how the transmission took place including transmissions over the following media:

- Wire
- Radio
- Electromagnetic
- Photo-electrical
- Photo-optical

The act was passed because law enforcement agencies had strayed when they wiretapped organized crime figures. It is illegal for a governmental agency to intercept any telecommunications, such as electronic funds transfers and electronic mail, without prior authorization.

The act defines which transmissions are protected and which ones are not. It mandates that public electronic communication providers, such as ISPs may not give the contents of the transmitted messages to anyone but the sender and the addressee. If proper provisions have been met, they can divulge this to law enforcement agencies.

The Computer Matching and Privacy Protection Act

The Privacy Act was further amended by 5 U.S.C. 552a (1988)—the **Computer Matching** and Privacy Protection Act. If an individual proves that a federal agency intentionally or willfully violated provisions of this act, they can recover monetary damages; if it can be demonstrated that that disclosure was deliberate, the fine can be substantial. The act requires federal agencies to follow specified procedures for information exchange.

While it applied strictly to federal information processing functions, it served to raise the overall **national awareness** of potential for misuse of the body of personal information collected on computers.

When the act passed, lawmakers were concerned about the increasing use of sophisticated information technology devices and computers to acquire and analyze information. This law limits compilation of information on citizens through data mining or data matching from separate databases by federal agencies. The act requires agencies to negotiate written agreements among all participants in information-matching enterprises, as well as obtain administrative authorization. Finally, the act establishes the oversight rights of Congress and the Office of Management and Budget (OMB) over computer-matching activity.

Individuals applying for and receiving federal aid were frequently the target of information matching and are protected specifically by this law. As such, the matching agency must notify applicants and beneficiaries that their records are subject to matching and verify the findings from a match before reducing, suspending, terminating, or denying an individual's benefits or payments.

The act is controversial because while it provides some protections it also institutionalizes data-mining activities conducted by federal agencies. The term data mining describes data analysis to discover patterns or signatures.

Information collected for one purpose can now be used legally for different purposes by other federal agencies as long as the proper procedures are followed. Although the act mandates assurance of the integrity of the data, it does not protect the privacy of the individuals matched in the process.

Recent events changed privacy law. In response to September 11, 2001, lawmakers sought to remove some legal protections established through laws, presidential acts, codes, and precedent for over 35 years. For example, the awkwardly named Uniting and Strengthening America by Providing Appropriate Tools Required to Intercept and Obstruct Terrorism Act of 2001, known as the USA PATRIOT Act, gives law enforcement and intelligence agencies authority to monitor private communications and access the personal information of individuals in order to safeguard against terrorism.

The PATRIOT Act apparently contravenes many federal government laws and common law legal precedents related to information; it has been extremely divisive. The arguments for the PATRIOT Act stress the importance of reacting promptly to emerging new cultural realities. A less controversial example of legislation driven by cultural phenomena, is the **CAN-SPAM Act (2003)**.

Canning Spam: The CAN-SPAM Act of 2003

The United States law currently regulating **spam** is the Controlling the Assault of Non-Solicited Pornography and Marketing (CAN-SPAM) Act of 2003, which took effect on January 1, 2004. It deals with the rapid increase of Internet junk mail, called spam. According to SpamCop, there were upwards of 158 million spam messages sent in the most recent year and it represented a constant send rate of between 5 and 15 messages per second. Controlling spam might not be a matter of grave national security importance. However, for the sake of alleviating the irritation factor, it is probably high on everybody's list of useful legislation.

This act is based on the concept of affirmative consent, which means that the recipient of a commercial e-mail message must give permission to be a recipient before the message can be sent. Under this law, it is illegal to:

- Send a commercial e-mail message with header information that is either false or misleading

- Spoof the originating address or relay a message from another computer to disguise its point of origin

- Failure to identify clearly that the message is an advertisement or solicitation

The law further requires that the message provides a conspicuous opportunity to decline further messages. If the recipient asks not to receive additional messages, it is illegal to send one that falls within the scope of that request or for others acting on behalf of the sender to do so.

Aggravated violations of CAN-SPAM can bring a substantial fine and imprisonment of one to five years. Federal enforcement of CAN-SPAM is vested in the **Federal Trade Commission (FTC)**, which prosecutes in the same way as other unfair or criminal trade practice. States enforce this law through their respective attorney generals, who may conduct their own investigations.

Cyber-Crime

Computers brought in a new type of criminal—the hacker. The term "hacker" is a catch-all phrase for any person who violates a computer or its information. Crimes associated with hackers range from simple trespass, to data corruption and destruction to distributed denial-of-service attacks costing companies millions of dollars.

Hackers seek unauthorized access to computer systems. Therefore, the correct term for **hacking** is more appropriately "cracking," since the point is to "crack" into a computer just like a safecracker in a bank. Hackers are motivated for different reasons. There are five reasons why hackers try to break into systems:

1. Curiosity or recreational attacks
2. Business or financial attacks
3. Grudge attacks
4. Intelligence attacks
5. Military or terrorist attacks

Types of **hackers** are differentiated based on four factors:

- Motivation—Why was the crime committed and how, where, when, and why was a particular victim selected?
- Method—Sequence of events and behavior of victims and offenders have to be considered.
- Outcome—What was the result of the criminal behavior? What was the degree of harm and was it intentional?
- Post-offense behavior—How does the offender act after committing the crime? Do they seek publicity or anonymity?

Motivation and Method

Motivation factors are classified into eight behavioral signatures or methods of operation (MOs): Those are: ego, exposure, deviance, monetary gain, extortion, sabotage, disinformation, and infowar.

- Ego—Behavior motivated by an inflated sense of pride or superiority to others.

- Exposure—Behavior motivated by a desire to learn or reveal information that the owner wants to protect; violates confidentiality principle.

- Deviance—Abnormal behavior, which does not fit societal norms and is unacceptable. Cyber stalking is an example of this.

- Monetary gain—The behavior is motivated by a desire to obtain money through socially undesirable actions, such as theft, fraud, or conversion. The motivates many targeted crimes.

- Extortion—The behavior is intended to force the victim to do something that he would be unwilling to do otherwise.

- Sabotage—The behavior is intended to damage or destroy the credibility of a resource. The most common example is attacks on databases.

- Disinformation—The behavior is intended to harm or for dishonest purpose by spreading untruths using the distributional power of the Internet. It harms reputations of individuals, companies, and nations.

- Infowar—Information Warfare is hostile strategic behavior in cyberspace conducted to achieve a national or organizational purpose by learning secrets or destroying an adversary's information assets.

Outcome

The outcome is a good way of classifying intent. Six factors describe intent. They are trespass, invasion, theft, harm, commercialization, and strategic use.

- Trespass is well defined in law. Trespass is the act of entering another's property without permission. This can be for the simple purpose of accomplishing that act or it can be to do harm.

- Invasion is shorthand for invasion of privacy. There are three categories of invasions of privacy in cyberspace: appropriation (of personal information), publication of private facts (confidentiality), and false light.

- Theft is obtaining something unlawfully. Theft include larceny, burglary, embezzlement, robbery, intrusion, fraud (theft by deception), and criminal conversion.

- Commercialization is the broad perversion or inappropriate use of a legitimate medium for profit. The commercialization must happen in such a way that the credibility of the medium itself is called into question.

- Strategic use is the employment of a medium to achieve the political purposes of a nation or an organization. The intent must be to achieve a long-term end. Strategic uses in the case of the Internet include spying and tactical disinformation.

Behavior

Finally, post-offense behavior is a strong indicator of the personality type of hackers and one of the best ways of structuring a criminal investigation. For instance, people who perform known ego-driven exploits eventually tend to brag about them. If that is the case the investigator usually only needs to listen to the chatter in the hacker community to identify the perpetrator. Post-offense behavior cannot be characterized as neatly as MO and outcome.

If we look at the motivations and goals of cyber-crimes, there are at least 12 distinct behavioral types. This is not an exhaustive list, but it illustrates the range of malicious behaviors that might be encountered. Table 11-1 summarizes these types.
Note the following points about the types in Table 11-1:

- *Kiddies* are technologically inept. They use pre-programmed scripts to trespass; their motivation is ego, but because they do not know what they are doing they can be destructive. Kiddies may be tracked by matching the crime to people who have downloaded a particular toolset from hacker websites.

- *Cyber-punks* are usually ego-driven counterculture members usually intent on trespass or invasion. If their act is invasion, the motive is exposure. Cyber-punks may engage in theft and sabotage, but only of what they perceive as legitimate counterculture targets. Cyber-punks are responsible for many virus, application layer, and DoS attacks targeted on establishment organizations, companies, and products.

- *Old-timers* are the most technologically proficient members of the hacker community. They are ego-driven. They are the last of the Old Guard whose interest is in proving their art. They are usually harmless since they usually know what they are doing and have benign motives.

- *Code warriors* are the first of the more destructive profiles. They may have been driven by ego or revenge; however, it is now primarily monetary gain through either theft or sabotage. Their crimes are built around code exploits, application layer attacks, and Trojan horses. Like old-timers, they are technologically superb with a long and visible history in technology.

- *Cyber thief*—The motive of this group is always monetary gain, either by learning something they should not know or by theft. Their crimes are means to that end. They are adept at surreptitious network attacks such as **sniffing** or **spoofing**. This profile uses tools and programming exploits such as Trojans and malware rather than targeted code. They are adept at **social engineering**. Individuals with this profile may be insiders.

- *Cyber hucksters* are the spammers and purveyors of malware motivated by monetary gain and commercialization. They are adept at social engineering and spoofing. This profile employs tracking cookies, spyware, and even data mines to find victims. This profile is more irritating than criminal and thanks to CAN-SPAM they are now criminals.

MOTIVATION	Kiddie	Cyber Punk	Old Timer	Code Warrior	Cyber Thief	Cyber Huckster	Unhappy Insider	Ex-Insider	Cyber Stalker	Con Man	Soldier	War Fighter
Ego	X	X	X	X					X			
Exposure		X					X					
Deviance									X			
Monetary Gain		X		X	X	X	X			X	X	
Extortion				X			X	X			X	
Revenge				X			X	X			X	
Sabotage		X		X			X	X				
Disinformation								X				
Infowar												X

INTENT	Kiddie	Cyber Punk	Old Timer	Code Warrior	Cyber Thief	Cyber Huckster	Unhappy Insider	Ex-Insider	Cyber Stalker	Con Man	Soldier	War Fighter
Trespass	X	X	X									
Invasion of Privacy		X			X				X			
Theft				X	X		X			X	X	
Harm		X		X			X	X		X	X	X
Commercialization						X				X		
Strategic Use												X

Table 11-1   Potential Cyber-Attack Profiles, by Motivation and Intent

- *Unhappy insiders* are perhaps the most dangerous group since this group is actually authorized to access the organization's information. Their motive is monetary gain, theft, harm, extortion, or exposure of organization secrets for revenge or sabotage. They can steal information or perform other malicious acts on the system. They are characterized by dissatisfaction with the organization. The only protection is to identify signs of discontent and closely monitor actions.

- *Ex–insiders* are hostile terminations. They are motivated by extortion, revenge, sabotage, or disinformation. They focus on harming the organization that dismissed them. If they anticipate dismissal, they might set logic bombs or perform other destructive acts. They will make use of insider information to harm or discredit the organization externally. The only protection is to plan a dismissal to ensure a clean break. A sure sign of the work of an ex-insider are attacks on organization vulnerabilities that were not public knowledge.

- *Cyber–stalkers* are motivated by ego and deviance with the intent of invasion of privacy to learn something to satisfy some specific need (like jealousy). This profile is differentiated from the other ego-driven profiles since their invasions of privacy are driven by a psychological need—their mental fingerprint. Identification of the need will often point to the cyber-stalker.

- *Conman*—This category is motivated by simple monetary gain with the intent of theft or milder commercialization motives. They are adept at social engineering and spoofing. Members of this group run traditional con games as well as newer exploits like phishing. These attacks are typically untargeted. The conman depends on the victim ignorance; the best defense is awareness.

- *The Soldier*—Organized crime's entry into the field of **cyber-crime**. It is differentiated from the other categories by its high level of determination and organization—second only to the warfighter. They achieve their ends by theft, extortion, and blackmail. Soldiers have the same distinguishing characteristics as the code warrior or con man. However, they always work in highly organized groups often with the best technology that money can buy. Most frequently this type works out of the Far East and Eastern Europe. Given the ease and profitability of Internet crime, it is expected that every organized crime group in the world will have soldiers in this field.

- *Warfighter*—This is not a criminal type when it is fighting on your side. However, when the warfighters are on the other side, their actions would be viewed as destructive. The warfighter is motivated strictly by infowar. Their aim is strategic advantage for friends and harm to the enemy. They are extremely dangerous since they can wreak havoc to the physical infrastructure of a country by attacking its electronic infrastructure. Warfighters can also spread disinformation through targeted attacks on media or social engineering. Warfighters are highly organized and frequently the best and brightest the country has to offer. They are technologically superb. Since this just describes the members of any government agency, the best defense against a warfighter is a friendly set of warfighters.

Types of Hacker Tools

Tools that hackers use fall into three categories: password cracking, technological exploits, and social engineering. The first of these, password cracking, relies on one of three approaches: password sharing, password guessing, and password capture.

Password sharing involves the simple disclosure of a password to others. This is the most common violation since workers in the workplace are very willing to share passwords with co-workers or friends. This is done out of ignorance of the dangers and awareness is a simple tool to prevent sharing. Shared passwords are dangerous; violations should be punished.

Password guessing is what the name implies. Hackers use software to automate this attack. The most common method is the brute force attack—where a program simply enters a series of characters until it finds the right combination. Another approach is a dictionary attack where the software enters a series of common words. Since people typically use simple names or words for their password, a dictionary attack is frequently sufficient. Safeguard against password guessing by limiting the number of logon attempts for the user.

Password capture is an advanced approach; the hacker obtains the password using malware or Trojan code. It is also possible to capture passwords using sniffers and other network monitors. Passwords should never be transmitted over a network in plaintext. Encrypt every sensitive item sent, since it is impossible to guarantee that no one is eavesdropping. Even with encryption, hackers have "password crackers," which allows the listener to decrypt a password or password file. If an attacker gains the right administrative privileges, every user password is exposed. Ensure that the system staff is properly vetted and controlled.

Technological Approaches of Attackers

Attackers may use sophisticated technological approaches to gain access, including spoofing and probe tools, which alters packet headers to make it appear as though a file came from an authorized source. Hackers use automated probe tools to explore remotely other's systems. They identify any vulnerability that might be exploited to gain access.

A port scanner is a good example of a probe tool. Port scanners try to connect to the ports on another machine; they are automated and sweep millions of machines seeking vulnerabilities.

Keyloggers and their password capture variants are also examples of remote exploration tools. If the aim is invasion of privacy they are keyloggers. If the aim is to intercept passwords they are "password capture" tools. They are placed on a host machine by Trojan code. Then these two types of spyware sit in the background recording all keystrokes. Once keystrokes are logged, they are hidden in the machine for later retrieval or shipped raw to the attacker.

However, probably the most dangerous hacker tool is the Remote Administration Tool (RAT). As its name implies, a RAT is Trojan code that allows the hacker to administer remotely another machine. This hands over control of another person's computer to a hacker, this attack is among the most popular exploits on the Internet for hard core hacker with dangerous profiles.

Statistically, the most popular form of RAT is some version of SubSeven. Since RATs are surreptitious, there is no way of knowing how many are out there. A survey conducted by PestPatrol indicates that RATs are the second most common form of malware after tracking cookies and infections on Windows machines are becoming as frequent as viruses. RATs can be placed directly on a machine, but they are most frequently delivered via e-mails and social engineering. This brings us to the final category of hacker tools.

Social engineering is "running a con game." The hacker uses a confidence swindle to "con" a victim into doing something the engineer wants. Classic social engineering activities include the "phone survey" and the "emergency situation." The defense is to know or verify the identity of the person you are talking to.

A popular low-tech approach is "dumpster diving." The criminal goes through an organization's garbage cans, dumpster, or trash bins to obtain important information such as discarded system documentation. The most effective countermeasure against this attack is a good shredder.

Computer Crime

There are other types of computer crime. There are crimes intended to harm or illegally obtain proprietary information or intellectual property. We discussed this type of crime in the section "Protecting Intellectual Property." Now we are going to look at crimes against property.

Crimes against property are not always technical in origin. Most criminal acts of this type do not directly involve the use of the hacking tools. For instance, the *use* of the computer to carry out a conventional criminal act like fraud is a cyber-crime and it is a growing menace.

Internet fraud increased drastically from 2001 to 2002. In 2002, federal officials arrested 135 cyber-criminals and seized over $17 million in assets. Criminal acts included phishing scams to steal account information from unsuspecting customers, auction fraud, and nondelivery of merchandise. According to the Computer Security Institute, dollar losses due to credit and debit card fraud alone appear to be increasing at a rate of around 300 percent per year as are the actual number of complaints referred to law enforcement.

Laws Designed to Control Computer Crime

There are laws and federal regulations that designed to deter computer crime. They have emerged as the crimes have developed rather than a preemptive body of law; as a result, the coverage of these laws is not comprehensive. It is clear from the current activities that as technology evolves, the body of legal responses will also evolve. Figure 11-2 illustrates the timeline of these laws.

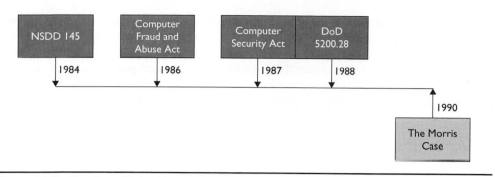

Figure 11-2   Timeline of federal laws and regulations related to computer use

The Computer Fraud and Abuse Act

An early law that directly addressed crimes committed using a computer is Public Law 99-474, the **Computer Fraud** and Abuse Act (1986). This act establishes that a person is in criminal violation of the law if they knowingly access a federal interest computer without proper authorization or exceed their permitted access privileges and subsequently:

- Use that access to cause a loss greater than $1,000

- Use that access to obtain sensitive governmental information

- Perform an act (DOS for example) that prevents other authorized users from using a computer

Prior to the Internet, the Computer Fraud and Abuse Act applied strictly to computers containing national defense or financial information. It established a range of serious penalties for the enumerated actions ranging from fines to up to 20 years in jail.

The interpretation of the term "federal interest computers" extends to computers are owned by the government or used by the government, as well as computer that access federal data or any set of computers located in two or more states. The law also applies to computers used by federally insured financial institutions such as banks. The definition extends federal jurisdiction into the private sector.

First Application of the Fraud and Abuse Act: The Morris Case

In 1990, Robert T. Morris, Jr., the legendary implementer of the first Internet "worm," was convicted and sentenced under this law. It was the first conviction for a true cyber-crime. His case serves as an illustration of the problem of assigning penalties for crimes involving intangible property. Although his acts were considered moderate, the judge gave Morris a light sentence. According to Mark Rasch, who prosecuted Morris, a new Justice Department policy now mandates that all defendants will be treated equally, without regard for personal history or other factors that might mitigate stiffer sentences.

The Supreme Court failed to overturn his conviction by deciding not to hear his case. It was their opinion that the wording of PL 99-474 was sufficient to define the facts of unauthorized access and the defendant had demonstrated sufficient intent to injure. This justified his conviction under the authorization to access provisions.

Federal Regulations for Classified and Sensitive Information

The protection of classified and sensitive information is a major national security interest and there has been extensive federal legislation and regulation. These laws apply exclusively to information deemed sensitive or classified by the federal government, organizations contracting with the government must be aware of their provisions.

The federal regulation that first applied to classified and sensitive unclassified systems and information is the National Security Decision Directive 145–1984 (NSDD-145). This directive vested authority to protect both classified and **sensitive but unclassified information** with the National Security Agency (NSA). It covers such items as

- Census Bureau statistics
- Air traffic control information
- Health and financial records

Over the past 20 years, a number of the federal directives such as NSDD-145 have become controversial when they reach into the private sector. This regulation gives the NSA the authority to "encourage, advise, and assist in the protection of information *in the private sector* that the federal government deems classified and/or sensitive."

This directive has application to the private sector and its oversight is given to an overarching System Security Steering Group. The group is composed of representatives from the following agencies, departments, and offices: the Secretaries of Defense, State and Treasury; the Attorney General; the Director of the Office of Management and Budget; and the Director of the Central Intelligence Agency (CIA). Because of its potentially invasive effect, the directive was revised to apply primarily to defense-related information and reissued in 1990 as NSDD-42.

Another regulation that raised concerns in the private sector was the National Telecommunications and Information Systems Security Publication 2. This directive, entitled "National Policy on Protection of Sensitive But Unclassified Information in Federal Government Telecommunications and Automated Systems," was intended to apply to all government agencies and contractors, but was withdrawn in March 1987 due to privacy concerns.

PL 107-347

The law that currently governs sensitive and **classified information** is the Federal Information Security Management Act of 2002 (FISMA, PL 107-347, sec. 301–305). In many instances, this law supersedes PL 100-235 (the Computer Security Act of 1987).

Under FISMA, agencies must demonstrate due diligence in compliance, making it one of the most influential federal information assurance laws. FISMA applies to all federal agencies and government contractors. It requires agencies and contractors to establish agency-wide risk-based information security programs. Programs include: periodic risk assessments, use of controls and techniques to comply with information security standards, training requirements, periodic testing and evaluation, reporting, and plans for remedial action, security incident response, and continuity of operations. An important provision of FISMA requires annual independent evaluation of federal agency information security programs.

The act charges the National Institute of Standards and Technology with the responsibility to issue information security guidelines for all federal information systems that are not national security systems. These documents include the Federal Information Processing Standards (FIPS) and the NIST SP 800 series.

The National Security Agency retains control of issuing information security guidelines for national security systems. National Security Systems are defined as "any information system (including telecommunications systems) used or operated by an agency, a contractor of an agency, or other organization on behalf of an agency of the federal government." FISMA applies where the function, operation, or issuance of that system involves (PL 107-347) any of the following:

- Intelligence activities
- Cryptologic activities related to national security
- Command and control of military forces
- Equipment that is an integral part of a weapon or weapons system
- Equipment that is critical to the fulfillment of military or intelligence missions
- Information specifically authorized under executive order, or an act of Congress as classified in the interest of national defense or foreign policy

The provisions of NSA doctrine do not apply directly to "a system that is to be used for routine administrative and business applications; including payroll, finance, logistics, and personnel management applications.

The National Computer Security Center (NCSC)

Although the Federal Information Security Management Act has superseded the majority of the Computer Security Act, one of the influences of the latter is the National Computer Security Center (NCSC). The NCSC is a component of the National Security Agency with the responsibility to evaluate and recommend computing equipment for high-security applications.

The NCSC evaluated commercial systems, conducted and sponsored research necessary in computer and network security technology, provided access to the verification and analysis tools used to develop and test secure computer systems. In addition, it conducted training in computer security by disseminating computer security information to other branches of the government. Its role ensured that all facilities processing classified or other sensitive material are making use of "trusted" computer approaches.

The organization worked with industry, education, and government agency partners to promote research and standardization efforts for secure information system development. The NCSC's computer evaluation directives are carried out by another NSA organization, the **Trusted Product Evaluation Program (TPEP)**, which tests commercial products against a comprehensive set of security-related criteria. NCSC issued the first Department of Defense (DoD) **Trusted Computer System Evaluation Criteria (TCSEC)** in August 1983 and now against the common criteria.

Historically, the **TCSEC**, more commonly referred to as the "orange book," was reissued in 1985 as a DoD standard with the goal of providing manufacturers with security-related standards to include as product features. The standard also provided DoD components with information about security metrics for the evaluation of trust levels to accredit products that processed sensitive material. Other books containing benchmarks and standards were published to supplement the orange book. Each was named and covered in a unique color. This series of publications is known as the Rainbow Series.

The Common Criteria

An important aspect of the mission is fostering and administering the use of Common Criteria Testing processes. The Common Criteria were discussed in Chapter 10. They are a standard model for certifying trustworthiness of commercial-off-the-shelf (COTS) products under the Trusted Product Evaluation Program (TPEP).

Vendors request an evaluation of their commercial-off-the-shelf (COTS) products from the TPEP is to get a specific level of trust rating. Evaluators working under TPEP use the Common Criteria to assess how well the product meets the requirements for the targeted rating.

The outcome of this process is an Evaluation Assurance Level (EAL) defining where the product falls on a scale of assurance as defined by the Common Criteria. TPEP evaluations are published quarterly in the Evaluated Products List (EPL) and used by all government entities to guide the selection of trusted products.

Ensuring Contract Compliance

Although conformance with legal and regulatory requirements is critical to compliance, the most common application is the assurance of contract compliance. A contract is a legally enforceable agreement formed by a meeting of the minds of at least two parties, a mutual agreement resulting from an offer by one and an acceptance of that offer by the other accompanied by an exchange of value. Contracts may be explicit, between a customer and a supplier. Contracts might also be implicit, for instance between a supplier and an in-house customer. In every case, however, if a binding agreement exists, then the terms of that agreement must be met. Compliance ensures that the terms have been met.

The Body of Law Regulating Contracts

A contract can be made for any product or service; there is no single way to define how compliance should be ensured. The principle for defining compliance, rights, and obligations of parties is called **contract law** and it standardizes commercial agreements.

Best practice dictates that agreements for software work should be derived from formal conditions of the work, including a specification of the outcomes demonstrating how the requirements will be judged. The contract should spell out the obligations of each party. The conditions become elements of the contract. Contract agreements are monitored through systematic **reviews** or audits of the results.

Consequently, formal reviews and inspections assure legal and **regulatory compliance**. Review processes serve as the basis for identifying the status activity and product within the conditions of all contracts, laws, and regulations. Therefore, it is necessary to understand the elements of the contract review process to implement a competent compliance system.

Formal Contract Reviews

Reviews are scheduled based on the level of assurance desired. Keep two points in mind. First, these reviews have to be formally planned and scheduled as part of the overall information assurance process. Second, planning has to be based on the level of integrity required.

The legal and regulatory compliance of a critical national security system will have a higher level of assurance than would a simple business application. The number and rigor of the scheduled reviews would differ between the two situations. An overall compliance assurance plan defines of how areas of non-compliance will be reported and resolved.

The continuous monitoring of technical activities based on embedded inspections ensures the timely reporting of deviations and failures as well as facilitating management oversight. They are resource intensive and costly since they involve human evaluators. They are the only way that compliance with contract conditions can be validated directly.

For instance, in mission-critical projects or ones involving classified information, a third-party audit might be required in cases where compliance is an essential condition. The audit monitors contracts and certifies that they are fulfilled. Because an audit is the essential element of legal and regulatory compliance, the following section provides a brief, overview of how compliance audits are done.

Compliance Audits

Auditors perform compliance audit to ensure the strict conformance of an organization to a contract condition, law, or regulation. A properly performed audit proves due diligence in the management of the use, design, development, maintenance, or operation of an information resource.

The **audit process** requires a complete definition of the requirements of a given compliance situation. All observable criteria serving concrete proof that a requirement was met and must be itemized on a list that used to assess compliance.

Audits are initiated for many reasons including that a client or regulatory agency requests it or it may follow up an earlier audit. Another reason is the implementation of significant changes since the last audit. An organization or unit may perform internal audits to confirm or improve their compliance. This is common in the case of high integrity requirements.

Chapter 11 Review

Chapter Summary

- It is almost impossible to ensure that the intellectual property kept in public repositories like the Internet will not be stolen.

- The legal issue rests with the concept of intangible property. Real property has substance and obvious value. It can be seen and counted. Intellectual property is abstract, so it is hard to value.

- The most important step in counteracting the theft of intellectual property is to increase the level of lawmaker awareness that the item of intellectual property has actual value.

- The deliberate act of stealing software is called piracy. Piracy is a major world-wide problem because programs are so easy to copy and duplicate.

- When you "buy" software, you buy a license to use it. Therefore you must be able to produce a valid license for all of the software you are running.

- Piracy is a particular concern to corporate America because there are so many PCs and so much software to keep track of.

- Companies that egregiously violating license agreements can expect to pay monetary damages on top of having to buy the correct number of licenses.

- Loss of personal information is serious if a malicious person accesses that information.

- Human error is the most likely cause of problems with computerized information, so safeguarding it is an important concern.

- The current United States law regulating spam is the "Controlling the Assault of Non-Solicited Pornography and Marketing Act of 2003" or the "CAN-SPAM Act of 2003." It took effect on January 1, 2004.

- Congress in 1998 created PL 105-318, The Identity Theft and Deterrence Act (18 U.S.C. 1028a).

- The use of the computer to carry out a conventional criminal act, like fraud, fits within the category of cyber-crime.

- A common form of computer-based crime is hacking.

- There are five reasons why a hacker might try to penetrate a system: recreational attacks, business or financial attacks, intelligence attacks, grudge attacks, and military or terrorist attacks.

- Tools that the hacker uses to penetrate a system fall into three categories: **password sniffing**, spoofing, or social engineering.

- The Freedom of Information Act (FOIA) (5 U.S.C. 552 PL 890554), 1966, provides the first electronic age protections for privacy.

- PL 93-579, better known as the "Privacy Act," defines the rights of individuals with respect to the computerized information that is kept about them.

- The Privacy Act was further expanded by the Right of Financial Privacy Act (1978), which establishes that a depositor's bank accounts are private and can only be accessed by court order and due and proper notification.

- The Electronic Funds Transfer Act (1979) that followed it then specifically safeguarded the privacy of transmissions related to funds using electronic funds transfer (EFT).

- The Electronic Communications Act offered a single clear statement of the rights of individuals with respect to electronic information.

- The Privacy Act was further amended by 5 U.S.C. 552a (1988), which is entitled the Computer Matching and Privacy Protection Act.

- The "Uniting and Strengthening America by Providing Appropriate Tools Required to Intercept and Obstruct Terrorism" Act, commonly known as the PATRIOT Act, greatly extends the authority of law enforcement and intelligence agencies.

- The first real law that directly regulates the crimes that are committed using a computer is Public Law 99-474, the Computer Fraud and Abuse Act (1986).

- The Fraud and Abuse Act further prohibits unauthorized or fraudulent access to government computers.

- The law makes it a felony to alter or destroy information in computers that falls under that designation.

- The Federal Information Security Management Act of 2002 (PL 107-347)—FISMA focuses on ensuring the security, confidentiality, privacy, and integrity of the information contained in federal computer systems.

- FISMA establishes information security requirements for federal agencies.

- The role of compliance is to ensure that contract terms have been fulfilled.

- This is called contract law. It serves as the basis for standardizing all commercial agreements.

- Best practice dictates that contracts for software work should be drawn up based on formal specifications of the work to be done, including a stipulation of the outcomes that will demonstrate how the fulfillment of the various requirements will be judged.

- The overall purpose of the audit process is to ensure the confidentiality, integrity, availability, and compliance of a given organizational function or element.

- A properly performed audit ensures that due diligence is carried out in the management, use, design, development, maintenance, or operation of an information asset.

Key Terms

audit process (303)
awareness (290)
CAN-SPAM (291)
classified information (300)
compliance (283)
computer fraud (299)
computer matching (290)
contract law (302)
copyrighted works (286)
cyber-crime (296)
Federal Trade Commission (FTC) (292)
hacking (292)
human error (288)
intangible property (284)
intellectual property (284)
legal system (284)
licensing agreement (285)
password sniffing (304)
permissions (286)
real property (283)
regulatory compliance (303)
reviews (303)
site licenses (286)
social engineering (294)
software license (286)
software piracy (285)
spam (291)
spoofing (294)
Trusted Computer System Evaluation Criteria (TCSEC) (302)

Key Term Quiz

Complete each statement by writing one of the terms from this list in each blank. Not all terms will be used.

1. Non-delivery of items purchased over the Internet is a form of _____.

2. Data mining in the federal government is underwritten by _____.

3. Unsolicited bulk e-mail messages are called _____.

4. The best defense against social engineering is _____.

5. The most common type of cyber crime is _____.

6. The reason why intellectual property is so difficult to control is because it is not _____.

7. The document that grants the permission to use a piece of software is called a _____.

8. The use of a piece of software without permission is called _____.

9. Compliance is assured by a _____ or an _____.

10. The _____ or TPEP evaluates products using the _____ or TCSEC.

Multiple Choice Quiz

1. The study of the impacts of computers on our legal framework is important because
    a. computers are important
    b. they are not well understood
    c. they are costly
    d. they are the same as those for documentation

2. The NSA
    a. is in charge of space exploration
    b. is in charge of spying
    c. is charged with the protection of classified information
    d. is a TV network

3. Regulation of the disposal of old computers is important because
    a. they contain toxic material
    b. it is hard to do
    c. they cannot be recycled
    d. the materials in them do not get into the ecosystem

4. Spam is
    a. software placed on your computer without your permission
    b. a virus
    c. a means of monitoring your behavior
    d. a form of junk mail

5. Compliance is most frequently applied in the case of
    a. the legal system
    b. computer forensics
    c. the courts
    d. contracts

6. People who use pre-programmed attack scripts are
   a. script kiddies
   b. code warriors
   c. cyber-punks
   d. soldiers

7. Data-mining is
   a. like digging for gold
   b. the use of attack scripts
   c. based on the use of sniffers
   d. an attempt to discern a pattern

8. The purpose of the FOIA is to
   a. regulate access to records
   b. allow individuals to alter data kept about them by federal agencies
   c. allow individuals to see data kept about them by federal agencies
   d. underwrite certification of security competence

9. The purpose of the FISMA is to
   a. regulate access to records
   b. allow individuals to alter data kept about them by federal agencies
   c. allow individuals to see data kept about them by federal agencies
   d. underwrite certification of security competence

10. The term compliance process applies to
    a. any formal process to assure compliance with contracts
    b. any formal process to assure subcontractor responsibilities
    c. any formal process to prevent cyber-crime
    d. any formal process to monitor behavior

Essay Quiz

1. Why is the rapid evolution of computer technology a problem for the legal system?
2. What is the relationship between identity theft and the availability of large amounts of personal information?
3. What is the definition of piracy? Why is it so easy to pirate software as compared to more tangible things?

4. What are some of the penalties for piracy? How do these apply to individuals and to organizations?

5. How can an organization safeguard itself from piracy? Why is it so essential that this be properly organized?

6. Why is intellectual property so susceptible to theft?

7. Why is it important to have a formal compliance function in place in an organization? What does it protect against?

8. What is the focus of the Computer Fraud and Abuse Act? What does it seek to prevent and how can it be complied with?

9. Why should regulations for controlling classified and sensitive information be a factor in a compliance scheme? When do they apply?

10. Why is there likely to be strict regulation of the disposal of computer equipment? What makes that equipment hazardous?

Case Exercise

Complete the following case exercise as directed by your instructor.

Refer to the Heavy Metal Technology Case in Appendix A. You have been assigned the responsibility to catalogue all relevant laws and regulations that might apply to the project to upgrade the target acquisition and display (TADS) for the AH64-D Apache Longbow attack helicopter. You know that to start the process you must first understand all of the compliance problems that HMT faces. Therefore, using the project materials outlined in the case, perform the following tasks:

- Identify all of the federal regulations that will have to be observed.
- Identify all other compliance areas, such as contracts.
- List the requirements that will have to be undertaken to ensure the necessary compliance.
- Ensure that there is a mechanism in place to audit the compliance with each requirement.

Devise a standard operating procedure for doing that.

Network Security Basics: Malware and Attacks

In this chapter, you will learn how to:

- Work with connection control and transmission control concepts
- Develop the planning and control techniques associated with network security
- Work with the various types of threats to networks

The global information grid offers enormous opportunities with endless challenges. It is possible to deliver everything from SPAM to cyber-terror, directly to your desktop along with your daily e-mail. Everybody from individual user to the largest corporation has to ensure that they have effective and persistent safeguards in place to protect networks.

In the information assurance process, the network security function guards against threats to electronic communication. Those threats come from any place in the world at any time and are unimaginably diverse; that challenge is one of the most difficult portions of the entire information assurance process. It is a critical responsibility since our economy and national defense relies on safe, stable, and accurate electronic data communication.

Network security protects electronic communication from unauthorized modification, destruction, or disclosure and ensures that an increasing number of diverse attacks do not harm the distributed critical information infrastructure. It is the range, diversity, and extent of those attacks and the complexity of the medium that makes securing a network a compelling and difficult task.

Network security has a dual mission. First, it must ensure the accuracy of the data transmitted. Second, it must also protect confidential information processed, stored on, and accessible from networks, while ensuring the network is always available to authorized users.

The role of the network security function is to ensure the components of the network operate correctly, satisfy design requirements, and the information transmitted retains its fundamental integrity. The latter implies that all network hardware and software elements, as well as the media that record and retain information, are maintained in a secure state.

A well-designed network security function should incorporate a range of mutually supporting activities. When people think of network security, they often think about just the technological aspect of the operation, since it is the most visible. In fact, the network security function has a broad range of responsibilities. Many of these do not directly entail technical work. However, they all contribute to the assurance of a secure network.

The organization must provide proper supervision and have effective procedures in place to ensure that the operators are trustworthy. Plan-and-execute routine functions such as systematic training and awareness to ensure that everybody knows how to operate the network properly. We will not approach network security as a technical assurance function in this chapter. We will present network security from the perspective of how it fits within the information assurance process.

Engineering the Network: Ensuring a Proper Design

A network must obey all of the rules of any system. All components must be designed properly, implemented correctly, and overseen effectively. The physical infrastructure of every network should be designed deliberately to ensure all required security functions are present.

The term "network" describes one of three electronic communication systems—an organizational intranet, an extranet, or the Internet. These are usually merged to achieve organizational missions. To ensure security, security architects implement technological countermeasures such as **firewalls**, **intrusion detection systems (IDSs)**, and strong **authentication**.

Network infrastructures share the security issues associated with computers because the physical infrastructure of a network is hardware-based and enabled by software. The difference between the two is that the sole responsibility of the network is communication rather data processing. Networks employ hardware and software that is designed to channel data between senders to receivers.

The unique physical components of networks are *switches, hubs,* **routers**, and *cables.* Switches and hubs are physical components interconnecting computers within a network while routers connect that network to a common resource such as the Internet. The cables are the physical link among these elements.

Physical security practices for network components were discussed in Chapter 8. However, there are software components as well they are **connection control** and **transmission control**. Figure 12-1 illustrates how these two relate.

Connection Control

Connection control establishes and regulates the relationship between a computer and a network. Connection control ensures reliable transfer of messages between a sender and a receiver and performs some transmission error correction. Connection control operates just like an old-fashioned telephone switchboard operator, plugging the calling parties into the right sockets to set up conversations and then breaking the connection after the call is over.

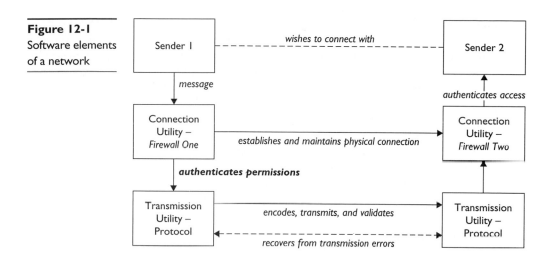

Figure 12-1
Software elements of a network

To create the temporary communication link and manage the transmission process, connection control uses specialized software functions built into the network operating system. Those functions must be installed, maintained, and configured by an individual who understands the drivers and **network access protocols** well enough to ensure secure operation.

The configuration process is the responsibility of the **network administrator**, who establishes the authentication rules that the connection control function enforces. The rules for connection control center have a single consideration, the specification of whom the network will trust. The administrator must tell the network in advance who will be allowed immediate access and who will require further authentication.

Specifications of rules for the authentication of a trusted source balance the need for confidentiality and integrity with **availability**. If the rules are not strict enough, unknown and potentially malicious people might be granted access. If the rules are too strict, then authorized users might not be able to gain timely and efficient access. Both instances would violate a fundamental principle of security.

Enforcing Connection Control: The Firewall

Firewalls enforce **access rights** and protect the network from external systems. Firewalls regulate access between trusted networks and untrusted ones, such as the Internet. To ensure a high level of security the organization may array multiple firewalls in a defense-in-depth configuration.

A *firewall* is essentially a filter dedicated to securing network connections. Firewalls are high-level software utilities that sit on the router end of the physical network. **Network security policies** embedded in the firewall software dictate access. Consequently, the presence of a verified set of policies for **access control** is as important to information assurance as is the system engineering work that establishes and maintains them.

Firewalls vary in terms of their robustness and the services provided. The simplest form is the *personal firewall*. It regulates connections between a single computer and external sources such as the Internet. The regulation is a simple task compared to establishing other more complex types of firewalls, networks, and applications.

Two types of network firewalls are stateful and stateless. The earliest firewalls were packet based *stateless firewalls*. Packets are a basic unit of data transmitted across a network. They are routed between a sender and a receiver based on embedded address called an Internet Protocol (IP) address. Stateless firewalls accept or discard incoming packets based on whether the IP address seems to correspond with services known to the protected network. This primitive discrimination approach caused many rejected packets until stateful firewalls were implemented.

A *stateful firewall* tracks of the status of network traffic traveling across it in a "state table." The firewall is programmed to distinguish legitimate traffic for different types of connections using that table. Only the network traffic that matches the right "state" for a given connection is given access. Other traffic is rejected.

Firewalls have to be able to distinguish between unsolicited traffic and inbound traffic requested by an internal user. A stateful firewall logs the external IP address of all outbound requests and when the external address responds, it allows access. At the same time, it continues to reject all inbound requests not in its table or not requested by an internal source.

Transmission Control

The other software-enabled function in a network is transmission control. It regulates the actual transmission process. Transmission control ensures that the communication between two devices is flowing properly. Effective transmission control supports the integrity and availability of network data.

Transmission control programs are machine-level functions that encode the data, detect, and recover transmission errors. Transmission control ensures that the components doing the encoding and transmission are correctly configured and that the software required to assure a reliable transmission process is installed and working properly.

Transmission control is facilitated through firmware drivers built into communications devices and software in the operating system. These functions are invisible to the average user. The drivers transmit data from one device to another through the network. To ensure effectiveness, both devices must be able to agree on the rules that will be followed during the transmission process. That includes such critical things as

- The mode in which the data will be transmitted
- The format of the data
- The rate of transmission
- The type of **error checking**
- The data compression method
- How the sending device will indicate that it has finished sending a message
- How the receiving device will indicate that it has received a message

This agreement is a *protocol*. Transmission protocols are built into the communications devices. In the past, there were a variety of standard transmission protocols such as the old Xmodem, Kermit, and CCITT's X25 and V42. A common modern transmission control is based on the OSI reference model that defines seven layers for communication among computer systems. The model was defined by the International Organization for Standardization as ISO standard 7498-1 allows interoperability among platforms offered by vendors. The **TCP/IP** protocol used by the Internet is frequently shown with five layers: Application Layer, Transport Layer, Network Layer, DataLink Layer, and Physical Layer. TCP/IP was fundamental to interoperability on ARPANET.

Defending Networks from Attacks

A unique security problem with networks is their level of interconnectedness. For example, according to the SANS Institute, when you connect your private network to the Internet, you are physically connecting it to more than 50,000 **unknown networks**. Therefore, networks have to be secured by specialized and very robust technologies and practices.

There are two broad categories of networks threats—malicious code and direct attacks. Malicious code is broad a problem; however, there are commercial screening products that safeguard against common examples of malicious code. Direct attacks are entirely different because they can be launched in many ways and places.

Threats to Information: Malicious Code

Malicious code is virulent. According to the University of California at Berkeley, a virus called Sapphire/Slammer infected 90 percent of vulnerable hosts worldwide within 10 minutes. Its infection footprint doubled in size every 8.5 seconds. That exploit, as well as other more destructive threats, emphasizes the importance of knowing about and responding to malicious code.

There are three categories of malicious code transmitted through networks: **viruses**, **logic bombs**, and **Trojan horses**. Viruses are common; they are pieces of code attached to host programs and propagate or replicate when the host is executed. Logic bombs are programs installed in a system by individuals and only activated based on specified parameters. They are frequently destructive because individuals with malicious intent installed them for a purpose. Trojan horses are another means of attack; like their namesake, they introduce harmful things under the guise of a useful program. Figure 12-2 shows the types of malicious code and their means of propagation.

Not all malicious codes share the same intent; each achieves its aims differently. Although viruses might be harmful, their primary purpose is **replication**. Viruses attempt to replicate themselves in the infected host and then perform other actions. With logic bombs, the purpose is to affect a given target based on defined circumstances, like the date or a system condition. With Trojan horses, the aim is to deliver a hidden payload using the ruse of an attractive or apparently benign package. What that payload does varies but the delivery method is always the same surreptitious means: Trojan code.

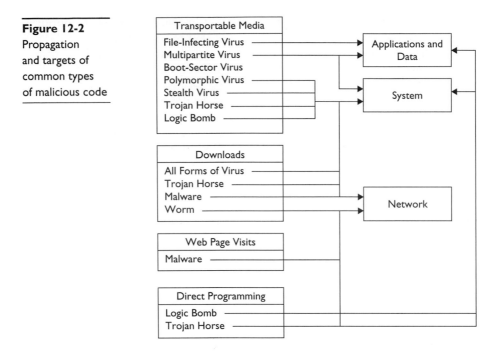

Figure 12-2
Propagation
and targets of
common types
of malicious code

Viruses

An appropriate countermeasure to a common virus is a **virus checker** that detects and removes viruses from programs launched by the computer. As virus writers have become more sophisticated, virus checkers have had to respond and become more powerful.

Most virus checkers examine files in memory or storage for recognizable code fragments or key words. The checker compares scan results patterns **(virus signatures)** with signatures of known viruses. The checker takes action when an identifiable pattern is detected. Sometimes the **antivirus application** performs an automatic repair by placing the suspected malicious code in a quarantine space while awaiting further user instructions. Subsequent repair actions depend on whether the virus can be easily removed from the attacked system.

Virus signatures are stored in the antivirus application's signature database and must be updated frequently to remain effective. In addition to maintaining the real-time virus-screening capability in most commercial antivirus products, it is best practice to conduct a complete scan of a computer's storage locations at least once a week.

Impact of Viruses   Some viruses are more ingenious and dangerous than others. They cause varying degrees of harm. Some are inoffensive, while others are destructive; it is important to distinguish between various types of viruses. Viruses usually target specific system functions or applications, such as the operating system or e-mail. They have to be programmed to perform the task they carry out, so their destructive potential is dependent on the malicious intent of the designer.

A virus is destructive if it damages a system function. The ones that do the most damage affect the operating system in undesirable ways. The most malicious acts include corrupting or deleting files, reformatting the hard drive, and executing denial-of-service attacks. In most cases where a harmful virus is launched, the system becomes unusable, its data or files are lost, and cannot be repaired automatically.

With less malignant viruses, the effects are not as destructive or are not permanently harmful. There may be minor modifications to data, unknown programs might be executed, or security-related applications like antivirus checkers or firewalls might be disabled. The effects of these attacks can be repaired and in most cases, functions and data are recoverable using tools or through reinstalling the operating system. Remember, data modification is a serious integrity violation and such modification can have significant repercussions.

Categories of Viruses   Viruses fall into six general categories: file infecting, boot-sector, multipartite, macro, polymorphic or stealth, and worm.

File-infecting viruses affect executable programs, replicate, and spread by infecting other host programs from the infected program. File-infecting viruses are considered non-destructive, because their principal purpose is replication. However, some file-infecting viruses deliver payloads. A **payload** is an additional piece of code that invokes additional actions.

Payloads do deliberate damage, such as intentionally overwriting part of the host program's code. They may also plant malicious logic bombs that might wipe the hard drive at a predetermined date, for example. Most file-infecting viruses can be identified and removed by virus-checking software because they are relatively unsophisticated. However, it is important to keep virus signatures up to date, since the number and sophistication of viruses increase daily.

Boot-sector viruses are more insidious; they infect the boot sector or **partition table** of a system. These are virulent since a computer infected by a boot sector virus attempts to infect everything it accesses. Boot-sector viruses may be identified and removed successfully by a virus checker with up-to-date virus signatures. Boot-sector virus that is not caught at the time it is introduced is likely to cause some form of harm because of where it takes up residence.

Multipartite viruses infect both the boot sector and the executable programs and files simultaneously. If the virus infects the boot sector it affects the system files, and when the virus attacks files, it will in turn infect the boot sector. The threat lies in the versatility of being able to infect both the system or its files, depending on which is the most vulnerable. Most of these of viruses can also be detected and removed by a good virus checker, but the signatures have to be available.

Macro viruses "infect" systems through an application such as Microsoft Word. When a data file (document) is opened, it causes a sequence of actions to be performed by the internal macro language. They are not specific to one type of operating system (they are a function of the application), or dependent on local sources, like CDs or floppy disks, for their introduction. They are hidden within data that must be opened by an application for the virus to be executed.

Macro viruses are activated at a variety of points including file open, program launch or upon a save, close, or deletion. They propagate through most forms of transport medium including e-mail, downloads, file transfers, and applications. They are hard to detect and destroy because they become active after they have been introduced to the system.

Polymorphic and **stealth viruses** are difficult to detect because they seek to conceal their presence, as well as the changes they might make. These changes are replication and file infection, but each time they occur, the virus changes its form at the code level so that its pattern is unique and undetectable. This defeats most signature-based countermeasures.

Worms are currently the malicious code of choice on the Internet because of their virulence. A worm is a self-contained program capable of spreading copies of itself or its segments to other computer systems via network connections or e-mail attachments. The common type of damage caused by a worm is a **denial-of-service attack (DoS)**. The "denial of service" results from the fact that legitimate users are prevented from using their servers and networks because of the actions of the worm.

The malicious code causes harm by replicating itself and creates undesirable levels of traffic on a network. In many cases, a worm absorbs enough bandwidth to cause a widespread denial of service. Worms frequently are destructive and dangerous infections because they attack the transmission medium itself. Fast-moving network worms can propagate across continents within minutes.

Logic Bombs

Logic bombs are an early form of malicious code. The Internet is now the delivery mechanism of choice; however, logic bombs date back to the early days of computing. They were occasionally programmed into mainframes by system programmers who wanted to create a job security for themselves.

Logic bombs get their name from the fact that they are activated when some prescribed set of criteria is met such as time, date, or status of the system. Logic bombs are a special concern when it comes to hostile terminations. The bomb can be set prior to the termination and activated afterward for revenge. A programmer in California included code in the payroll system that would delete all files from the system if his name failed to appear on the payroll file.

Logic bombs differ from viruses in that they do not perform acts that alert virus checkers or other system monitors to their presence. They are dormant blocks of undocumented code in a system until the criteria are met to trigger them. When they activate, they carry out a malicious act.

Logic bombs should be aggressively hunted down and eliminated because of their destructive potential. This requires extensive, expensive, code reviews by high-level professionals. Logic bombs are resurfacing as an important part of the cyber-terrorist's bag of malicious tricks because of their destructive potential,

Trojan Horses

A Trojan horse operates like its namesake. Trojan horses come in attractive packaging, such as a piece of apparently useful freeware. Hidden within that appealing gift is code with a malicious purpose. Trojan horses are not viruses because they do not replicate; however, they may transmit viruses or spyware. Nevertheless, they make your computer vulnerable to external sources and are usually harmful.

Trojan horses can deliver a number of unwelcome payloads. Recently a Trojan horse was inadvertently introduced by a major online retailer, when one of their suppliers offered customers an Internet accelerator. The accelerator redirected all their communications through a program that logged the customer's activities and compromised their privacy.

The Trojan horse may assist in propagating denial-of-service (DoS) attacks, which absorb available system resources. Subtle Trojan horse payloads open a stealth port in a computer allowing unauthorized access to a system. These attacks are sometimes called back doors.

Spyware and adware are common Trojan horse payloads. A common Trojan horse payload is **spyware** that propagates from websites. It is estimated that this type of malicious code affects more PCs than viruses. Once it is installed, spyware may monitor the user's computing habits and personal information, and it sends data to a third party.

The implications of this for personal privacy and confidentiality are serious. Since spyware is not a virus, it is not normally identified by the virus-checking security software. There are numerous commercial tools designed to find and remove spyware.

Some types of spyware are more harmful. Five categories of spyware cross the line into invasion of privacy. These are spamware, password capture, **keyloggers**, and cookie trackers. Spamware turns an individual's computer into a remote spam mailer for a third party (BOT). It is not common, but it can lead to criminal prosecution if a computer is identified as the source of illegal spam. In early 2006 an individual was sentenced to 5 years in prison for unleashing BOTs. Password-capture programs record and send passwords to external sources. Password-capture programs are highly dangerous. These will be discussed at greater length later in the section on password attacks.

Keyloggers are an insidious form of spyware. Once this spyware is installed, it allows external agents to view what an individual types into the computer. A benign form of keylogger is the cookie tracker, which allows others to track your private life by following your Internet viewing habits.

Adware is a common form of spyware that opens a computer to ads delivered from the Internet. Like an unwanted telemarketer, adware is not directly malicious; it does use up valuable time and system resources.

Malicious Attacks

Last year, 70 percent of all companies suffered some sort of loss due to attacks. According to the most recent CSI/FBI statistics, the average cost of a network attack ranged from $10,000 for a small business to more than $2.5 million for a large business. It is important for every organization to understand these attacks and what to do to prevent their occurrence.

The best way to counteract a network attack is to anticipate it and have the measures in place to either stop it or mitigate the harm. It is helpful to know what the common attack types are. Network attacks fall into seven general categories:

1. Password attacks
2. Insider attacks

3. Sniffing

4. IP spoofing

5. Denial of service

6. Man-in-the-middle attacks

7. Application layer attacks

Password Attacks

A **password attack** attempts to access a computer by **password guessing**. A successful password attack is a dangerous breach because once an attacker gains access, he or she has exactly the same rights as the authorized user. This is a primitive exploit, which succeeds with surprising frequency because most people have a hard time remembering sufficiently complicated passwords. As a result, users make their password easy to guess or will write it down, or never replace a familiar old one.

Password attacks are harmful because they open the door to attacks that are more destructive. For example, a stolen root password provides access to the entire table of passwords for the system. Imagine the harm if an attacker had all of the passwords for a banking system. If the compromised password enjoys a sufficient privilege; attackers could perform modifications including back doors, to enable them to control of the network.

Dictionary Attacks If guessing does not work, a **dictionary attack** trys common words from the dictionary and common password names in an attempt to "hit" the correct one. Dictionary attacks can be a very efficient shortcut because most users prefer to use easily remembered passwords.

The other, more resource-intensive approach is called a **key search**, or sometimes an **exhaustive search** or **brute force attack**. In this version, the attacker systematically tries all potential text and numeric values until the right combination is found.

Like dictionary attacks, these attacks are supported by software; an individual does not enter each guess since that would be hopelessly time-consuming given the permutations possible.

Social Engineering The easiest way for attackers to obtain a password is to have the user give it to them. The same social engineering techniques mentioned elsewhere in this book are the mechanisms for achieving this goal. Social engineering attacks depend on persuasion rather than technology; frequently, the attacker uses claims of authority and other of misrepresentations to dupe users into disclosing passwords. The countermeasures for social engineering exploits are education and awareness.

Password Sniffing **Sniffers** are software based network management tools. They may be part of the regular system management function; however, sniffers can also intercept passwords. Sniffers let attackers examine network traffic in real time; they intercept poorly secured passwords as they are transmitted. A good countermeasure for sniffers is **encryption**. It is particularly important to encrypt password information that is sent through a network.

Insider Attacks

The primary source of breaches is insider action (CSI, 2004; DTI, 2003, for instance). Approximately three-quarters of all misuse incidents originate from the intentional or inadvertent actions of employees. When an insider is disgruntled, even more harm can ensue.

As the litigation potential increases, liability issues make prevention of insider attacks a matter of survival for most organizations. The first line of defense is good management supported by monitoring to prevent **insider attacks**.

Supervisors are a key security control points for employee monitoring. The supervisor is best positioned to observe signs of the uncharacteristic behavior that indicate an impending insider attack. Examples of uncharacteristic behavior may be such sudden changes in work hours or work habits, signs of dissatisfaction, and visibly searching for jobs while at work. There are also automated software agents called policy managers or **policy enforcement systems** that help.

The Role and Use of Policy Managers

Automated policy managers are effective tools for defending organizations against unauthorized access to confidential data and proprietary information; they provide the ability to filter network transactions through custom policies. Automated policy managers provide an effective way to monitor a large number of online transactions that cross a network.

Policy enforcement systems control the distribution of unsuitable or offensive content and inappropriate activities. Without some mass monitoring, organizations would be at risk of losing intellectual property, source code, and trade secrets to external competitors.

The policy manager enables central control and efficient management of network access and use. Network administrators can embed rules in the policy manager to determine which file attachments can be accepted and delivered to recipients. Managers can define rules governing access if a message will be blocked, quarantined, rerouted, or dropped if it comes from a competitor domain or is associated with malicious code. It is invisible to end users and unobtrusive unless a violation occurs.

The major advantage of a policy manager is that it regulates the enterprise's e-mail traffic. Administrators can define and enforce spam rules, filter content, and implement encryption and digital signature policies at the network gateway. The software then enforces this consistently. Content filtering is ensured by scanning each message for keywords, text strings, and text file attachments. Some policy managers allow the system to filter messages based on priority, send date, message size, senders, and recipients.

The Use of Sniffers

Earlier we discussed **sniffing** as it applies to passwords; however, it has broader application. Sniffers are common utilities, employed to read any information in packets transmitted over a network. Sniffers are usually a software utility, which monitors data traffic through a network or server. It is easy for a third party to develop packet sniffers because the specifications for common network protocols are well known. There are many freeware and shareware examples available on the Internet, which do not require the user to understand anything about TCP/IP.

Although programs like NMAP automate the process, sniffing can be used to map the entire network topology. It will capture all of the information necessary for a network administrator—or an attacker—to determine how many computers are on the network, what they access, and which clients run what services. This information can be acquired by viewing the packet exchanges as they pass back and forth.

Sniffers filter packets for items of interest to the user. When the sniffer identifies a packet fitting user set criteria, it logs it to a file for later examination. When used for malicious purposes sinffers identify interesting packet containing words like "login" or "password." Network sniffers may capture sensitive information from the data transmission stream. For instance, plaintext items such as user account and password information are easy game for a network sniffer. Sniffers can also be very effective if sensitive information is sent over a network in plaintext.

Sniffers and their extensions can also be used to compromise the integrity of the data stream by injecting new information or modifying existing packets. An attacker with that access can control of the system. The attacker can read, corrupt, or even destroy the information within it, without the owners being able to prevent it.

Sniffers are passive on the network, so they are hard to detect. They sit on a network and accept or capture all packets independent of destination. Malicious users can monitor network traffic without sending out suspicious packets that would identify them to security systems.

The defense against sniffing is encryption and strong physical security. If it is particularly important for sensitive information not to be read by a sniffer, it should be a routine practice for all information to be encrypted before being transmitted. An encrypted packet is nonsense to a sniffer because its content cannot be compared against the sniffer's programmed criteria. The sniffer is likely to let the encrypted packet pass unnoticed. Of course, the simplest countermeasure is good physical security. If it is impossible to install the sniffer, the system is more secure.

Sniffing does not belong exclusively to the "black hat" community. Although the hacker community frequently uses sniffers, they are also used by law enforcement to detect computer crimes. Internet-facing sniffers are a good countermeasures for many network intrusion. Agencies of the federal government use sniffers for national security monitoring and as a means to "wiretap" suspicious individuals. Network administrators routinely use them to ensure that the network functions properly and to identify connected devices.

IP Spoofing

IP spoofing is an address attack in which the malicious agent electronically impersonates another network party through its IP address. This technique is sometimes called *cloaking*. It is considered highly unethical and it is perhaps illegal. The intruder gains access to the target system by altering the sequence numbers of a packet's IP source address to make it appear as though the packet originated from a trusted site or one with the right access privileges. Figure 12-3 illustrates this.

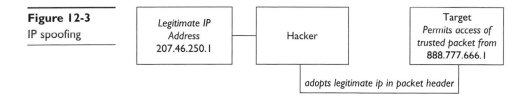

Figure 12-3

IP spoofing

One form of IP **spoofing** attack occurs when an established session is intercepted and co-opted by the attacker. A network outsider pretends to be a trusted computer facilitated by using an IP address within the range of IP addresses for the target device or by using an authorized external IP address that is trusted.

Normally, an IP spoofing attack is limited to activities such as adding data or commands to a data stream. However, if the attacker is able to change the routing tables in the target system to point to the spoofed IP address, he will be able to hijack network packets addressed to the spoofed address.

These packets pass through the network just like those from a trusted user, and thus could prove to be embarrassing. For example, an attacker could spoof an internal user to send messages that appear to be authentic. These messages could have malicious intent.

Routers and firewall mechanisms can be programmed to identify IP spoofing attacks by detecting discrepancies in the sequence numbers received. However, the most effective response to IP spoofing is not to rely on simple address-based authentication schemes. Instead the network should rely on encrypted systems such as SSH (secure shell) for authentication services.

Methods such as SSH use public key **cryptography** for both connection and authentication, which protects passwords by allowing the network to encrypt all data traveling from clients on the network to the server. It reduces IP spoofing by ensuring that both ends of the client/server connection are authenticated using digital certificates. This is discussed in Chapter 13.

Denial of Service

Denial-of-service (DoS) attacks are different from other attacks because they do not directly affect network information. DoS attacks are a problem because they affect the availability transmission media. When a network is flooded with traffic, it cannot respond normally, so service is curtailed or denied.

A denial-of-service attack usually does not result in the loss of information. Instead, it is an information assurance compromise because DoS attacks degrade the *availability* of information. A DoS attack is designed to cost the target organization time and money by preventing the network from responding to normal requests. They are a favorite technique of network saboteurs because denial-of-service attacks originate across the Internet.

Denial-of-service attacks can be launched in numerous ways. A common form of DoS attack is to overload the system's servers, routers, or DNS to the extent that service to authorized users is delayed or prevented. The overload may focus on exceeding some resource limitation of the network by flooding the target system with phony requests for attention or service. This prevents firewalls from servicing normal and legitimate requests. That type of attack is called a *DoS flood*.

DoS attacks involve disabling a particular network service, such as temporarily bringing down the website or the e-mail system. In a worst-case scenario, it can put an organization's e-commerce site out of business. If an organization's site is normally accessed by millions of customers, this can adversely affect many users and cost the organization money. Occasionally a denial-of-service attack destroys programs and files.

Although DoS attacks are usually conducted with malicious intent, some denial-of-service attacks are accidental. For instance, a network's router can be misconfigured or the website can be accidentally brought down during routine maintenance. Both of these restrict availability and therefore they meet the fundamental definition of a denial of service.

Man-in-the-Middle Attacks

A **man-in-the-middle (MITM) attack** is an exploit where the attacker is able to read and modify all messages passed between two parties without either party knowing the link between them has been compromised.

Possible outcomes of such attacks include theft of information, hijacking of an ongoing session to gain access to a network resource, traffic analysis to derive information about a network and its users, denial of service, corruption of transmitted data, and introduction of new information into network sessions. Figure 12-4 illustrates this.

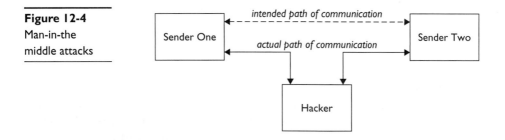

Figure 12-4
Man-in-the middle attacks

By appearing as a trusted party to each side, an intermediate attacker can do harm, including launching the usual attacks against the confidentiality or integrity of the data passing through the system. MITM attacks often use network packet sniffers or modification of routing and transport protocols directly as their means of attack.

MITM attacks can be also launched through intermediate parties who function as proxies for the clients on either side, such as an ISP. If such an agent is trustworthy, then there is little cause to worry. If they are not, then the clients on both sides of the communication link are in jeopardy.

Application Layer Attacks

Application layer attacks take advantage of weaknesses in popular applications and application services. These are usually Internet-based exploits of web-facing applications on servers. They include common attacks as such **buffer overflows**, which exploit poorly written code that improperly validates input to an application. A buffer overflow allows attackers to seize control of the system. These flaws have been a known problem for at least 35 years, yet remain the number one source of compromise of Internet resources.

Another type of defect is the **cross-site scripting flaw**, which allows web applications to drop attack scripts on a user's browser. These can then lead to account hijacking, changing of user settings, cookie theft, cookie poisoning, or false advertising. These attacks are the source of much of the **malware** currently on the Internet.

There is also the problem of **invalidated parameters**, which are web requests that are not validated before being used by the application. These allow attackers to perform unauthorized back-end manipulations.

There are also **command injection** attacks. These happen when web applications are allowed to pass parameters containing malicious commands to be executed on an external system. This problem originates from use of interoperable protocols, which use the data formats of the eXtensible Markup Language (XML).

These attacks are exploitations of design flaws in a application software and center on the server. By taking advantage of weaknesses, attackers gain access at the same level of permission as the account executing the application. This is dangerous in the case of system-level authorizations.

These vulnerabilities can be addressed by good application design and secure coding practice. One frustrating aspect of this problem is that none of it is new, yet software developers still make the same mistakes. These errors jeopardize the security of the customers running the flawed applications and threaten the security of the entire Internet. They are rapidly becoming an industry and government-wide concern.

Technically, these are web security rather than network security concerns, so they cannot be fixed by tinkering with the firewall. Consequently, one of the most widely favored approaches to securing the network against Internet-based attacks is to use a layered architecture based on concentric firewalls—termed a **defense-in-depth** strategy. By using multiple security layers, intrusions can be headed off before they infect the entire system.

Cyber-Terrorism

The topics of cyber-warfare and **cyber-terrorism** are elements of this network security because they represent future challenges. The goal of cyber-terrorism is to harm or control key computer systems or computer controls to achieve some indirect aim, such as to destroy a power grid or to take over a critical process. Potential targets for cyber-terrorists are power plants, nuclear facilities, water treatment plants, and government agencies. Many of these systems have an additional network vulnerability since they use Supervisory Control and Data Acquisition (SCADA) systems to directly control operations. However, any site that has implemented Internet-facing monitoring and control systems is vulnerable.

Cyber-terrorism is not a new phenomenon. In 1996, the threat was so credible that the federal government created the Critical Information Protection Task Force and later the Critical Infrastructure Protection Board. The Federal Information Security Management Act sets security requirements for all government systems built around three major national objectives:

- **Prepare and Prevent**—Identify critical infrastructure assets and shared interdependencies

- **Detect and Respond**—Respond and recover based on creating better detection and response technologies, as well as building up the capabilities of the nation's intelligence and law enforcement services and the better sharing of information about attacks.

- **Build Strong Foundations**—Enhance the nation's research and development efforts; engage the academic community to increase the awareness, training, and education of its workforce; and create and adopt legislation to support enforcement

The National Strategy Document only suggests an overall direction to combat cyber-terrorism. It assumes that substantive solutions will be developed by the businesses, federal, and state agencies responsible. Since 2002, these actions have been coordinated by the Department of Homeland Security.

Managing and Defending a Network

Just as it is with other processes, good management is an essential factor in defending a network. Good management involves the specification and enforcement of policies and practices to assure proper access as well as the effective use of the network.

Network security management involves all actions to ensure **authorization** and use. Those actions include the development and documentation of the method to authorize access to network files and **network directories**. It requires specification of an approach used to ensure the reliability of the data resources accessed or used over the network. Finally, good management involves implementation of safeguards to ensure the users of the network are protected from all network-based security threats.

These steps require planning. A strategy must be developed to fit the organization and environment. To implement that approach, the means must be specified for **threat assessment**, cryptography, and network access control. Planning also involves the development and maintenance of an active, robust, and continuous network operation to ensure the confidentiality, integrity, and availability of data and the rights of all users.

Network Security Management and Planning

Network security is based on a plan defining the approach to assuring of the physical components of the network. In addition, it must detail the steps to be taken to ensure that information stored, processed, and transmitted by the network is secure. The plan must specify all technology and practices to implement and maintain effective network security. The high-level steps required to implement an effective network management process are

1. Create **usage policy statements**.

2. Conduct a risk analysis.

3. Formulate a security team.

Creating Usage Policy Statements

If the requirements and conditions applying to network use are not clearly communicated, it is hard to enforce security. The first step in the process is preparing a statement that details the proper uses of each network component.

The policy development exercise is a top-down activity. It starts with the statement of a general policy about system use outlining the thinking that defines the organization's network management philosophy. This step makes the purposes and application of the network clear. For instance, the security philosophy for an e-commerce system will be different from the philosophy for a network that transmits top government secrets. This direction has to be clear to start developing the policies that define how to secure each network component.

Usage statements are a frequently overlooked part of the process because everybody has to adopt the same perspective to ensure correct practices in day-to-day use. If usage statements are not documented, the organization risks misunderstandings and conflicting approaches to the same requirements.

Once agreement is obtained, the next step in the process is to tailor the rules for each component. The tailoring should detail clearly the acts considered to be security violations and actions to be taken if a security breach is detected. At this stage the organization defines the behaviors used to protect against insider attacks. Subsequently, these rules will serve as the basis for the controls implemented in the automated policy management system.

In the final stage of the process, the organization defines the acceptable use policies (AUP) to define procedures that serve as the foundation of network administration including rules for account administration, policy enforcement, and privilege review. In this final stage, the organization must pursue an aggressive training and awareness program to ensure that the members of the organization understand and will follow each rule.

Risk Analysis

A classic risk analysis process is executed to identify the risks to a particular network, its equipment, resources, and data. The analysis involves identifying and labeling network assets and placing them into a network asset baseline.

Each baseline item is assessed and prioritized to define the appropriate level of protection to be applied. Detailed procedures are specified, which will be used to secure each baseline item. This risk assessment factors in three levels of threat. If the system were compromised:

- **Low Risk**—the breach would not constitute a significant interruption and the threatened system does not permit access to other systems.

- **Medium Risk**—the interruption would cause a minor business loss or financial impact. Some effort would be required to restore the system and/or the compromise could provide restricted access to other systems.

- **High Risk**—there would be a major interruption causing a significant business and/or financial loss. In addition, substantial effort would be required to restore the system and/or a compromise would provide direct access to other critical functions.

Once a risk level is determined for each component, the next step is to identify the types of users and their privileges. The compromise potential depends on the types and level of privilege assigned to individual users. The five most common types of users are

- Administrators responsible for managing network resources
- Privileged internal users needing an elevated level of access
- Internal users with general access
- Trusted external users needing access some resources
- Other untrusted external users or customers

The use of a process that aligns user types against system criticality requirements can be an effective method for allocating the right resources to ensure all components. The resulting integrated understanding serves as a point of reference for developing the security scheme. For instance, a high-risk component requiring nothing but administrator access would be secured differently than a high-risk component that is accessed by untrusted users.

Establishing the Security Team

Once the network security requirements are fully understood, the organization assembles and trains the people responsible for the actual implementation. They are a network security or NETSEC management team.

This team implements and maintains the network configuration and is responsible for evolving the network as conditions change. The process requires a detailed specification of security requirements for each network component and the continued refinement of the requirement statements over time. The network **security team** establishes and maintains the network security configuration from these requirements.

Network Defense in Depth:
Maintaining a Capable Architecture

Defense in depth is an influential concept used protecting computer systems. It is discussed further in the chapter on secure use (Chapter 14); however, the requirement for ongoing security is satisfied through a formal process that maintains a segmented topology. That topology prevents intruders from exploiting other areas of the system, should one segment be breached. Protection is established by controlling access through a number of boundaries, which have been termed a *defense in depth*.

The components in this topology are the routers and firewalls that secure the perimeter of each layer. Figure 12-5 illustrates this.

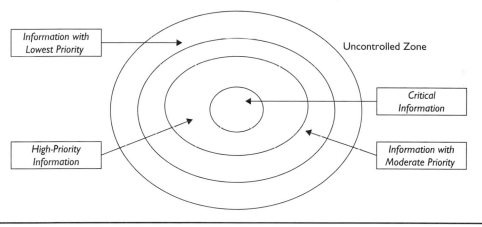

Figure 12-5 Elements of a defense in depth

From a **network topology** standpoint, the outermost perimeter is the dividing point between the assets that the organization wishes to control and the ones that it does not. Within that perimeter, each succeeding layer has increasing levels of criticality. In many ways, the components of each layer work like the guards at a gate to a medieval city. They inspect all inbound traffic for anything that may cause harm.

The inspection takes place at the point that divides a more trusted network from a less trusted one. Consequently, the outermost perimeter of the network is by definition the least secure; the outer perimeter is the easiest to access. It is the most frequently attacked point. Sensitive information should never be placed close to the logical boundaries of the system; it should always behind the largest number of defensive tools including firewalls and routers.

The network security operation must have the ability to monitor, control, evaluate, and evolve the actual network configuration over time because it uses ever-changing technology; the configuration has to be maintained to reflect evolving best practice. Naturally, a number of elements are included in the process, but the primary issues are those of *trust, boundaries, assumptions*, and *human factors*.

Defining Trust

In network security, the first issue to be decided is how to interact with trusted, untrusted, and unknown networks. The decision is essential for maintaining network operations since networks must communicate among hosts. Always maintain an accurate reflection of which network connections can be trusted.

Trusted networks lie within the defined security perimeter of the organization, that means that these networks within the organization's security scheme. A trusted network falls within the defined security perimeter.

Untrusted networks are outside of the security perimeter and are not controlled. Although an organization's trusted network may communicate with untrusted ones, it needs to be protected from possible damage that originates from untrusted sources. Therefore, firewalls are set on the perimeter of a trusted network to filter incoming messages from untrusted networks based on threats are known to originate from them.

Unknown networks are neither trusted nor untrusted. By definition they are outside of the security perimeter. It is not possible to tell the perimeter defense, specifically the firewall, what to do in advance of being contacted because their chrematistics are unknown. In most cases, handle unknown networks in the same fashion as an untrusted network.

In the case of untrusted networks, likely threats are known and it is possible to build actions into the firewalls to handle incoming traffic. That is not the case with unknown networks; contact from them is always treated with restriction and suspicion.

Establishing Boundaries

Security boundaries define the area to be protected and dictates the level of organizational resources required to perform the security function. Wide boundaries imply a large of resource commitment, while narrower boundaries indicate fewer resources. The boundary setting process is an important part of the network security operation.

A good defense makes sure that each security policy is enforced. To do that properly, set the boundaries of the system so that it is possible to implement defined policies.

To ensure that resources fit the information sensitivity requirements, it may be necessary to create a series of interconnected perimeters within the system to accommodate the different types of data. These perimeters function like the concentric walls in Figure 12-5. The perimeter rules can be set to enforce different degrees of security depending on what they protect. If the overall network contains multiple perimeters it is defense in depth; several perimeter defenses must be breached for harm to occur.

Formulating Assumptions

Security system designs are based on assumptions, so unidentified and undocumented assumptions are potential security vulnerabilities. The design of the network defense strategy and the necessary security policies should be guided by an understanding of the requirements of the situation.

Security designs require the organization makes assumptions about the attacks expected and the intruders it faces. Success requires a continuous refinement of the threat picture.

The designer has to anticipate who might want to breach the current security measures and why.

The anticipation relies on identifying the malicious agents in the environment and their motivations. No security measure can be expected to protect the network absolutely. Security measures delay the inevitable long enough for the proper response to be developed. The countermeasure deployment process identifies and establishes the right responses based on the likely motivations and capabilities of known attackers.

Deploying an effective response is as much a people problem as it is a technical design issue because most security measures impact ease of use. For instance, an innocuous as a virus checker takes time to perform its services, which requires the user to wait. If security measures are not carefully justified and explained thoroughly, unsophisticated users see network security countermeasures as unproductive and costly. The design and deployment of a network security scheme has to be done while justifying the likely costs and benefits.

Chapter 12 Review

Chapter Summary

- Network security operations revolve around the responsibility to identify emerging threats and then develop appropriate responses.

- The role of network security is to protect an organization's electronic communications from unauthorized modification, destruction, or disclosure.

- The primary function of network security is to make certain that the components of the network operate correctly and fulfill their intended purpose.

- In addition, it must ensure that the information that is transmitted through the network retains its fundamental integrity.

- The network security function comprises the various formal steps that must be taken to protect the aspects of the business that are involved in the transmission of electronic data.

- This can entail deliberate managerial actions to ensure that the business has the right personnel available to respond appropriately to threats as they emerge.

- It can involve the formulation of the policies and procedures that guide those activities.

- It can even include direct safeguards that are not electronic, such as the measures that a business might take to prevent social engineering exploits.

- Good network security management primarily entails the stipulation and enforcement of policies to assure proper authorization and effective use.

- It involves specification of the precise methods that will be employed for threat assessment, cryptography, and network access control.

- Managing the network security function involves establishing the processes necessary to ensure that only authorized users have physical and/or electronic access to the network.

- This implies the creation and maintenance of an active protection strategy, the purpose of which is to ensure the reliability of data and the appropriate rights of all potential users.

- Network security entails the actions taken to control access from untrusted sources.

- Connection control is the means by which the connection between a computer and a network is established and supervised.

- The component most closely associated with connection control is the firewall.

- Transmission control oversees the actual message transmission process.

- Transmission control normally embodies a standard set of machine-level operations for encoding the data and for detecting and recovering from transmission errors.

- Password attacks are executed in one of three typical ways: **password sharing**, general password guessing, and password capture.

- Viruses and other kinds of malicious code such as worms, Trojan horses, attack applets, and attack scripts represent the most common threats to information.

- Most virus checkers operate in the same way. They scan a file in memory for recognizable fragments of code or key words.

- Virus signatures are stored in the antivirus application's database and must be frequently updated, usually over the Internet, for the virus checker to remain effective.

- In general virus types fall into six categories: file-infecting, boot-sector, multipartite, macro, polymorphic or stealth, and worm.

- A computer worm is a specialized form of macro virus. It is currently the malicious code of choice on the Internet because of its virulence.

- Logic bombs get their name from the fact that they are activated when some prescribed set of criteria is met.

- A Trojan horse comes in attractive packaging such as a piece of useful freeware. Trojan horses can deliver a number of unwelcome payloads.

- There are four general categories of spyware: spam mailers, password capture, keyloggers, and cookie trackers.

- The essence of protecting from insider attacks lies in the monitoring function. The obvious first line of defense in this lies in supervisory action.

- Automated policy enforcement systems provide the ability for the business to build a custom set of policy definitions into network transactions.

- Sniffing is the technological process that is employed to read packets that are being transmitted over a network.

- Sniffers are dangerous because they can be used to snag sensitive information.

- The primary defense against sniffing is encryption.

- IP spoofing is an exploit where the malicious agent attempts to impersonate another network party through its IP address.

- The most effective response to IP spoofing is to implement encrypted systems such as SSH (secure shell) for authentication purposes.

- Denial-of-service (DoS) attacks are different from most other attacks because they are not targeted at access to the network or at the information on the network. Instead, they create a situation where the network can no longer respond to normal requests.

- A man-in-the-middle (MITM) attack is an exploit in which the attacker is able to read and modify all messages that are passing between two parties without either party knowing that the link between them has been compromised.

- Application layer attacks take advantage of weaknesses in popular applications and application services. They normally include such common attacks as buffer overflows, **cross-site scripting flaws**, invalidated parameters, and **command injection flaws**.

- The generic steps that are required to put an effective network management process into practice are: create usage policy statements, conduct a risk analysis, and formulate a security team.

- A defense in depth centers on controlling access. This is usually based on the use of a number of perimeters.

- In the domain of network security, the mechanisms for dealing with trusted, untrusted, and unknown networks have to be defined.

- No security system will succeed unless the designers fully understand how the users will use it. Consequently the designers of security systems have to keep human factors in mind when they create the protection scheme.

Key Terms

access control (313)
access rights (313)
adware (319)
antivirus application (316)
application layer attacks (325)
authentication (312)
authorization (326)
availability (313)
boot-sector viruses (317)

trusted networks (330)
unknown networks (315, 330)
untrusted networks (330)
usage policy statements (327)
virus checker (316)
virus signatures (316)
viruses (315)
worms (318)

Key Term Quiz

Complete each statement by writing one of the terms from this list in each blank. Not all terms will be used.

1. _____ is responsible for creating a temporary link between computers using an electronic transmission facility like the Internet.

2. A network defense based on a segmented topology is called a _____.

3. There are essentially _____ generic types of threats to networks: _____

4. The software systems that ensure that network policies are being followed are called _____

5. The information that a network is trying to protect falls within the boundaries of the _____.

6. The type of malicious code that prevents use of network services is called a _____.

7. The Internet transmission control protocol is _____.

8. Threats can be anticipated through a _____.

9. The commonest form of direct attack on a network is the _____.

10. Connection control enforces _____.

Multiple Choice Quiz

1. The proper response to the virus problem is

   A. good procedure

   B. virus checkers

   C. transmission control

   D. malware

2. Responses to attacks are based on formulating a good set of

   A. plans

   B. controls

    C. assumptions

    D. documents

3. Transmission control regulates

    A. TCP/IP

    B. protocols

    C. communication between devices

    D. access

4. Stealth viruses are dangerous because they are

    A. hard to find

    B. very destructive

    C. invisible

    D. constantly changing

5. Application layer attacks are caused by

    A. poor connection control

    B. bad design

    C. weak encryption

    D. TCP/IP

6. Keyloggers are a form of

    A. malicious code

    B. tracking device

    C. policy enforcement

    D. network protocol

7. Policy managers ensure

    A. malicious code checking

    B. network sniffing

    C. policy enforcement

    D. network defense in depth

8. The role of network security is to

    A. make sure that all of the components work right

    B. perform regular audits of equipment

    C. monitor network traffic

    D. protect electronic communications from harm

9. Transmission control relies on:

   A. connection control

   B. firmware

   C. defense in depth

   D. policy enforcement

10. Application layer attacks are

    A. targeted on the topology of the network

    B. targeted on the system

    C. targeted on user software

    D. types of spyware exploits

Essay Quiz

1. Why is network security particularly difficult to achieve?

2. Why are network vulnerability assessments important?

3. Why is IP spoofing always unethical? What are some examples from real life?

4. What is the basis for defining trust in networks, and what does that imply in terms of the protection approach/requirements?

5. Why are perimeters so important to the physical design of secure networks?

6. What differentiates network equipment from other kinds of computer equipment? What unique security issues does this difference raise?

7. How does connection control differ from transmission control? Why are both of these functions essential to secure transmissions?

8. Why is configuration an important aspect of both transmission control and connection control?

9. What is the purpose of a virus? Why is it harmful? What property of a virus might make it even more harmful?

10. What potential ways can a Trojan horse attack your computer? How are Trojan horses delivered over networks? What special property of a Trojan horse makes it particularly dangerous to Internet users?

Case Exercise

Complete the following case exercise as directed by your instructor.

Heavy Metal Technologies (HMT) is a defense contractor headquartered in Huntsville, Alabama. HMT was recently contracted by the Army to upgrade the fire control system for the MH64-D Apache Longbow attack helicopter. This is a high-security project. The actual manufacturing will take place at the Oceanside Main building; however, the operational testing will take place in Buffalo. It is assumed that the fire control system must be tested in its operating environment and the Buffalo facility can more easily work in conjunction with Army pilot inspectors based at Fort Drum in Watertown, New York. The actual factory acceptance tests will be done there and the DoD inspectors will grant the approvals from the Buffalo facility.

Consequently, the project managers in the Oceanside Main facility will teleconference daily with the managers in Buffalo from the time that the project begins operational testing to the time it obtains final approval and signoff. This is likely to include the production managers from the Jackson Street facility as well as the DoD project managers when approvals are required. The Army has voiced seven concerns with respect to this arrangement, which we would like you to address by identifying the problems and then either suggesting the solution or coming up with an acceptable design.

1. The teleconferences will be over the Internet.

2. The teleconferencers have not been identified yet.

3. Internal network usage is not controlled at Oceanside.

4. Sensitive designs will be exchanged between facilities.

5. The Buffalo facility is not a trusted network.

6. Jackson Street is not within the network boundaries of Oceanside.

7. The Fort Drum network is unknown.

Cryptology

In this chapter, you will learn how to:

- Understand the purpose and importance of cryptology
- Describe the fundamental elements of the encryption process
- Differentiate symmetric and asymmetric encryption
- Explain key management

Cryptology is the scientific discipline that guarantees secure communications. The word comes from the Greek words *kryptós,* "hidden," and *lógos,* "word." Cryptology creates a level of trust in electronic messages. The study of cryptology is composed of two complementary subdisciplines, cryptography and cryptanalysis.

Cryptography is the mathematically based science of disguising information. It ensures the security of an electronic communication by scrambling the text in such a way that the message is unreadable by anyone but the person who should legitimately read it.

The other aspect of the field of cryptology is cryptanalysis. **Cryptanalysis** is a specialized aspect of cryptology. Cryptanalysis breaks **encryption** by changing scrambled information (Cyphertext) into readable form (Cleartext). It is the art of reading somebody else's mail. Cryptanalysis is also a mathematical discipline. Cryptanalysts perform analysis without knowledge of the mechanism used to scramble the message. Therefore, another term for cryptanalysis is **code breaking**.

Cryptologic services have long been in demand in the shadowy domain of spies and the military; however, in an era of mass network communications and competitive business intelligence, cryptology has become a mainstream science. In this chapter, you will learn the basic principles of cryptology as well as the common mechanisms for implementing cryptographic systems. Finally, we discuss the ways to apply cryptography for conventional use.

Cryptography Principles

Cryptography is an important aspect of information assurance since it guarantees secure transmission of electronic data. Global commerce relies on trust; the secure message transfer capability provided by cryptography ensures that trust. Cryptography ensures that no one but the authorized recipient can read an electronic communication.

As post-industrial society becomes more and more dependent on networks, the importance of cryptography as a safeguard against eavesdroppers and malicious individuals grows.

Cryptographic services are important in several technical areas of information assurance, most notably application and network security because these are closely associated with transmitted data. The conduct of cryptographic services is an important part of day-to-day operations, because the principles of confidentiality, integrity, **authentication**, and non-repudiation all depend on the assurance cryptography provides.

For example, in any business transaction, the sender and the recipient both want to have the assurance that the information contained in the transaction is confidential and that the content of the message was not changed or altered—*integrity*. The recipient of an inquiry must be able to confirm that it came from the right person—*authentication*. In addition, if the recipient acts on the inquiry the sender must be prohibited from subsequently claiming that they did not send it—*non-repudiation*. All five attributes are ensured by cryptography.

Integrity and Authentication

The integrity of communication processes is a primary concern to organizations. It would be a bad thing, if for example, a customer's order for 1,000 units were to be accidentally changed to 100 or 10,000. The conduct of global commerce relies on the capacity to confirm the accuracy of the message.

The ability to authenticate senders is also important. Even if the message can be proven accurate, the order for 1,000 units is useless if the receiver cannot confirm it was from an authentic source. In the faceless Internet world, every routine transaction requires authentication.

It must be possible to authenticate the sender, as well as validate the contents of every important message. Two situations involving senders and recipients illustrate why this is important.

- **Authentication without integrity**—when the sender is communicating with a recipient, an adversary may intercept an authenticated message. If the message has no means of guaranteeing its integrity, the adversary could alter the message contents but leave the authentication intact. Upon receipt, the recipient would see the authentication and believe that the message came from the original sender, but would not know the contents had been altered.

- **Integrity without authentication**—In this case, an adversary would be able to send a false message to a recipient, which appeared to originate from a trusted source. The message would have integrity because it was not changed in transit; however, it would lack authentication because the recipient could not confirm the sender's identity.

Digital Signatures

To ensure trust, every electronic transaction must be documented to ensure the parties involved cannot deny its authenticity. In normal business operations trust is assured by written documents, signed, witnessed, and notarized to provide binding authentication.

A document of this type cannot be denied later. Similarly, electronic communications are documented using a form of signature—a *digital signature*.

A digital signature is impossible to fake. Using cryptographic techniques discussed later, the sender transforms the text of a message into a block of data called a "digest." That digest is calculated using a cryptographic key. It is attached to the message as a form of electronic "signature." The recipient can use the same cryptographic technique to authenticate the asserted source and integrity of the message.

Digital signatures cannot be repudiated because they are authenticated by the calculations built into the encryption. When an organization acts on the assumption that a digitally signed electronic message is genuine, it does so based on specific and undeniable proof. Digital signatures are required if the organization uses electronic communications to conduct business. In fact, digital signatures are currently more legally acceptable in court than written signatures because of the robustness that the encryption process enforces.

How Cryptography Works: Codes Versus Ciphers

No element of the information assurance process is as mysterious to the average person as cryptography. This is understandable since the aim of the process itself is confusion. On the surface, encryption and cryptography appear to be interchangeable terms. This confusion stems from the long history of the use of encryption.

Encrypted items are disguised from view, and encryption techniques range from backward writing to steganography (the art and science of hiding information by embedding messages within other, seemingly harmless messages). Many techniques have been in use since ancient times; the Persians, Greeks, and Romans were as expert in their own way as most modern practitioners. In the modern world of electronic messages however, the term "cryptography" denotes a mathematical technique.

Cryptography makes a message unreadable by transforming the plaintext. **Plaintext** is the term for an original, clearly intelligible message, which will be scrambled into a secret form. The "scrambling" is called *encryption*. The protocol employed for **encrypting** and **decrypting** a message is a **cryptosystem**. Cryptosystems make use of a shared algorithm to process the original plaintext. The process of transforming the plaintext into a secret message is called either **enciphering** or **encoding**, depending on the approach used.

The outcome is a **ciphertext** or a **codetext**. The secret message is the **cryptogram**, which is just the enciphered form of the message. Individuals who legitimately possess a **codebook** or key and use it to reveal the original message are **decoding** or **deciphering** the cryptogram. This is in contrast to the **cryptanalysis** process, wherein a person who does not have the key or codebook attempts to solve or "crack" the cryptogram.

The Intricacies of Codes

A *code* is distinguished from a *cipher* in that a code uses whole words, phrases, and **code-groups** (numbers and words) to substitute for words and phrases in the plaintext. Whereas, a cipher replaces each character with a letter, or symbol that theoretically cannot be associated with the character that it replaces.

Most codes are so complex and involved that it is impossible to memorize them. That is the reason why individuals who want to read an encoded message require a codebook. To encode a message, the sender represents each word or group of words with a distinctive group of words, phrases, or symbols obtained from the codebook. The sender and receiver of the message must have identical codebooks to communicate. Figure 13-1 illustrates this.

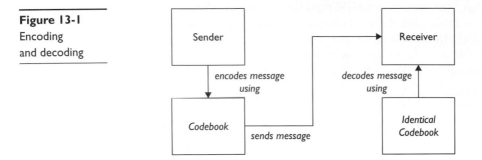

Figure 13-1
Encoding
and decoding

A codebook might be an ordinary book, such as a standard dictionary. For instance, the numbers 3223114 might indicate that the encoded word is on page 322, column 3, eleventh line, fourth word in some textbook (this all has to be in a specific order for the coding process to work). In this case we are using the Comprehensive Information Assurance Dictionary (http://niatec.info/pdf/NIATECV30d.pdf) that specific word is "defend." If a person wished to send an encoded message that says "Defend NIATEC," using this system, they would send 3223114-0191012-2372155-4161123-3871241-0833334-1283132-0622244. Only a person understanding the protocol and possessing a copy of the same dictionary could accurately decode the message.

This technique might seem secure; however, this example is easy to break. There are numerous methods. An approach would be to identify patterns in the code. For example, if a good cryptanalyst were attempting to crack the message traffic from an automobile manufacturer, they would assume that words peculiar to that industry were more likely to occur.

Alternatively, in the case of our "defend NIATEC" example, since the fourth value is always a "1," a "2," or a "3," an experienced cryptanalyst would probably guess that this designated a column in a book. If so, then the first three numbers would be perhaps a page number and the last numbers may designate words. Then the only issue would be determining which codebook was used to encode the message.

The Intricacies of Ciphers

The more common approach to encryption is the cipher. This process replaces the individual letters in the basic plaintext with different letters, numbers, or symbols, and then employs a key to "decipher" the meaning of the message.

The message would then be transmitted in the form of those replacement values. That distinguishes a cipher from a code. In a cipher, the basic unit of transformation is the letter, number, or symbol, whereas selected words or phrases are used to form codes. Figure 13-2 illustrates this.

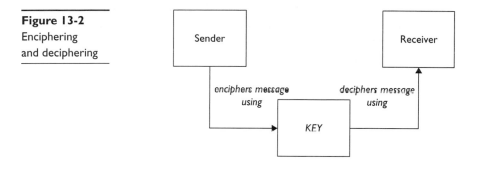

Figure 13-2
Enciphering
and deciphering

Two processes may be used to transform plaintext into a cipher: transposition and substitution. **Transposition** is the process of rearranging the letters of the plaintext out of their normal order. For example, "NIATEC" might be rearranged to "ENIACT." **Substitution** means replacing the letters of the plaintext with numbers, letters, or symbols. Using substitution, "message" might appear as 13051919010705 or some other unreadable combination where the characters relinquish their individual meaning, but retain their relative positions. Transposition and substitution can also be used together to transform plaintext into a secret message.

One or more keys are required to decipher a message. A *key* is nothing more than a symbol or sequence of symbols that is known only to the sender and receiver, which is used to encrypt or decrypt a message. Keys are always based on a mathematical system that rearranges the order of letters or substitutes characters according to a specific pattern. For example, the old-fashioned Morse code is not a code at all but an encryption cipher. The term SOS (which has coded meaning itself) is flashed, beeped, or keyed letter by letter as: [Dot Dot Dot] [Dash Dash Dash] [Dot Dot Dot]. In its simplest form, a cipher might represent each letter by a letter or number (called a substitution alphabet), as in the following:

A	B	C	D	E	F	G	H	I	J	K	L	M	N	O	P	Q	R	S	T	U	V	W	X	Y	Z
1	2	3	4	5	6	7	8	9	10	11	12	13	14	15	16	17	18	19	20	21	22	23	24	25	26

Anything encoded in this cipher is easy to compromise, even if the number sequence was less obvious. Therefore, to complicate the cipher, messages undergo a second transformation process using an encryption key.

Keys are based on algorithms. An **algorithm** is a systematic process that is used to solve a problem or accomplish a (frequently mathematical) goal. For instance, let us see how the urgent message "hold the fort" would be encrypted using a key. The obvious first requirement would be to have a key, which as we saw can be any random combination of letters, numbers, or symbols. For our example, let us use the 11-letter word "outstanding" to perform the actual encryption. That would produce the following encryption values:

8	15	12	4	20	8	5	6	15	18	20	*(hold the fort)*
15	21	20	19	20	1	14	4	9	14	7	*(outstanding)*
23	36	32	23	40	9	19	10	24	32	27	*(encryption)*

In this case, the plaintext "HOLD THE FORT" is converted to its numerical equivalent based on our substitution cipher (which converts a letter to its corresponding numerical position in the alphabet) as: 8-15-12-4-20-8-5-6-15-18-20. Then using the encryption key "OUTSTANDING," which the substitution cipher translates to: 15-21-20-19-20-1-14-4-9-14-7, these values can be added to the message to produce the encrypted message 23-36-32-23-40-9-19-10-24-32-27.

This example is basic, but two fundamental things should be noted. First, a person would have to have both the correct algorithm (substitution and addition) and the correct key ("outstanding") to decrypt this message. To crack this cipher, then, it would be necessary to know the key, which in our case was the word "*outstanding*," as well as the processing algorithm, which is that the values are *added* to the substituted plaintext values. Most algorithms are publicly available, yet they can be used with confidence because each requires a unique key.

Although this encrypted message would not take a long time to figure out, it does illustrate the effectiveness of the key approach. Unlike our straightforward example, the algorithms for most common keys entail a variety of permutations, including such activities as dividing, multiplying, and **hashing** the encrypted message.

For instance, the numerical values of encrypted letters might be multiplied by a random number, the product squared, and the key subtracted from the product. Repetition may improve things slightly. Remember, complexity alone does not improve the resistance to decryption, but additional passes to permutate the message may.

There are many supposedly "uncrackable" algorithms commercially available and in the public domain. The mathematics in these algorithms is quite complex. The degree of complexity is necessary because the techniques that are dedicated to **cracking** them are also extremely sophisticated.

Nonetheless, the wide availability of an algorithm also serves as a means to validate its strength because there will have been millions of attempts to crack it. If no one has succeeded, cryptographers use that algorithm with confidence. Several commercial techniques are examples.

Keys for Encryption

The cryptographic process begins when an **encryption algorithm** is used to process a plaintext message. When that activity is complete, the message will be scrambled into a form that will require the same algorithm to decipher it. When the resulting ciphertext message reaches the receiver, the specific decryption algorithm has to be known to change the message back into its plaintext form.

There are a finite number of encryption algorithms, so the inability to select a unique one is a weakness in the process. For example, whether a substitution cipher has been developed for use by the Central Intelligence Agency, Julius Caesar, or a Spiderman decoder ring, it involves some form of displacement. The only problem involved is determining how the plaintext was displaced. Therefore, if the algorithm were the only part of the encryption process, there would never be any real security.

Consequently, an additional component must be amalgamated with the algorithm to produce a secure ciphertext, namely, keys. The key builds the meaning into the message. Accordingly, although somebody might guess the algorithm, if the key is kept secret then the message is secure.

This can be illustrated through a home security system. While many people use home alarms, which have exactly the same design and which are made by the same manufacturer, each individual alarm uses its own specific key combination to activate or deactivate it. The key combination for the alarm is the equivalent of the key used in the encryption process. Even though the alarm is one of many, only the people authorized to control that particular alarm know what the key sequence is.

There are two basic types of cryptographic keys: **secret key** (symmetric), and **public key** (asymmetric). The difference between these two is that in secret key cryptography, the same key is used for both encryption and decryption. Hence, the key is used symmetrically. In public key cryptography, the encryption and decryption operations are the same, but they use different keys. In other words, the keys are used asymmetrically. Figure 13-3 illustrates this.

Both types of systems provide a degree of privacy, but public key systems are the mechanism of choice for secure communication in business because they support the transmission of messages between unaffiliated parties.

Secret Key (Symmetric) Cryptography

The simplest form of encryption is **symmetric**, or "secret key," which is also sometimes called "single key" encryption because it uses the same key to encrypt and decrypt a message. The key and the plaintext are combined to yield a ciphertext. When a symmetric encryption algorithm is used, decryption is the mathematical reverse of encryption. This process is illustrated in Figure 13-4.

Secret key cryptography uses a common key for encryption and for decryption. The sender encrypts the message using a key that only that sender and recipient share. The key is typically preloaded into each party's cryptosystem or sent between the two parties as a separate transmission. The secure transmission of a secret key is a challenge by itself, and will be treated in a separate section. The recipient uses the shared key to decrypt the message.

Consider the case of Bob and Sue. Bob wants to send Sue a secure message. He encrypts that message using a specific previously agreed-upon key. The resulting ciphertext is then sent to Sue, who authenticates the sender. She then takes her duplicate key out of her secret key lockbox and uses it to decrypt the message. The authentication is valid if Sue is able to decrypt the message correctly, since if the key is truly secret, then by definition only Bob could be the sender.

Figure 13-3
Symmetric versus
asymmetric keys

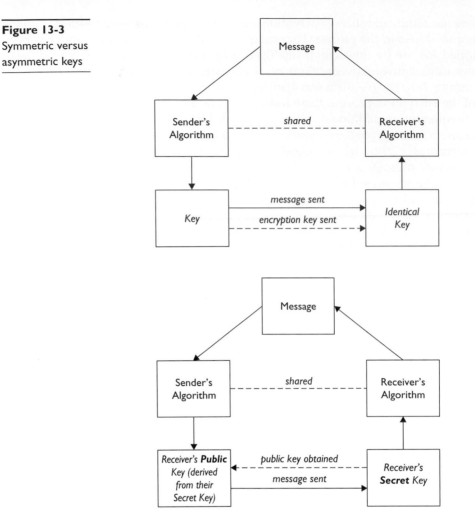

Historically, secret key algorithms have been the most efficient way to do encryption. There are fewer steps involved in establishing the relationship and in computing the encrypted values. Once the key is agreed upon, each party can securely encrypt messages intended for the other. The authentication of the message is ensured because each party knows that they are the only two who have the key. Therefore, when a message arrives, there is only one person who could have sent it. The *exchange* process can continue for some given period until the secret key is changed by mutual agreement. Thus, there is less intermediate coordination required for the overall process. From a processing standpoint, secret keys are more efficient, because there is no "other" calculation involved in transforming the ciphertext.

Figure 13-4
Symmetric or
secret key
encryption

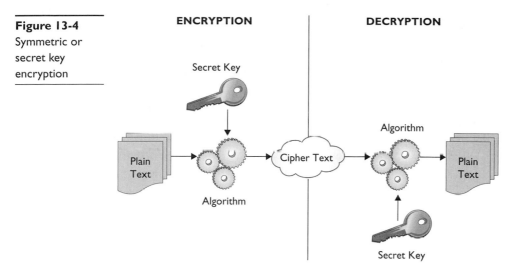

ENCRYPTION   DECRYPTION

The weakness of secret key cryptography is that both the sender and receiver have to use the same secret key, without divulging it to a third party. Therefore, if both the sender and receiver are involved in a remote two-way conversation to determine what type of key to use, there is a risk of eavesdroppers learning what that key is. If that happens anyone, who has overheard the exchange of the key information, will also have that secret. Moreover, the eavesdropper would then be able to intercept and read any messages between the two parties.

This is the traditional problem that military and intelligence services have with secret keys, and many world events have risen or fallen based on either the interception or cracking of a secret key. For instance, the British success against U-boats during the Second World War was materially aided by the fact that their cryptanalysts had a German code machine (that is, the German's secret key—called an Enigma machine) in their physical possession.

Secret Key Management

The secret key approach is flexible and practical for one-to-one exchanges. The only problem is ensuring that the two communicating parties are the only ones who know the secret. Nonetheless, the **key management** and exchange process is critical and is a limiting factor in systems that involve a large and diverse number of parties.

Safe distribution becomes a cumbersome task in large networks with a large number of participants because the organization has to ensure that all parties have the right secret key at the time of use. This is a logistical nightmare if the secret key is changed frequently. The nightmare is further complicated by the fact that users can communicate securely only with people who hold the matching key. Fortunately, public key cryptography helps the key management problem.

Public Key (Asymmetric) Cryptosystems

Public key or **asymmetric** cryptography is a practical means to ensure electronic transactions because it does not require the use of a shared key. Instead, it employs two different keys—a **private key** that only its owner may access, and a **public key**, which is available to other users or distributed on request.

Anyone desiring to send a secure message encrypts it using the receiver's public key. Recipients use their private key, which only they know, to decrypt the message. These keys correspond to each other; in that they share a predefined mathematical relationship, which allows any message that is encrypted with one key to be decrypted using the other. That relationship is illustrated in Figure 13-5.

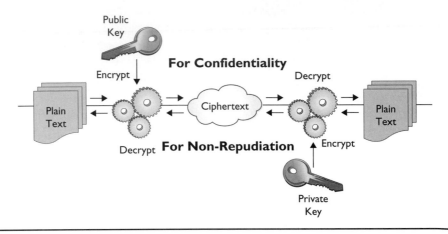

Figure 13-5 Asymmetric or public key encryption

This type of encryption is called "asymmetric" because it involves the use of a different key at each end of the transmission. The public key uses a public transformation algorithm and the private key uses a personal one. Each of these keys undertakes a mathematical process to transform the text. These functions are inversely related to each other. That is, if one is used to encrypt the message, the other must be used to decrypt it.

For instance, let us assume that Sue wants to send a secure message to Bob. Sue would encrypt that message using Bob's public key. However, even though that public key is widely available, the only way to decrypt the message would be through the private key, to which only Bob has access. This ensures that Sue's message was securely transmitted to Bob and it does not require the negotiation or transmission of a shared key, as a secret key encryption process would. It requires only that Sue know Bob's public key.

An old example illustrates how Bob would use his private key to decrypt the message. Imagine that Bob has a mailbox with a key chained to it. The mailbox is the place where people place messages for Bob. The key can be used only to lock the mailbox. It is Bob's public key. Anyone who wishes to send Bob a message puts the message in the box and sends it (or locks the box) using the attached key. Bob has in his possession the only key that will unlock the mailbox. This is his private key. The key chained to the mailbox will not open the box once locked; only Bob's secret key can do that.

The advantage of a public key cryptosystem is that two users can communicate securely without exchanging keys. This enables a large number of people to use public key encryption for secure communication. Most public keys are readily available. They are generated with the encryption software and stored in a downloadable location such as on an organization's website or on a public key server. Many public key servers are available on the Internet. One example is the implementations of Pretty Good Privacy (PGP).

The two keys employed in this process are derived as a pair through a mathematical function based on hard-to-solve problems such as large primes, discrete logarithm, and factorization. What makes the discrete logarithm problem hard, and hence the discrete algorithm approach desirable, is that it is easy to raise a number to a power to generate a large number, but hard to derive the identical power to generate the same number on the back end of the process.

The factorization problem is hard because it is easy to multiply numbers to generate a large number, but difficult to determine those factors when it is time to turn that number back into something meaningful. The difficulty of these problems ensures that, given the current state of mathematics, it is extremely difficult to derive one key from knowledge of the other. It should also be noted that the secrecy of the public key is not relevant to maintaining the integrity of the public key structure. However, the ability to associate a given public key with its user is critical to the function of the overall process.

Public Key Management

From a processing standpoint, a public key system is inefficient compared to its secret key counterpart because another key is involved in the calculation, so the computation process that encrypts the data requires more time. Depending on the algorithm employed, this process may produce a ciphertext that is considerably larger than the plaintext. Consequently, public key cryptography is not an efficient way to encrypt large messages. Moreover, because public key cryptography involves posting public keys to an accessible location, those keys may not be changed as often as they should, yielding a potential vulnerability.

Another disadvantage of a public key system is that since a recipient's public key must be used to encrypt the message, it can only be sent to a single recipient. While it is possible to send an authenticated message that cannot be repudiated to multiple recipients, one person at a time, it is currently not feasible to send a single confidential message to a distribution list because each recipient will employ a unique key. In addition, due to its slower response time, public key cryptography is not usually used to encrypt entire messages; however, it is used to generate digital signatures and transmit private keys.

Digital Signatures

Digital signatures ensure the integrity, authentication, and non-repudiation of a message. A hash value is derived from the original text of the message to generate a digital signature. A hash value is the output of a well-defined mathematical function, which uses a discretionary input value to produce the output value. The MD-5 (Message Digest) algorithm is a widely used example of a hash algorithm. MD-5 produces a unique 128-bit "signature" value from any message of arbitrary length. Although the MD-5 cryptographic algorithm has been shown to be weaker than it was once thought to be, for the present it is the tool of choice for producing digests of messages.

Because the signature value produced by the hashing process is substantially smaller than the text, it is often called a **message digest**. In addition, the input values for the hash cannot be inferred from any value that it produces; functions such as MD-5 are sometimes referred to as *one-way algorithms*. The digital signature is the hash value, which is then encrypted by the sender's private key. That "signature" can then be sent attached to an unencrypted (plaintext) message, or embedded in an encrypted message.

If the signature is embedded in an encrypted message, the actual process of encrypting the message will be done symmetrically. It is common to use a symmetric algorithm for confidentiality with an embedded **digital signature** for integrity and non-repudiation. If encryption is not used, the digital signature serves as the integrity check. That element also ensures the non-repudiation. To verify the integrity and **nonrepudiation of origin** of the message, the receiving party

1. Generates its hash value by running the plaintext message through the same hash algorithm used by the sender

2. Decrypts the digital signature, revealing the hash value computed before the message was sent

3. Compares the two values

This process is illustrated in Figure 13-6.

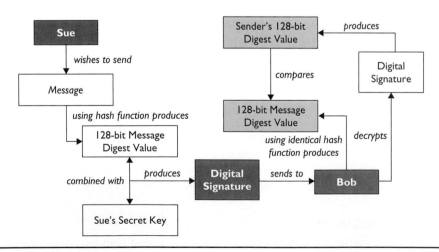

Figure 13-6   Digital signatures

The receiver knows the message is from the right sender and has not been altered when the hash values match. If the receiver finds the hash values to be different, he or she knows the message has been altered in transit.

The following example illustrates that process. It assumes two users have agreed upon a hash function, **checksum algorithm**, and key for the verification process in advance. Then, if Sue wants to send a digitally signed message to Bob, Sue will perform the following steps:

- Generate a digest for the message
- Compute a digital signature as a function of the digest and her private key
- Transmit the message and the signature to Bob

Upon receiving the message, Bob will

- Generate a new digest for the received message
- Using Sue's public key, decrypt the attached digital signature
- Compare the value he calculated with the value he decrypted

If Sue's digital signature can be verified, the following can be assumed:

- Bob is assured that the message was not modified. If even one bit of the original message was changed, the digest generated using the received message would differ from the decrypted value, and cause the signature verification process to fail.
- Bob is assured that Sue sent the message. Public key transformation functions cannot be duplicated by any practical means; therefore, only a signature generated by the originator's private key can be correctly decrypted using the originator's public key.

One problem remains, to verify Sue's digital signature with confidence. Although the integrity of the message is assured, there is no authentication supporting non-repudiation unless Sue's public key can be proven to belong to Sue only.

For example, if Pam were able to establish an alias for herself as Sue, she might masquerade as Bob's friend Sue, when in fact she is his enemy Pam. That problem is resolved by using an authentication service. An authentication service is a third party who vouches for the identity of a public key owner. The formal mechanism for accomplishing this is known as **Public Key Infrastructures (PKI)**.

Public Key Infrastructures

In the previous section we noted that users of a public key system have to access the public keys of other users; using PKI eliminates that need. PKI provides the public-key encryption and digital signature services necessary to verify, enroll, and certify users of a secure application. Consequently, PKI includes the entire collection of technologies, protocols, and policies that maintain, distribute, create, and validate public keys and their associated information.

PKI serve as the trusted third party in a secure transaction. The infrastructure is composed of a **Certificate Authority (CA)**, a key directory, and associated management rules. Other components such as key recovery and registration procedures may be included in a PKI. As outlined in Figure 13-7.

Figure 13-7
Public key
infrastructures

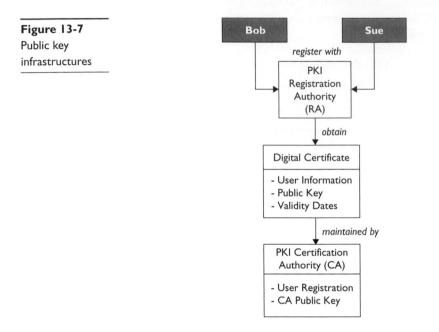

The CA function is to verify and register the identity of users through a **Registration Authority (RA)**. Once registered, each user is given a digital certificate that is maintained through a CA. A **digital certificate** is a public document that contains information that identifies a user, as well as the user's public key, the period during which the certificate is valid and other information. The digital certificate is unique to the individual user.

The following illustrates the method by which these certificates are generated and distributed. Bob and Sue register with a CA. During the registration process, they provide their public key information to the CA. The CA, in turn, provides each user with the following information:

- A signed certificate containing the user's public key
- The public key information of the CA

The users store these certificates in a public directory. The commonly used repositories are based on the ITU X.509 standard. At some future time, Bob sends a signed message to Sue. The message is signed using Bob's key. When she receives Bob's message, Sue queries the public directory to obtain Bob's public key certificate. Sue first uses the CA's public key to validate the certificate's signature, and then verifies Bob's message signature using the public key contained in his certificate. One advantage of this technique is that while insecure data channels might be used for the communication, the digital signatures assure the integrity and authenticity of the information.

A problem is that there are many CAs. This makes it difficult to establish trust between users of different CAs. In the case where two different CAs certify two different users who communicate frequently, the CAs might certify each other. In other words, the two CAs may store each other's public keys in certificates signed by the certifying CA. This concept is called *cross-certification*. In scenarios where there are large numbers of users and CAs, it is more practical to arrange the CAs into a structure of certificate services than to require every CA to cross-certify every other CA.

The long-term goal of the PKI initiative is to create a global directory of people who can communicate securely using (primarily) ITU X.509 certificates. That would produce standard worldwide certification assurance of public key information. Currently there are a number of different types of standard certificates, including

- X.509 public key certificates
- Simple Public Key Infrastructure (SPKI) certificates
- Pretty Good Privacy (PGP) certificates
- **Attribute certificates**

The reader should keep in mind that each of these certificates has a separate and unique format. However, in most environments, when people use the term "public key certificate" they are talking about the ITU X.509 digital certification.

At present, the problem with X.509 is that it is not fully standardized. Consequently, companies such as Microsoft and Netscape have implemented X.509 differently. The outcome has been that an X.509 certificate generated by Microsoft may not be readable by a Netscape browser and vice versa.

Key Management

Key management is a process that assures the secure generation, distribution, and storage of keys. Key management must be a secure method, since once a key is generated it must remain secret. A good avenue for attack—particularly in the case of a public key system—is on the key management process because cryptographic keys are extremely robust. Key management must be robust also as well.

All legitimate users must be able to generate securely and distribute keys that are suitable to their communication and security needs. There must be a way for users to find others' public keys as well as efficiently publicize their own.

If someone's key is lost or compromised, it must be possible to alert other users to prevent them from encrypting messages using the now-invalid public key, or accepting messages signed with the invalid private key. Users must also be able to store private keys securely, but keep them readily accessible for legitimate use. Finally, like passwords, to ensure security, expiration dates for keys have to be both assigned and enforced rigorously.

There are a number of practices associated with good key management. They include the determination of a proper **key length**, the development of a secure process for **key generation**, the enforcement of an effective **key life cycle**, and the development of effective **key storage** procedures. These factors are interrelated , so it is important to understand the issues pertinent to each to do the necessary trade-offs to arrive at an optimum solution.

Key Length

The efficiency of the encryption process is usually dependent on key length. Key length is a function of encryption requirements; the longer the key, the more robust the encryption. However, key length also affects the speed of the processing, because each bit in the key sequence has to be processed.

If the security demands of the encrypted information require a long, complex key, then it can be anticipated that the time it will take to encrypt and decrypt that information will be longer. However, if the key is too short, it can be easily cracked and so it will not fulfill its purpose. Remember, if a key is kept in use too long, the likelihood of it being broken increases. Therefore, the length and complexity of the key is dictated by how long it will be kept in use. Key length determination is a purposeful design activity.

There are security **best practices** that can be used to determine appropriate key length. In any **key-based cryptosystem**, remember the longer the key, the more time the **attacker** needs to crack it. Today, the common recommendation for symmetric cryptosystems is a minimum 75-bit key length in the case of data that will be kept a short time, and a 90-bit key length for information that will be kept for 20 years or more.

Asymmetric cryptosystems are susceptible to shortcut attacks, such as factoring, which make it possible to avoid trying all of the possible key combinations. Therefore, the period of the attack is much shorter. Consequently, those keys have to be much longer. RSA keys, for example, are usually 768 or 1064 bits long.

Key Generation

Key generation is based on random numbers, whether for a secret key cryptosystem or a public key cryptosystem. A good random number source produces numbers that are unknown and unpredictable by adversaries. Computer programs do not generate random numbers—only pseudorandom numbers.

Random numbers obtained from a physical process are in principle the best; many physical processes appear truly random. One option is to use a hardware device, such as a cryptographic accelerator. Another one is to use physical movements of the computer user, such as inter-key stroke timings measured in microseconds. Clearly numbers generated by radioactive decay are even stronger. An unsophisticated technique uses spinning disks to generate random data, rather like an (honest) slot machine. However, these are not truly random, as the movement of the disk platter is not truly random.

Whatever method is used, the random numbers might still contain some artifact, which would reduce statistical randomness. Some recommend, it is best to run whatever random numbers are obtained through a good hash function before using them. Since programmatic random number generators are based on algorithms, it is important to use one that can be guaranteed cryptographically secure.

Random seeds for programmatic random number generators are important. A *random seed* is the starting point for generating the random array of sample data. The seed must be sufficiently complex to deter attacks based on trying all possible seeds. Obviously, the starting point will determine what will be derived in the form of the data set. Therefore, changing the random seed will essentially produce a different random sample.

Key Lifetime

Keys have limited lifetimes for many reasons. The most important one is to safeguard against cryptanalysis. Each time the key is used, it generates a number of ciphertexts. Using a key repetitively allows an attacker to build up a store of ciphertexts (and possibly plaintexts), which they can place under analysis to crack the cryptosystem.

Another reason for limiting the lifetime of a key is to minimize the damage from a compromised key. It is unlikely a user will discover that an attacker has compromised his or her key, particularly if the attacker remains "passive," so the best defense is to frequently change the key. Doing so ensures against the potential that a key was compromised. Of course, if it can be confirmed that an attacker has compromised a key, the use of that key for encryption should be immediately discontinued.

Key Storage

Private keys must be stored securely, since unauthorized duplication leads to increased risk in the communication process. Measures taken to protect a stored private key should be at least equal to the level of desired security of the messages that are encrypted with it.

A private key should never be stored anywhere in plaintext. The simplest storage mechanism is to encrypt a private key under a password and store the result somewhere. However, passwords are sometimes guessed. If a simple password protection scheme is followed, the storage password should be chosen very carefully because the overall security of the key is tied directly to the robustness of the password.

Many hacker exploits are aimed at obtaining keys accessible from the Internet. Therefore, it is a good idea to store the encryption key somewhere that is not accessible from cyberspace. These places include CDs, floppy disks, flash storage, or local hard drives. It is good practice to store the key in systems that are inaccessible to other users or on media that the user can remove when using a particular computer. Private keys may also be stored on portable hardware, such as a smart card. Users with extremely high security needs, such as certifying authorities, should use tamper-resistant devices to protect their private keys.

Key Distribution

As we saw, because of the computation requirements imposed by using two keys, public key systems do not encrypt large messages very efficiently. That is their drawback; in common practice, cryptographic systems employ a secret (or symmetric) key to encrypt the message, and public key cryptography to distribute the secret key.

The secret keys used in conventional cryptosystems are small and easy to process. If a secret key is viewed as a kind of message, then its encryption using a public key algorithm, and the subsequent employment of that process to exchange symmetric key information, would not place an unnecessary burden on the processing. The combined use of secret and public key cryptography efficiently underwrites all the authentication, integrity, and secrecy services necessary for most users. The following illustrates that concept.

Returning to Sue and Bob for a minute … Sue needs to send a signed, confidential message to Bob. She first computes a digital signature as a function of her own private key and a digest of the plaintext. Second, she generates a conventional secret key, and uses this key to transform the plaintext into ciphertext. However, then she encrypts the secret key using Bob's public key. Sue appends that encrypted secret key and the digital signature to the ciphertext, and transmits the information to Bob. Figure 13-8 illustrates this.

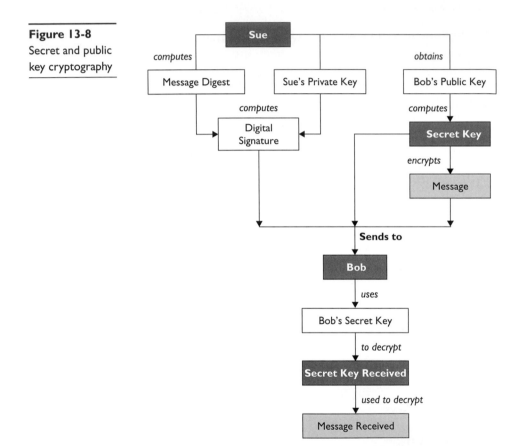

Figure 13-8
Secret and public key cryptography

Upon receipt of the message, the secret key is decrypted using Bob's private key. The secret key is then used to decrypt the ciphertext. Once the plaintext is obtained, Bob validates the signature using the normal authentication process. Confidentiality is guaranteed because only Bob's private key can be used to decipher the secret key necessary to decrypt the message. Integrity is guaranteed because the digital signature was generated using a digest of the original plaintext message. Finally, authentication is certain, because the digital signature provides irrefutable evidence that Sue generated the plaintext message.

This approach overcomes two disadvantages of a public key system: performance and the inability to send a message to multiple recipients. Performance degradation is minimized because a conventional secret key algorithm is used to encrypt and decrypt the message. The only use of the public key algorithm is to encrypt the secret key itself. If the message is transmitted to several recipients, the originator encrypts the secret key one time per recipient, using that recipient's public key. For example, if a message were to be sent to five recipients, there would be five different encryptions of the secret key appended to the message. We are now going to look at some typical commercial encryption products.

Attacking a Cryptosystem: Cryptanalysis

It is important to have a robust encryption process because most cryptosystems will be attacked. As we saw in the beginning of this chapter, these attacks fall under the heading of "cryptanalysis."

The aim of cryptanalysis is to find a hole in a code, cipher, protocol, or key system. There are somewhere between 60 and 70 common types of cryptanalysis attacks, which span the alphabet from "acoustic cryptanalysis" to "XML attacks." However, only four conditions serve as the basis the approach. These are:

- Ciphertext-only
- Known-plaintext
- Chosen-plaintext
- Chosen-ciphertext

Ciphertext-Only Attack (COA)

Ciphertext-only attacks assume that the attacker only has access to the ciphertext. The aim of a ciphertext-only attack is to deduce the plaintext, or at least usable, information from the ciphertext alone. Occasionally a good ciphertext-only attack can even work out the key.

These types of counting and observational techniques are actually very old since ciphertext in one form of another has been around since the beginning of writing. The common defense against such an attack is complexity, permutation, and iteration. That is because the methods used in ciphertext-only attacks center on frequency analysis and pattern recognition. The other option is non-repetition in the message transfer process, since any kind of successful ciphertext attack requires a very large amount of ciphertext to analyze.

Known-Plaintext Attack (KPA)

Known-plaintext attacks are the central theme in many of the spy movies from the 1940s. In a known-plaintext attack, the cryptanalyst has access to a message in both its ciphertext and plaintext form. The aim of a known-plaintext attack is to deduce the secret key.

Once an analyst is able to do a comparison between a known plaintext within any part of an encrypted system, it is likely that they will be able to figure out the rest of the encryption. Therefore, a known-plaintext attack can bear fruit long after the initial event.

The common defense against such an attack is key or encryption system management. It should never be possible to obtain a matching plaintext rendition of a ciphertext. Conversely, it should also never be possible to use cracked encryption to obtain any further useful knowledge. Therefore, the encryption system ought to be changed on a random basis as a matter of standard operating procedure.

Chosen-Plaintext Attack (CPA)

In chosen-plaintext attacks, the cryptanalyst has access to an arbitrary set of plaintexts along with their ciphertext forms. The aim is to deduce the secret key from the material at hand. These types of attacks are not as likely to break cryptosystems as known-plaintext attacks since the analyst only has access to a piece of the puzzle.

Chosen-plaintext attacks are not a matter of the intended victim handing a selected set of their encrypted plaintexts to an attacker (as the name might imply). What actually occurs is that the attacker monitors communication traffic over a set period to snag occasional parts of encrypted messages, which might be broadcast unencrypted due to error or bad practice. The alternative is to either guess the contents of a given message, or obtain it from other sources. From various intercepts, the attacker assembles a usable set of comparable messages to base the cryptanalysis on.

The common defense against a CPA is randomness. At best, a chosen-plaintext attack is seeking to assemble pieces of things into a logical structure to improve understanding. If the basis for that understanding is constantly changing, then the attack is much less likely to gain anything meaningful within a reasonable period.

Chosen-Ciphertext Attack (CCA)

In chosen-ciphertext attacks, the cryptanalyst has the ability to decrypt an arbitrary set of ciphertexts using an unknown key. Traditionally, the most common way to do that is by using a physical decryption device left unattended, hence the other name for these types of attacks—"lunchtime attacks."

If a device can be forced to provide decryptions of selected ciphertexts, the generic term used to describe it is "decryption oracle." With the advent of software agents plantable on unsuspecting hosts surreptitiously means that gaining stealth access to a software decryption oracle is increased dramatically.

If attackers can decrypt enough ciphertexts, they can deduce the secret key. As such, chosen-ciphertext attacks are considered especially harmful to cryptosystems and must be carefully countered. The most common way of doing that is by "padding" all ciphertext with extra data. These are sometimes also known as redundancy strings.

Public Key Products and Technologies

Public key encryption systems are commercial software because they are an important feature of electronic commerce systems—not to mention the ubiquitous e-mail function. There are several public key security products on the market. An informed person should know about the commonly used products in this non-exhaustive survey of influential ones.

RSA

The best known is from RSA developed in 1977 by the team of Rivest, Shamir, and Adleman (RSA) and now owned by RSA Data Security, a subsidiary of Security Dynamics. Many browsers and software packages incorporate RSA making the RSA algorithm the most commonly used encryption and authentication algorithm on the market. It serves as the *de facto* standard for public key encryption. It is included as part of the web browsers from Netscape and Microsoft. It's also part of Lotus Notes, Intuit's Quicken, and many other products.

RSA is a public key cipher used for both encrypting messages and making digital signatures. When the patents expired (in the USA) in 2000, RSA released the algorithm into the public domain making it more common. It underlies public key cryptographic systems like PGP.

RSA is popular because of its one-way computational security. Earlier we pointed out that it might be easy to multiply two huge prime numbers it is not so easy to decompose the outcome of that process to determine the two original prime numbers.

Once the keys have been developed, the original prime numbers are no longer important and can be discarded. As we have seen, both the public and the private keys are needed for encryption and decryption. However, using the RSA system, the private key never needs to be sent across the Internet.

DES

The **Data Encryption Standard (DES)** was developed by IBM with government encouragement during the 1970s. DES was first published in 1976 by the U.S. National Bureau of Standards. DES is an ANSI standard adopted by the U.S. government in 1976 as Federal Information Processing Standard (FIPS) Publication 46-1. DES was most recently reaffirmed in 1999 by FIPS 46-3.

DES is the most widely used symmetric encryption system in the world. It uses a private key that was judged so difficult to break by the U.S. government that it was restricted for exportation to other countries. This is a 56-bit key sequence that maps a 64-bit input block of plaintext onto a 64-bit output block of ciphertext.

DES is an old algorithm and 56 bits is a small key for today's computing power. The algorithm is still considered practically secure as triple DES; it is beginning to reach the end of its useful life.

IDEA

The International Data Encryption Algorithm (IDEA) is a block cipher that was first published by Lai and Massey. IDEA was developed in 1991 at the Swiss Federal Institute of Technology Zurich (ETHZ). IDEA is based on a 128-bit key—longer than the DES key. IDEA's **key size** ensures greatly enhanced security. The IDEA algorithm performs a series of non-linear transformations on a 64-bit data block.

IDEA was designed to replace the Data Encryption Standard. As such, IDEA's structure is very similar to DES; it performs 17 rounds, each round taking 64 bits of input to produce a 64-bit output, using individual round keys that are generated from the 128-bit key.

The operation of a round is more complicated than that of DES. It involves hashing input and per-round keys together in a one-way process. The advantage of IDEA over DES is faster performance in software. In addition, it has the advantage that aside from per-round key generation, decryption is identical to encryption.

Secure Sockets Layer (SSL)

Secure Sockets Layer (SSL) is a security protocol that provides privacy, integrity, and authentication services for Internet communications. SSL Handshake Protocol establishes the relationship between communicating parties (an SSL client and a server). When the parties first make contact, they exchange electronic "hellos" that are secret numbers that enable them to select encryption algorithms, exchange keys, and authenticate each other. Symmetric encryption algorithms, such as are what enforce the privacy. The identities of communicating parties are authenticated using asymmetric encryption algorithms, such as RSA. Message integrity is checked by a hash function.

Elliptic Curve

Victor Miller and Neal Koblitz first proposed **elliptic curve cryptosystems** independently in the mid-1980s. As in all public key cryptosystems, the security of elliptic curve cryptosystems relies on mathematical formulas. The difference between this algorithm and other public key cryptosystems is that it is based on a special subset of numbers originating from an elliptic curve function rather than factoring.

Other algorithms such as ElGamal and Diffie-Helman use the discrete log problem. The elliptic curve subset can be applied to any algorithm based on that problem. Therefore, elliptic curve systems can achieve a high level of security with shorter keys than systems relying on the difficulty of factoring. Elliptic curve (EC) systems are newer and have not yet survived years of intense scrutiny as DES and RSA have. EC continues to be tested against various forms of attack. However, elliptic curve systems are beginning to be adopted within the cryptographic community because of their advantages.

Chapter 13 Review

Chapter Summary

- The study of cryptology makes up two complementary subdisciplines: cryptography and cryptanalysis.
- Cryptography is the mathematical science of disguising written communication.
- Cryptanalysis, which is often referred to as "code breaking," entails all of the techniques that might be employed to break somebody else's encryption.
- Cryptanalysis is a very highly involved mathematical discipline.
- Cryptography underwrites the confidentiality, integrity, authentication, and nonrepudiation of origin of anything that is transmitted between two parties.

- The process of transforming the plaintext into a secret message is called either enciphering or encoding, depending on the approach that is used.

- A code is distinguished from a cipher in that a code consists of letters, whole words, and phrases with code-groups (numbers and/or words) that replace the plaintext.

- The more common approach to encryption is the cipher. These replace the individual letters in the basic plaintext unit with different letters, numbers, or symbols, and then employ a key to "decipher" the meaning of the message.

- There are two basic processes used to transform plaintext into a cipher: transposition and substitution.

- One or more keys are required to decipher a message.

- A key is nothing more than a symbol or sequence of symbols, which is known only to the sender and receiver and which, when applied to the text of the message, either encrypts or decrypts it.

- Keys are based on an algorithm, which is just a step-by-step process for solving a problem or accomplishing a goal.

- A person would have to have both the correct algorithm and the correct key to decrypt a message.

- There are two basic types of cryptographic keys: secret key (symmetric), and public key (asymmetric).

- The difference between these two is that in secret key cryptography, the same key is used for both encryption and decryption.

- In public key cryptography, the encryption and decryption operations are similar, but use different keys.

- The security weakness of any symmetric, or secret key, encryption system is in the distribution of the key.

- The advantage of a public key system is that two users can communicate securely without exchanging secret keys, which makes it possible for the largest number of people to employ a secure method for communication.

- The disadvantage of public keys is that they are computationally inefficient compared to their more conventional, symmetric counterpart.

- Message digests are generated by **hash functions**.

- Public Key Infrastructures (PKI) is the common approach that has been adopted to allow users of a public key system to access the public keys of other users.

- PKI is an integrated collection of technologies, protocols, and policies that are implemented to control the maintenance, distribution, creation, and validation of public keys and their associated identification information.

- PKIs serve as a trusted third party in a secure transaction and entail a Certificate Authority (CA), a key directory, and associated management rules.

- Their function is to verify and register the identity of users through a Registration Authority (RA), and then to provide each registered user with a digital certificate through a Certification Authority (CA).

- A digital certificate is a public document containing information identifying a user, the user's public key, a period during which the certificate is valid and other information.

- There are a number of different types of standard certificates, including: X.509 public key certificates, Simple Public Key Infrastructure (SPKI) certificates, Pretty Good Privacy (PGP) certificates, and attribute certificates.

- Key management deals with the secure generation, distribution, and storage of keys.

- Because public key systems underwrite most electronic commerce, they are very much a part of the domain of commercial products.

Key Terms

algorithm (343)
asymmetric (348)
attacker (354)
attribute certificates (353)
authentication (340)
best practices (354)
Certificate Authority (CA) (352)
ciphertext (341)
code breaking (339)
codebook (341)
code-groups (341)
codetext (341)
cracking (344)
cryptanalysis (339)
cryptogram (341)
cryptography (339)
cryptology (339)
cryptosystem (341)
Data Encryption Standard (DES) (359)
deciphering (341)
decoding (341)
decrypting (341)
digital certificate (352)
digital signature (350)
elliptic curve cryptosystems (360)
enciphering (341)

Key Term Quiz

1. _____ scrambles _____ into ciphertext.

2. A system for making public keys available is called a _____.

3. There are essentially _____ types of encryption.

4. The encryption method where sender and receiver share the same key is called _____.

5. The _____ method and the _____ method are examples of encryption algorithms.

6. The _____ provides proof that the message was not altered.

7. The _____ determines the degree of long term robustness of the encryption.

8. PKIs provide _____ , _____ and _____ services.

9. The function that ensures that a sender cannot deny that they sent a message is called _____.

10. The key that can only decrypt a confidential message in a public key system is called the _____.

Multiple Choice Quiz

1. The main problem with secret key systems lies in
   a. keeping the key secret
   b. negotiating the key
   c. computation
   d. hashing

2. The main problem with public key systems lies in
   a. keeping keys secret
   b. negotiating the key
   c. computation
   d. hashing

3. Because it is used so much, the de facto standard for public key encryption is
   a. TCP/IP
   b. IDEA
   c. RSA
   d. one-time pad

4. Key length determines the
   a. degree of protection
   b. private key
   c. encryption
   d. level of secrecy

5. The codes differ from ciphers in that codes require a
   a. key
   b. book
   c. encryption algorithm
   d. third party

6. The difference between symmetric and asymmetric cryptosystems is
   a. with symmetric systems the key is symmetric
   b. with symmetric systems the key is public
   c. with symmetric systems the key is shared
   d. with symmetric systems the key is encrypted

7. From a processing standpoint, the most efficient key approach is
   a. cipher
   b. code

    c. public

    d. private

8. The correct term for a secret message is a

    a. encryptogram

    b. codegram

    c. cryptogram

    d. telegram

9. A message digest can be

    a. used for integrity checking

    b. used to disguise the plaintext

    c. used to transmit the public key

    d. used to spoof the sender

10. The advantage of a public key cryptosystem is that:

    a. they are much faster processing

    b. they allow the sender to send messages to multiple recipients

    c. they are perfectly secure

    d. two users can communicate securely without exchanging keys

Essay Quiz

1. The essence of a digital signature is that it ensures authentication. Explain how and why it does that.

2. What is the role of the Certificate Authority in a PKI? How are certificate authorities authenticated?

3. Why is randomness so important to key generation? What does a truly random system ensure?

4. What is the possible advantage of using a joint public-key/secret-key approach to key distribution?

5. Why is the ability to disguise the content of messages an important part of modern business practice?

6. Why are authentication and integrity checking such important dual functions? What would be the outcome if one or the other was missing?

7. What is the role of digital signatures in modern organizations? What would be the impact on e-commerce if it were not possible to authenticate an electronic document?

8. Key distribution is an important part of both kinds of encryption. What are the chief concerns associated with distributing keys in a secret key and in a public key cryptosystem? What causes each?

9. Elliptic curve cryptography appears to provide a very robust solution. However, it is not currently the system of choice. Why is that the case and why is that justification logical?

10. Having a message and its encrypted version in your possession is an easy way to break a cipher. Why is that true and what should the approach be if only the ciphertext was available.

Case Exercise

Complete the following case exercise as directed by your instructor.

Heavy Metal Technologies (HMT) is a defense contractor headquartered in Huntsville, Alabama. HMT was recently contracted by the Army to upgrade the fire control system for the MH64-D Apache Longbow attack helicopter. This is a field upgrade of a current analog system used in the Apache, thus the pilots of this helicopter want to have significant input into the requirements for the redesign of that system. Since the pilots want so much involvement, the Army is pushing to have individual field personnel, whom they will authorize, involved in the development process.

Consequently, there will be considerable teleconferencing from the Oceanside Main building between the HMT engineering staff and a selected group of pilots based at Fort Drum in upstate New York. There is concern that these teleconferences might be eavesdropped, so the Army would like HMT to propose a method for protecting these sessions. As such, you must propose a secure method for protecting these transmissions. Also, suggest an implementation approach for that proposed method. The Army would like as much detail as possible in this part of the proposal because this is a high-security national defense project.

Ensuring the Secure Use of Software

In this chapter, you will learn how to:

- Define the requirements of application and system software security
- Use processes for securing operating systems
- Structure and execute an operational process to secure applications
- Describe software assurance methods

The subject of **software assurance** appears more often than many topics in this text because the security of electronic information assets depends on the software that processes it.

Software is the weakest link in electronic security process because it both intangible and complex making it hard to ensure and trust. In Chapter 9, we presented several approaches for ensuring software against exploitable defects during development or acquisition. Prevention of defects in a commercial product does not worry most people. The chief concern for ordinary users is the secure *use* of their software.

Most successful attacks result from the exploitation of defects in commercial software. Many defects, such as buffer overflows and command injection flaws, are beyond the user control. However, there are important user actions including secure operating system configuration, secure network management, and ensuring that applications software does not breach security and integrity. Other concerns include secure management of databases, data transmission services, and encryption.

This chapter does not discuss every topic associated with effective software use. We focus on issues associated with using software securely including the secure configuration and maintenance of *system* and *application* software. It is important to understand and reliably operate the security-related functions embedded in a software portfolio.

A problem with application software is the number and diversity of commercial products available. Any product might contain serious, exploitable defects and the interaction of many products increases the risk. We discussed ways of avoiding the pitfall of diversity in Chapter 9 and we discussed attacks that target the application layer in Chapter 12. In this chapter, we examine the considerations associated with the configuration and subsequent maintenance of the security and integrity of both system-level and application software.

The types of software discussed in this chapter are in two categories—**system software** and **application software**. Systems software is a set of programs to control and support operations of a computer system. Systems software includes the communications control programs, compilers, program loaders, database management systems, operating systems, and service and systems utilities. Although not precise, the term "system software" is used interchangeably with the term "operating system." An **operating system** is a large, complex set of programs that coordinates and controls the internal functions of the machine including memory management and job scheduling. Application software is a program or group of programs designed to provide or support specific functions such as word processing, games, and graphics. Like system software, application software has security issues; however, the problems that relate to securing particular applications are different and usually less complex than those associated with systems software including the operating system.

Configuring the Operating System for Security

For most of the history of computing, operating systems were machine specific because the **hardware architecture** and the software designed to ensure its proper operation were inseparable. This is still true today in most mainframe situations. However, when users hear the term operating system, they think of either the Windows or the Macintosh environments and perhaps UNIX or Linux because of the influence of the personal computer on practically every aspect of information processing and use.

Because operating systems are a bundle of common, interacting, machine-level functions, the programmed configuration of that bundle determines the services the operating system provides. Consequently, if the programming of the operating system does not enable a certain function, it will never be available unless developed independently. Thus, the architectural design of the operating system determines the effectiveness of its security functionality.

The design process is the step when and where the security architecture is established. The overall security capability of the operating system is out of the hands of everybody but the architects and programmers who built it. Different security issues are linked to different operating systems and some operating systems are considered more or less secure than others.

In addition to providing basic preprogrammed functions, most commercially available operating systems also offer the capability to adapt functions provided by the system to meet the needs of a given environment. In the case of security, this is done by setting or altering the configuration settings. The settings determine how the services of the operating system will be made available to client applications. The coordination of operating system services should be transparent to the end user, so the administrator of the system usually configures the required security functions.

Security configurations vary with the requirements and it is possible that it will not be necessary upon installation to change the common assumptions built into the software by the manufacturer. One question must be answered in the configuration of all operating systems–How will access to the subjects and objects within the system be controlled?

Operating systems allow security administrators to embed trust relationships into the system processes by setting the access criteria for the files, directories, devices, and other data or code that reside within the system. That control involves the establishing and maintaining of the **access rights** of every user and process in the system.

One of the most important characteristics of good operating system architecture is the ability to easily and effectively establish and regulate access. That ability is tied directly to the administrator's ability to define an appropriately granular set of *types* and associated *rights* of the system's users and processes. We discuss these elements next, and then review **policies** and how they relate to operating system configurations.

Types: Assigning the Proper Label

Access control at the system level requires the definition of access types. The term **type** is a label. That label may apply to a structure, class, module, defined interface, or user. Types serve as the basis for making the automated decisions about the form of the access and the **permissions** that will be assigned to each request. This decision is made at the point where the request for access is presented.

The system must be able to associate a preprogrammed access decision with every type and mode of access when each request arrives because the decision-making that underlies access control is automated. Consequently, all types of users and access rights have to be established prior to accessing the system. This activity assigns the appropriate privileges and other permissions. These **rights** are configured by the system administrator within the operating system environment. The typing function establishes the identity and characteristics of all the objects within that environment.

Typing sets an appropriate label on the object for use by the system. The type is determined based on the attributes, roles, and relationships that each object possesses within the system when that an access is requested. The security concerns center on the correct specification of an accurate type label and the determination and enforcement of the associated privileges.

Establishing types is an ongoing function for system administrators. It is not visited once at system setup and never revisited. Access privileges have to be assigned at the permission level for each type and updated, monitored, and revoked as conditions change. If done correctly, it should be possible for the operating system to determine what access to provide from a range of potential **access permissions** assigned to a given user or process type.

The criteria for making that decision are maintained within the operating system. The mechanism for implementation is called a *reference monitor*. The reference monitor is software that is interposed between all subjects and objects within the system.

The reference monitor regulates how subjects can access objects within the environment. A reference monitor first automatically logs a request for access and then provides explicit **authorization** for access by referencing a self-contained database of stored criteria. The reference monitor is always invoked, tamper-proof, and small/verifiable.

The reference monitor is a programming abstraction. In most cases, the concrete instantiation of the actual reference monitor may be as simple as an application program interface (API) that between the requesting function and the operating system kernel. However, the formal definition of the reference monitor requires it to be integral to the operating system. To ensure that system-level requests for access are handled without interference, it is vital to ensure an efficient interaction between the reference monitor and the operating system. In that respect, the reference monitor might be instantiated in hardware, firmware, or software as part of the overall operating system environment.

Reference monitors provide four types of service:

1. They link access control to a set of specified policies.

2. They monitor and regulate access based on policies.

3. They allow policies to be updated easily.

4. They log the degree of conformance of the accumulated requests.

Decision criteria embedded in the policies can enforce temporal, transactional, or even mandatory access control. Access permissions are granted based on those criteria, monitored during the period of access, and automatically enforced by the operating system. Figure 14-1 illustrates this process.

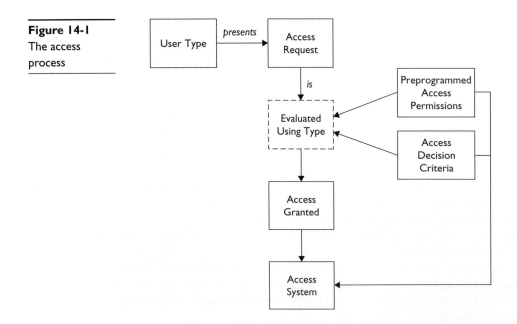

Figure 14-1
The access process

Rights: Ensuring the Proper Access

Access authorization is only part of the control issue. The other part is rights management. A user's right to access the system is not tied to their right to view or use the information assets on it. *Rights* are the specific controls, restrictions, and rules granted to a given subject upon access or which apply to a particular object. Essentially, the rights a subject is granted define the amount of information and the level of detail that can be accessed.

To be secure, those rights are assigned and managed for each access attempt. Rights are granted by the administrator. The administrator pre-establishes the actions that a subject takes with respect to an object. That includes the classic read, write, execute, or delete actions. A common way of doing this is through internal access control tables, which may be part of the reference monitor. This is similar to the access control lists (ACL) discussed in Chapter 6 that controlled network access. Nevertheless, they are also a prime means of regulating access to objects within the system itself. The process of assigning rights within that table enforces the separation of privilege function for each user and process.

Every object has a unique identifier or label associated with it. The label identifies the object to all relevant ACLs within the system. It specifies the level of permission or privilege required to access, read from, write to, or execute the object.

A system administrator should be the only one authorized to configure and maintain an ACL, because system-based access control lists are intricate and difficult to maintain. For the system to work properly, the ACLs have to be updated regularly. This becomes more complex since ACLs are set up and maintained differently in different operating systems. A reasonable degree of technical proficiency is required.

An access control list can be applied to any subject or object, such as a file, a directory, or some other means of encapsulating information. Although they are an efficient way of contain the properties to regulate access, they do not provide the granularity necessary to ensure that access rights have been assigned correctly in all cases. That is a security concern since the assignment of rights must be correct under all conditions.

The assignment of rights determines the access privileges granted to a given object at a particular time. That is not as simple as it sounds since the rights granted depend on all of the variables associated with the process making the request. Processes are tasks that are executing within the operating system at a given time. The operating system balances all running processes to allow them to work together in a safe and predictable fashion.

To make the decisions about what system resources to grant, the operating system has to know what rights the process has at that time given the conditions of the request. Therefore, the information about each object and running process within the system is kept as a dynamic entry in a system table. The entries in those tables specify the access rights of each current user, or group of users, with respect to the specific resident objects within the system at that time including running applications, processes, and files.

Policies and Operating System Configuration

Policies establish the access control requirements implemented and enforced by the operating system at its **interfaces**. As we said in Chapter 3, policy is critical to the security process because it determines and shapes the form of the control environment. For instance, access control actions will be considerably different if the policies that guide the access are based on a model such as Bell-LaPadula or Biba or both. Policy clearly exists outside of the software environment, proper policy setting is essential to maintaining the secure software environment.

Both the reference monitor and the concept of operating system control are driven by policies. Every attempt to access the system must be evaluated and acted upon through a deliberate policy implemented by the software within in the computer's control function. Subsequently, the criteria for ongoing satisfaction of those policies continue to be enforced by the operating system. Once access is granted, the session is monitored and controlled to ensure the ongoing compliance of all running processes with all requirements. Compliance is based on the ongoing ability of each process to satisfy all the criteria set for it, as well as the satisfaction of other conditions that might be set to identify conformity. Detected violations must invoke some form of automated corrective action within the system.

From an operating system standpoint, if no criteria are available to judge conformity, the result will be to do nothing. Absent policy, if a violation occurs the most likely consequence would be that it would not be detected and no corrective action would be taken. Since a lack of action is an undesirable security condition, it is important to ensure that every reasonable action of the system can be related to an established policy. Remember, policies do not happen by chance; they have to be created and maintained. An element of any process to ensure secure configuration and software use is a management commitment to establish an inclusive set of reference policies.

A complete and correct set of policies ensures a high degree of organizational control at the automatic or system level because they guarantee that system operations will be aligned with the **security requirements** of the organization. In addition to the level of assurance this approach provides, the benefit of developing and embedding security policies directly into the operating system is that it makes the management of systems resources more efficient. A high level of automated assurance is an important consideration when it comes to the organization's applications operations.

Application Management Software and Security

Up to this point, we have discussed the operating system. Operating systems control the basic functions of the machine. However, the value of the computer lies in the applications that it runs. Applications are written to carry out a required task. Although they are highly complex, the instances of operating system software are limited to a few commercial products. Application software programs, on the other hand, are as varied as the tasks they perform, so the number of commercial applications is large.

In the case of applications, the aim of the security function is to minimize harm that might occur through malicious action or misuse of the software. Application security includes the measures installed to secure the applications themselves, as well as the practices to configure and manage securely subsequent application use. Both minimize the likelihood that malicious individuals will be able to modify, delete, or steal information assets associated with a given application.

Application assurance is an increasingly critical area of concern because Internet applications no longer load and operate in isolation. Now, many interactions of applications have to be assured, both within the enterprise's own operating environment and from the actions of external agents. This assurance is gained by first identifying threats and then ensuring against application vulnerabilities by patching them or reconfiguring the system to prevent exploitation.

As we said in Chapter 12 when discussing network security, the primary means for external attack against applications comes through exploitation of faults in the application layer. Those faults are exploited in one of two ways: they can be the subject of a direct attack by outsiders over the network or they can be attacked from within the machine by insertion of malicious code.

The Scope of Application Security

The easiest way to secure an application is to ensure that security vulnerabilities are not created in the first place. However, the problem is that most developers focus on establishing functionality, rather than security. Since it is possible to write a program that operates properly, but is insecure, the distinction between these two issues has to be kept in mind when the application is created.

Ensuring Applications: The Necessity of Secure Use

In Chapter 9, we explained the importance of testing and review processes to assure code under development. There is a second, perhaps more critical, area of software assurance, which is *secure use*. Secure use is made up of the actions that must take place to ensure the security of the software while it is in the operational environment. Secure use provides assurance that the software will continue to achieve its confidentiality, integrity, and availability goals. Secure use establishes the appropriate level of confidence in the entire portfolio of software items because all software is inter-connected.

The process of secure use assures an adequate level of confidence by guaranteeing the organization's ability to identify and record problems; analyze those problems; take the appropriate corrective, adaptive, perfective, or preventive action; and then confirm the restored capability. The process of secure use for any software item ends when it is retired.

Forms of Secure Use

The secure-use process can be either **proactive** or **reactive**. Proactive activities include the identification of threats and vulnerabilities; the creation, assessment, and optimization of security solutions for software that within the architecture of the system; and implementation of organizational controls to protect the software and the information that it processes. Reactive activities include threat response, the detection of and reaction to external or internal intrusions or security violations, and disaster recovery.

Operational assurance, **operational analysis**, and **problem-resolution** processes underlie and ensure both proactive and reactive security. Operational assurance detects intrusions, violations, inappropriate use, and latent vulnerabilities. The operational analysis function involves operational monitoring, testing, and assessment of software performance to determine the form of a resolution. The problem-resolution process ensures that a proper solution is in place to address all identified weaknesses.

The operational analysis function facilitates understanding of the risk represented by any threat detected through the operational **assurance process**. It assesses the frequency of occurrence and impact. It identifies and evaluates all risk avoidance, risk mitigation, and risk transfer options. The problem-resolution process then selects the appropriate remediation option. Problem-resolution also monitors and assures any changes required and ensures the correct reintegration of these changes to the code, settings, or associated policies.

Types of Response

In the case of proactive assurance, the response can be *preventive, perfective,* or *adaptive.* In the case of reactive assurance, the only option is some type of *corrective* or *emergency* response.

Preventive action is the identification and detection of vulnerabilities. Perfective action involves the improvement of the performance, dependability, and maintainability of the software. Adaptive action adapts the software to a new or changed environment, for example, a new operating system with enhanced security. On the other hand, corrective action involves the identification and removal of vulnerabilities and correction of errors while emergency response involves unscheduled corrective action.

Security requires complete, accurate, and unambiguous understanding of the software, at its most basic level as well as how the software interconnects with the entire portfolio. The way the software receives, processes, or transmits data must be a matter of certainty. The certainty must extend to the status of attached users and software. Figure 14-2 illustrates this. Examining each element of the diagram would produce

Figure 14-2
High-level representation of the elements of software interaction

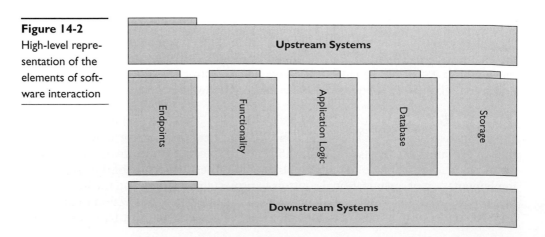

a detailed understanding of the actual nodes with their installed components and interrelationships.

Operational Assurance

Operational assurance is a proactive function. Operational assurance uses defined policies, procedures, tools, and standards to monitor, test, and review the software within its operational environment to detect vulnerabilities or violations. This function should be performed on a continuous basis.

Operational assurance identifies and resolves latent security and control weaknesses present within the software, the data it processes, or its associated policies. Operational assurance is not limited just to application software but extends into the operating environment surrounding applications because vulnerabilities can arise from defects in the application software, operating system software, network or device configurations, policies and procedures, security mechanisms, physical security, and employee usage,.

As we said in Chapter 9, technical assurance practices include intrusion detection, penetration testing, and violation processing using clipping levels. Periodic performance **reviews** are also a required activity; they evaluate the software, the system, the policies and procedures, and the users' activities against established standards. Those reviews consist of walkthroughs, **inspections**, or managerial and technical audits.

Detected threats, vulnerabilities, and violations are managed using a defined problem reporting and problem-resolution process. The problem-resolution process must be tailored to allow decision makers to authorize appropriate responses based on their risk assessment.

To do operational assurance correctly, the software must already be in a known and assured state. The state must be understood and documented fully. To start the operational assurance process, validate every aspect of the security functions in the current software configuration, as well as assure that the security functions are enabled.

Operational assurance is accomplished by monitoring the ongoing function of the software within the operational environment. Thus, operational assurance is carried out in a disciplined and regularly scheduled fashion using a continuous operational testing plan.

Threats are always in the environment. In addition to the software function, the operating environment that surrounds the software has to be monitored to identify security threats, exposures, vulnerabilities, and violations as they arise. This part of the process is termed "threat identification." Threats are identified using threat models. Many current threat-modeling techniques are derived from a Microsoft-originated process based on data flow diagramming.

Once an incident is identified, it must be reported through a standard process. This process responds as rapidly as possible to problems arising from an attempt to exploit a vulnerability or malfunction. That process must have standard procedures, and must be fully documented. The process must also be well understood within the organization. Therefore, the institutionalization of a systematic trouble-reporting procedure is a requisite of good practice.

Trouble reporting is a controversial part of the process. If vulnerability is not reported promptly, it may be exploited. On the other hand, if the vulnerability cannot be repaired immediately, a leak of the trouble report may stimulate exploitation. The current thinking is that vulnerabilities should be reported to a secure central entity designated to coordinate the response. However, widespread disclosure should be discouraged.

Ensuring Operational Effectiveness: Making the Assurance Case

The operational assurance function is important to security. Therefore, the conduct of the process should also be assured. To ensure that operational assurance is done correctly, the organization should assess and audit the policies, procedures, tools, and standards used for operational assurance. The organization should document those assessments and audits and make recommendations for improvement of the operational assurance process.

Various types of proof can be used to maintain an assurance case for the operational assurance process. That includes evidence that

- An organizationally standard procedure manual is in place, which details the steps for every activity in the operational assurance process. That should include the itemization of expected results and a measure to determine that they have been achieved.
- A set of organizationally sanctioned actions, procedures, or protocols that can be invoked when an *anticipated* threat occurs has been established.
- A set of organizationally sanctioned actions, procedures, or protocols that will be invoked when an *unforeseen* hazard occurs has been developed.
- The specific method for incident reporting or requesting change and the procedures for responding to each report have been documented.
- A process is in place to ensure that the Business Continuity Plan is kept up to date.
- All of the relevant members of the organization know precisely what activities they have to carry out with respect to secure use and the timing requirements for performing them.
- The precise steps taken to build awareness of correct practice, including a formal employee education and training program, have been documented.
- Each employee's specific education, training, and awareness activities have been documented.
- The explicit enforcement requirements and consequences for non-compliance for every job title have been documented.
- Specification and evidence of personal agreement to the consequences for non-compliance have been documented.
- Enforcement has been practiced on a continuous basis and as an organization-wide commitment.

Operational Analysis

Operational analysis directly supports operational assurance. It evaluates the consequences of vulnerabilities or violations identified during the operational assurance process. The goal of operational analysis is to understand the effect of identified threats along with the impact of recommended responses. For the analysis to produce valid results, all software, systems, policies, processes, or objectives affected by that threat must be included in the evaluation.

This wide range of consideration is necessary to ensure a coordinated response. The operational analysis process identifies the software components influenced by a given threat. That identification extends through all cascading or ripple effects. The specific items of software selected are then examined to determine the impacts of any prospective response. The analysis must be comprehensive, including not only technical considerations but such related questions as the return on investment.

All impacts on existing software and the security implications must be fully analyzed and communicated to the problem-resolution function. Documentation should be standardized to ensure the communication is complete. It may be necessary to replicate or verify the existence of the problem to understand the nature and implications of the vulnerability and to develop a response strategy.

A specific response strategy must be developed for each software components to be changed. The response strategy must ensure the integrity of each interface associated with the software. Relevant security policies should be identified in that process. Areas of consideration in the development of a response strategy might include

1. The effect of any response on the assurance case

2. The type of violation, exposure, or vulnerability, and the threat that might exploit it

3. The scope of the impact of the violation, exposure, or vulnerability

4. The **criticality** of the violation, exposure, or vulnerability

5. The feasible options for response

6. The likelihood and feasibility of occurrence

7. The safety and security impacts if a response *is not* implemented—based on the likelihood of occurrence and financial and operational impacts

8. The implications of any proposed response as they affect the organization's procedural infrastructure

9. The resource requirements, staff capability, required to implement the response

10. The feasibility and timelines for implementation

Once all considerations relevant to the operational analysis are addressed, communicate the body of evidence developed to the decision maker for authorized resolution. The results of the analysis should be reported with a full explanation of the required remediation. This report must clearly outline the effect of each option while being plain and understandable. Because it is not the function of the operational analysis process to make the decision, all feasible remediation options must be presented. Finally, the recommendations must be fully and demonstrably traceable to the business case.

Problem Resolution

The problem-resolution process ensures the integrity of the system or software product is maintained throughout its life cycle. The activities associated with problem-resolution revolve around establishing and maintaining control mechanisms sufficiently rigorous to ensure that defects or problems reported and documented will be resolved in the shortest time possible.

The people responsible for ensuring problem-resolution do not actually do the work; they oversee the effort. The problem-resolution process provides a timely, reliable, and explicit means of assuring that problems identified during operational assurance are resolved via some other formal organizational process such as software development. Because software solutions are dynamic and subject to changes in the technology, problem-resolution ensures that any new information or emerging trends arising out of the actual implementation of the authorized solution are reported, recognized, and remediated.

The problem-resolution process guarantees the satisfactory resolution of reported threats or violations brought to its attention. Therefore, the problem-resolution report must provide a detailed description of the threat or violation as well as the analysis and decision-making process adopted to resolve it. As part of the **problem resolution**, the process must confirm the long-term effectiveness of the proposed solution. Finally, the problem-resolution process must maintain a full set of documentation items sufficient to warrant that the integrity of the software has been satisfactorily assured.

The Importance of Problem-Resolution in Application Assurance

Problem-resolution is sometimes established by contract. However, its purpose is to ensure that concerns involving threats arising from the operational use of software do not persist. As such, problem-resolution is normally conducted as a closed-loop activity. Reported instances of threat, violation, or non-conformance must be resolved and signed off on before the problem-resolution can be concluded. The process must ensure that each reported problem is resolved quickly and that participants know what that resolution was. The knowledge gained from the elimination of given problems ensures the ongoing improvement of the security and safety features of a software product. This final requirement implies the need for ongoing comprehensive analysis and tracking of problems as well as careful record keeping.

Although it is a small and isolated function, problem-resolution is the basis for organizational assurance of the entire software portfolio and thus it is a critical process. That is one reason why, where security is concerned, the requirement for a formal problem-resolution process is always embedded in the contract.

Problem-resolution ensures coordination and assurance of the chosen remediation option. Remember, problem-resolution does not do the actual remediation. With software that is most often done through the software development process. Instead, it is the role of problem-resolution to oversee and then warrant the correctness of the remediation solution. Since problem-resolution plays a key oversight role, the policies, tools, and standards that are employed by it must also be continuously assessed so that recommendations can be made to enhance the process.

Responsibilities of the Process When Resolution Is Not Required

There may be operational justification for not resolving a problem or for not resolving it as soon as possible. Those reasons might be established by factors such as the amount of time and resources required to implement the resolution. The justification might include lack of current resources, difficulty, or infeasibility of the repair, or an unwillingness to take down a critical operational system. In addition to assuring a proper solution, another responsibility of the problem-resolution process is to ensure that known vulnerabilities are continuously monitored for changes in the conditions that supported the original decision to avoid addressing the risk.

In the case of the decision not to address a risk immediately, the role of the problem-resolution function is to maintain a continuous and complete record of all publicly and privately known vulnerabilities. The operational behavior of the system must be monitored to detect the presence of attempts to exploit an identified vulnerability. One way of doing that is to automate alarms to inform the problem-resolution process of attempts to exploit a known weakness. The process should also maintain a systematic and well-defined preplanned response to attempted exploit of an identified weakness. That requires the system staff to maintain continuous awareness of the correct response to attempts to exploit a vulnerability that is already being tracked.

Ensuring the Effectiveness of the Resolution

The process must ensure that the agent who is doing the actual work fully understands the requirements and restrictions of the solution because problem-resolution does not actually construct the solution. Thus, the problem-resolution process must convey all the technical, behavioral, and qualitative requirements of the remediation option to the agent providing the solution. Therefore, organizationally persistent controls have to be established to ensure that the correct information is transmitted. Consequently, it is good practice to always

- Identify the appropriate change agent—this may be either an acquisition or a development entity within the organization.
- Develop and document a statement of work (SOW) and communicate it to the selected change agent.
- Develop and document the criteria that will be used to test and evaluate the software to ensure that the remediation was successful.
- Communicate these criteria to the change agent prior to institution of the change process.
- Develop and document criteria for ensuring that the elements and requirements of the software that must not be modified remain unaffected.

Reintegration: Operationalizing the Solution

Eventually, every solution must be reintegrated into the array of day-to-day functioning applications. The decision maker who authorized the resolution in the first place must provide the approval to perform the reintegration of the solution into the operational system functions. This approval must be accompanied by proof that the issues from the last section were satisfactorily resolved.

Once the authorization to re-integrate is obtained, the resolution or repair is embedded back into the operational system. Because a lot of things that looked perfectly acceptable during the testing process can suddenly look different when a piece of code is reintroduced into its operating environment, it is necessary to undertake a technically rigorous process to ensure that the reintegration is successful and satisfies all security goals. As such, all reintegrations are supported by a comprehensive testing program.

The reintegration testing program must be designed at the beginning of the resolution process. Reintegration testing is specified when the change agent puts together the actual plan to do the work. The reintegration testing must certify that the resolution is satisfactory and that the software and the interfaces function properly.

In addition to certifying the correctness of the reintegration, it is also necessary to update and fully document the new software **baseline** configuration. This baseline is then maintained under strict configuration management control. As such, prior to placing the changed item under **configuration management**, it is good practice to confirm that the reintegration has achieved the desired level of integrity and security. Then the documentation is updated to reflect the new level of integrity and security of the software.

Ensuring the Integrity of the Solution Post-Change

Changes to software may eliminate vulnerabilities. However, changes also create new ones. Consequently, attackers examine any changed code to decide about new or different exploitations. Therefore, the system staff must also continue to oversee and analyze the effects of problem-resolution after the solution has been implemented. This requirement is fulfilled by performing operational testing regularly on the changed code and reporting test results to the appropriate decision maker.

Monitoring and evaluation must continue to occur even after a resolution has been provided. The goal is to understand the long-term consequences of changes. Therefore, it is good practice to ensure an in-depth follow-up examination of the changed code. This examination must take place within the operational environment of the software to identify potential points where the resolution was not satisfactory or where future exploitation might take place. This can be done by penetration-testing, load-testing, or other stress-testing methods. The idea is to identify any new points of weakness or potential failure. The examination process continues until the designated decision maker determines that the resolution is satisfactory.

In addition, the problem-resolution process should update the range of countermeasures deployed to enforce the security status and requirements of the software. It might be necessary to modify the assurance case to ensure that the resolution is persistent and addresses the weakness identified by the operational assurance process.

Although the change is implemented through the agency of another process, either acquisition or development, it is the responsibility of the problem-resolution process to ensure that the resolution has met all established criteria.

The post-change analysis process is often continuous because changes are complex. It can even involve the joint review of the solution and any additional problem resolutions between representatives of the change agent and representatives of the stakeholders. It is good practice to monitor the resolution development through joint reviews because they encourage wider perspectives and promote buy-in. These reviews are specified in an overall statement of work.

In addition, problem-resolution must ensure that all reviews specified by the project plan are conducted at their scheduled checkpoints. Finally, problem-resolution is also responsible for ensuring that any action item that issued out of a checkpoint review is recorded, overseen, and then closed out.

Management Responsibilities for Problem Resolution

Problem-resolution ensures that a review or audit specified by the statement of work is properly resourced and satisfactorily executed. As the name implies, the duty of problem resolution is to ensure that testing, audit, or review findings involving non-concurrence are satisfactorily resolved. That might include official activities such as monitoring service levels as specified in the statement of work that supports the resolution, as well as overseeing the execution of specific actions to ensure that service levels are maintained.

In particular, problem-resolution ensures that problems identified through testing, reviews, and audits are resolved. The decision maker responsible for managing the resolution process must certify that non-concurrences identified in the testing and review process were addressed and that the problem-resolution process was properly managed are performed.

That includes providing documentary evidence that resource considerations were factored into the initial authorizations. It might also require evidence that the resolution was authorized by the proper organizational authority and documentation of an approved schedule or timetable. It might include providing evidence of a capable status-accounting function that involved the use of established baselines for each software item and the ability to document the current state of the software at all times.

Certification and Accreditation of Applications

To ensure confidence in a software portfolio, the critical applications should always be assessed and identified as secure by an appropriate agent. This must be done using a commonly accepted process. The findings of that process are accredited by formal certification. To ensure that the security is persistent, re-accreditation of the results obtained by an initial certification process should be confirmed on a periodic basis. This ensures continuing confidence in the software. Intervals for re-accreditation are specified by organizational policy and/or external regulation.

Good practice requires that a legitimate third-party agency conduct formal certification audits. The audit standard should be established by regulation or contract. Assessments for certification/recertification of accreditation must be performed by properly certified lead auditors, and adequate resources must be provided to ensure the effectiveness of the audit process.

The independence of the auditing/accrediting organization must be assured and consistent use of a standard audit method must be guaranteed. Recertification audits should be performed on a timely enough basis to ensure that the software continues to function as intended.

The Role of Audit in Certifying Applications

Because of its rigor and thoroughness, an effective audit process is the best mechanism for ensuring the integrity of the applications within an organization's software portfolio. An organization employs the *audit* process when it has to certify beyond a doubt that a system or software product has met the requirements for safety and security.

Audit is normally a responsibility of the customer organization at the time of system acceptance; thus, audit and **acceptance testing** have tended to be seen in the same terms. However, because of the increasing importance of security in application deployment and use, ongoing certification audits are increasingly important in the assurance process.

The principal condition required for the audit process is the independence of the auditing agent. This entity must be empowered and able to operate independent of the group undergoing the audit. It must be guaranteed that an audit is based on objective evidence and that it is conducted in a completely unbiased fashion. Accordingly, the auditing agent must be situated sufficiently far enough from the group being audited to ensure impartial execution of the audit procedure.

To that end, the Common Criteria, discussed in the next section, has established a formal certification infrastructure of trusted independent evaluation labs for the universal certification of the security levels of application software. This initiative is called the National Information Assurance Partnership (NIAP) conducted under the sponsorship of the National Security Agency (NSA).

The NIAP provides a third-party organization independent evaluation and certification of software products and producers. Third-party agencies are accredited through the National Voluntary Laboratory Accreditation Program (NVLAP), which is operated in conjunction with NSA and the National Institute of Standards and Technology (NIST). The NVLAP serves as the accreditation body for certification of NIAP Common Criteria Testing Laboratories (CCTLs).

Organizing the Audit Process for Security

To be correct, the audit must be based on accepted auditing standards. An accepted standard for auditing application security is the Common Criteria, but this varies based on the situation. Once an auditor has been identified and the audit arranged, the auditing entity is responsible for planning the audit work. That work must be done in accordance with the applicable audit standard and it must address the specified audit objectives. The task of the auditor during the course of the actual audit is to gather sufficient reliable, pertinent, and practical evidence to demonstrate that the audit objectives can be achieved.

At the point where the audit is deemed complete, objective data and conclusions obtained by the audit must be authenticated by a suitable analysis and justified through a careful consideration of the meaning of that evidence. Upon the completion of the audit work, the auditing agent is responsible for providing a report in correct form to the appropriate recipients.

The audit report describes the scope, objectives, and duration of the examination, as well as the particulars of the work performed. The audit report identifies the organization audited and the intended recipients of the report and states restrictions on circulation. The report presents and clarifies findings. In addition, it contains a set of logical conclusions drawn from the analysis of the data, as well as the recommendations that flow from the evidence.

Common Criteria: Ensuring Confidence in Commercial Software

Because the ability to certify security is particularly important with commercial application software, an international standard is used. That is the ISO 15408 standard, which has been dubbed the Common Criteria, discussed from the developer's standpoint in Chapter 9. Now we would like to examine the same standard from the perspective of how the right set of security attributes is certified for the software itself.

The Common Criteria provides a catalogue of attributes that should be present in any secure application. As a result, the standard can serve as the basis for assessment and formal certification of any software product. For instance, a Common Criteria assessment level, or evaluation assurance level (EAL), is often required for formal software acquisitions by the federal government.

As the name suggests, the Common Criteria are a set of commonly recognized characteristics found in trusted systems. The aim of the Common Criteria evaluation process is to provide a rigorous examination of the security capabilities of software products by testing for an exhaustive set of useful attributes employed to benchmark the required security behaviors. The Common Criteria enumerate known security attributes that can be confirmed through direct observation. The standard is considered complete and satisfies overall security requirements for most applications.

What Does the Common Criteria do for Application Security?

The Common Criteria provide an encyclopedic collection of standardized security properties, any one of which might be adapted to a situation depending on the requirements driving the process. The eleven generic areas of security in the standard are

1. Security audit
2. Data communication
3. Cryptographic support
4. User data protection
5. Identification and authentication

6. Security management

7. Privacy

8. Protection of the security function

9. Resource utilization

10. Access

11. Trusted path/channels

These categories are elaborated in detail by 68 criteria for evaluation. The categories range from requirements such as security-audit data generation through cryptographic key management and fault tolerance. The influence of the Common Criteria continues to grow because of its importance as a tool for commercial software certification and government backing.

Ensuring an Effective Security Architecture

Security functions do not magically appear in software. They have to be designed and coded into both operating system and applications programs. That process is a **security architecture**, which is the way the security requirements are represented while "architecture" describes the discrete, formal process that assures the development of a tangible structure from a set of intangible requirements. Figure 14-3 illustrates security architecture.

Figure 14-3
Security
architecture

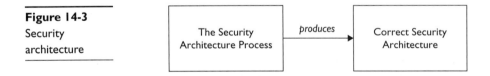

Security architecture maintains a dynamic response to security threats and implies the ongoing development, deployment, and continuous maintenance of the most appropriate set of tools, frameworks, and components to assure the security of software. Security is planned, designed, and administered within a structure of control elements.

The purpose of security architecture is to ensure that the organization's software assets are protected by an effective defense. The current thinking with respect to the form of that architecture is to develop a defense in depth. In practical terms, a defense in depth secures the system at every potential level of access. Figure 14-4 illustrates this process.

Figure 14-4
Software defense
in depth

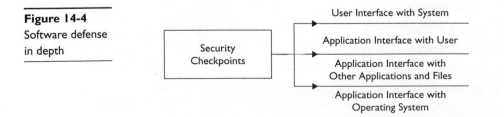

The idea behind a **defense in depth** is to slow potential attackers by forcing them to take the time to solve defenses of every level. While this is happening, the defenders can defend effectively.

Defense in depth applies to application software security in the same way that it applies to the assurance of networks. The aim of a defense in depth is to prevent one compromised element from infecting another part of the system through **segmentation**. Segmentation is easy when designing something like a castle but more difficult when the medium is software. Therefore, defense in depth, segmentation, and compartmentalization should be viewed as an exercise in elegant architectural design.

Database Security

Since the objective of information assurance is to protect the organization's data, the security of the database management system is a paramount concern. Given the issues of access and **interoperability**, databases are a major source of risk because they are secured by security functions built into the applications that access them. This works well if the source of the access is internal and well controlled. It is a problem if the access is from external sources or originates from a place that is not properly controlled by the organization, such as the Internet.

To ensure the security of databases, it is necessary to develop a system architecture that implements robust security functions within the database software. This security function is developed from a comprehensive risk and **vulnerability assessment** and is refined further by the installation of **real-time detection** capabilities within the database management system (DBMS). These real-time safeguards alert database operators of unauthorized access attempts or efforts to change database contents. The detection and warning system is always established based on a predefined set of rules, which are set by the database administrators.

The detection and warning capacity is implemented by software utilities capable of discriminating between various types of data and selectively exercising the controls assigned to each of them. This is based on criteria built into the security programming for the database. A content-driven access model often defines that process.

The definitions of the data to be controlled are set using the modeling techniques that we have just discussed. The access restrictions are based on the usual set of access control functions, such as logins/accounts, passwords, roles, and privileges. This capability is further supported through rigorous logging of database actions and the performance of ongoing audits of those logs to confirm that the protection is secure.

Chapter 14 Review

Chapter Summary

- Software comes in two functional categories: system and application.
- System software is made up of those programs that are specifically designed to control internal functions, including loading, storing, and executing other programs.

- System software is understood in terms of the operating system.
- The operating system contains the necessary instructions that the computer must have to correctly manage its own resources.
- Application software is the entity that is responsible for fulfilling the specific functional or business needs of the user.
- The term "application" describes a program or program group that is specifically designed to achieve a desired operational outcome.
- Defects that are introduced into a piece of software in the construction phase always constitute a potential security vulnerability.
- To have a possibility of developing a successful, defect-free piece of software, a disciplined set of practices has to be adopted and followed.
- The conventional area of the industry that is responsible for doing this is called software assurance.
- Software assurance, in the context of this text, warrants that the security and control features are collectively and individually free of vulnerabilities.
- Software assurance is nominally made up of six large processes: Software Quality Assurance (SQA), Configuration Management, **Verification**, **Validation**, Audit, and Problem Resolution.
- Security architecture describes the formal design and approach that is used to build the system in such a way that it satisfies specified security requirements.
- **Specifications** are almost always developed as part of a formal software engineering process.
- The outcome of the process is an explicit understanding and documented description of every design element, what will be required to implement each function, and the inherent relationships between elements that are embodied in the design.
- A lot of the particulars of good architecture are oriented toward defining and implementing the modes of operation needed to adequately secure the operating system.
- Accordingly, the common-sense approach to correct security architecture is to embed the security functionality directly into the system kernel itself.
- In practice, operating systems implement the security policies that are set for them.
- In security, types are used to guide the decision that the system will make about the appropriate access mode.
- It should be possible to define a range of possible access permissions for a given user or system type based on criteria that are set for it. These criteria can be temporal, transactional, or even defined.
- Permissions are then monitored and automatically controlled by the operating system.

- Breaches can occur in a system unless adequate consideration is given to security issues during the development and implementation phases.

- The essence of defense in depth is segmentation of the protective array.

- The only way that this can be assured is through proper software design.

- Reliability is underwritten by the probability that a component or system will operate without failure for a given time, in a given environment.

- **Causal analysis** allows an organization to tell what software structural and development characteristics are predictive of vulnerabilities, both in a causative and symptomatic sense.

- The easiest and most effective way to obtain a security reliability estimate is to employ one of a number of useful modeling approaches to underwrite the understanding of **system behavior**.

- To ensure the security of the organization's databases, the overall system architecture has to be developed to embody a set of security functions that lie within the database itself.

Key Terms

acceptance testing (382)
access permissions (369)
access rights (369)
application software (368)
assurance process (374)
authorization (370)
baseline (380)
causal analysis (387)
configuration management (380)
criticality (377)
defense in depth (385)
hardware (368)
inspections (375)
interfaces (372)
interoperability (385)
operating system (368)
operational analysis (374)
operational assurance (374)
permissions (369)
policies (369)
problem resolution (378)
reactive (373)
real-time detection (385)
reviews (375)
rights (369)

Key Term Quiz

Use terms from the Key Terms list to complete the following sentences. Not all terms will be used.

1. The _____ describes how the system operates.

2. _____ is a process that attempts to predict vulnerabilities from defects.

3. There are essentially _____ types of software: _____ and _____.

4. The function that ensures that changes to software are rationally controlled is called _____.

5. The term that describes the functionality that will be built into the software is called _____.

6. _____ is the basis for establishing a defense in depth.

7. _____ are the privileges assigned a given access.

8. The establishment of privilege is based on a label, which is also termed a _____.

9. The process that has to do with ongoing assurance of the software portfolio is called _____.

10. The process that supports decision making about changes to the software is called _____.

Multiple Choice Quiz

1. A vulnerability is a defect that should be
   a. found
   b. fixed by the manufacturer
   c. eliminated
   d. ignored

2. The main problem with using applications to secure operating systems is

   a. there are none

   b. they have defects

   c. inefficient processing

   d. cost

3. Security is best established by following a disciplined and comprehensive

   a. program

   b. project

   c. process

   d. routine

4. Databases are hard to secure where the accesses come from

   a. outside

   b. inside

   c. people

   d. networks

5. Validation assures that the product

   a. meets specifications

   b. works right

   c. is secure

   d. is built right

6. Secure use processes can be either reactive or

   a. not present

   b. efficient

   c. effective

   d. proactive

7. Operating systems are

   a. a bundle of inter-operating programs and services

   b. similar to applications in their purpose

   c. the basis for must security

   d. scary

8. The process that ensures rapid response to threats is called:

   a. firefighting

   b. eternal vigilance

   c. trouble reporting

   d. risk assessment

9. The reference monitor ensures

   a. the proper references are assigned

   b. the proper privileges are assigned

   c. that policies are maintained

   d. that the system functions efficiently

10. The primary problem with applications security is that it is possible to write a program that

    a. will not run properly

    b. will run properly and then stop

    c. will run properly and is secure

    d. will run properly and be insecure

Essay Quiz

1. The essence of software assurance lies in following good software engineering procedure. Specifically, how does that procedure aid security?

2. Defects cause vulnerabilities, but are defects vulnerabilities? If not, why not? Give an example.

3. What is the role of the configuration manager in subcontractor work? Why is it important to security?

4. SQA and configuration management are the cornerstones of defect prevention. Why is that the case? What does each process contribute?

5. Why is defense in depth important in application and system software security? What does it provide and how easy is it to obtain? What are some of the obstacles?

6. The essence of operational assurance is the presence of a reviews and inspections. How do these processes ensure operational assurance?

7. The purpose of operational analysis is to support decision making about how to react to problems. How exactly does operational assurance do that and what is the primary element that underlies the process?

8. The conclusion of the problem-resolution process must be authorized. Why is it important to do that? What would be the consequences if it were not?

9. Policies are essential to establishing and configuring the reference monitoring function. Why is that true? What would happen if a policy were not available to guide reference monitoring?

10. The occurrence of incidents should be reported through a well-established and standard process. What is likely to happen if the process was not standardized?

Case Exercise

Complete the following case exercise as directed by your instructor.

Heavy Metal Technologies (HMT) is a defense contractor headquartered in Huntsville, Alabama. HMT was recently contracted by the Army to upgrade the fire control system for the MH64-D Apache Longbow attack helicopter. HMT has determined that about 9,000 source lines of code (SLOC) will have to be developed and/or modified. The condition of the existing legacy software is not known and the customer wants formal documentation of the security of the interface between legacy and new software modules. The Army (acquirer) has contracted to supply a System/Subsystem Specification (SSS), a System Design Description (SSDD), and an Operational Concept Document (OCD). HMT will be responsible for the following areas of assurance:

- Software and Interface Security (SS & IS)
- Software and Interface Design Assurance (SDA & IDA)
- Software Test Planning (STP)
- Software Test Description (STD)
- Software Test Reporting (STR)

SQA and SCM will be part of the development effort. Here is some other information you may need:

- There are five application interfaces involved.
- There will be a subcontract for modifications to some of the code.
- This is a life-critical application.
- There is a moderate need for management visibility.
- Because it is a life critical application, sufficient testing needs to be done to assure that the functional requirements have been reliably met.

The areas for concern are human safety, the level and formality of the design, and the unknown complexity that could exist in the interface code. On examining the project characteristics, the project manager requires you to address the following issues:

- Reliability metrics will be stressed during testing. HMT needs to come up with two quantitative ways to measure reliability.
- There is a need for in-process reviews for this project. HMT must specify where.

- It will be important to track progress on the coding for this project. Suggest three ways to do that.

- Although the risk management practices will be used, there is no idea about where to apply them. Define the places in the process where risk assessments should be done.

- The program integration needs to be carefully controlled throughout that phase of the development effort. Justify why that should be done and suggest a method.

- Set up the review requirements to allow for in-process reviews of the execution of the project. These should be fully documented.

Human Factors: Ensuring Secure Performance

In this chapter, you will learn how to:
- Work with models of the body of knowledge in information assurance
- Structure the content of awareness, training, and education programs
- Instill and ensure proper information assurance discipline

As you now know, information assurance requires that each credible threat has to have a countermeasure. The problem is that it is hard to think of all of the threats and worse, the threats come from many directions. They can be "sophisticated" incidents, like electronic penetrations of the network; however, threats may also originate from "low-tech" sources such as insider theft, or simple human error.

Technological **countermeasures** are reliable and trustworthy measures if executed properly. They achieve information assurance objectives and if well maintained, they execute their preprogrammed instructions with reliability. People are a different challenge; the actions of people are hard to predict and even harder to control. The information assurance function has to guarantee that the people empowered to access and manage information do so in a predictable and disciplined way. These countermeasures provide safeguards against unpredictable human behavior threats, as simple as reformatting hard drives and sending unauthorized data.

It is essential to make certain that the people who use information and are responsible for its information assurance adopt and follow secure practices, as shown in Figure 15-1. That requirement for secure practice must be shaped and sustained by a set of designed activities, aimed at ensuring the performance of each worker's information assurance duties. The means for ensuring consistency is the focus of this chapter.

Assuring Reliable Performance

The root of unreliable performance is fact that information is a complex and dynamic asset. Due to this, organizations should adopt procedures designed to ensure that secure practices are reliably performed.

Secure procedures regulate the way people perform their assigned duties. However, human factors influence how closely an individual follows a given procedure.

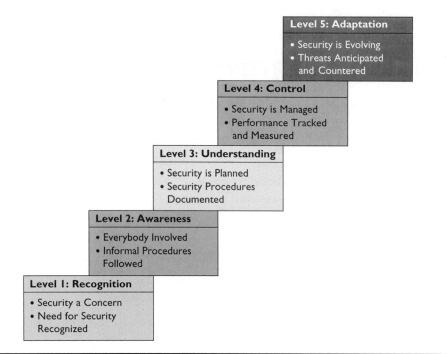

Figure 15-1   The Information Assurance hierarchy of secure practices

For instance, most organizations have robust firewalls to protect their information from external threats; however, they sometimes fail to provide training that defines the steps an authorized individual should follow to secure the information in the system.

Consequently, critical or classified information can be modified, stolen, lost, or even given away, through ignorance of information assurance performance requirements. A key aspect of the information assurance process is the need to ensure that the people follow the defined procedures.

The requirement for consistent performance implies the need to ensure information assurance discipline. The term **discipline** indicates that a practice is performed consistently. Information assurance requires discipline because procedures have to be executed in a coordinated fashion by all participants at all times. The first steps in establishing a systematic information assurance process is to define and document disciplined practice among the trusted individuals who access information or manage the process.

Disciplined practice encourages information assurance, but imposes additional work requirements. Remember that because of workload, people will not do everything that they should to be secure; they have to be motivated to perform those tasks.

Motivation is essential to the information assurance process by initiating, directing, and sustaining all forms of interaction. Motivation ensures a person's willingness to execute a task consistently or achieve a goal, even if it is personally inconvenient.

It defines the level and persistence of a person's commitment to information assurance. Motivation establishes disciplined performance.

Motivation is geared to accountability defined by **appropriate use policies**. Appropriate use policies are developed and documented by the organization to guide everything from the use of computers to the use of expense accounts. They are monitored for compliance and the accountability system rewards appropriate actions and discourages inappropriate ones. It is impossible to have **accountability** if the policies are not known or understood. The organization also has to ensure that its employees know performance expectations and the consequences of non-compliance.

Ensuring that everybody in the organization understands his or her exact role, responsibility, and function is critical in managing human performance. No matter how flawless the information assurance scheme might be, if the people responsible for executing it do not understand the expected behavior, there is little chance that the organization will be secure.

Every organization has to make a deliberate effort to maintain the knowledge of information assurance duties and accountabilities for each employee. The need to ensure a satisfactory level of information assurance knowledge is essential in light of the fact that employees are constantly changing—trained workers leave or change jobs and untrained people are added. Therefore, another aim of the assurance function is to make certain that the knowledge management system operates as intended.

The organization is responsible for ensuring that its employees are knowledgeable about their assigned duties and associated performance standards. The mechanism is an **awareness**, **training**, and **education (AT&E)** program.

The Body of Knowledge in IA

AT&E programs are based on a body of knowledge that provides scope, sequence, and content to be taught during instruction.

Early attempts at defining a body of knowledge for information assurance centered on the description of the operational tasks associated with securing computer equipment, such as how to do backups and perform physical security protection tasks.

This knowledge was adequate before distributed computing and the Internet. However, in today's wide-open and information-intensive environment, information assurance professionals discovered a need to keep up with a rapidly changing technological and threat landscape. That led to the development of a new concept for information protection. This is called information assurance (IA). The Committee on National Security Systems (CNSS) defines IA as:

> Information operations (IO) that protect and defend information and information systems by ensuring their availability, integrity, authentication, confidentiality, and nonrepudiation. This includes providing for restoration of information systems by incorporating protection, detection, and reaction capabilities.

The concept of **information assurance** (IA) expands the scope of the responsibilities and accountabilities of information assurance professionals. It incorporates the traditional array of computer security (COMPSEC), communications security (COMSEC), and information security (INFOSEC) defensive measures with a new set of proactive approaches, such as "active network defenses."

IA also fosters a view of information protection as a seamless process incorporated into the operations of the organization. That vision has reinforced the perspective that information assurance is pervasive in IS management. Figure 15-2 illustrates the time-line of this development:

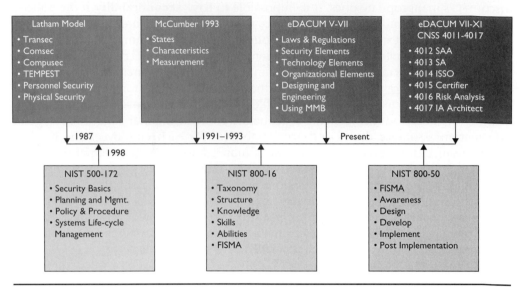

Figure 15-2 Timeline for the development of the IA body of knowledge

Latham Model (1987)

Donald Latham, U.S. Assistant Secretary of Defense for Command Control, Commu-nications, and Intelligence, offered one of the earliest representations of the body of knowledge. In *Security in the Information Age* he described an integrated six-category concept of information security. He pointed out that the mass of information is acted on by a series of enablers constituting the information security process, as shown in Table 15-1.

NIST 500-172 (1989)

In response to federal legislation, the National Institute of Standards and Technology (NIST) developed Special Publication 500-172, Computer Security Training Guidelines. It specifies a fundamental definition for the training to be provided in accordance with PL-100-235, The Information Security Act of 1987. This approach, called the Todd and Guitian model, establishes four activity levels:

1. Awareness—Need for security is recognized.

2. Policy—Policies define response.

Category	Description
TRANSEC	Transmission security—the protection of transmissions from interception and exploitation
COMPUSEC	Computer security—the protection of computer systems by electronic, software and procedural techniques
COMSEC	Communications security—the protection of communications by electronic techniques
TEMPEST	The means, usually through system design, to inhibit the unwanted emission of electromagnetic radiation from electronic systems such as cryptographic devices, telecommunications equipment, computers, and so on
Physical security	Physical measures to safeguard information
Personnel security	Measures to ensure the integrity of people handling sensitive or classified information

Table 15-1 Six-Category Concept of Information Security

3. Implementation—Policies are implemented by plan.

4. Performance—Security functions are performed.

The model then specifies which activities are appropriate for each of the following five training areas:

- Computer security basics
- Security planning and management
- Computer security policy and procedure
- Contingency planning
- Systems life-cycle management

In addition, the model defines five audience categories

- Executives
- Program and functional managers
- Information Resource Management security and audit
- Automated Data Processing (ADP) management and operations
- End users

The Todd and Guitian model broke the barrier of thinking about security in terms of a simple set of discrete personal activities applied to a single aspect of the operation.

Instead, it adopted a holistic view of security as an enterprise-wide function. It placed a greater emphasis on protecting the technologies upon which the information resides— "information technology security." However, it did not offer sufficient guidance about implementing the process, nor did it address the fundamental differences between awareness and training.

McCumber Model (1991, 1993)

The next stage in the evolutionary chain encompasses a much broader vision of security. John McCumber of the United States Air Force developed this concept. His view integrated the complete range of security functions into a single model that described assurance across the enterprise. The McCumber Model defines three dimensions of security:

- **Information states**
- **Information characteristics**
- **Security measures**

Each of these dimensions has a set of fundamental characteristics, as shown in Table 15-2. McCumber asserts that every security function can be understood by viewing it as an element of a cube with three dimensions and those nine characteristics. From an awareness, training, and **education** standpoint, the intersection of these three dimensions and their nine categories produces 27 potential functional subcategories or security conditions. These 27 subcategories represent a set of knowledge areas.

Information States	Information Characteristics	Security Measures
1. Transmission	1. Availability	1. Policy and Practice
2. Storage	2. Integrity	2. Technical
3. Processing	3. Confidentiality	3. Education and Training

Table 15-2   Dimensions and Characteristics of the McCumber Model

The model was extended to accommodate the Canadian Trusted Computer Product Evaluation Criteria (CTCPEC), which splits the criteria for defining where this model ought to be applied into two distinct domains: *functionality* and *trust*. Both of these are legitimate targets for an AT&E program.

The Intermediate Models: eDACUM and NIST 800-16

In the early 1990s, an International Federation for Information Processing (IFIP) publication proposed a model of a mature body of knowledge. It compiled, distilled, and enhanced existing attempts by a variety of organizations to define an Information Assurance Body of Knowledge (IABK) for information systems security. It also provided a taxonomic structure for the contents of that IABK that has been used in industry and government training standards.

Appropriate knowledge, skills, and abilities (KSAs) were placed within that taxonomy, after which they were associated with each of the elements in that IABK. Finally, verbs from Bloom's classic learning hierarchy were assigned to each Knowledge, Skill, and Ability element. That step allowed the user to write appropriately focused performance standards for each KSA. This model was used during the development of NIST SP 800-16 in 1998 and the CNSS standards.

This stable IABK incorporates the axioms, lore, and methods of the trade. As implemented, the IABK represents knowledge integral to the way professionals carry out their work. A series of eDACUMs (V through VII) was employed throughout the end of the 1990s to develop this into an IABK. This work has continued to expand and revalidate the IABK.

The term *eDACUM* stands for *electronic Develop a Curriculum*. An eDACUM involves groups of subject matter experts who cooperatively analyze solutions to issues of importance using electronic tools to support this brainstorming. Their products are comprehensive and authoritative because they incorporate so much expert input.

The IABK contained in early eDACUM work condensed over 1,100 individual knowledge elements into a listing of 385 behavioral descriptions. These were partitioned into two major taxonomic categories: Things You Need To Know and the Things You Need To Do. This process, which was defined by Schou and Maconachy (IFIP 1993, IEEE 2004), details the methods used to define the IABK.

Information systems security topic areas were divided into "Encyclopedic Knowledge" and "Process Knowledge"—where Encyclopedic Knowledge describes facts, technologies, and principles; and Process Knowledge describes *how* encyclopedic knowledge is used. The resulting Unified Taxonomy is useful as a reference point by both curriculum developers and authors.

The taxonomy codifies those elements of knowledge, skill, and ability that define the core knowledge requirement. The Unified Taxonomy also serves as a guide to job classification, career development, and professional development activities. Building on this conceptual framework, the eDACUM group developed a model accounting for the behavioral descriptions. The two major categories are subdivided into six partitions, as shown in Table 15-3.

Things You Need to Know	Things You Need to Do
Laws and regulations	Designing and engineering AIS to be secure
Fundamental security elements	
Technology-oriented security elements	Using and operating AIS securely
Organization-specific security elements	

Table 15-3 The Six Partitions of Behavioral Descriptions

Recent Standards Development

Recently, NIST has published a special publication, SP 800-50, which details how organizations should meet the requirements of the Federal Information Security Management Act of 2002 (FISMA). The Committee on National Security Systems (CNSS) has also continued the development of government-wide standards derived from additional eDACUM research, as detailed in Table 15-4

These standards have been developed and continuously improved over the course of more than 15 years of study. They represent the state of the art in information assurance.

Standard	Description
CNSSI 4011	National Training Standard for Information Systems Security (INFOSEC) Professionals, dated 20 June 1994, and is under current revision for publication in 2006
CNSSI-4012	National Information Assurance Training Standard for Senior Systems Managers, dated June 2004; supersedes NSTISSI No. 4012, dated August 1997
CNSSI-4013	National Information Assurance Training Standard for System Administrators (SA), dated March 2004
CNSSI-4014	Information Assurance Training Standard for Information Systems Security Officers, dated April 2004; supersedes NSTISSI No. 4014, dated August 1997
NSTISSI-4015	National Training Standard for Systems Certifiers, dated December 2000
CNSSI-4016	National Training Standard for Risk Analysts, dated March 2005

Table 15-4　Additional Government-Wide Standards

Extending the McCumber Model—The MSR Model

Maconachy, Schou, and Ragsdale (MSR) extended the McCumber model to provide recommendations for how to protect the Critical Information Infrastructure (CII) in an age of terrorism. The MSR model extends the importance of three classes of countermeasures: Technology, Policy/Practice, and People. It encourages using people in the organization into effective countermeasures. The MSR model shown in Figure 15-3 illustrates that three-dimensional integration of countermeasures, **states**, and services.

The MSR model expands the services category by adding non-repudiation and authentication. More importantly, the model introduces a fourth dimension, time. The time dimension demonstrates that the introduction of new technology and threats over time requires modifications to other elements of the integrated model to restore a system to a secure state.

This work changed the way IA solutions are developed. The process no longer focuses on creating and deploying static countermeasures. It can now focus on the development of safeguards that offer deterrence and prevention, in addition to simple

Figure 15-3
The MSR information assurance model

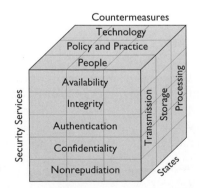

protection and response. Now, a well-designed assurance process is obligated to secure information from the time it is collected until it is no longer contained in the system. That expands the role of information assurance to include activities that must occur throughout the life cycle of the entire operation. This model is now included in some ACM curriculum recommendations.

Delivering the Body of Knowledge

The models discussed in the prior section outline the body of knowledge. They do not provide advice about dissemination. That is the role of the delivery process. There are three approaches to teaching secure practice, which are **awareness**, **training**, and **education**–the **AT&E program**.

Each of these delivery models represents a different approach to learning. Each has a distinct application and each is characterized by progressively more rigorous and extensive learning requirements. Because of that progression, these approaches are depicted in a hierarchy.

At the basic level, *awareness*, the application of the learning is broad but the learning requirements are limited. The next level is *training*, which builds on awareness. However, the application of training is restricted to fewer people and the learning is more in depth. Finally, at the top of the hierarchy, which is *education*, the application might be limited to a few key people but the learning requirements are very broad and in depth.

Awareness Programs

Awareness is the lowest level in the hierarchy. Effective awareness programs ensure that all employees at every level in the organization appreciate the need for, and are capable of executing disciplined information assurance practice, in a coordinated manner.

This meets basic information assurance aims. However, the requirement for awareness varies across the organization. Awareness at the highest levels of the corporation sets the "tone at the top." Awareness programs at the executive level focus on ensuring strategic awareness of the assurance issues facing the organization, as well as the costs, benefits, risks, and implications of information assurance.

At other levels, it is necessary to maintain a relatively high degree of awareness of relevant assurance practices. Therefore, everybody in the organization must be made aware of the information assurance requirements that apply to their position. Remember, they have to be motivated to practice information assurance in a disciplined fashion. A good awareness program will

1. Strengthen motivation—The program must motivate all users to practice information assurance.

2. Ensure effective focus—The program must concentrate on relevant and appropriate topics.

3. Maintain participant interest—The program must ensure that individual participants will continue to be interested in information assurance.

4. Underwrite capable performance—The program must ensure effective actions with respect to information assurance

5. Integrate the content—The program must ensure the full integration of the proper set of practices into the organization.

Awareness alone does not assure reliable information assurance. It is necessary to ensure that individuals responsible for executing information assurance functions are knowledgeable in the requirements of their role. It is essential to ensure that every information assurance function is performed correctly. That implies a greater degree of knowledge and capability than is provided by an awareness function. This increased knowledge is delivered thru formal training.

Training Programs

Training is organized instruction that produces a defined outcome emphasizing job-specific skills. The purpose of training is to make sure that organizational functions, which are required to ensure a safe and secure environment, are performed correctly.

Training ensures that all participants in the process have the skills necessary to carry out their assignments and that the level of organizational capability is continuously maintained. Training can be expensive, but it is an effective way to guarantee long-term execution of information assurance processes.

Training is too narrow to ensure the security of the entire organization; it is based on skills rather than abstract concepts. Training prepares individual workers to execute a series of steps without concern for the context or the reasons why those might be necessary.

Training provides a quick and satisfactory outcome if the situation never changes or if adaptation is not required. However, most information assurance situations are dynamic and complex. Therefore, training does not provide the overall strategic **understanding** necessary to establish a lasting information assurance solution. Consequently, a program of formal education is also required.

Education Programs

Education is oriented toward knowledge, rather than the acquisition of short-term skills. It ensures an intelligent, rather than rote, response. It establishes understanding of the principles of information assurance as well as the critical thinking abilities needed to move the organization through a continually changing and uncertain information assurance landscape. Therefore, a formal and in-depth education program is essential for individuals who are responsible for the long-term guidance of the information assurance function.

Education can be distinguished from training by its scope, as well as the intent of the learning process. In a training environment, the employee acquires skills as part of a defined set of job criteria. In an educational context, the employee is taught to think more about the implications of what he or she is learning.

The learner must be able to analyze, evaluate, and select the optimum information assurance response from all alternatives. Learners are encouraged to examine and evaluate critically the problem and to respond by tailoring fundamental principles into a solution that fits the situation.

The aim of education is to integrate new knowledge and skills into day-to-day information assurance practice. The outcome of an institutionalized education process is the ability of executives, managers, and workers to adapt to new situations as they arise. Given the constantly changing nature of threats and vulnerabilities in cyberspace, this is an essential survival skill for the leadership of any organization.

Increasing Organizational Capability Through AT&E

The outcome of a well-executed AT&E program is an increased level of organizational capability. This is a strategic concept based on the achievement of five progressively more capable **states** of security:

- **Recognition**—the organization recognizes the need for information assurance.
- **Informal Realization**—the organization understands informal information assurance practices.
- **Understanding**—the information assurance practices are planned and monitored.
- **Deliberate Control**—decisions about information assurance practices are based on measurement and data.
- **Continuous Adaptation**—information assurance practices can adapt to changes as they occur and are continuously improving.

The levels of capability are progressively achieved through targeted AT&E processes.

Information Assurance Recognition

The fundamental level is simple *Recognition*. Here, the majority of the participants are able to recognize that information assurance is valid and necessary. This state can be achieved by implementing a basic awareness program.

Until the state of recognition is achieved, the organization is defenseless. Once recognition is established, however, individual members begin to understand that information assurance is a concern. It involves a persistent appreciation that information assurance practice is necessary.

Informal Realization

At the next level, *Informal Realization*, members of the organization become more conscious of information assurance in their day-to-day work. Every worker is aware that concerns exist. Workers might follow rudimentary procedures in response to that appreciation. A more elaborate awareness program supports this level.

The awareness program supporting informal realization presents information assurance issues that have been identified as concerns. It presents sound practices to address these concerns on an *ad hoc* or informational basis. The practices are not specific and their performance is not organized well enough to ensure that information assurance is embedded in the standard operation. That happens in the next step.

Information Assurance Understanding

The third stage, *Understanding*, is the first level where a consciously planned and formal information assurance effort takes place. At this stage, the organization understands and acts on a commonly accepted knowledge of the need for formal information assurance. The response might not be extensive and it is dependent on individual willingness, but it is recognizable in that information assurance procedures are planned and documented.

The fact that information assurance procedures have been formally documented allows the organization to implement a training program. Training is done to enforce understanding of the information assurance practices associated with each role.

For instance, there might be targeted programs for executives, a different one for managers, and another for line workers. The line worker programs might be subdivided by operation. These programs foster knowledge of the information assurance procedures appropriate to that role or function. They do not impart skills beyond the understanding of the information assurance practices required to carry out basic work. That is done in the next stage.

Deliberate Control

The fourth stage, *Deliberate Control*, is typical of a well-organized information assurance operation. Deliberate control is characterized by an institutionalized information assurance response built around a defined set of skills. These skills are defined and managed based on knowledge of the requirements of each individual's role in the organization.

The execution of information assurance tasks is monitored with quantitative measures of performance, such as intrusion detection. Deliberate control is enforced by defined accountability. Because it is objectively monitored, the information assurance operation is fully managed by the organization's top-level executive team. At this level, the organization can be considered both safe from common threats and actively practicing the steps needed to maintain the required level of security.

This state is a targeted mix of training and education. Coordination and administration of the program is designed to achieve defined assurance outcomes. The training and education program communicates the knowledge and skills needed to perform correctly information assurance practices required by each function. This is reinforced through periodic retraining.

Training at this level is a planned activity that uses many of the activities performed by the personnel security function, such as job definition, job classification, and privilege setting, to make it successful. The outcome provides a high level of carefully controlled information assurance. However, this is not yet the highest level possible.

Continuous Adaptation

The organization is fully optimizing at the fifth level, *Continuous Adaptation*. It carries executes the practices needed to ensure security that the situation requires, but it continues to evolve as conditions change. Organizations at this level adapt easily to new threats as they arise. This allows the organization to maintain consistently effective countermeasures as well as an active response to incidents. They are less vulnerable to harm because they are protected from all but the most unforeseen events and are capable of a rapid reaction to a threat that might occur.

This stage is achieved by helping workers master the critical thinking skills needed to identify and solve problems. This requires a high level of knowledge of the elements and requirements of information assurance, as well as the thought processes to allow people to adopt these principles to new situations as they arise.

The mechanism for reaching this level of competence is a well-designed educational program. Skill training might also be needed to achieve this level. Nevertheless, the integration of that knowledge into the capability to respond correctly to new or unanticipated events falls within the realm of education.

Building Effective AT&E Programs

In the case of the employees, effective information assurance can be achieved only through a systematic AT&E program, which is structured around achieving the desired information assurance outcomes. Table 15-5 summarizes the AT&E practices and the

Capability Levels	AT&E	Resultant Processes and Practices
Recognition	Awareness events designed to heighten information assurance awareness among staff.	Periodic consideration of information assurance-related issues in performing job functions.
Informal Procedural Realization	Targeted awareness events designed to introduce understanding of information assurance issues	Overall information assurance considerations become part of job performance.
Planned Procedural and Information assurance Understanding	Information assurance practices are defined, standardized, documented, and publicized through extensive awareness programs with ad-hoc training.	Members of the organization practice information assurance as day-to-day routine and demonstrate individual information assurance initiative.
Controlled	Internal best practices are characterized and formally communicated through role-based training—workers are educated in information assurance principles.	Information assurance program is complete and implements a managed information assurance process.
Adaptive	Training and communication supports information assurance best practice	Best practices are employed and continuously improving.

Table 15-5 AT&E Practices

expected outcomes that must result in order to achieve the various levels of information assurance capability that we discussed.

Steps to Achieve the Basic Recognition Level

Obviously, there is a level below the recognition level best described as "chaos." However, since this is the natural state of things, it does not require a program to achieve it. The first step above chaos is **recognition**.

An organization must meet two conditions to satisfy the learning requirements needed to ensure responsiveness to information assurance issues. First, information assurance issues have to be publicized through simple mechanisms such as posters, handouts, or reference cards. The outcome must be that the members of the organization are aware of and informally discuss topics related to information assurance. This does not need to be in a formal setting; it is most likely to happen in informal settings, such as a lunchroom.

The second step is to increase the level of community understanding and discourse. The outcome that indicates that this has been achieved is that members of the organization are aware that information assurance procedures should be followed. Posters and handouts can also accomplish this.

The aim is to foster a minimum level of understanding of proper information assurance practice. This does not need to go beyond employees thinking to take simple precautions. Nevertheless, they should be able to make some association between common information assurance threats and the steps taken to prevent or avoid them.

Although the Recognition level provides little substantive protection, it creates the potential that adverse events can be detected and mitigated. For example, until people are able to recognize that worms exist they will consistently launch one if it is presented to them. Once that recognition is created, whether through a posted reminder or by discussions around the coffee pot, they are more likely to think twice when they are offered the opportunity to... "Take a look at this!" That level of knowledge may not carry over to other information assurance practices related to viruses, but it is a step in the right direction. Awareness is a better state.

Steps to Achieve the Informal Procedural and Realization Level

Targeted awareness of information assurance concerns characterize the *Informal Procedural Realization* level. Awareness programs should reach everybody in the organization, and should alert the membership to hazards peculiar to the organizational environment. Two conditions must be met to achieve this level of information assurance.

First, analytic work must be done to understand and characterize the risks resident in a particular organizational setting. This analysis is necessary since awareness programs have to be planned and the effective level of awareness will vary depending on the line of business. For example, the awareness program at a "mom and pop" Internet business has different requirements and addresses different concerns than the one at NASA. The measure for success is that the awareness function is focused on the problems in that environment.

The other requirement of a sound informal procedural program is common knowledge and **acceptance**. That is, there has to be an intuitive understanding by every member of the organization of the fundamental need for uniform information assurance practice. This does not require a rulebook. Nor does it demand rigid and uniform adherence to detailed requirements. Rather, the awareness level requires a basic consistency in execution.

To illustrate, if the members of a unit have a range of perceptions of the threat level varying from none to outright paranoia, they will approach information assurance differently. If they are completely independent in implementing their approach to the information assurance goals, none will be achieved because the response will not be coordinated and there is the potential for dysfunctional infighting.

Focused and coordinated collective understanding of the information assurance goals of the organization supports that level of awareness. Learning is tailored to the needs of the situation and learner. Accordingly, procedural awareness programs are designed based on learner-centered and situational requirements.

The learning program is resourced, planned, and deployed from those requirements. There has to be a formal organized effort to develop and publicize all best practices. These are promoted in the form of adages, like "always back up your hard drive," rather than explained in depth. The intention has to be embedding commonly accepted correct practices into the workplace.

Procedural awareness programs begin to concentrate and direct the response. They are minimally effective in mitigating adverse happenings. The value of procedural awareness is that organizations establish a base level of information assurance with a small commitment of resources. It will not guarantee that costly breaches will never occur, but a good awareness program raises the level of information assurance performance for the entire organization and is valuable.

Procedural awareness programs create the critical mass of consciousness necessary to move to the next level. In some respects they may be more cost-effective than the more formal responses because they ensure a fundamental level of preparedness without significant commitment.

Steps to Achieve the Planned Procedural and Information Assurance Understanding Level

The next stage is the first institutionalized response—the *Planned Procedural and Information Assurance Understanding* level. This stage is frequently established by training programs because a minimum level of controlled information assurance practice must be present. Deliberate programs instill the proper skills.

There are two conditions associated with training at this level. The first is that the information assurance requirements of the organization are understood. Everybody in the organization must know the information assurance requirements and everyone has access to material that explains how they operate.

The second condition is that information assurance practices are standardized, based on formally acknowledged and commonly accepted best practices implemented by clear procedures.

The design of the training program necessary to achieve this level is supported by the current needs of the organization. This is based on an inventory of known and documented security incidents. The outcome of that inventory is an identified set of vulnerabilities to be targeted by focused training exercises.

An in-house staff may not necessarily deliver this content. A primary difference between this level and the Controlled level is the fact that training is not institutionalized as a process at the Planned Procedural level.

Instead, training is often left up to the initiative of individual managers and process owners within the organization. Although some of the goals of training are achieved, others go unmet because they were not recognized as necessary or the functional area was too busy doing something else.

The Planned Procedural level represents an advance over the Informal Procedural level because it establishes information assurance functions as a consciously delivered and continuous process. It allows an organization to target its most persistent needs, and it usually delivers some resolution to information assurance problems. The lack of uniformity in addressing all threats is a continuing concern, but if one assumes the old adage that 20 percent of the vulnerabilities produce 80 percent of the problems, this level can still provide considerable benefit.

Where these programs fail, however, is in the lack of consistent application. They are not deliberately overseen or coordinated because they are not a part of the routine organizational planning and management. Consequently, they are not able to adapt to new threats quickly to provide trustworthy assurance, which creates the potential for some nasty surprises.

Most of the recent highly publicized breakdowns in information assurance have resulted from changes in the technology or the culture that surrounds it. AT&E programs at the Planned Procedural level do not deal with such change adequately because they are reactive. In essence, they are only deployed after the building is already on fire. Because the ideal outcome for an information assurance function is fire prevention rather than firefighting; dependable oversight and repeatable outcomes are a much more attractive alternative. The Planned Procedural level of understanding does not offer that; however, the Controlled level does.

Steps to Achieve the Controlled Level

The *Controlled* level is the fully managed stage in the hierarchy of AT&E programs. It implies that the solution is comprehensive, and institutionalized as part of the organizational planning and decision-making function. Consequently, where actions at the prior level are established by training, this level is based on satisfaction of a legitimate education requirement.

Organizational control can be achieved only by using a planning and deployment process. That process entails an organized risk assessment and planning activity. Risk assessment and planning are complex activities. They are driven by circumstance rather than being routine. The only way to achieve the level of critical thinking necessary to do this properly is an education program supported by a training program to enforce accountability.

The Controlled level is managed by accountability. It conveys a set of commonly best practices. These address the current information assurance needs of the organization.

This requires that three conditions are met. The first is that the roles for information assurance are assigned and understood among the organization's staff and management and that the overall responsibilities are assigned and placed within a management accountability system.

The second condition is the existence of a complete and correct set of best practices and control objectives implemented by procedures. These must be defined, documented, and tailored to fit the entire range of known information assurance requirements of the organization.

The third condition is that the set of practices and control objectives are accompanied by a valid and objective set of measures and metrics. These quantitative measures are needed to characterize the ongoing performance of the information assurance function.

A systematic risk assessment process establishes this level. That assessment process creates a set of vulnerabilities that are targeted by control objectives. These are monitored and assessed. The response is a mix of procedures, technologies, and methods integrated by design into a complete organizational system. The requirements for proper execution of that system are delivered as a comprehensive education program.

This process is programmatic in that it functions as an established institution within the operating structure. The administration of the education program must be supported by the relevant managers. Third-party suppliers might be part of this process, but an institutional stakeholder always performs the coordination of their work.

Accountability for the success or failure of the education process is vested with the stakeholder. The organization must demonstrate a commitment and an ability to perform the education function by ensuring that the staff is empowered and that an adequate educational capability is maintained.

The advantage gained by an effective organization-wide education program cannot be overstated. Information assurance is a complex and multidisciplinary challenge rooted in individual behavior than technology. Most of the problems with information assurance arise directly from failures by the members of the organization to follow correct procedure, or from their inability or unwillingness to comply with information assurance requirements.

It is important to be able to both convey the message as well as reinforce the behavior. A properly functioning information assurance education program does this. It provides the individual worker with the knowledge to do his or her job correctly and it reinforces the cultural and behavioral norms associated with the information assurance operation. Then, if an individual employee subsequently violates those norms, the organization will be able to assign and enforce accountability. That combination of knowledge and motivation allows the overall information assurance goals of the organization to be both assured and maintained with confidence.

The fourth stage, *Controlled*, represents a major advance over the prior planned procedural level because it establishes the information assurance function as a systematic process. It places the information assurance operation on a day-to-day footing and addresses all known problems.

It institutionalizes the ability to respond to incidents in a timely fashion and ensures that breaches will be contained with minimal damage. That is because the operation produces data that can be used by managers to identify anomalies as they appear and initiate remediation or problem-resolution actions.

If there is a criticism of programs at this level, it is that they do not anticipate problems. A program of this type builds a static defense that is effective as long as the threats are known and countermeasures face the attack. However, if the attack comes from a new or unanticipated direction, they can be more of a hindrance than help because they engender a false sense of security.

Consequently, attacks from a new direction can make headway before they are recognized and someone responds appropriately. The ideal would be for the defense to respond to an attack as it is presented. However, that requires a level of understanding capable of supporting that type of anticipation. That is the role of the final stage.

Steps to Achieve the Adaptive Level

The final stage, *Adaptive*, implies that the organization can recognize information assurance events as they occur and respond appropriately. This ability implies a high level of comprehension and systematic operation requiring both total understanding and refined practice. Among other things, this requires adoption of a mature and highly developed body of knowledge. At the same time, it also relies on the ability to attract, develop, motivate, and retain the individual staff **capabilities** necessary to meet those goals.

This stage lays the foundation for continuous enhancement of information assurance capability by increasing the competency of the personnel who operate the system. That assumption presupposes a deliberate quantitative assessment mechanism exists that allows the organization to predict its information assurance requirements with accuracy. If that is the case, then the organization will be able to develop the knowledge and skill capabilities among the staff necessary to address those exact challenges.

This is an important advantage because, in the end, an information assurance scheme is only as good as the abilities of the staff. No matter how well intentioned those people might be, without sufficient advanced knowledge in that area, those capabilities will be limited.

For instance, no matter how competent and highly trained an individual programmer is, without knowledge of secure coding practice he or she is as likely to create vulnerabilities as the most naïve end-user. The primary distinction between this level and the one that precedes it is that it establishes a **culture of continuous improvement** in information assurance practice.

The aim of this stage is the disciplined evolution of fundamental information assurance knowledge, skills, and motivation within the work force. It is based on an identification of the information assurance requirements of the roles that make up the operational structure of the organization.

There is one caveat: To reach this level of function the prior level must be well established, that is, the roles for information assurance are assigned and well understood, and the responsibilities are assigned, operationally managed, and accountable. The procedures derived from those practices have to be tailored to fit the known information assurance requirements of the organization. Furthermore, quantitative data must be available.

The training process is initiated by a review of the information assurance require-ments for each staff category within the operation. This review is done to determine the approach that the organization will adopt to develop the knowledge, resources, and skills needed to ensure proper information assurance performance. That determina-tion is based on matching the types and levels of training required to the categories of personnel needing training. The aim is to produce optimally skilled and knowledge-able personnel ready to execute their day-to-day work securely. The implication of this requirement is that this knowledge must also be incorporated into the ongoing hiring process, particularly if none of these identified skills and behavior are currently avail-able in the organization.

This is developed as a training plan that provides a strategy and a mechanism for leveraging current personnel assets through a focused training process or for acquiring the right personnel through targeted hiring. This plan is a documentation artifact and it is placed under configuration control. It states the precise training requirements for each staff category, along with a schedule and the associated resource requirements for each identified training need. This document is refined as new information is obtained.

The plan leads to the training program. This is the work of the training staff and con-stitutes the execution of the process. The training staff deploys a program to meet the information assurance requirements and competencies associated with each staff role. That involves both the operational, managerial, and technical tasks of the position.

The types and levels of training required must be planned for each role based on the current capabilities of the incumbents. This includes the development of a detailed set of training materials, manuals, and presentation media. That fact implies the need for a continuous assessment or rating process to determine the learning needs of each indi-vidual. It is normal practice for organizations at these levels to do annual performance reviews of every employee. It is at these times that the considerations for supplemental education need to be addressed.

To keep materials consistent with organizational requirements, the process of modi-fying the training program is iterative. The documentation required for each role must be specified along with the materials and media that will be used to conduct the train-ing. That understanding is refined over time as performance is assessed. The materials are then modified to make them responsive to change as it occurs. Since the assess-ment of individual performance is the basis for directing and refining the process, the performance data is also maintained as an organizational resource. It is kept under configuration management and subject to quality assurance practice. This is all directed by a formal set of training plans developed for the organization, as well as individual training protocols developed for each individual role.

The implementation is prescribed in the training plan. This is a closed loop process. That means that feedback obtained from the day-to-day operation, is factored into the refinement of the competency requirements and reflected in the programmed response. The actual training activities take place regularly. The key to refining this activity lies in constant formal evaluations and reviews that take place because of people entering and exiting the process.

The data generated by these assessments can be used to fine-tune the training process. It can also provide workforce management feedback to the organization about the progress it is making toward obtaining the right mix of trained resources. This is an important operation because managers can only coordinate plans for information assurance operations based on the availability of personnel matching their needs. As an example of these concepts at work, it would be pointless to institute a rigorous network security or computer forensics operation if nobody trained in that discipline were available at the time.

Assessments support the efficient allocation of resources. The right people can be hired, or people with the required skills can be moved from other jobs when needed. Assessments form the basis for good team building, because the right people can be developed or acquired before they are required.

This dynamic approach is an ongoing commitment. It cannot be stressed enough that the entity given the responsibility for training must constantly monitor and control the development of the training program and the personnel resource base through formal assessment and review.

The maturation of the training program is a continuous activity that flows from the refinement of information assurance requirements as well as new knowledge gained through performance of information assurance activities. The training operation requires a total commitment by the organization to maintaining a dynamic and complete understanding of requirements and capabilities. This is necessary to develop the programmatic responses necessary to meet these requirements. However, if this mandate is adhered to, this level of AT&E provides the personnel necessary to ensure that the organization will stay secure.

Chapter 15 Review

Chapter Summary

- Information assurance can only be possible if participants understand the requirements for good practice.

- Awareness, training, and education programs (AT&E) are important countermeasures.

- Any kind of coordinated work depends on an adequate understanding. So, whether formally acknowledged or not, it is the duty of the organization and its leadership to ensure that all participants in the information assurance process understand precisely what is expected of them.

- This understanding can only be communicated through a formal learning process, one that teaches everybody about the commitment that his or her role represents.

- Thus, it is the implicit responsibility of the corporation's leadership team to formally institute and conduct a proper AT&E program.

- This also means that every implementation scheme for each security system must be accompanied by a proper AT&E plan.

- AT&E programs target the chief vulnerability in the establishment of an information assurance program, which is the lack of recognition of the need for information assurance procedures.

- Effective information assurance programs are based on the capabilities of the people who execute them, not on methods or technologies.

- Accordingly, the correct response to an overall lack of knowledge about assurance is a formal and comprehensive program of training and education.

- All organizations must view information assurance as a planned integrative systematic process, which is deployed at the highest level of organizational functioning.

- Awareness warrantees that the information assurance consciousness of everybody in the organization has been raised to a proper level.

- Training produces relevant and required information assurance skills and competencies.

- Education integrates the necessary information assurance skills and competencies into a single information assurance common body of knowledge (IABK).

- There are five possible levels of knowledge associated with information assurance practices.

- The most fundamental of these is simple recognition.

- At the awareness level, participants become more conscious of information assurance measures in their day-to-day practice.

- The first stage that embodies a consciously planned and deployed effort is the understanding stage. That is where the organization understands and acts on a mutually understood need for formal information assurance.

- The fourth stage in the process is typical of a well-organized information assurance operation.

- It involves an institutionalized information assurance response built around a complete and analytically derived knowledge of the requirements of the situation

- Accordingly, it is frequently supported by quantitative measurement and reporting. It is operated under the full and complete control of the organization's management team.

- At the fifth stage of understanding, the organization carries out the practices necessary to ensure its security within the terms of the current situation.

- When formulating an Awareness, Training and Education program the first and most critical issue that must be resolved is the question of the form of the body of knowledge.

- Early attempts at defining a body of knowledge for information assurance centered around describing the operational tasks that were associated with securing computers.
- IA incorporates both the traditional array of information security (INFOSEC) defensive measures, with a new set of proactive activities.

Key Terms

acceptance (407)
awareness, training, and education (AT&E) (395)
capabilities (410)
countermeasures (393)
discipline (394)
education (398)
motivation (394)
recognition (406)
states (400)
understanding (402)

Key Term Quiz

Use terms from the Key Terms list to complete the following sentences. Not all terms will be used.

1. Because they build awareness of security requirements, AT&E programs are legitimate _____.

2. _____ instills critical thinking.

3. The Body of Knowledge is fully integrated at the _____ level.

4. Organizations at the proactive level are continuously _____.

5. The McCumber model defines three _____ for information as well as three _____.

6. Attacks that are behavior oriented are caused by _____.

7. _____ characterize the various forms in which information might exist.

8. The effectiveness of the response is dictated by the _____ of the people who operate the system.

9. The _____ dictates the behavior of the people within the organization.

10. The provision of job-centered skills is called _____.

Multiple Choice Quiz

1. Cognitively, awareness operates
   a. at the highest level
   b. in short-term memory
   c. infrequently
   d. by plan

2. At the training level the requirements of the organization are
   a. known
   b. yet to be defined
   c. concrete
   d. varied

3. The criticism of the understanding (managed) level is that
   a. it doesn't react to incidents
   b. it doesn't anticipate incidents
   c. it is hard to do
   d. it is expensive

4. The information assurance principle
   a. protects selected information
   b. is hard to understand
   c. embodies restoration concepts
   d. is iterative and feedback oriented

5. Information assurance programs are based on
   a. people capabilities
   b. IDS technology
   c. inspection processes
   d. quantitative management concepts

6. The basic recognition level allows the organization to
   a. maintain information assurance functionality
   b. respond to incidents as they occur
   c. plan a information assurance response
   d. be aware of information assurance requirements

7. The continuous adaptation level allows the organization to

    a. maintain information assurance functionality

    b. respond to incidents as they occur

    c. plan a information assurance response

    d. be aware of information assurance requirements

8. The planned procedural level allows the organization to

    a. maintain information assurance functionality

    b. respond to incidents as they occur

    c. plan a information assurance response

    d. be aware of information assurance requirements

9. McCumber structures security AT&E around

    a. things you know

    b. things you do

    c. things you recognize

    d. both things you know and things you do

10. In eDACUM the IABK is structured around encyclopedic knowledge and

    a. information assurance knowledge

    b. practice

    c. process knowledge

    d. professional knowledge

Essay Quiz

1. Why is human behavior a factor in assuring reliable protection?

2. Why is proper understanding so important to effective information security?

3. How are levels of advanced knowledge reached? Why is a capability hierarchy necessary?

4. Differentiate Awareness from Training and then from Education.

5. Why is it necessary to consider information states when developing an IA solution?

6. What is the difference between Encyclopedic Knowledge and Process Knowledge? How do these two apply?

7. What is the usefulness of a disciplined approach?

8. What is the primary human factor that influences the degree of discipline practiced?

9. Planning is the mechanism employed to implement higher levels of information assurance performance. Why is it especially necessary for human factors based issues?

10. Most of the breakdowns in information assurance happen because of poor performance of the process rather than bad planning. What factors make it harder to execute the process long-term?

Case Exercise

Complete the following exercises as directed by your instructor:

Refer to the Heavy Metal Technology Case in Appendix A. You have been assigned the task of ensuring that all employees of HMT follow proper information assurance procedures. Management has decided that the best way of doing by undertaking an extensive AT&E program at the Walton Beach facility. Your job will be to

1. Make a comprehensive list of all of the different types of employee categories at all facilities.

2. Decide what degree of information assurance knowledge will be necessary for them to perform their jobs.

3. Categorize each employee category by whether it would be most efficiently served by an awareness, training, or education program.

Justify your selections.

Information Ethics and Codes of Conduct

In this chapter, you will learn how to:
- Explain the role of ethics in information assurance
- Identify the fundamental elements of a professional code of conduct
- Define and apply an ethical system

This final chapter examines the role of ethics and ethical **behavior** in the information assurance process. **Ethics** is an important topic in information assurance because, like members of every other profession, information practitioners need guidance in correct behavior. That guidance is particularly important in the case of information work, because the commodity is abstract and information assurance professionals have unprecedented access.

If the rules for working with information were as clear as they are for jobs in traditional fields, ethics might not be as important. The elements of professional practice in long-standing areas such as electrical engineering or even physical security are well established and have not changed much over time. The stability is not the case with a new and rapidly changing discipline such as information work. The rules but not ethics are always changing because of continuous advances in the technology. Frost in an IFIP paper points out that the Internet gives the user the "ring of Gyges" described by Plato. The ring provides invisibility—no one knows what the wearer is doing or who he is.

Given anonymity, the intangibility of the product, and the evolution of the technology, there are an ever-increasing number of places where ethical grey may areas appear. For example, the Internet allows individuals to do things that they could not have done 25 years ago, like send massive amounts of e-mail to millions of people worldwide. That ability may be a blessing as a communication tool. However, it is also the source of spam, which is an unpleasant fact if you have a valid e-mail address.

Although spam has always been irritating, the question of whether it was ethical required a framework. Crimes like fraud or robbery are intuitively easy to evaluate, so the need for regulation is clear. It takes time for society to recognize and make a decision about the ethics of spamming because the technology is new. In the case of spam, an entire industry appeared before that decision was made.

If spamming were the only grey area, the consideration of the ethical use of cyberspace might not be as critical. Unfortunately, innumerable unique concerns develop as technology evolves and lack an ethical reference point.

Technological advances usually come without ethical instructions. Absent a clear understanding of the implications of a particular capability, it is hard to draw conclusions about its proper use. Thus, the list of grey areas associated with technological advances seems endless. These grey areas range from minor issues like third-party cookies up to institutionalized data gathering that is central to some corporate strategies. Ethical behavior is a constant; however, the application always needs evaluation and understanding. The lack of understanding causes ethical failures to fall through the cracks.

Ethical violations of cyberspace occur regularly without widespread recognition or response because nobody has thought through what a particular capability or activity represents in terms of right and wrong. As such, it is important for individuals and corporations to develop and use a frame of reference to ensure correct behavior. That is the role of ethics in information assurance.

What Is Ethics?

Ethics is a global term describing the system by which individuals distinguish right from wrong. An **ethical system** describes the duties and behaviors commonly considered correct for a given circumstance. There are both personal and organizational ethical systems.

Ethical systems are documented by an ethical guideline that aids in behavior evaluation and as a framework to judge behavior. Ethical systems are also necessary for every profession because the ethical guideline provides the basis that will allow practitioners to differentiate right from wrong in their profession.

Ethical systems allow members of a profession to make appropriate choices and evaluate proper conduct. They formalize the principles of proper communal behavior. That foundation gives the group's decision makers a yardstick to evaluate the conduct of employees and peers, and communicates the philosophy, beliefs, and **values** of the group to colleagues, prospective clients, and partners.

In a discussion about something as abstract as values, definitions are important. The term "ethical" is frequently used interchangeably with the terms "moral" and "legal." However, that is not correct. Ethics benefit information assurance because they are applied morality. Ethics are logical assumptions about how moral principles should be applied in practice. Ethical systems represent an organization or an individual understanding of what is morally correct. Ethical systems become legal systems when the morality they capture is formalized into law. Laws are different from morals and ethics in that they are explicitly stated and have **enforcement** mechanisms and sanctions built in.

The distinction between these three terms is in their degree of formality. Ethics represents the middle ground. Morals encapsulate beliefs. Ethical concepts are practical descriptions of desired behavior. **Legal frameworks** are prescriptive and proscriptive in that they define and enforce defined standards of behavior. We discussed the legal implications of information assurance in Chapter 11.

Ethics and Information Assurance

Although ethics are abstract, the requirement for an ethical system is a critical part of the information assurance process. Ethics establish the foundation of group trust and trustworthiness is the basis for assurance. Thus, a common ethical frame of reference ensures the trust relationship between individuals and organizations.

Ethical foundations are important because the policies that shape the assurance process should be formulated based the **ethical values** of the organization and not contradict the principles of individual. This implies that an organization should have an established ethical standard that guides the approach to the preservation of confidentiality, integrity, and availability. Moreover, that ethical standard must be clearly articulated and understood throughout the organization.

Ethics and Technology

Technology creates serious problems when it comes to ethics because technology has advanced at a rate that exceeds society's ability to decide about its appropriateness. As a result, people who might have a desire to do the right thing have no guidance beyond the "golden rule" about where to draw the line between correct and incorrect.

For example, many third-party cookies are part of spyware and are placed on a system surreptitiously to gather data without the owner's consent. There would more outrage if the average person understood that the purpose of third-party cookies is to track Internet usage without individual consent. Users assume ethical behavior by others and should be disappointed.

The data-mining industry is another example of organizations operating without an ethical compass. Data mining accumulates detailed records about every person who buys something, sells something, or has a bank account. In fact, people with high consumer activity have forecasts of shopping and credit behavior actually attached to their files. In an increasing number of important instances, such as job interviews and credit, this body of information is utilized to form judgments about an individual's personal trustworthiness. At a minimum, privacy concerns should raise question of the ethics in this context; it violates the principle of confidentiality. Yet at this time, there is very little awareness and almost no regulation of that industry.

More grey areas are likely to develop because the technology evolves faster than society can develop the needed awareness and understanding. Therefore, it is essential for the information profession to consider, adopt, and use robust and effective **ethical guidelines** to regulate their professional practice.

Without ethical guidance it is difficult to expect effective control of information workers' behavior. The immediate payoff for a consideration of ethics will probably not be an improved society; it will be the ability to establish and enforce expected conduct within the entire organization. Expectations of will provide the foundation for statements of proper behavior and will lead, through policy, to measurement and enforcement among its personnel. It will also allow the organization to judge behavior that is incorrect and act accordingly based on established principles.

That discussion is the focus of this chapter. We will examine the role that ethics and ethical systems play in the specification of proper personal behavior. We will also examine how ethical systems may regulate professional conduct. Finally, we are going to discuss the practical application of ethics to underwrite and regulate security functions within the organization.

Practical Ethical Systems: Enforcing Proper Individual Behavior

A formal ethical system helps individuals make correct day-to-day behavioral decisions. These choices balance what is good for the individual and for the group versus the greater good of society. The balancing act is dynamic; there are few correct answers. The compilation of a system depends on the ability to develop a commonly accepted set of beliefs, principles and rules of thumb to guide behavior.

Those principles make up the value system of the society or group and must be documented, as well as commonly accepted by the organization. The interpretation of how these principles should be applied is up to the individual. That interpretation requires an understanding of the ethical implications of each situation.

A communal set of values provides the framework to ensure that individual decisions reflect the group's common **ethical principles**. That implies that the group has a common value system, which is known to everybody. It assumes that all actions that constitute **unacceptable behavior** can be recognized. To ensure this common understanding, group values have to be formally documented.

The formal documentation of the values of an enterprise or organization is an **ethical code of conduct**. An ethical code of conduct is the organization's **standard of behavior**. It defines the **accepted values** and principles of the people who operate within its domain. Codes of conduct dictate the **duties and obligations** of individuals relative to group norms. The code of conduct is either **normative**, that is, they establish an understanding of right and wrong, or they are **descriptive**. Descriptive norms define what the group believes and how the members of the group should act in reference to that belief.

Enforcing Behavior Norms: Aligning Personal and Group Perspectives

Although the decision about how to behave is the right of the individual, the means for judging proper behavior is established by society as a community. Group norms are the measuring stick for evaluating individual behavior. The mechanism employed to communicate those norms is an essential component of an ethical system.

The formally documented code of conduct dictates the minimal moral tone and actions of an organization. It is the only framework used to judge the organization's ethical stance. It is important to ensure that each individual understands the organization's code of conduct as part of the screening and hiring process.

It is the code of conduct that dictates how individual workers act within an organization. For example, individuals working at a credit-reporting agency may have a different ethical perspective than the actual code of conduct required for its members. If that is the case, the behavior of the individual employee must align with the code of conduct established by the organization. If that is not the case, then the ethical choice is to leave.

Ethical systems delineate the correct choices for individuals relative to the group norms. More importantly, from a personnel security standpoint, a defined ethical code also helps an organization decide when an individual is not behaving correctly. Proper behavior characterizes "… the individual's capacity to make consistently correct decisions in the light of the **normative values** of the organization." A properly designed ethical system always provides a concrete reference for that decision making as well as an explanation of the consequences of **deviation from group norms**. In practical applications of codes of ethics, an explicit enforcement mechanism is a necessity.

It must be recognized, though, that because codes of ethics define group norms and all groups are different, there is probably no such thing as a universally valid set of rules. For example, the code of conduct for the hacker community is different from the code of conduct of the Business Software Alliance. Although the legitimacy of the former group's ethics may be questioned, nonetheless, their code represents their accepted group norms. The underlying basis and intent of the supporting ethical system has to be understood when judging what a code of conduct means.

Ensuring Professional Conduct

Professional codes of conduct define the values and beliefs of a profession. They state the duties and obligations the members of the profession owe each other and their clients. Professional codes of conduct describe the way members of a practitioner group to relate to each other. Finally, they define how the overall profession proposes to interrelate with society.

Professional codes of conduct communicate the formal models that make up the norms a group has chosen to adopt. Those models are based on each organization's understanding of **correct professional behavior**. In the case of the assurance process, the professional code must describe the organization's position with respect to safeguarding the confidentiality, integrity, and availability of data assets, as well as the policies for appropriate use.

Professional codes of conduct are essential in information assurance because they speak to a broad range of fundamental concerns raised by the ever-increasing and changing use of information and the proliferation of technology. They provide guidance relative to significant issues such as the privacy rights of individuals, the protection of intellectual property, and the legitimate boundaries of efforts to ensure integrity and confidentiality of information.

Establishing a Basis:
Formal Codes of Conduct for Cyberspace

As we have said throughout this text, information is an intangible asset. That lack of tangibility can make it difficult for honest people to determine whether they are violating an ethical rule, or even breaking a law. This is particularly true in the case of the use of information in cyberspace. The entities that have been very helpful in addressing that problem are accepted global authorities who have published formal codes to define correct behavior.

In that respect, a formal code for cyberspace was published as far back as 1989. Its sponsor was the Network Working Group of the Internet Activities Board (IAB). The IAB has its roots in the Defense Advanced Research Projects Agency (DARPA) and in the actual origins of the Internet. To reinforce its authority in the area, the IAB was renamed the Internet Architecture Board in 1992 to reflect its new placement within the Internet Society. The Internet Society serves as the worldwide catalyst for Internet-based initiatives and is the recognized body responsible for providing international oversight and guidance in the use of the Internet. Its code of conduct is authoritative.

The IAB directive entitled "Ethics and the Internet" (RFC 1087) outlines five simple principles that are meant to serve as the basis for judging unethical or unacceptable use of cyberspace. These principles state that it is unethical

1. To seek to gain unauthorized access to the resources of the Internet

2. To disrupt the intended use of the Internet

3. To waste resources (people, capacity, computer) through such actions

4. To destroy the integrity of computer-based information

5. To compromise the privacy of users

Since its publication, RFC 1087 has had a broad impact on how we as a society have subsequently defined proper usage of the Internet. For instance, item 2 serves as the basis for the information security principle of *availability*, while Item 4 underwrites the *integrity* principle and Item 5 supports *confidentiality*.

Organized religion has even weighed in on the ethical use of the Internet. In 2002, the Pontifical Council for Social Communications, which is an arm of the Vatican, promulgated a formal set of recommendations and conclusions. This document outlines the Roman Catholic Church's views on proper behavior with respect to the Internet. It emphasizes the role of **personal responsibility** in governing acceptable use, while suggesting that the United Nations or some other international body has a duty to ensure regulation of the Internet so it cannot be used for criminal or immoral purposes.

Large initiatives such as these imply that the eventual responsibility for overall ethical guidance should rest with international bodies; however, there are also national bodies who have established formal codes of conduct. That includes such influential societies as the Association for Computing Machinery (ACM), the Institute for Electrical and Electronics Engineers (IEEE), and other industry and interest groups. As might be expected, these codes are specific to the profession. They communicate the ethical responsibility of information professionals to perform their duties in a capable manner. In addition, they set the minimum expectations with respect to the level of capability required. Finally, they serve as a basis for judging whether that standard has been adequately met.

In addition to national societies, a number of professional societies have also taken on the responsibility for stipulating codes of ethical practice. For instance, professional societies such as the Information Systems Audit and Control Association (ISACA), the International Information Systems Security Certifying Consortium (ISC), and the SANS Institute have outlined detailed requirements for ethical practice for their members, and each has an ethical code of conduct. Finally, countless proprietary codes of conduct exist, which have been developed by individual organizations.

A major concern is that there is not a single universally recognized code of conduct for the information assurance profession. The issue of whether ethical behavior will be enforced by external regulation or whether it will have to rely on internally motivated compliance is also still controversial. However, the need for formally documented points of reference for professional conduct has been clearly established.

Certification: Ensuring Professional Capability

To protect the organization from charlatans, one should consider certification as a method of identifying individuals committed to ethical behavior. A code may formalize is the level of capability required for an information assurance professional. The expression of a minimum level of capability is called a *standard level of professional competence*. It characterizes the degree of proficiency that a reasonable person might expect from an assurance professional under a given set of circumstances. Additionally, a statement of expectation is attached to each of these proficiencies.

A formal definition of competency is important to the profession, because there is an assumption that practitioners have the necessary level of expert skill, training, knowledge, and experience in assurance work. Other professions where public trust has to be guaranteed—such as medical practitioners–have a formal statement of expectation and associated with licensure.

For doctors, the minimum standard level would be that a medical condition would receive the proper diagnosis and treatment. Doctors are held to a high standard of expectation in that respect because of their elevated skills, training, and knowledge. Their medical license attests to that and that they will uphold a standard of ethical conduct. Similarly, lawyers are held to a higher professional standard in matters related to the law because they have to pass state bar exam. These both ensure confidence in the profession. Their licensure is a function of the state, not of the profession.

The same degree of capability cannot be assured for information assurance professionals because the assessment of professional capability level is not licensed. There are expectations, but there is no mandated external mechanism to underwrite professional competence, as there are with the American Medical Association (AMA) and the American Bar Association (ABA).

There *are* certifications based on a number of representative common bodies of knowledge (CBK), but no single system guarantees that the practitioner responsible for protecting an organization's information is competent nor a common code of ethics.

This uncertain state of professional practice persists because there are few formally agreed-on definitions of the knowledge or competencies necessary to ensure the successful performance of information assurance work. Some forward-thinking organizations have specified the minimum level of education and training that an IA professional must have to work within that particular company. However, there is variability in skills and competencies required within the profession as a whole. That lack of definition has an effect on the type and degree of protection expected the potential for misunderstanding and miscommunication is obvious.

Therefore, consumers who have faith in the ability of a security professional to safeguard the availability, confidentiality and integrity of their information have no guarantee that their confidence will not be misplaced. Managers who trust the ability of IA professionals to safeguard the availability, confidentiality, and integrity of their information assets have no guarantee that this will be done correctly because there are no universal standards to ensure professional competence.

One consequence of that lack of trust has been litigation over breakdowns in security under current tort laws and negligence. If some minimum standard of competency is not voluntarily adopted and enforced by the profession, the expectation is that there will be increased litigation in the IA area.

On the positive side, however, professional certifications exist that provide a basic definition of competency. Establishing the value of each of these certifications requires understanding the process, the integrity with which the process is followed, and the time dependencies of the capabilities that the certificate attests.

It is thought that certification that attests to an individual's ability to think critically about an identified problem space, not to a technical skill, provides the most valid proof of competence (Ryan 2005). Certifications that attest that an individual is competent to manage version 1.4a of a firewall become obsolete when version 1.5 is released. A certification that attests that an individual has been taught how to examine complex options against a set of requirements will never be obsolete. Some of the decision criteria that might be used to determine the value of a certification include the following:

- How long has the certification been in existence?
- Does the certification organization's process conform to established standards?
- How many people hold the certification?
- How widely respected is the certification?
- Does the certificate span industry boundaries?
- What is the probability that 5 or 10 years from now, the certificate will still be useful?
- Does the certification span geographic boundaries?
- Does the certification require attestation to a defined ethical behavior?

Answers to each of these questions provide insight into the value of the certificate and the expected competence of the individual practitioner.

Information Ethics

Information ethics specifically deals with the ethical questions that relate to the use of information assets. It explores and evaluates the development of ethical principles in information assurance. It examines ethical concepts that support information assurance theory and practice, as well as their relevance to everyday information security work.

Information ethics is a timely and important area because the philosophical frame of reference that we have employed for thousands of years to define ethical and legal behavior is quaintly out of date when it comes to the information industry. That is, information technology has extended individual and institutional capabilities beyond any physical horizon ever imagined by traditional moralists and philosophers, and far beyond ideas captured in the precedents and principles of our legal system.

From an ethical perspective, computing may suffer from the bombardier syndrome; actions in cyberspace are one-step removed from the consequences. It is hard to form a sense of the ethical or moral implications of the behavior because the outcomes are not experienced firsthand. For instance, in the process of delivering bombs on a target, deciding where they should land is both intellectually absorbing and abstract. Unless something unforeseen and undesirable happens, the people in the bomber are insulated from what happens to the people on the ground. It is hard to develop a sense of the consequences of a bombing run and to understand the ethical ramifications of the action because of that abstract distance.

Technology builds an insulating factor into information work by separating the outcomes from the act itself. For example, breaking into a computer store in the middle of the night and stuffing software into a bag is hands-on. It is easy to see that you are doing something wrong; the consequences are concrete. Pirating the same software requires knowledge, skill, and *savoir-faire*. The crime can be perpetrated in the privacy of your own home; you do not have to go anywhere, smash windows, or get your hands dirty. It is a harder to grasp the moral implications.

Individuals who use the computer unethically are shielded from thinking about the appropriateness of their actions by the intangibility of the commodity and the anonymity that computing provides. Information is the only resource that can be stolen without anybody knowing that it is missing. This raises the ethical question: "If you could commit a crime that nobody knew about, would you?" The right answer depends on the ability to recognize that what you are doing is incorrect.

There are four areas where guidance about ethical behavior should be provided. These are *invasion of privacy, unauthorized appropriation of information, breach of confidentiality,* and *loss of integrity.* Because these represent the foundation of ethical behavior in information assurance work, we are going to discuss each of these qualities separately.

Invasion of Privacy

A common violation is an **invasion of privacy** that is the act of obtaining information to breach an individual's reasonable expectation of privacy. Legally, the Bill of Rights does not actually guarantee a right to privacy from other individuals except in specific cases. Nevertheless, privacy is an important and desirable quality in modern life because privacy is fundamental to personal freedom. On the other hand, a society's need to know something about each of its citizens requires that records be kept and information gathered. The concern with respect to the information industry is finding the proper balance between knowing enough about a person, but not too much.

This kind of issue was less important 70 years ago because it was not possible to efficiently collect and retrieve information about each individual. Times have changed and while people in a highly mobile society are difficult to track. Large organizations have developed an insatiable appetite for data. Throughout the 1990s, every company in the Fortune 100 dedicated enormous economic and staff resources to developing a better understanding of every person in the United States. That thirst for data has spawned an information industry that can provide complete, aggregated, in-depth, up-to-date information about every person in the United States. That is the problem.

The Ethics of Invading Your Privacy for Profit: The Data Mine

The foundation of our ethical system rests on commonly understood individual rights. Among these is the reasonable expectation of protection from unwarranted searches by the government. However, the intent and purpose of the industrial data-warehousing and data-mining activity that characterizes modern business practice legally violates that expectation in many ways, without any regulation.

Data aggregation and data mining augments an organization's ability to understand its customers better. This is a benefit by itself; however, in doing so these data-mining methods may intrude too far into people's personal lives. There is little moral outrage over the things that the information industry does to gather data because technology masks the actions. As such, nobody really knows what is happening. Earlier we used the example of tracking cookies to illustrate this.

It is common practice to place tracking cookies surreptitiously on most computers. Although they have valid uses for the session, their primary purpose is to record the viewing habits of individual using the machine. The information can then be used by those who have been granted access to generate reports that will be sent elsewhere when the system is idle.

A similar act the physical universe would be to tap a person's home telephone to find out what kind of pizza orders was placed. Most people would view that as a violation of privacy because they know enough about wiretapping to understand this is not a legitimate business practice. However, there is so little knowledge about spyware and cookies that the average citizen does not understand their significance and use.

The willingness of society to condone anti-social institutional behavior is understandable, given that few understand the threats to privacy in cyberspace. The leading edge in information technology has progressed to a point that the general population does not have a concept of what is happening to their personal life because of computer use. An ethical solution is to build an understanding across society and grapple with the essential question, "What is the limit to the acquisition and use of knowledge by institutions?"

The point to note is that institutional monitoring is taking place without individual knowledge. That degree of stealth may be justified if personal information were necessary to protect the greater good. However, harvesting the Internet browsing habits of the citizen in general for no particular reason is a questionable practice. The simple distinction between justified corporate surveillance and common snooping should define the limits of proper use of information. Ethically, information obtained without permission, which allows a person, corporation, or a government access into the private affairs of an individual, falls outside of the bounds of correct behavior.

There are many instances where invasion of privacy takes place for example, credit-monitoring services. These agencies collect more than credit history. They know the legal, marital, employment, and medical histories of most individuals in the U.S., right down to the magazines they read. Despite Family Educational Rights and Privacy Act (FERPA) requirements, many of these services even have access to school records (see, your second-grade teacher was right when she said, "This will go on your permanent record!"). The question yet to be answered is, "what can other people know without violating your privacy?" The resolution of that question remains a distant and rapidly fading goal because the technology is so fast moving.

What Are You Doing at Work?
Invading the Privacy of Your Employees

Data mines are not the only organizations crossing the ethical line. Employers frequently do too much prying. A common form is workplace monitoring. An employer may reasonably monitor its employees because it is implied that when people come to work, they have sacrificed some of their rights to privacy for the good of the organization. Thus the organization has an unstated right to oversee employee behavior and communications on the job. The typical example of that is recording phone conversations or monitoring e-mail. There are also more subtle activities, such as keylogging of employees and even observing them through workplace video cameras and closed-circuit television.

This is not an express violation when the employee is informed about the measures being taken. However, where the steps taken to monitor are intentionally surreptitious, such as placing a keylogger on an employee machine that action may cross the boundary into invasion of privacy. This may be the case because personal e-mail and any other type of communication that does not fall within the organization's rights will be captured as well.

The point to remember with this section is that, because of the widespread harvesting of electronic information, large institutions, such as state and federal governments and corporations, know a lot about every citizen in the United States. More important, from the standpoint of this chapter, the right of access to that information was never expressly granted. Where this violation occurs, it is known as unauthorized appropriation.

Unauthorized Appropriation

Unauthorized appropriation is the use of a computer to obtain something under false pretenses. Unauthorized appropriation is a crime if an item of concrete value is taken. It is an ethical compromise where the value is either intangible or cannot be estimated. Unauthorized appropriation typically takes place when another person's intellectual property is either stolen or misused.

We talked about the problems associated with monitoring and enforcing the theft of intellectual property in Chapter 11. In that respect that it is always an ethical compromise to appropriate another person's intellectual property. However, it is not necessarily a legal one unless the value of the property can be assessed and proven and there are local laws to point.

Misappropriation of intellectual property presupposes that an identified piece of intellectual property exists. However, there is one piece of property that everybody possesses that is a more frequent target of misappropriation. That is the personal information of each individual. We talked about personal information in the prior secretion under the heading of violations of privacy. Here we address that topic from the standpoint of the ethics of how that information is obtained.

The information industry is a billion-dollar-a-year business lurking in the shadows. It is dedicated to learning as much as possible about everybody in the U.S. This knowledge is kept in repositories—data warehouses and used to develop facts about individual citizens. Those facts are used to support commercial activities. For that purpose, the information industry maintains data warehouses, where data mining is conducted 24 hours a day.

A consequence of uncontrolled data mining is that individual and aggregated consumer information is bought, sold, and traded like commodities on the Chicago Mercantile Exchange. In the case of ethics, such activity crosses the line if the data that is kept in these warehouses has not been not expressly authorized or provided by the individuals themselves.

This activity raises the question of how and where those data were obtained. Frequently, personal data are acquired under false pretenses. That is, individuals who supply the data are not aware that they are providing it for use by others. Individuals may think, for example, that they are filling out an online registration form or a job application, or they are navigating a website. Instead, they may be supplying one more item of information about themselves to some faceless data warehouse.

The representation of an untrue fact or circumstance calculated to mislead to obtain money or goods is the classic legal definition of false pretenses. Information is an asset, in that respect; information obtained by false pretenses by the information industry is not subject to legal remedies since the courts have consistently upheld that an *individual's personal data does not belong to them*.

Therefore, although deception schemes that are designed to feed the data-mining industry might be unethical, they are NOT illegal. The condition that would make the act illegal would be when an individual's private data was made public. Whether that leak was an accidental or intentional, it is a direct violation of confidentiality and may have explicit legal remedies.

The Ethics of Confidentiality

If gathering information about the private life of a person is not bad enough, the actual existence of that data in readily available repositories raises another concern, namely, *breach of confidentiality*. Breach of confidentiality can be intentional or unintentional. It is not just an ethical issue, since the disclosure of private information is a matter of civil and even criminal liability in some states.

There are two well-known examples of the way the federal legal system addresses breach of confidentiality. Those are the Health Insurance Portability and Accountability Act (HIPAA), which is the first comprehensive federal protection for the privacy of personal health information. The other is the Family Educational Rights and Privacy

Act, 1974 (FERPA), which limits the personal information that educational institutions can release to the public.

Litigation about confidentiality lies in the fact that an organization that holds personal data also has a legal duty to prevent unauthorized or harmful viewing or use of the data. As an example, most video stores keep the rental history of their customers on file. Most video-viewing habits are of interest only to themselves, but if, for example, this information were intentionally leaked to reveal lurid facts about a political candidate's viewing habits, it may be illegal, constitute an invasion of privacy, and a breach of confidentiality.

An organization in possession of personal information should pass the legal test of whether the organization took reasonable precautions to protect the information—a form of **due care**. If it is found that the organization failed to exercise due care in the protection of personal information in their possession, then the custodian of the data may be liable for damages that ensue. There are many cases illustrating this principle. For instance, if the custodial party, such as a credit-reporting agency, is breached and damage ensues for the people whose information was in their files they are liable. The legal liability has been consistently found to rest with the keeper of the information.

Remember, legal is not the same as ethical. The ethical test is simpler. An individual dealing with an organization has a right to assume that the information provided will be kept confidential. Breach of confidentiality violates that reasonable presumption.

The failure to protect private information is always an infringement of ethical expectations independent of the court finding. Thus the protection of the confidentiality of information one of the prime directives within information assurance, has both a security and an ethics aspect. Therefore, no matter what concerns there might be behind issues of invasion of privacy or unauthorized appropriation of information, the ethical obligation to ensure confidentiality is clear cut and unambiguous.

The Ethics of Integrity

A responsibility of information assurance professionals is to ensure that the information that they safeguard maintains integrity. The term **integrity** implies that the information is correct. That is, the information has not been accidentally or maliciously altered or destroyed. This is a critical element of the information assurance process. The ethical issue can be characterized by a legal term, "**false light**."

False light is a circumstance where information that is being kept either is false or harmfully misrepresents something about the individual. From a legal standpoint, this is related to libel or slander, in that the person is falsely portrayed. Nevertheless, although they are similar, the two situations are not exactly the same.

The difference lies in the fact that libel is an intentional act, whereas false light may be accidental. As such, in the case of false light there is a requirement for integrity in the process of assuring the information under a particular organization's control. The requirement for integrity means that the information must always be assured to be accurate and that it has not been altered accidentally or maliciously.

Unfortunately, for information assurance there are two sides to that coin. Depending on the circumstances, the person incorrectly characterized may *actually gain* from the misrepresentation. An example is the case where a person with a criminal record might not be entered into a law enforcement database because of a data entry error. The outcome of that failure would be that an organization might hire that person for a position of trust. In that case, the obligation to ensure the accuracy of all information is a matter of ethics as well as one of good security practice.

Consequently, it should be noted that it does not matter if the falsely portrayed individual gains or loses by that misrepresentation; the breach of professional ethics is in the failure to maintain the integrity of the record. The motivation behind that failure can be either intentional or inadvertent; but the ethical compromise applies in both cases.

Unintentional Errors

Typical **unintentional errors** are incorrect or missing values. Incorrectly entered values are a cost of doing business in the information industry, since employees cannot be 100 percent accurate. The ethical response to the inevitable inaccuracy is the establishing a well designed and adequate set of error-trapping functions in the system, as well as embedding rigorous audit and control mechanisms within the process itself.

Although capable error trapping and audit mechanisms should be addressed at design time for the system, they are frequently overlooked through sheer ignorance. Because both of these functions impose overhead on the human resources of the organization as well as on the system, they are often the first things sacrificed on the altar of profitability.

Cost cutting makes good sense, but it is not ethically acceptable if it increases the probability that an individual suffers from inadvertent errors. Imagine the effect of having your checking account accidentally debited a thousand dollars instead of ten dollars because the data entry clerk was having a bad day and you will understand why controls over these types of errors are as important as the ones that check for malicious actions.

Intentional Errors

A less frequent occurrence is the **intentional error**. Intentional errors come from three sources; all such errors have ethical implications. The first source is the insider who alters data to portray the facts of a given situation incorrectly. The second is the insider who accepts and records incorrect information. The third is the outsider who hacks into the system in order to change the integrity of its data.

In the first case, the organization is ethically and legally liable because of its failure to screen and supervise its employees properly. The legal liability of the organization for intentional employee misuse of the system has well-established precedents and has been applied numerous times; there is a legal term to describe this type of liability: "negligent hiring."

The ethical issues are simpler. No matter how personal data is obtained, third parties in possession of such data are ethically bound to ensure its integrity. If the custodian of the data is unable to ensure that their employees will not alter an individual's information, then the custodian is guilty of an ethical compromise. This obligation is critical when the data may be used to influence the person's life, for instance in the case of credit or background checks.

The legal term for this relationship is "bailment," which describes the binding relationship established when a person gives property to someone else for safekeeping. To create a bailment, the other party must knowingly have exclusive control over the property and that party must use reasonable care to protect the property. Consequently, any deliberate action that a corporation takes to obtain personal data establishes a legal requirement to ensure its integrity and safekeeping.

The circumstance of accepting incorrect information has less legal liability attached to it. However, it may actually be a greater ethical compromise. The courts have upheld the idea that an organization that keeps incorrect data about an individual is not liable for misrepresentation, if they accepted it from a known source in good faith.

The fact remains, however, that in this instance, the third-party custodian is not in possession of accurate information. Therefore, if that custodian then provides incorrect information to another organization—the credit or employment community, for example—they are violating the integrity principle as they would if they had been responsible for the inaccuracy. As such, the same ethical conditions apply.

The failure of the organization to validate data that it has received, recorded, and provided, is a serious ethical compromise. That violation is not diminished by the fact that the organization was deceived. This is true when the organization did not assign sufficient staff or define explicit procedures or screening devices to check incoming data for validity and accuracy.

The term that most information assurance professionals use to describe breaches in integrity due to the action of hackers is "data diddling." Legally, the organization is not held liable if they established "reasonable measures" to protect the information from being misrepresented and modified. This is true in the ethical sense because, assuming they took reasonable precautions, the organization is as much a victim of the breach as the individual whose data was altered. As such, it can be assumed that the people who are responsible for the protection of the data lived up to their professional obligations.

The key to that decision rests with the phrase "reasonable measures." "Reasonable" is a slippery term because what might seem reasonable in one situation may be inappropriate in another. For instance, in the case of top-secret data, an organization would be considered to violate that presumption both legally and ethically, if it took the same measures as it did to protect routine information assets.

Every situation has different criteria for determining if the protection measures were ethical, reasonable, and adequate. Consequently, every information assurance solution has to be tailored to the circumstances. Remember, if the solution and the circumstances are not aligned properly, there is the likelihood that, even though the organization itself was victimized, it will be liable of an ethical or legal breach.

Exercising Due Care

In the final analysis this discussion comes down to one principle—due care. That term is a legal concept that describes the degree of thoroughness of the effort to detect and prevent problems that may occur, before they happen. It refers to the process of maintaining the availability, integrity, and confidentiality of information contained in a system.

In information assurance, due care is characterized by a careful attention to detail in the process of designing, assessing, updating, and monitoring data and systems. It has control implications as well. The assumption is that an ethical organization will always exercise due care in the enforcement of confidentiality and integrity requirements. In an information technology operation, the measures that demonstrate due care are the user authentication and access controls and audit mechanisms within the process.

All organizations are required to exercise due care in the practice of information assurance. There may not be legal consequences if they do not, but the ethical implications are clear. An ethical organization will practice due care in all instances. Unfortunately, this is not always a well-defined requirement. Therefore, it is important that there is an organizationally sponsored definition due care in the practice of information assurance. This definition must provably fit within that organization's particular setting.

The existence of a **statement of due care** is necessary to protect the organization from liability concerns as well as to ensure good ethical practice. This statement should be developed at the very top of the organization and both executive management and the company's board of directors should sponsor it. It should make plain the level and degree of commitment of the firm to the exercise of information assurance practice and, as such, it should serve as the code of ethics for all instances.

Chapter 16 Review

Chapter Summary

- The function of ethics is to increase the ability of people to distinguish between right and wrong.

- An ethical system is important for professions because it helps people decide what is right or wrong.

- Ethical systems differentiate proper choices and behavior from the improper ones in the execution of daily work.

- The function itself centers on the description of a concrete set of collective duties that dictate how an individual should behave in a given circumstance.

- Ethics implies a logical consideration of how **moral values** should be applied in the real world. In that respect, ethical systems represent an organization's or individual's tangible understanding of what is moral.

- Ethics is an extremely important part of information assurance, because the overall process should always be structured in the light of a formal statement of the ethical values and principles of the organization.

- The way that an organization defines its basic commitment to confidentiality, integrity, availability, non-repudiation, and authorization depends on its ethical perspective.

- The delineation of group values for running an organization enterprise is called an ethical code of conduct.

- An ethical code of conduct is, in effect, the organization's standard of behavior.

- It defines the accepted values and principles of its particular ethical system. It dictates the duties and obligations of individual workers in reference to the group norms.

- Thus, it offers the ability to manage the ethical behavior for that particular group.

- These dictates are either normative—that is, they establish right and wrong—or descriptive; in essence, descriptive codes define what the group believes and how people should act in reference to that belief.

- The established code of conduct dictates the moral tone and actions of an organization and it is the reference point in judging its ethical stance.

- Codes of conduct are intended to delineate the correct set of choices for individuals in relation to the overall norms of the group.

- Therefore, in a practical sense, a defined ethical code underwrites the ability to tell when an individual is not behaving correctly.

- Professional codes of conduct define the values and beliefs of a particular profession.

- They delineate the duties and obligations that the members of the profession owe to each other and their clients.

- In addition, they specify the proper way for the group's members to interrelate with each other.

- Finally and most importantly, they define how the overall profession proposes to interact with society as a whole.

- Information ethics deals specifically with ethical questions as they relate to the use of information.

- It explores and evaluates the development of moral values in the field of information assurance.

- It examines ethical concepts that underwrite information assurance theory and practice, as well as their relevance in everyday information security work

- The first and most common type of ethical compromise is an invasion of privacy, that is, the use of information to breach an individual's reasonable expectation of privacy.

- Ethically, information that allows a person, corporation, or a government to intrude improperly into the private affairs of another individual falls outside of the bounds of correct behavior.

- Information about every citizen in the U.S. is kept in large repositories and then used to develop facts that even the individuals themselves may not recognize.

- Most of this data has not been not expressly authorized or provided by the individuals that it describes.

- The primary concern with the existence of this data is an accidental or intentional breach of confidentiality.

- The assurance of integrity of data is a critical element of information assurance process. The most typical violations of integrity are incorrect or missing values.

- In the final analysis this discussion boils down to one principle, which is due care.

- That term is a legal concept that describes the degree of thoroughness of the effort to detect and prevent problem that may occur, before it happens.

- In the case of information assurance, due care is characterized by careful attention to detail in the process of designing, assessing, updating, and monitoring data and systems.

- In an IT organization the normal mechanism for determining due care is through the presence of sufficient user authentication and access controls and audit mechanisms.

Key Terms

accepted values (422)
behavior (419)
correct professional behavior (423)
descriptive (422)
deviation from group norms (423)
due care (431)
duties and obligations (422)
enforcement (420)
ethical code of conduct (422)
ethical guidelines (421)
ethical principles (422)
ethical system (420)
ethical values (421)
ethics (419)
false light (431)
integrity (431)
intentional error (432)
invasion of privacy (427)
legal frameworks (420)
moral values (434)
normative (422)
normative values (423)
personal responsibility (424)
professional codes of conduct (423)
standard of behavior (422)

statement of due care (434)
unacceptable behavior (422)
unintentional errors (432)
values (420)

Key Term Quiz

Complete each statement by writing one of the terms from the Key Terms list in each blank. Not all terms will be used.

1. _____ provides the ability to distinguish right from wrong.

2. The use of information to breach a person's reasonable expectation of privacy is called _____ .

3. The legal term for intentionally, or unintentionally, misrepresenting a person is _____.

4. The information assurance term for intentionally, or unintentionally, misrepresenting a person is a breach of _____.

5. There are two ways an ethical code of conduct can be expressed: _____ and _____.

6. The mechanism that protects companies from legal liability for breaches in confidentiality is a _____.

7. The advantage of an ethical guideline is that is specifies _____.

8. Ethical frameworks are different from _____ because they do not have formal enforcement systems.

9. A description of the correct behaviors for a given circumstance is called a _____.

10. Providing information about a person that is incorrect and might lead to harm is called _____.

Multiple Choice Quiz

1. A professional code of conduct communicates ethical

   a. norms

   b. morals

   c. laws

   d. regulations

2. The maintenance of confidentiality is an ethical issue in

   a. data modeling

   b. data mining

   c. database design

   d. data dictionaries

3. The ethical problem with technology is that it separates the act from the
   a. circumstance
   b. individual
   c. outcomes
   d. process

4. The assumption is that an ethical IT organization always exercises
   a. due care
   b. control
   c. specified criteria
   d. technology management

5. Capability standards are expressed in a statement of minimum professional
   a. objectives
   b. competency
   c. goals
   d. work

6. Information presents particular ethical problems mainly because it is:
   a. valuable
   b. portable
   c. transmittable
   d. intangible

7. The norms of a particular group are embodied by a
   a. standard
   b. code of competency
   c. code of conduct
   d. code of ethics

8. Unauthorized appropriation obtains information by
   a. stealth
   b. software
   c. false pretenses
   d. false light

9. From an ethics standpoint, data mining is a form of
   a. invasion of privacy
   b. violation of availability

    c. breach of integrity

    d. denial of service

10. Guidance is particularly important in information work because

    a. the commodity itself is dangerous

    b. the commodity itself is abstract

    c. the commodity itself is illegal

    d. the commodity itself is dynamic

Essay Quiz

1. A generally accepted universal code of conduct would be very useful, but it would have to be self-enforcing. Why is that the case, and how effective do you think that may be?

2. How does the existence of too much information potentially affect the rights of individuals? Given that, how can those rights be assured?

3. In what situation could an organization be held liable for unintentional errors? What would be the basis for that liability and how can the possibility that it may occur be addressed?

4. The code of conduct rather than personal ethics defines the accepted behavior of an organization. Explain that statement and provide an example where the two may conflict.

5. What is the difference between moral, legal, and ethical?

6. What is a normative code? What is a descriptive code?

7. Why is an ethical system particularly important to information assurance?

8. What is the ethical problem that technology raises for organizations?

9. Why is it important to keep the individual and group ethical norms aligned?

10. Why is professional competency an ethical issue? When would it become a legal one?

Case Exercise

Complete the following case exercise as directed by your instructor.

    Heavy Metal Technologies (HMT) is a defense contractor headquartered in Huntsville, Alabama. HMT was recently contracted by the Army to upgrade the fire control system for the MH64-D Apache Longbow attack helicopter. Because HMT wants to avoid liability issues, it would like to have both a professional code of conduct as well as a statement of the standard level of professional competency for every individual who handles corporate information. These codes will be both certified by the comp and authorized by the people working on the project. However, the comp does not presently have either of these codes formalized. Therefore, you have been assigned to the task of preparing a standard code of conduct for this project and an accompanying statement of minimum competency for each of these job categories:

- Project Manager
- Project Lead Software Engineer
- Project Software Engineer
- Project Information Assurance Officer
- Project Software Quality Assurance Officer

APACHE LONGBOW AH-64D: Target Acquisition and Display System (TADS) Upgrade Project

Heavy Metal Technologies (HMT) is a defense contractor headquartered in Huntsville, Alabama. It is a relatively small company by Pentagon standards (approximately $350 million a year), but it has an exceptionally good record of accomplishment in the area of upgrading operational electronic combat systems to new or improved equipment standards. As such, it enjoys an extremely strong, relationship with virtually all branches of the Department of Defense (DoD), as well as several defense prime contractors. It has a very large installed base of products, a number of sole-source contracts, and a strong management and advisory team.

Its Electronic Combat Systems Group is located in several places in North America, specifically Kanata, Canada, which specializes in the design and production of electronic warfare (EW) training systems and Buffalo, New York (which provides circuit-card assembly, electromechanical assembly, and environmental testing). However, the main production operation is in Ft. Walton Beach, Florida, which actually constitutes four facilities:

- **Jackson Street**—the Jackson Street Facility does manufacturing and engineering functions. The main building is dedicated to electrical, software, and mechanical engineering and documentation control. Four other buildings are dedicated to machine shops (consisting of CNC milling, lathes, sheet metal brakes, and coordinated inspection stations).

- **The Sunnyside Street Main Building**—this building houses the complex's administration, purchasing, finance, main shipping and receiving, quality assurance, contracts, legal, information technology, stockroom, program management, and business development functions.

- **The Oceanside Facility**—This facility houses the bulk of the electrical manufacturing facilities including printed circuit-board component insertion, soldering, surface mount assembly/soldering, light painting and silkscreen, electrical/mechanical assembly, chassis wiring, subsystem/final system testing, environmental stress testing, stockroom, industrial engineering, and production management. It performs the same function as the Buffalo facility does for the entire company; however, it is focused strictly on work at the Walton Beach site.

- **The Sunnyside West Facility**—this facility houses the engineering staff for the electronic warfare unit.

The Project

HMT was contracted by the Army to upgrade the target acquisition and display fire control system for the AH64-D Apache Longbow attack helicopter. This is a field upgrade of the current analog system used by the Apache, thus it is considered a modification of an off-the-shelf (COTS) product. However, even though the work is done on a legacy system, modifications to the code will be necessary in order to integrate a GPS and enhanced communication capability into the aircraft. Revisions of the current system will need to be written (and/or modified) to support the following functional requirements:

1. Integrate the GPS into the existing navigation system.
2. Display updated navigation information on the pilot's Head-Up Display (HUD).
3. Allow the pilot to be able to input and modify navigation and fire control data through an onboard Control Display Unit (CDU).
4. Communicate GPS and targeting information to ground control and to other aircraft in the mission. (Note: No equipment upgrades are planned to support the increased communications requirements.)

In the case of the GPS/CDU upgrade, the product will be a working GPS interface with the CDU. This project can also be viewed in terms of its constituent management processes. In this case, the major processes are project management, software development support, software development, software qualification, and postdevelopment support.

The requirements of the GPS interface are well known. The software in the current onboard navigation system and interface software is written in C, and due to the nature of the changes required for the navigation components, no change in language platform is being considered. The contractor who will supply the GPS system will make modifications to the GPS software that will allow it to be interfaced directly to the overall system. This will be done on a subcontract to HMT. HMT will provide a specification of the modification requirements to the subcontractor. This will reduce the cost and risk associated with that aspect of the overall system development process.

HMT has determined that about 9,000 source lines of code (SLOC) overall will have to be developed and/or modified in order to integrate the GPS into the current fire control system. Because configuration management has not been practiced in the past maintenance of the system, the existing navigation software has not been fully validated and the customer wants formal documentation. Therefore, it was assumed in the initial planning that the development process itself would most closely resemble that for a new project.

The Army (acquirer) has contracted to supply a valid System/Subsystem Specification (SSS), a System Design Description (SSDD), and an Operational Concept Document (OCD). The Army will modify the OCD during development to reflect any requirements or changes that might emerge as the process progresses downstream. HMT will be responsible for the following technical documents:

1. Software and Interface Requirements Specifications (SRS and IRS)

2. Software and Interface Design Descriptions (SDD and IDD)

3. Software Test Plan (STP)

4. Software Test Description (STD)

5. Software Test Report (STR)

HMT will also be responsible for the following management and support documentation:

1. Software Development Plan

2. Software Transition Plan (STP)

3. A Software Version Description (SVD)

Project Requirements

Based on the preliminary project planning, it is estimated that the software effort will take approximately 3.25 person-years over a period of 12 months. The development, test, and technical documentation effort will be approximately 2.25 person-years; the remaining 1.0 person-year will be dedicated to software project management, managing the support documentation, SQA, and SCM. User documentation will be produced as part of the new CDU development effort. The GPS subcontractor will develop the SRS and SDD for the GPS from existing materials created for the product.

The pilots for this aircraft dislike the old CDU and want a replacement. The pilots would like to add new query capabilities. The pilots also want an opportunity to help determine the requirements for the TADS and to have significant inputs to the changes to the user interface. Because the pilots want so much involvement, the Army is pushing to have individual field personnel, whom they will authorize, involved in the actual development process.

Since that is the case, HMT feels that prototyping will be useful to support the user interface development. In addition, it is not known how many new capabilities will be added to implement the pilots' query requirements. HMT is assuming that the new CDU will have all new software. The Army wants the new CDU to be implemented in Ada, and the existing code is in assembly language, so it is assumed that there will be no software code reuse. Furthermore, the Army is requesting significant amounts of formal documentation.

Based on HMT's knowledge of the existing CDU and a rational appraisal of the possible new requirements, HMT assumes that the new CDU will require about 20,000 SLOC to implement. Given the unknown nature of the new requirements, this is a soft estimate. The customer wants the new CDU to be a significant improvement from the current version, so there may be some flexibility to renegotiate the terms of the contract when the first sets of prototypes are completed and approved by the pilots. In both parts of this upgrade project, software supportability is a primary concern. Thus, planning for the software transition to the government and for Post-Deployment Software Support (PDSS) is stressed in the acquisition. This may add labor to the existing software estimates from HMT.

Project Characteristics

Here is some information that you might need as you make decisions for this project:

1. The project size is approximately 29,000 SLOC.
2. There are five interfaces involved between the user, the GPS, and the CDU.
3. One hundred and fifty aircraft in the inventory are to be upgraded. There will be one user for each aircraft. It is assumed that the aircraft will remain in service for at least another decade.
4. There are approximately 800 pages of documentation.
5. There will be a subcontract for modifications to GPS code and for new (or modified) GPS documentation.
6. There is minimal technical complexity.
7. It is a life-critical application.
8. There is a moderate need for management visibility.
9. Because the application is life critical, assurance needs to be employed sufficient to assure that the aircraft requirements have been reliably met.

The areas for concern are security, human safety, the level and degree of formal software engineering methods that will have to be employed, the need for formal reviews and signoffs among a number of dispersed entities, and the relationship with subcontractors. On examining the project characteristics, the project manager noted the following regarding these issues:

1. Adding the GPS to an existing aircraft is a known problem and the system will be small; thus, a waterfall life cycle can be used.
2. System Reliability factors will be stressed during testing. These are already documented in the corporate handbook on metrics for life-critical or safety-critical systems.
3. There is a need for in-process reviews for this project.

4. Since the security assurance process is new to the organization, it will be important to track progress and results for this project.

5. The metrics practices are internal; they do not cover sharing data with the acquiring organization (e.g., the Army).

6. Although risk management practices will be used, nothing in the approach to risk management has been defined for this application.

7. The project manager is responsible for maintaining all compliances and for developing the risk and continuity management plans.

Production Details

The bulk of the initial engineering design work will be done at the Sunnyside West Facility, which houses a Sun server farm. However, there will be a requirement to involve the Kanata staff from the beginning since they are doing the training plans. This will be done by teleconference from the Oceanside Main building. It is not anticipated that the pilots will be involved in any part of the initial engineering setup, but that assumption cannot be confirmed. Therefore, the Army would like to have a contingency procedure in place to ensure that their field personnel will have access to this site if necessary. The layout of **Sunnyside West** is shown in Figure A-1.

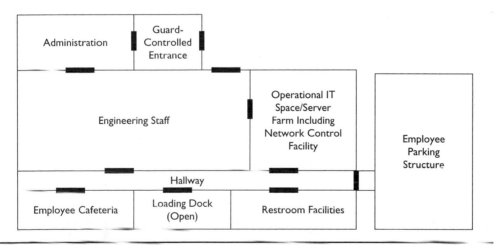

Figure A-1   Layout of Sunnyside West

After an initial inspection by the Army's consultant, five areas of concern were identified. In order of relative priority these are

1. Entrance from the parking structure is controlled by swipe card access.

2. Entrance from the loading dock is not secured.

3. None of the support employees have a security clearance.

4. Access to the server farm is available from the hallway.

5. Access to the network is controlled through a single firewall.

6. Access to the employee facilities is not monitored.

7. Engineers can come and go through their own entrance.

8. There is no fire suppression equipment in the machine room.

9. There are no disaster contingency plans for this facility.

Although the initial system design will be carried out in the Sunnyside West facility, the actual engineering of the software and the electromechanical engineering and subsequent integration will take place at the Jackson Street facility. Since prototype development will take place there, that is also the location of the joint reviews and pilot advisory visits.

These visits are integral to the design function, so the engineering staff in Sunnyside West will be required to come to these meetings. It is assumed that the engineers in Kanata will also occasionally need to attend these sessions.

In addition to the Army pilots, there is a requirement that the civilian project administrators from the DoD side of the operation (as well as their support staff) attend all meetings where final agreements are made regarding design. That means that the actual attendance at meetings at Jackson Street will involve at least three different constituencies: HMT engineers and staff, DoD engineers and staff, and the Army representatives. It is assumed that documentation and media utilized during these meetings will be developed and maintained by the Documentation Control Center located at Jackson Street. The overall layout of that facility looks like Figure A-2.

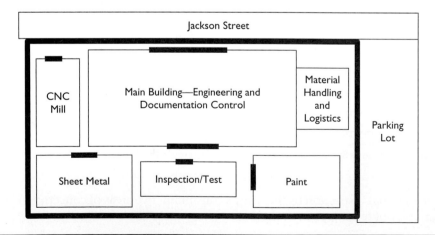

Figure A-2 Layout of Jackson Street

The detailed layout of the Jackson Street Engineering Building looks like Figure A-3.

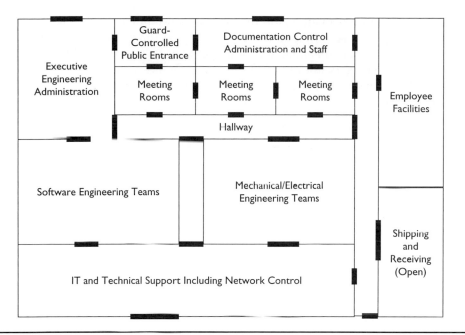

Figure A-3 Layout of Jackson Street Engineering Building

After an initial inspection by the Army's security consultants, nine areas of concern were identified. In order of relative priority these are

1. Entrance to the meeting rooms is open from the central hallway.

2. The central hallway is not monitored or controlled.

3. Entrance from the loading dock is not secured.

4. Access to the IT control center is available from the loading dock.

5. Access to the Documentation Center is available from the loading dock.

6. Access to the employee facilities is not monitored.

7. IT staff can come and go through their own entrance.

8. Documentation staff can come and go through their own entrance

9. Administrative staff can come and go through their own entrance.

The actual manufacturing will take place at the Oceanside Main building; however, the testing will take place in Buffalo. It is assumed that the fire control system must be tested in its operating environment and the Buffalo facility can more easily work in conjunction with Army pilot inspectors based at Fort Drum in Watertown, New York. The actual factory acceptance tests will be done there and the approvals will be granted by the DoD inspectors from the Buffalo facility.

Therefore, the project managers in the Oceanside Main facility will teleconference daily with the managers in Buffalo from the time that the project begins operational testing to the time it obtains final approval and signoff. This is also likely to include the production managers from the Jackson Street facility as well as the DoD project managers when approvals are required. The layout of the Oceanside Main Facility looks like Figure A-4.

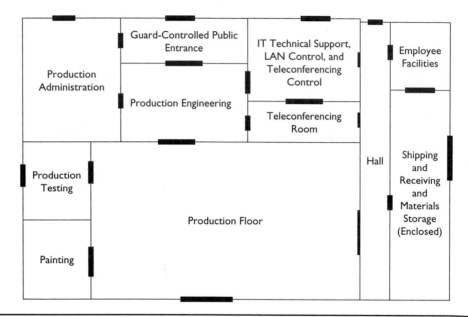

Figure A-4   Layout of the Oceanside Main Facility

After an initial inspection by the Army's security consultants, 14 areas of concern were identified. In order of relative priority these are

1. Entrance to the hallway is only controlled by swipe card.
2. Access to the production floor is only controlled by swipe card.
3. Entrance to the IT facility is open from the hallway.
4. Access to the IT control center is available from the production floor.
5. Access to teleconferencing is available from the production floor.
6. The hallway is not monitored or controlled.
7. Entrance from the shipping/receiving dock is not secured.
8. Access to the IT control center is available from the receiving dock.

9. Access to the teleconferencing room is available from the receiving dock.

10. Access to the employee facilities is not monitored.

11. IT staff can come and go through their own entrance.

12. Testing staff can come and go through their own entrance.

13. Administrative staff can come and go through their own entrance.

14. Production staff can come and go through their own entrance.

Finally, all legal, regulatory compliance, fiscal, and DoD reporting work is handled at the Sunnyside Street Main building. This is the nerve center of the Walton Beach operation. It is also the place where the company's executives are located. It provides all of the management oversight services for the other units as well as interfacing with DoD in terms of the details of management and accountability.

It is also the central repository of all administrative data for the entire corporation. It has a large and highly professional mainframe based IS unit as the central part of its operation. In addition, it provides all of the operational support for the administrative systems at the Walton Beach site. Finally, the project management staff, as well as the executive project managers, is located there. When there are DoD projects in process, the DoD also has representatives headquartered in this building. The layout of Sunnyside Street Main looks like Figure A-5.

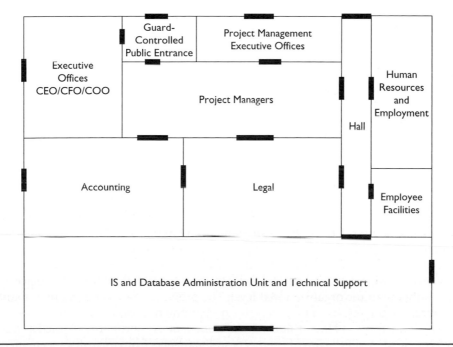

Figure A-5   Layout of Sunnyside Street Main

After an initial inspection by the Army's security consultants, various areas of concern were identified. In order of relative priority these are

1. Entrance to the hallway is only controlled by swipe card.

2. Entrance to the IT facility is open from the hallway.

3. Access to the data center is available to people seeking employment.

4. Access to legal is available from the hallway.

5. The hallway is not monitored or controlled.

6. Access to the employee facilities is not monitored.

7. IT staff can come and go through their own entrance.

8. Accounting staff can come and go through their own entrance.

9. Executive staff can come and go through their own entrance.

10. Project management staff can come and go through their own entrance.

The Organization

HMT is run like a typical corporation. Its organization is top-down and looks like Figure A-6.

Early software project planning is stressed at HMT, and project plans are developed to integrate effectively with the other engineering plans within each project. There is strong informal communication among all the engineering disciplines, and a single program manager manages each new project from an integrated system view. Software estimates are derived through expert analysis and documented for use throughout the project's life. These estimates are backed up with outputs from estimation tools that are used to provide a "reality check" to the experts' initial idea. Actual project data is retained to support an estimation improvement effort under way at HMT but it is not used in a formal feedback sense.

Software project management metrics are used to provide visibility into project performance at the project level. When performance deviates from the initial plans, the project manager is responsible for either making changes to the way the project is being handled (in order to bring the project back into conformance with the plan), or replanning. Software subcontracts are managed using a set of defined policies and procedures. Software requirements, design, and code inspections are used to support development. Defect metrics from the inspections are maintained. Other product-related metrics are identified and maintained for each development effort to help keep reasonable visibility into the development effort. These metrics also are used to support software project management and risk assessment. The only problem is that all of this takes place at the project rather than the organizational level. The program manager and upper management never see the results of this extensive measurement process.

The review culture at HMT is not well developed. SQA is primarily defined as testing. There is no SCM. A SEPG team of engineers and managers from the software engineering

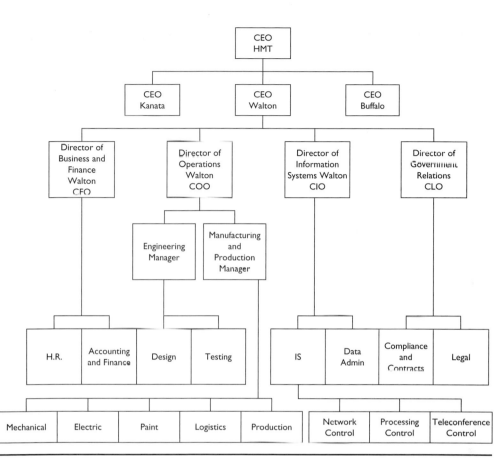

Figure A-6 HMT organizational chart

organization are responsible for keeping the approved software engineering processes up to date, and identifying new opportunities for improvement. This team reports to the manager of software engineering and to the corporate vice president of engineering. The vice president of engineering maintains a keen interest in the software engineering processes for the corporation. The manager of software engineering and the vice president of engineering are responsible for providing quarterly reports to the company president on the state of software engineering and software process improvement. The problem is that most of this is rumor rather than fact-based.

The Problem Facing the Organization

Because the contracted enhancement is so important to the continuing success of the main ground attack helicopter program and thus because of its importance to national defense, the Army wants a total commitment from HMT that the integrity, confidentiality, and availability of the project information will be assured. In order to do that HMT must address the areas of concern listed. In addition, the Army would like HMT to address the following 10 concerns. Provide a security plan that will adequately address all of these concerns.

1. The Army requires a procedure to assure that all applicable IS functions will be adequately controlled.

2. The Army requires a procedure to assure that all security concerns will be identified and addressed.

3. The Army requires a procedure to assure that control of IS functioning will be continuous.

4. The Army requires a procedure to assure that the control processes will be cost-efficient.

5. The Army requires a procedure to assure that employees are trustworthy, without violating their rights.

6. The Army requires a procedure to assure that all storage and communication of data will be secure.

7. The Army requires a procedure to assure that all security controls will be cost-efficient.

8. The Army requires a procedure to assure that the product will incorporate security functionality.

9. The Army requires a procedure to assure that the company will be able to satisfy its contractual and legal obligations.

10. The Army requires a procedure to assure that the integrity of the design and testing process will be maintained.

11. The Army requires a procedure to assure that all security incidents will be responded to effectively.

12. The Army requires a procedure to assure that all third-party work will meet security criteria.

    a. The integration needs to be carefully controlled throughout the software development effort.

    b. The review requirements should be set up to allow for in-process reviews. These should be fully documented.

    c. The metrics practices and the means for external distribution of metrics data should be specified. This should be fully documented.

    d. Where no reviews exist to cover a specific process area, those reviews will need to be supplied.

Abadi, M. "Security Protocols and Specifications." *Foundations of Software Science and Computation Structures, Second International Conference,* March (1999): 1–13.

Amatayakul, Margret. "A Reasonable Approach to Physical Security." *Journal of AHIMA* 73, no. 4 (2002): 16A–C.

Anderson, J. P. *Computer Security Technology Planning Study.* Technical Report ESD-TR-73-51, Air Force Electronic Systems Division, Hanscom AFB, Bedford, MA, 1972.

Anderson, Ross. *Security Engineering.* New York: John Wiley & Sons, 2001.

AR 12-15, SECNAVINST 4950.4, AFR 50-29. *Joint Security Assistance Training (JSAT) Regulation.* Departments of the Army, Navy, and Air Force, June 5, 2000.

AR 380-19, *Information Systems Security.* Department of the Army, February 27, 1998.

Asch, B. J. *Ensuring Successful Personnel Management in the Department of Homeland Security.* IP-235-NSRD, 2002.

Ashton, Gerry. "Cleaning Up Your Security Act for Inspection." *Computer Weekly,* January 18, 2001.

Audit Commission. *Opportunity Makes a Thief—An Analysis of Computer Abuse.* London: HMSO Publications Centre, 1994.

Barkley, John. "Comparing Simple Role-Based Access Control Models and Access Control Lists." *Second ACM Workshop on Role-Based Access Control,* ACM, 1997.

Bell, D. E., and L. J. LaPadula. "Secure Computer Systems: Mathematical Foundations." MITRE Technical Report 2547, MITRE Corporation, Bedford, MA, 1973.

Bell, D. E., and L. J. LaPadula. "Secure Computer Systems: Unified Exposition and MULTICS Interpretation." Revision 1, U.S. Air Force ESD-TR-75-306, MITRE Technical Report 2997, MITRE Corporation, Bedford, MA, March 1976.

Bellovin, Steven M., and William R. Cheswick. *Firewalls and Internet Security: Repelling the Wily Hacker.* Boston: Addison-Wesley, 1994.

Biba, K. J. "Integrity Considerations for Secure Computer Systems." ESD-TR-372, ESD/AFSC, Air Force Electronic Systems Division, Hanscom AFB, Bedford, MA, April 1977.

Bishop, Matt. "Writing Safe Privileged Programs." Network Security Conference, 1997.

Bloom, Benjamin S. "Taxonomy of Educational Objectives: Cognitive Domain." Fifty-Seventh Yearbook, Part II, National Society for the Study of Education, Chicago: University of Chicago Press, 1999–2000.

Bloom, Benjamin S. *Taxonomy of Educational Objectives*. Boston: Allyn and Bacon, 1984.

Bois, Justin. "Protect Yourself." *SANS GSEC* 1, no. 3 (April 2002).

Bragg, Roberta, Mark Rhodes-Ousley, and Keith Strassberg. *Network Security: The Complete Reference*. Burr Ridge, IL: McGraw-Hill, 2004.

British Security Industry Association. *Physical Security*. London: BSIA, 2004.

Brooks, Fred. *The Mythical Man-Month: Essays on Software Engineering*, 20th anniversary ed. Reading, MA: Addison-Wesley, 1995.

BS ISO/IEC 17799. *Information Technology: Code of Practice for Information Security Management*. British Standards Publishing Ltd., 2000.

Business Continuity Institute. *Business Continuity Management: Good Practice Guidelines*. Caversham, UK: BCI, January 2002.

Cebrowski, A. K., and J. J. Garstka. "Network-Centric Warfare: Its Origin and Future." *Naval Institute: Proceedings*, January 1998.

CERT/CC. "CERT Survivability Project Report." Computer Emergency Response Team Coordination Center, 1996.

Circular A-130, "Management of Federal Information Resources, Office of Management and Budget." U.S. Federal Register, February, 1966.

Clark, David D., and David R. Wilson. "A Comparison of Commercial and Military Computer Security Policies." *Proceedings IEEE Symposium on Security and Privacy*, 1987.

Committee for National Security Systems (CNSS). "National Information Systems Security Glossary." CNSSI 4009, Fort Meade, MD, September 2003, <http://www.cnss.gov/instructions.html>, (August 8, 2005).

Committee for National Security Systems (CNSS). "National Training Standard for Information Systems Security (INFOSEC) Professionals." NSTISSI 4011, Fort Meade, MD, September 2003, <http://www.cnss.gov/instructions.html>, (August 8, 2005).

Committee for National Security Systems (CNSS). "National Information Assurance Training Standard for Senior Systems Managers." CNSS 4012, Fort Meade, MD, June 2004; Supersedes NSTISSI No. 4012, dated August 1997.

Committee for National Security Systems (CNSS). "National Information Assurance Training Standard for System Administrators (SA)." CNSS 4013, Fort Meade, MD, March 2004.

Committee for National Security Systems (CNSS). "Information Assurance Training Standard for Information Systems Security Officers." CNSS 4014, Fort Meade, MD, April 2004; Supersedes NSTISSI No. 4014, dated August 1997.

Committee for National Security Systems (CNSS). "National Training Standard for Systems Certifiers." NSTISSI 4015, Fort Meade, MD, December 2000.

Committee for National Security Systems (CNSS). "National 1 Information Assurance Training Standard for Risk Analysts." CNSS 4016, Fort Meade, MD, November 2005.

Computer Security Institute (CSI). "Results of 2001 Joint Survey on Computer Security (with the Federal Bureau of Investigation—FBI)." San Francisco: CSI, 2002.

Critical Infrastructure Taskforce. "National Strategy to Secure Cyberspace (Draft)." Department of Homeland Security, September 18, 2002.

Cross, Stephen E. "Cyber Security, Testimony before the Senate Armed Services Committee." U.S. Armed Services Committee, Subcommittee on Emerging Threats and Capabilities, March 1, 2000.

Cross, Stephen E. "Cyber Threats and the U.S. Economy." Testimony before the Joint Economic Committee, U.S. Congress, February 23, 2000.

Cukier, K. "Critical Information Infrastructure Protection. A Report of the 2005 Rueschlikon Conference on Information Policy." Kennedy School of Government, Working Paper No. RWP05-055, October 2005.

Dart, Susan A. "Achieving the Best Possible Configuration Management Solution." *Crosstalk* 9, no. 3 (September 1996).

Defense Security Service (DSS). "DD1879 DoD Request for Personnel Security Investigation." Military, Civilian, and Industrial Contractor Requests, EPSQ 2.2, DSS, 2002.

Defense Security Service (DSS). "SF86 Questionnaire for National Security Positions." U.S. Office of Personnel Management, 2002.

Denning. Peter J. *Computers Under Attack: Intruders, Worms, and Viruses*. Boston: Addison-Wesley, 1990.

Department of Trade and Industry. "Information Security Breaches Survey." Great Britain: DTI, 2001.

Dorofee, A. J., J. A. Walker, and R. C. Williams. "Risk Management in Practice." *Crosstalk* 10, no. 4 (April 1997).

Ellison, C. and B. Schneier. "Ten Risks of PKI: What You're Not Being Told About Public Key Infrastructure." *Computer Security Journal* 16, no. 1 (2000): 1–7.

Federal Emergency Management Agency. "Capabilities Assessment for Readiness." Washington, D.C.: FEMA, 2000.

Feiler, Peter. "Configuration Management Models in Commercial Environments." Tech Report CMU/SEI-91-TR-7, March 1991.

Fischer, Lynn F., and Ronald W. Morgan. "Sources of Information and Issues Leading to Clearance Revocations." Defense Personnel Security Research Center, Monterey, CA, 2002.

Friedlob, T., and C. Schou. *An Auditor's Guide to Encryption*. Institute of Internal Auditors, 1997.

Galvin, Peter. "Designing Secure Software." SunWorld, April 1998, <http://sunsite.uakom.sk/sunworldonline/swol-04-1998/swol-04-security.html>, (August 21, 2005).

GAO Report, "Critical Infrastructure Protection Significant Challenges Need to Be Addressed." July 24, 2002, <http://www.gao.gov/new.items/d02961t.pdf>, (May 16, 2004).

"Generally Accepted System Security Principles (GASSP)." International Information Security Foundation, February 2003.

Giuru, Luigi. "Role Templates for Content-based Access Control." 2nd ACM Workshop on Role-Based Access, Fairfax, VA, 1997.

Hay, Ryan. "Physical Security, a Biometric Approach." SANS GSEC Practical Track 1-C, November 2003.

Hershey, Bob. *Cryptography Demystified*. 1st ed. Burr Ridge, IL: McGraw-Hill, 2003.

Honeynet Project, ed. *Know Your Enemy: Revealing the Security Tools, Tactics and Motives of the Blackhat Community.* Boston: Addison-Wesley, 2001.

HR 3162 RDS. "Uniting and Strengthening America by Providing Appropriate Tools Required to Intercept and Obstruct Terrorism." 107th Congress, October 24, 2001.

Humphrey, Watts. *A Discipline for Software Engineering.* Reading, MA: Addison-Wesley, 1995.

Humphrey, Watts. *Managing the Software Process.* Englewood Cliffs, NJ: Addison-Wesley, 1993.

Information Systems Audit and Control Association (ISACA). *Audit Guidelines.* Arlington Heights, IL: IT Governance Institute, 2003.

Information Systems Audit and Control Association (ISACA). *COBIT, Management Guidelines,* 3rd ed. Arlington Heights, IL: IT Governance Institute, 2002.

Information Systems Audit and Control Association (ISACA). *COBIT, Control Objectives,* 3rd ed. Arlington Heights, IL: IT Governance Institute, 2002.

Information Systems Audit and Control Association (ISACA). *Framework, COBIT,* 3rd ed. Arlington Heights, IL: IT Governance Institute, 2000.

Institute for Electrical and Electronic Engineers, *ANSI/IEEE 1042, Software Configuration Management, Guidelines.* New York: IEEE, 1990.

Institute for Electrical and Electronic Engineers, *ANSI/IEEE 12207.0, Industry Implementation of International Standard ISO/IEC 12207-1995.* New York: IEEE, 1996.

International Standards Organization (ISO). *ISO/IEC 9126, Software Product Evaluation—Quality Characteristics and Guidelines for Their Use.* Geneva, Switzerland: ISO, 1996.

International Standards Organization (ISO). *ISO/IEC 12207, Information Technology—Software Lifecycle Processes.* Geneva, Switzerland: ISO, 1995.

International Standards Organization (ISO). *ISO/IEC 15288, Systems Engineering—System Lifecycle Processes.* Geneva, Switzerland: ISO, 2005.

International Standards Organization. *ISO/IEC 15408-1, Information Technology—Security Techniques—Evaluation Criteria for IT Security, Part 1: Introduction and General Model.* Geneva, Switzerland: ISO, 2005.

International Standards Organization. *ISO/IEC 15408-2, Information Technology—Security Techniques—Evaluation Criteria for IT Security, Part 2: Security Functional Requirements.* Geneva, Switzerland: ISO, 2005.

International Standards Organization. *ISO/IEC 15408-3, Information Technology—Security Techniques—Evaluation Criteria for IT Security, Part 3: Security Assurance Requirements.* Geneva, Switzerland: ISO, 2005.

Internet Business News. *CSI Survey, FBI/Computer Security Institute.* January 20, 2006, <http://www.eweek.com/article2/0,1895,1913633,00.asp>, (February 13, 2006).

Irvine, C. E. "The Reference Monitor Concept as a Unifying Principle in Computer Security Education." *Proceedings of the IFIP TC11 WG 11.8*, First World Conference on Information Security Education, Kista, Sweden, June (1999): 27–37.

Killcrece, Georgia, Klaus-Peter Kossakowski, Robin Ruefle, and Mark Zajicek. "State of the Practice of Computer Security Incident Response Teams." Technical Report, CMU/SEI-2003-TR-001, ESC-TR-2003-001, 2003.

Koller, Mike. "Accurate ROI Requires Impartiality." *Internet Week,* September 25, 2001, <http://internetweek.cmp.com>, (March 13, 2005).

Lang, Eric L., and Katherine L. Herbig. "Model for a Future Defense Personnel Security System." Defense Personnel Security Research Center, Monterey, CA, 2002.

Latham. Donald C. "Security in the Information Age." *SIGNAL* May (1987): 173–180.

Lawrence, L. G. "The Role of Roles." *Computers and Security* 12, no. 1 (1993).

Lee, E. "Software Inspections: How to Diagnose Problems and Improve the Odds of Organizational Acceptance," *Crosstalk* 10, no. 8 (1997).

Lim, W. C. "Effects of Reuse on Quality, Productivity, and Economics." *IEEE Software*, September 1994.

Louridas, P. "Some Guidelines for Non-repudiation Protocols." *Computer Communication Review* 30, no. 4 (October 2000).

Maconachy, W. Victor, Corey Schou, Daniel Ragsdale, and Don Welch. "A Model for Information Assurance: An Integrated Approach." *Proceedings of the 2001 IEEE Information Assurance and Security*, United States Military Academy, West Point, NY, June 5–6.

Maiwald, Eric. *Fundamentals of Network Security.* Burr Ridge, IL: McGraw-Hill, 2004.

Maiwald, Eric. *Network Security.* Burr Ridge, IL: McGraw-Hill, 2003.

Marshall, Alexa. "Software Configuration Management: Function or Discipline?" *Crosstalk*, STSC, Hill Air Force Base, Utah, October 1995, p. 21.

Mayor, Tracy. "Value Made Visible." CIO, May 1, 2000.

McConnell, Steve. *Code Complete: A Practical Handbook of Software Construction.* Redmond, WA: Microsoft Press, 1993.

McCumber, John. "Information Systems Security: A Comprehensive Model." *Proceedings of the 14th National Computer Security Conference, National Computer Security Center,* October (1991): 334.

McGraw, Gary, and Edward W. Felten. *Secrets and Lies: Digital Security in a Networked World.* New York: John Wiley & Sons, 1999.

Mel, H. X., and Doris M. Baker. *Cryptography Decrypted.* Boston: Addison-Wesley, 2001.

Menezes, Alfred J., Paul C. Van Oorschot, and Scott Vanstone. *Handbook of Applied Cryptography.* New York: CRC Press, 2001.

Moya-Quilas, Roberto, and Stefano Zanero. "IT Contingency Plans, More Than Technology." *Upgrade* 4, no.6 (December, 2003): 3–5.

National Computer Security Center (NCSC). "Trusted Computer System Evaluation Criteria (TCSEC)." Department of Defense, DoD 5200-28 STD, December 26, 1985.

National Fire Protection Association. *NFPA1600–Standard on Disaster/Emergency Management and Business Continuity Programs.* NFPA, Quincy, MA, 2004.

Networking Services and Information Technology, NSC. *Physical Security Principles.* Chicago: University of Chicago, 2004.

Northcutt, Stephen, and Judy Novak. *Network Intrusion Detection: An Analyst's Handbook.* 2nd ed. Indianapolis, IN: New Riders Publishing, 2000.

OMB Bulletin No. 90-08. "Guidance for Preparation of Security Plans for Federal Computer Systems Containing Sensitive Information." Office of Management and Budget, July 6, 1988.

ORISE 02-0225. *Personnel Security Assurance Program: Profile 1992–2001.* U.S. Department of Energy, Office of Security, February 2002.

President's Commission on Critical Infrastructure Protection. *Critical Foundations: Protecting America's Infrastructures.* October 1997.

Public Law 93-579. "Privacy of Social Security Numbers." 5 U.S.C. 552a, 1974.

Public Law 99-474. "The Computer Fraud and Abuse Act." 18 U.S.C., 1986.

Public Law 99-508. "Electronic Communications Privacy Act." 18 U.S.C. 2510, 1986.

Public Law 100-235. "The Computer Security Act." 100th Congress, 1987.

Public Law 104-191. "Health Information Portability and Accountability Act (HIPAA)." 104th Congress, August 21, 1996.

Public Law 108-187. "Controlling the Assault of Non-Solicited Pornography and Marketing Act of 2003." 117 STAT.269. 108th Congress, December 16, 2003.

Public Law 890-554. "The Freedom of Information Act (FOIA)." 5 U.S.C. 552, 1966.

Raines. Paul S. "Slaying Cerberus." Softwaremag.com, July 2001, <http://www.soft-waremag.com/L.cfm?Doc=archive/2001jun/PRaines.html>, (March 24, 2004).

"Redefining Security." Report: Joint Security Commission, February 28 (1994): 124.

Rogers, Larry. "Cybersleuthing: Means, Motive, and Opportunity." *InfoSec Outlook* 3, no. 3 (Summer 2000).

Sandhu, Ravi. "A Lattice Interpretation of the Chinese Wall Policy." *Proceedings of the 15th NIST-NCSC National Computer Security Conference*, Baltimore, Md., 1992.

Schneider, Fred B. "Enforceable Security Policies." *ACM Transactions on Information and System Security* 3, no. 1 (February 2000).

Schneier, B. "Risks of Relying on Cryptography." *Communications of the ACM* 42, no. 10 (October 1999).

Schneier, B. "Security in the Real World: How to Evaluate Security." *Computer Security Journal* 15, no. 4 (1999): 1–14.

Schou, C. K., K. Trimmer, K. R. Parker, and Corey Schou. "The Design Reference Monitor Concept in Systems Analysis and Database Design Courses." *Proceedings International Conference on Informatics Education and Research*, Las Vegas, NV, December 9–11, 2005 (pp. 321–331).

Schou, Corey, and J. Frost. "Homeland Security and Information Assurance." In *Biomedical Informatics Systems, IEEE Engineering in Medicine and Biology*, January/February 2004.

Schou, Corey, W. V. Maconachy, and James Frost. "Organizational Information Security: Awareness, Training and Education to Maintain System Integrity." In *Proceedings Ninth International Computer Security Symposium*, Toronto, Canada, May 1993.

"Security-Audit's Frequently Asked Questions (FAQ)." Jeff Graham (maintainer) 1999, <http://www.l0t3k.org/biblio/faq/english/lsap_faq.txt> (November 11, 2005).

Simpson, S. "PGP DH vs. PGP RSA." Sam Simpson, September 1999, <http://www.scramdisk.clara.net/pgpfaq.html>, (July 31, 2004).

Singhal, Mukesh, and Niranjan Shivaratri. *Advanced Concepts In Operating Systems*. 1st ed. Burr Ridge, IL: McGraw-Hill, 2003.

Skamarock, Anne. "Quantifying ROI." *NetworkWorldFusion*, July 9, 2001, <http://www.servicesweb.org/syndication.en.php3?id_syndic=13>, (February 13, 2006).

Spafford, E. H. "One view of a critical national need: Support for information security education and research." 1997. <http://www.fas.org/irp/congress/1997_hr/h970211s.htm> (August 11, 2005).

Sturgeon, Will. "Time to Marry Network and Physical Security." <http://www.Silicon.com>, April 28, 2004 (November 7, 2005).

Swanson, Marianne, and Barbara Guttman. "Generally Accepted Principles and Practices for Securing Information Technology Systems." National Institute of Standards and Technology, Computer Security Special Publication 800-14, 1996.

Swanson, Marianne. "Security Self-Assessment Guide for Information Technology Systems." National Institute of Standards and Technology, Computer Security Special Publication 800-26, 2001.

Technical Support Work Group. "Intrusion Detection Assessment and Delay, Physical Security Technology." Washington, D.C.: TSWG, 2004.

Todd, Mary A., and Constance Guitian. *Computer Security Training Guidelines*. NIST Special Publication 500-172, U.S. Department of Commerce, National Institute of Standards and Technology, November, 1989.

Tomayko, James. "Software Configuration Management." Software Engineering Institute, Carnegie Mellon University, Pittsburgh, 1997.

Treasury Board of Canada. *Physical Security Standard*. Ottawa: Treasury Board of Canada, November 1995.

Viega, John, and Gary McGraw. *Building Secure Software: How to Avoid Security Problems the Right Way*. Boston: Addison-Wesley, 2001.

Voas, Jeffrey, and Gary McGraw. *Software Fault Injection: Inoculating Programs Against Errors*. New York: John Wiley & Sons, 1997.

Welch, I., and R. J. Stroud. "Re-engineering Security as a Crosscutting Concern—Experience with a Third-Party Application." *The Computer Journal* 46, no. 5 (September 2003): 578–589.

Williams, Phil, Casey Dunlevy, and Tim Shimeall. "Intelligence Analysis for Internet Security." CERT-CC, Carnegie Mellon University, Software Engineering Institute, February 10, 2006.

Wilson, Mark, Dorothea E. deZafra, Sadie I. Pitcher, John D. Tressler, and John B. Ippolito. *Information Technology Security Training Requirements: A Role- and Performance-Based Model.* NIST Special Publication 800-16, U.S. Department of Commerce, National Institute of Standards and Technology, April 1998.

Winslett, M, N. Ching, V. Jones, and I. Slepchin. "Using Digital Credentials on the World-Wide Web." *Journal of Computer Security*, 1997.

Zelkowitz, Marvin V. "Perspective on Software Engineering." *Computing Surveys* 10, no. 2 (June 1978).

Zimmerman, Michael. "Configuration Management, a Fashion or a Profession?" White Paper. Munich: usb GmbH, 1997.

Zimmerman, Scott C. "Secure Infrastructure Design." CERT/CC, Carnegie Mellon University, 2002.

INDEX